MW00569708

CRITICAL INSIGHTS

Absalom, Absalom!

by William Faulkner

CRITICAL
INSIGHTS

Absalom, Absalom!

by William Faulkner

Editor
David Madden
Louisiana State University

Salem Press
Pasadena, California   Hackensack, New Jersey

Cover photo: © Maureen Rigdon/Dreamstime.com

Copyright © 2012 by Salem Press,
a Division of EBSCO Publishing, Inc.

Editor's text © 2012 by David Madden
"The *Paris Review* Perspective" © 2012 by Nathaniel Rich for *The Paris Review*

All rights in this book are reserved. No part of this work may be used or reproduced in any manner whatsoever or transmitted in any form or by any means, electronic or mechanical, including photocopy, recording, or any information storage and retrieval system, without written permission from the copyright owner except in the case of brief quotations embodied in critical articles and reviews or in the copying of images deemed to be freely licensed or in the public domain. For information address the publisher, Salem Press, at csr.salempress.com

∞ The paper used in these volumes conforms to the American National Standard for Permanence of Paper for Printed Library Materials, Z39.48-1992 (R1997).

Library of Congress Cataloging-in-Publication Data
Absalom, Absalom!, by William Faulkner / editor, David Madden.
    p. cm. — (Critical insights)
Includes bibliographical references and index.
    ISBN 978-1-58765-834-1 (alk. paper) — ISBN 978-1-58765-821-1 (Critical insights : alk. paper) — ISBN 978-1-58765-833-4 (set-pack b : alk. paper)
    1. Faulkner, William, 1897-1962. Absalom, Absalom! 2. Historical fiction, American—History and criticism. 3. Plantation life in literature. 4. Families in literature. 5. Mississippi—In literature. I. Madden, David, 1933-
PS3511.A86A66 2012
813'.52—dc23

                                                                    2011022416

Contents_____

The Book and Author_____

Critical Contexts_____

Critical Readings_____

Resources_____

About This Volume _____

David Madden

The purpose of this collection of essays on William Faulkner's multifaceted novel is to provide the reader who has read or is about to read *Absalom, Absalom!* with as much of a multifaceted perspective as space will allow. Writing about this exceptionally ambiguous novel, these critics are exceptionally clear. The objective is to be as clear as possible without denying readers the exhilaration of working through the process on their own. Criticism does not replace reading a novel; it encourages repeated readings by providing new dimensions to the first experience.

This volume's opening original essays offer basic, clearly stated perspectives: a brief view of Faulkner's life and works, two close readings of *Absalom, Absalom!* that apply specific critical methods, the novel in a cultural-historical context, the novel compared and contrasted with another novel, and the novel's critical reception. These original essays are a worthy addition to the one thousand or so already published.

Lorie Watkins Fulton sketches Faulkner's life in chronological order (see also the chronology at the end of this book), from his early life in the small town of Oxford, Mississippi, through his death, alluding to but not discussing his works, and citing people in Mississippi, New Orleans, and Hollywood who influenced his life and writings.

In "From Mapmaker to Geographer: Faulkner's Sense of Space in *Absalom, Absalom!*" Nicole Moulinoux offers a unique close reading from the perspective of cartography, examining the various versions of the map Faulkner drew of Yoknapatawpha County to guide the reader through the events in *Absalom, Absalom!*, comparing his map with maps other writers have drawn for their novels. She corrects errors in the various versions of the map in different editions to help the reader avoid becoming confused, and she stresses Faulkner's shifting map omniscience as he made changes on his own and in response to editorial pressures; she notes errors and variations that arose from publishing exigencies.

In "Cultural Context: *Absalom, Absalom!*" Ted Atkinson describes and analyzes in unusual detail the novel's cultural and historical contexts. He examines cultural perception, North and South, as a problem of identity. With the advent of multiculturalism, readings of Faulkner steeped in feminism, African American studies, and new directions in American and southern studies, including global contexts, have reassessed and critiqued the monolithic view of "the South." The reader may want to keep in mind that critical assessments that stress facts are one thing, and the realities of a mass culture that stresses facts meshed with imagination, which has the more universal appeal, are another.

Randy Hendricks, in "Tragedy and the Modern American Novel: *The Great Gatsby, Absalom, Absalom!*, and *All the King's Men*," demonstrates that comparison and contrast constitute a vibrant technique for seeing the novel in sharp relief. His comparison of the image of the loom in *Absalom* with the famous image of the spider web in the Civil War chapter of *All the King's Men* is especially useful as the reader reads both the novel and the critical essays about it. He convincingly argues that Gatsby, Stark, and Sutpen are tragic figures, and that the novels should be read as modern tragedies of the American Dream turned nightmare. Many scholars have compared *Absalom* with other novels, but *Gatsby* and especially *All the King's Men* offer the most revealing comparisons.

Kevin Eyster's "The Critical Reception of *Absalom, Absalom!*" provides a detailed historical survey and analysis of the seven-decade, astonishingly varied critical reception of the novel, considered generally not only to be Faulkner's greatest work but one of the greatest novels in literary history. "According to John Bassett," Eyster says, by way of introduction and summary, "studies of the novel have fallen into 'two major categories, one focusing on the nineteenth-century story of Thomas Sutpen and the other the twentieth-century dilemma of Quentin Compson. The first is concerned with social themes, myth and legend, tragic form and character; the second deals with narrative techniques, epistemological issues, and the novel's connection, through Quentin . . . to *The Sound and the Fury*' (276)." Those "two categories suggest the range of topics that critics have written about in discussing *Absalom, Absalom!* over seven decades." No other essay quite like Eyster's has previously been published on Faulkner. It is worth noting that in the pieces Eyster surveys, very little mention is made of Wash Jones and other poor whites.

Rounding off the original essays is Aimee E. Berger's "Gates and Doors and Metaphors: Materiality and (Dis)Embodied Sexuality in *Absalom, Absalom!*" Berger provides a close reading of the novel from the critical standpoint of feminist theory. Observing that the novel speaks to the reader even before the reader understands it, she offers an unusual approach, taking her own reader through the intellectual process that produced her essay, beginning with and pursuing a question: "The starting point for this essay was the question 'Why Quentin?' I was in good company for asking this; Quentin asks it himself, wondering why in the world he should have been 'summoned' by Rosa Coldfield to be the recipient of this story (6). Later, in conversation with his father, he twice demands, 'Why tell me about it?' (7)." Berger focuses on Quentin's identification with Henry and Judith Sutpen's incestuous longing as parallel to his own feelings for his sister Caddy, carried over from *The Sound and the Fury*, written ten years earlier.

In addition to the new essays commissioned for this volume, ten previously published essays have been carefully chosen to provide a wide range of perspectives on such subjects as those Eyster surveys in his essay: theme, protagonists, feminism, storytelling, race, style, Civil War, and time, among others. In "Past as Present: *Absalom, Absalom!*" Hyatt H. Waggoner provides in a rather informal style a relatively simple guide through the novel's characters and structure, dealing with the theme of the past as it is active in the present. Waggoner is one of the few critics who thinks of the novel as a poem, leaving that idea to be developed further by others.

The main argument of my own essay "Quentin! Listen!" is that Quentin is the protagonist of *Absalom, Absalom!* This view challenges the prevalent conviction that the novel is primarily about the "tragedy" of Sutpen's rise and fall. If we examine the various artistic techniques Faulkner employs, mostly in innovative ways, we find that most of them contribute to a growing awareness that they focus upon Quentin, by implication when not explicitly. Miss Rosa in the present and Quentin's father, both in the present and in the past, and many others in his family and small community repeatedly tell him about Sutpen, the epitome of the ideals of the antebellum plantation society and of the Civil War fought to protect and preserve the southern way of life, ideals further eroded during Reconstruction and the Jim Crow years. They seem to rely on Quentin, as a young man of an aristocratic society, to preserve and pass on the memory of the lost cause. His dilemma is that he knows that he feels nothing and is psychologically incapable of the act of historical memory, in spirit, spoken word, or in writing.

In "Subverting History: Women, Narrative, and Patriarchy in *Absalom, Absalom!*" Susan V. Donaldson begins by admitting that "such a reading requires a self-conscious determination to resist the various entanglements offered by a text as compelling as *Absalom, Absalom!*" She is partly motivated by the assumption that "all those aspects of the text . . . have been repressed in earlier readings to accommodate interpretive conventions required by cultural priorities." The stories of women are "muted stories," what I have called submerged narratives. Going beyond the scope and focus of Donaldson's essay, one might well add Wash's daughter, Bon's mulatto wife, Clytie's mother, Rosa's mother, Rosa's aunt, Mrs. Compson. Ironically, a critic's focus on voiceless women results in inattention to another current privileged critical perspective, black studies. Voiceless also are Sutpen's male slaves, Bon's son (considered black), and so on. Rich contexts of the story that the storytellers tell and of their own personalities and histories enable the reader's imagination to give voice to the mute women in the shadows, and, if one is inclined, also the men who are voiceless in the novel: Henry Sutpen and Charles Bon, obvious examples. For the telling process, the wording is major in the novel as written, and so imagining the telling voices of the mute characters is as important as the stories the reader may imagine about them. What Faulkner imagines as told is enhanced by what readers imagine that Faulkner does not tell. Donaldson concludes that "what we learn in the end from such a double reading, one that concentrates both on what *is* told and *not* told, is not just the seductions of patriarchy but its limits and weaknesses as well."

In "*Absalom, Absalom!*: Story-Telling as a Mode of Transcendence," Richard Forrer stresses how each storyteller imagines most of what he or she tells, even Mr. Compson regarding Wash Jones. More than most critics, Forrer discusses the role of Faulkner as narrator, who seems to become one of the characters very like all the others. The storytellers' experience of telling demonstrates "that self-transcendence is possible because men have within themselves a spiritual reality that transcends—and requires their transcending—all social and cultural barriers" through storytelling, that self-transcendence is "realized—when the narrator imaginatively repossesses the values of others as expressions of their own deepest self." One might add that although the triumph of the imagination may not be followed by transcendence, the triumph in itself is a value.

Philip Goldstein conducts a very interesting and useful comparison in "Black Feminism and the Canon: Faulkner's *Absalom, Absalom!* and Morrison's *Beloved* as Gothic Romances." Having established the fact that both works go beyond the conventions of the gothic novel, Goldstein compares and contrasts the two, illuminating both in ways that attention to each separately cannot. He succinctly reviews the range of critical perspectives on the novels and concludes: "I have argued that, while *Beloved* and *Absalom, Absalom!* both depict gothic romances, Faulkner's novel shares the modernist disillusionment with liberal notions of progress and freedom, whereas Morrison's novel forcefully suggests that the community can overcome these horrors and reintegrate its alienated members. Since *Beloved* proves the better romance, it justifies the black feminism supporting it even as it denies the autonomy of both African American and traditional criticism."

In "'A Shape to Fill a Lack': *Absalom, Absalom!* and the Pattern of History," Deborah Wilson discusses the ways women are sidelined in the writing of the history in which they played a role. Having compared Faulkner's view of the role of women in history and in telling the stories of the past with Robert Penn Warren's *All the King's Men*, Wilson explores the biblical story of David compared with Sutpen's story. She examines each storyteller and listener, including Rosa, with attention to Judith and other women who have no voice in the novel— "drowned out by male voices." Faulkner focuses finally upon Quentin and Shreve, a marriage of two voices, made possible in part by Rosa's having relinquished her role as poetic, historical storyteller to a young male, Quentin. "For Faulkner, the shape of history in his narratives compensates for the loss of the patriarchal Old South, restoring authority to men who tell the stories over and over while the women listen silently from the grave."

In "Faulkner's Prose Style in *Absalom, Absalom!*" Robert H. Zoellner's intricate analysis of Faulkner's complex style may seem initially as difficult to follow as the style he is explaining, but understanding Faulkner's style is so important for fullest enjoyment of the novel that time and effort spent carefully reading Zoellner's essay is well worthwhile. The style of *Absalom* is its essence. Readers with background in any one of the nonliterary disciplines (music, engineering, mathematics, for example) may fall in quite comfortably with this kind of analysis. Very little criticism sets out to explain Faulkner's famous style—which is often too complex for some readers—the words that create the novel, the words from which all interpretations, and the words to express them, derive.

Linda Wagner-Martin, in "Rosa Coldfield as Daughter: Another of Faulkner's Lost Children," brings Rosa alive, gives her story, including her childhood years apart from Sutpen, but in the shadow always of Sutpen's effect on other men, especially her oblivious father, whose behavior combined with Sutpen's robbed her of childhood and maidenhood. Wagner-Martin sensitively and meaningfully pieces Rosa's life together from fragments strewn throughout the novel in the course of her own storytelling and that of Mr. Compson, Quentin, and Shreve as they take over her story, subordinate it to the Sutpen saga. There is much we can learn from Rosa's story, Wagner-Martin points out, and she teaches us a good deal. For one thing, she moves among and observes the lives of the other women who lived in the shadows of men.

In "War and Memory: Quentin Compson's Civil War," Lewis P. Simpson places Quentin Compson in the context of literary history, especially with Huck Finn, as the protagonist, as the only character who imagines an answer to the question, Why did Henry Sutpen kill his idol, his older half brother Charles Bon? He also examines the role of the omniscient narrator, Faulkner.

Beginning with the theme of time in the novel, in "The Dead Father in Faulkner" John T. Irwin slips from applying Freud into the Old Testament. He traces the continuity between Quentin's struggle with time in *The Sound and the Fury* and *Absalom*, focusing on the relationships between all the fathers and sons and the question of incest. Irwin's essay is the most demanding of reader concentration among those presented here; his is the most sustained argument, from point to point. The alert reader does well to carry over memory of the first fifteen pages into the final five, keeping in mind that Irwin continues to draw a parallel, though no longer overt, between father and son in the two Faulkner novels and Abraham and Isaac and God and Christ (and the Holy Spirit).

In the general spirit of helpfulness that guides this book, I need to caution readers about the page references to *Absalom, Absalom!* in the various essays. Most of the authors of the reprinted essays state that they refer to page numbers in the Modern Library edition. The original essays (those in the section headed "Critical Contexts") refer to later editions. Readers should be aware that the 1986 corrected edition was retypeset for the 1990 edition, thus changing the page numbers.

* * *

Something about our vision of the act and art of reading critical essays may be useful here. We realize that readers may disagree with some parts of the various forms of criticism offered here about *Absalom*, but from no one of them is the reader likely to fail to derive some useful insight. Faulkner's own myriad-mindedness created a novel so complex that every interpretation of his "little postage stamp of native soil" is as valid as a single postage stamp in a postal system.

Each piece is limited by its premise, but that very limitation enables the critic to focus the reader's attention on a particular aspect of this multifaceted novel. The value of each of these pieces lies not only in what it reveals but also in what it does not reveal, enabling the reader to participate in the process of elucidation by questioning, disagreeing, conjuring his or her own insights along the way.

A perhaps grander view is that one value of this collection of new and previously published essays is that a certain unity among them emerges as the reader reads all of them. All the authors present insights that many of the other thousand or so critics who have written about this novel also present, with wide variations, in different contexts, so that the reader may see the novel from more than one vantage point, because no one of them obviously can tell all. The reader may become a pluralistic, myriad-minded interpreter who brings to the whole of them an overall balance.

Just as Faulkner as creator and his characters as delvers into the past and transmitters of what they discover dive into the experience of the novel at nonchronological places, one way to read the novel, even for the first time, is to dive into it at any point, as into a river, and swim up- or downstream, then sit for a while on the bank, watching the river flow. That is not true of most other great novels that are works of art, such as *The Great Gatsby* or even the multifaceted *All the King's Men.*

Readers of the criticism on *Absalom* do well to remember that many critics take readers through the process of storytelling as an effort to bring order to history, the present making sense of the past. But the reader of *Absalom* is first of all having the immediate experience of the act of storytelling in kinship with the storyteller's own immediate experience of telling in the very present.

While reading any genre, fiction or nonfiction, readers interrogate the text in various ways; so in reading critics who are questioning the text, the reader questions the questioner, and that experience is richer if the reader deliberately, very consciously does so. Like the listeners of the stories being told in *Absalom*, who say often, "Wait! Go back and tell about . . . ," the reader of criticism searching for answers does well to question, agree, and disagree.

Above all, if the reader's imagination has been inspired and is at work, the novel becomes more accessible, more enjoyable, and richer. One critic says that the reader of the novel must become a kind of writer; so reading that critic and all others, the reader must become a sort of writer of criticism. Because Faulkner is more myriad-minded in this than in any of his other novels, each point a critic makes stimulates an opposing argument, and that is where the imagination and mind of the reader of these pieces, who has read the novel, come into play.

In reading any critical essay, the reader should be aware that it is in the nature of writing criticism that once a critic lays out the grid of a premise, concentration upon that premise often causes him or her to spin off peripheral inferences and speculations to the erroneousness of which they are inattentive. For instance, if the premise is that the novel is about the storyteller's effort to trace the history of Sutpen's effort to create a patrimony, then the critic may be inattentive to all the evidence that Quentin is the novel's protagonist. The reader of a critical essay who is attentive has the last word.

Another general caution the reader should keep in mind is that far too many critical discussions, in classrooms as well as in publications, proceed to develop historic and/or thematic arguments without first identifying the techniques of fiction that the novelist employs to express those ideas. Foremost among techniques is the novelist's choice of point of view: first-person, third-person omniscient, or third-person limited (or "central intelligence," Henry James's phrase, which is more pertinent). Style evolves out of point of view. Confusion arises when the terms "point of view" and "narrator" are used loosely, as when Quentin, Rosa, and Mr. Compson are called narrators even by those who point out that Faulkner is the omniscient narrator. It is clearer to refer to these three characters as "storytellers," in the oral tradition, rather than as narrators in the art-of-fiction use of the term. Their acts of storytelling are embedded in the omniscient narration.

Related to that confusion is the fallacy of the often-employed term "unreliable narrator." It is in the nature of human communication and of literary first-person narration that all such narrators are to varying degrees unreliable and that their unreliability is an inherent part of the experience of reading them. Faulkner makes an unusual effort to make each of the *Absalom* storytellers unreliable. Facts are of little relevance in this novel. Knowing Sutpen through the distorting voices is the point; the primary experience is storytelling as distortion itself. Some critics try to make factual sense of it all by taking the reader by the hand and walking him or her through the storytelling sessions, plucking facts and fragments and assembling them into one theory or another, as if to say, See now, this is the truth. Even so, those theories are valuable if the reader keeps well in mind what Faulkner's point-of-view technique is and that questions about the unreliability of one character or another are unreliable or at least very limited guides through the novel. A rich subconscious life is implied by the conscious life of each character; in a community of telling and listening, those submerged feelings, imaginings, and thoughts overlap, intermingle, mesh, as it is also with the critics who read each other.

My experience, as editor making choices regarding what to include in this volume, has been quite simply thrilling, at moments exhilarating, even exalting. For the nearly one thousand articles on record about *Absalom* collectively one is inclined to use the word "magnificent"—even the run-into-the-ground word "awesome." Being informed by a select few—the present collection—is a delight.

THE BOOK
AND
AUTHOR

On *Absalom, Absalom!*:
A Guide Through Myriad-Minded Faulkner _____

David Madden

"Come into the dining room with me, David," said William Faulkner's niece, Dean, daughter of the brother who died in a plane crash. I did. "Now touch this table." I did. "It was at this table that Pappy worked on *Absalom, Absalom!* while I was still in my mother's womb." So ever since then, I have pictured my favorite novelist, haunted by the death of his younger brother, meditating and writing on the cherrywood dining room table in his mother's house where Dean Faulkner Wells now lives.

As reader, teacher, critic, and novelist, I regard Faulkner as the greatest of all novelists—greater than the others I most admire, Conrad, Joyce, Mann, Dickens, Hugo, Balzac, and Meredith. *Absalom* is my favorite novel, a work of art that I can reread many times. Compared with some of the world's great works—Balzac's *Cousin Bette*, Hugo's *The Man Who Laughs*, Dickens's *Bleak House*, Conrad's *Nostromo*, Brontë's *Wuthering Heights*, Tolstoy's *Anna Karenina*, James's *Portrait of a Lady*, Joyce's *Ulysses*, Melville's *Moby Dick*, Mann's *Magic Mountain*, Wolfe's *Look Homeward, Angel*, Gaddis's *The Recognitions*, Pynchon's *Gravity's Rainbow*—the myriad-minded Faulkner's masterpiece *Absalom, Absalom!* is much more complex and difficult.

Because of that difficulty, I decided that a practical guide through the novel as a work of art would prove to be a helpful supplement to the varied commentaries collected in this volume. Given that Faulkner's artistry created *Absalom, Absalom!*, it makes sense to begin a study of the novel with attention to the techniques of fiction that produced it. As he created this work of art, Faulkner made artistic choices; the reader, consciously or unconsciously, is aware that those choices were made and experiences the results of those choices. The reader experiences the techniques themselves as well as what they convey.

Each technique Faulkner chose enabled him to explore the possibilities of his raw material. In the various phases of the creative process, Faulkner consciously and deliberately employed basic artistic techniques in innovative ways. In *Absalom, Absalom!* all the elements of *the art of fiction* are active on the highest plane of achievement.

Every novel that is a fine work of art is created out of and controlled by the author's *conception*. Faulkner's conception is that Quentin Compson becomes immersed in the southern oral storytelling process and ends in a state of existential anxiety. A conception is a total grasp of the story that enables the author to control the development of the situation, the characters, theme, plot, point of view, style, and other techniques. It orders, interprets, and gives form to the raw material of the story and infuses it with vision and meaning.

The *charged image* is Quentin listening to Miss Rosa; superimposed upon it is the charged image of the story to which he listens: the gate to Sutpen Hundred. (It is like the double charged image in *The Great Gatsby* of the green light at the end of Daisy's dock and the eyes of T. J. Eckleburg in the Valley of Ashes.) The charged image is the dominant, controlling image-nucleus in a work of fiction. More vivid and simpler than the conception, it helps to illuminate the development of the conception. As the reader moves from part to part, the charged image discharges its potency gradually. After the reader has fully experienced the story, fully perceived it in a picture, that focal image (of Quentin listening to the story that ends at the gate) continues to discharge its electrical power. The device of the charged image provides the writer with one way of achieving coherence, synthesis, and organic unity: the important elements of a story are condensed and compressed into this charged image; it can evoke all the other elements—theme, character, setting, conflict, and style. The developing elements become integrated finally into a single image, which is really a tissue of many images: all the Quentin listening images and all the gatelike images (doors, windows, and so on).

In the act of listening, *the listener (Quentin) becomes the protago-*

nist, whose conflict is internal more than external. In making a character the protagonist whose primary act is to listen, Faulkner created a new dimension in fiction. If Quentin is the main character, the reader must consider why Sutpen, the subject of all the storytelling, is not.

Faulkner begins the *structure* with Quentin and Rosa and returns to Quentin after every instance of focus on a storyteller or major character within the stories.

1. Faulkner narrates Rosa, as insider, telling Quentin about Sutpen.
2. Father, as outsider, tells Quentin about Sutpen and Rosa.
3. Father tells Quentin more about Sutpen.
4. Father continues to tell Quentin about Sutpen.
5. Rosa tells Quentin more about Sutpen.
6. Shreve retells to Quentin what, Faulkner implies, Quentin has already told him and his father about Sutpen.
7. Quentin tells Shreve about Sutpen's early life via his father, who got it from his own father.
8. Quentin and Shreve as a duo tell the story of Bon and Henry and Judith Sutpen.
9. Faulkner narrates the storytelling aftermath of Quentin and Shreve.

Quentin is the listener in each chapter, even in chapters 7 and 8; having been a listener before the novel opens, he even listens to his own telling as he tells it. Faulkner chose Rosa only among the women to tell the story; all the other storytellers are men, mainly Mr. Compson, Quentin, then Shreve. Other voices are only reported as being storytellers, especially Sutpen via Grandfather Compson, and various townsmen a little now and then, and Ellen and Quentin's grandmother, and his grandfather.

Faulkner's *point-of-view technique* overall is omniscient, within which we experience the separate quoted narrations of Aunt Rosa, Mr. Compson, and Quentin. *Absalom, Absalom!* is a matrix of meditations. It is first of all Faulkner's own meditation on the meditations of the characters he was creating; even when they are telling stories, they speak in a meditative voice, like most storytellers in the southern oral storytelling tradition, but with a far more intense tone of meditation and in a style purely Faulknerian. Quentin is the only character whose thoughts we get directly, another signal that he is the main character. The *setting in time and place* affects the way the characters tell and listen to stories, especially Quentin in the hot, wisteria-soft South and in the cold, iron North. Faulkner wants the reader to plunge into this storytelling process, get involved, and become affected emotionally, imaginatively, intellectually.

The reader can feel that Faulkner has a compulsion to tell this story, and he evokes that compulsion in his characters, of whom Shreve may be the best example, for he has less reason to tell the story and so must feel a compulsion. Quentin feels no such compulsion. He makes few responses to Rosa—"nome"—and Father—"no sir"—often to Shreve, in the course of his long story about Sutpen.

All the storytellers are also listeners to stories, and all, especially Quentin and Shreve, identify themselves with some of the characters. "The eagerness of the listener quickens the tongue of the teller," says Jane Eyre.

Faulkner has realized all the basic potentials of the *omniscient point of view* and imagined innovations. The most important innovation is that the act of listening makes Quentin the protagonist. He uses the device of *interior monologue*, confined to Quentin's expressionistic meditation. The device of the *dramatic monologue* comes somewhat into play, most apparently in those long, uninterrupted storytelling passages, sometimes in paragraphs five pages long. By contrast, when storytellers stop to question Quentin, his replies are very short, usually "yes" or "no, sir." Quentin is telling the Sutpen story to himself, really, not to Shreve, or is he even aware of Shreve as listener?

Faulkner's omniscient voice is more psychological than narrative. In chapter 8, Faulkner comments on Shreve and Quentin and mixes in Quentin talking briefly and meditating as Shreve is telling the story back to Quentin. The main contribution of chapter 8 to Faulkner's concept is the voices of Quentin and Shreve imagining Henry and Bon riding toward the gate to the mansion where Judith waits and feeling intensely that they are actually there in that time and place, that they are riding with them, two and two, until they become Henry and Bon. That is one of the many artistic innovations in this novel.

While other authors have mingled several distinct point-of-view techniques (omniscient with first person, as in Joseph Conrad's *Lord Jim*, or three or four labeled first-person narrators), Faulkner's meshing of omniscient with four major quoted storytellers in *Absalom* is an innovation. Another innovation is that he violates the general practice of novelists whereby the omniscient author maintains a proper distance between himself and his material. By giving the storytellers the same style as his own omniscient narration, he deliberately narrows the distance between himself and his storytellers.

Faulkner makes his storytellers so extremely unreliable as to obliterate the concept of *the unreliable narrator* so often addressed in discussions of works of fiction. In his own relatively reliable omniscient narration, he tells as little as he can, mostly about how the characters feel about each other, refraining from telling about factual events.

The dynamics of telling and listening to stories are based in human nature. That everyone in the area is a storyteller is implied by the actual storytellers, talking and telling about all events, not just the key ones repeated in the novel itself. Faulkner sets every facet of the story in motion simultaneously, so all that was told before, literal and implied, goes forward into the next page and the next as one reads a given page, itself full of elements repeated or new. Even those facets we have not yet read about are already in motion for Faulkner to present more fully in a nonlinear sequence. What we read before is active in our subconscious as we attend to each new facet and we anticipate what is to come. The technique of *simultaneity* is one demonstration of Faulkner's myriad-mindedness. Faulkner sometimes *juxtaposes* telling, listening, talking, and meditation in a cluster.

In chapter 7, Quentin tells Shreve the story of Sutpen, quoting or paraphrasing his father, who told him, quoting and paraphrasing his grandfather telling his father the story of his life that Sutpen told him, with some details told by the grandmother and Major De Spain and passed on, all having told it many times before and probably to other listeners; and then Shreve retells parts of the story back to Quentin, until Quentin demands to continue telling it, Shreve still interrupting often, calling it play (which on one level it is) to conceal his deeper feelings. Through the general contexts of the novel, Faulkner implies that hundreds of other folk must have told fragments of the story of Sutpen outside the immediate context of the novel. Saying that "nobody knows" some things, all of them—Sutpen, Grandfather, Father, Quentin, Shreve—imagine much of what is not known, sometimes admittedly, saying, "I imagine." Quentin's father imagines Wash's thoughts, speeches, and actions and Bon's talk with Henry. If Father is more personal in the telling of stories than Quentin, we experience Quentin's subconscious.

Faulkner seems to have imposed no limit on his *imagination*, but, as his revisions prove, he has chosen every word with great care (see Langford). The power of the imagination is a major *theme*. Faulkner conveys the importance of memory and imagination in the South, with Shreve's northern lack of it for contrast. Out of his own memories of his family's history, Faulkner derives and enhances the memory of his cast of characters. Each storyteller imagines outright or says, "I imagine." Quentin says, "I can see it." Father says to Quentin, "As you put it." He paraphrases Quentin. "I can imagine them as they rode," says Father. Then Quentin and Shreve later imagine the same thing. Readers may imagine that even Bon's mother's lawyer is a storyteller who imagines. Each character imagines—Father, too, as a child listening, watching, waiting. For what? Why? Faulkner implies that he wants the reader to imagine the effect on Quentin of his father's tone of voice and rhetoric. The characters' memories, imaginings, and their storytelling crisscross, overlap, mesh. Father's motivations for telling Quentin stories so obsessively and Quentin's motivations for listening are complex. Father implies that the stories of the past are their stories, too, his and Quentin's. Quentin listens more to Father as his father than to the story itself. Father as medium is the message. Quentin is talking not to Shreve but to the letter that represents Miss Rosa, as if in the flesh.

Just as I claim that all first-person narratives are about the narrator, in this novel storytelling is about the storyteller. Faulkner's choice of and employment of his point-of-view technique expresses, in itself, major facets of his conception.

It is in the nature of the art of fiction that *style* is dictated by the point-of-view technique chosen for each work of fiction. And Faulkner's style is a major expression of his conception. Page-long sentences and four- and five-page paragraphs imitate the immersion of the storytellers in the flow of the telling and the listeners, especially Quentin, in the listening experience. That Quentin's style in telling Sutpen's story, gotten from his one-armed grandfather, via Sutpen, is simpler than elsewhere in the novel suggests that he feels little or no emotional involvement.

As Faulkner the omniscient narrator moves from one storyteller to another, his style remains the same, except for Shreve's northern wisecracking way of talking. To provide contrast to his general style, Faulkner meshes folk speech and slang. He emotionally, imaginatively, and intellectually chooses each word and phrase, mindful of how each relates to other words and phrases. His stylistic imagination is at work word by word, line by line.

Even though Faulkner's style is complex, his sentences and paragraphs often unusually long, his style generates *a sense of immediacy*. That style is to some extent a compound of word choices and phrases from other fiction (Sir Walter Scott's novels, for instance) and from the law, politics, religion, slang, and colloquialisms. His style is a mixture of humor, a sardonic tone, and philosophical-sounding and elegiac, lyrical passages. The effects are a variety of tones, not only sardonic but also tragic (although the novel is not a tragedy).

Faulkner's use, against the general practice in fiction, of *compound adjectival phrases and adverbial clauses* is deliberate. His style is mainly literary, but he mixes in the style of southern oral storytelling. His use of rhetorical *parallelisms* lends variety of syntax to his style. The rhetoric of storytelling expresses the sense of a community, but Faulkner and the storytellers are not captivated in the same way, so that we feel an artistic tension between Faulkner and the storytellers.

Because both Faulkner and the storytellers speak in the mode of community consciousness, *pronoun use* is deliberately ambiguous (it, he, they ["they will have told you"]).

His use of *punctuation* is controlled to achieve various effects. A major feature of his style is *parenthetical phrasing* that demonstrates the double-mindedness of southern storytellers eager to pull everything into the process. Some have thematic effect: in a world of fathers and husbands and sons, women are often parenthesized, expressing the idea that women, as vessels of the ideal, are often empty. (Parentheses often enclose Quentin, too, speaking or thinking.) Shreve interrupts Quentin sometimes in parentheses. *Italics* usually signal that we are entering Quentin's internal monologue.

The dynamics of Faulkner's style are such that seeming *digressions* turn out to be major developments. (See pages 114-24 in the 1990 Vintage International-Vintage Books corrected edition of *Absalom, Absalom!* All further page numbers cited here refer to that edition of the novel.)

The posing of *questions* is a device that stimulates the reader's attention and interest while being another expression of the concept. "But why tell me about it?" Quentin asks few questions, but Shreve, a surrogate for the reader, asks many. Readers raise far more questions than do the characters.

Fiction writers normally strive to play *short sentences and long sentences* off each other and vary the length of *paragraphs* to achieve rhythm. Faulkner does that in his own distinctive way, as, for instance, when, after a very long sentence or paragraph, he hits the reader with a staccato series of short sentences. *Sentence fragments* serve as emphasis but also as signals of a facet of the storytelling process: the gathering of fragments.

Basically when a writer *plays on words* or *contorts syntax*, the effect is to lend a sense of mindful liveliness to the style. Faulkner does that far more frequently than is usual, attributing that liveliness to the storytelling act and for stress.

Faulkner's style often seems *overwritten*, seems indulgent in abstract statement, overloaded with archaic or Latinate words. His distinctive syntax may seem too contorted, even awkward, but the reader's full attention will result in both delight and enlightenment. The paradoxical effect is that most of the novel is *underwritten* because so much of it arises in the reader's consciousness as implication.

The device of *contrast* is vital in a work of fiction. Faulkner's style contrasts severely with that of the characters living in the locale of the novel, even though all the storytellers are intelligent and well educated. Nobody tells stories orally in that style, which is full of words seldom used even in nonfiction. Faulkner decided that he wanted the artifice of having the characters speak in his own elevated, complex style as omniscient narrator. Like the reader, Quentin would not know the definitions of all the words his father uses.

There are three types of *context*, the effect of which is to enable Faulkner to imply far more than he states, drawing into the process the reader's participation. External to the novel's "action" are the general context of Europe, the United States, and the dreamy ideal of the South; the general internal context is the nightmare of the family. The immediate context is Quentin. Implications derive from these three contexts. And each paragraph creates an immediate context. Immediate internal contexts also enable Faulkner to transform clichés that, when presented straight, often dull a writer's style. All three contexts serve the conception described above.

The technique of *context and implication* enabled Faulkner to develop submerged narratives, about Judith mainly; about her mother,

Ellen, and Rosa, her aunt; about Wash's daughter; and about Bon's mother, his wife, and his grandson's wife. We may give them storytelling voices by imagining them, if we wish, hovering over, haunting the realm of their silences, haunting the voices of the males who are oblivious to the women.

Out of Faulkner's conception comes the role of *repetition* as technique and as meaning. The compulsion to tell a story results in repetition not only of the events of the story but also of words, phrases, and images within the story. The repetition device is, in this novel, expression. There are two general types of repetition in *Absalom*: Faulkner's and the storytellers' repetition of words and phrases in the style and their repetition of ideas and events. Here is a selection of words and phrases repeated throughout (see also Polk and Hart): "it," "because," "aghast," "outrage," "recapitulation," "but," "doubtless," "he," "they," "long since," "maybe," "and that was all," "so," "wait," "believe," "amazement." The word "amazement" means more to others than to Quentin, who is bewildered. "I" appears very seldom, suggesting a community of storytellers. Father uses "one," "all of us," "we." To draw in Quentin, he uses "you" often. The repetition of key words and phrases, events, and character relationships in *Absalom* goes beyond the norm, far beyond, so that the artistic device of repetition becomes a vital part of the essence of the reader's experience, the reader's own mental acknowledgment and sounding of what is repeated becoming also part of the repetition emotion. The reader's experience of repetition for emphasis is an enjoyment in itself. Faulkner knows that something about repetition, incremental with variations, delights both the teller and the listener.

The compulsion to repeat, Faulkner's and the characters', even the very same words (twenty or thirty times sometimes), and the satisfaction in the act of repeating, as in Homer and the Old Testament, give the style an incantatory tone, a trancelike aura, that sometimes hallucinatory effect. And Faulkner repeats some of the same artistic devices, in deliberately exaggerated forms, with and without variations. Sometimes parts of the story are repeated incrementally with variations and then we get a fuller version.

Faulkner often uses the technique of *withholding a scene*, delaying it, after alluding repeatedly to it—the scene in the tent with Henry and his father, Sutpen, the scene in the house with Rosa and Clytie and Henry.

Faulkner as narrator and his characters as storytellers employ many *allusions* of many types to enhance moments throughout the novel. There are historical allusions to the world, America, the South, the Civil War; to the Greeks and the Romans; to literature and the theater; and to the Bible. Literary allusions include allusions to the Greeks and Shakespeare, to Sir Walter Scott, to war, to Bon, to the climax. The teller may allude more than once to an event to come and, after telling about it in detail, allude to it as he moves forward into the story.

Faulkner's use of the technique of *parallels* enhances his depiction of characters and events. For instance, the origin of Wash parallels that of Sutpen, and Henry and Bon as roommates and friends are paralleled by Quentin and Shreve. Other parallels include Rosa's father hiding in the attic and Henry hiding in the bedroom of the house; conflict within the family and conflict in war within the United States; Shreve's pipe and father's cigar; Bon's scheme and Sutpen's design; deep breathing and panting; Rosa and wisteria, and Quentin and honeysuckle; Rosa well read and literary, a poet, like her father; Sutpen's cabin and Wash's cabin; Rosa/Clytie and Clytie/Wash. Parallels lend artistic unity of effect to the novel.

Ambiguity is a major technique, the positive effect of which is to enthrall the reader. Ambiguity arises out of Faulkner's conception. In the storytelling process, the storytellers are often unclear as to what really happened, especially the details, and their listeners pass on ambiguities when they retell the story. Vague pronouns (he, they, we, it) contribute to ambiguities. In his own voice, Faulkner engages in ambiguities that express the general aura of mysterious uncertainty. Ambiguity torments Quentin. His last speech, repeated with more passion than any of his other speeches, is ambiguous: Does he really mean that he does not hate the South? If he does not, in what ways does he regard the South and himself as a son of the South? Ambiguity expresses something about Quentin. Faulkner wants the reader to experience the many deliberate ambiguities as his intentions, not mistakes.

Faulkner cultivates an expressive ambiguity that is appropriate to the overall conception. His intentions are deliberately unclear. The reader does well to refrain from the effort to force everything to become clear. Faulkner seems to assume both too little and too much of his reader, creating confusion for many, but Faulkner actually assumes little or nothing, expecting the reader to plunge ahead, hand in hand with the storytellers, through a briar patch of ambiguities into a clearing of sorts.

Faulkner immerses the reader in *images* of every kind, activating all the reader's senses: sight, sound, taste, smell, and touch. All his descriptions of characters, setting, and objects are related to his conception.

It is expressive of the concept that many of the images are like *tableaux* because the characters are transfixed in time and place; but also they may be seen as components meshed into a tapestry, somewhat like the Bayeux tapestry.

The charged image of the novel is Quentin listening to Rosa; the charged image in the story the storytellers are telling is the gate to Sutpen's Hundred. The gate beyond which Bon must not go illuminates the function of front and back doors and windows throughout the novel. Key characters in the past have traumatic experiences at doors: Sutpen as a child is turned away from the front door of a mansion and in old age emerges from a cabin door and is slain; Clytie, Sutpen's half-black daughter, stops Rosa and Quentin at the front door of Sutpen's mansion and later at the foot of the stairs.

The gate and all images like gates (doors, windows) superimposed evoke all the other images as we read and remember what we have read: Quentin listening to Rosa in her office, to his father on the porch, to Shreve in the Harvard room; Sutpen riding the stallion; Henry and Judith watching the blacks fight; Sutpen putting his hand on Rosa's head; Mr. Coldfield tossing out the window the hammer he used to nail himself in the attic; Clytie barring the door, then the stairs; Bon and Sutpen in the tent; Bon's son, the son's son, Bon's wife, weeping at his grave; the Sutpen house; Rosa's house; the naked Negroes working; the French architect running; Sutpen and Eulalia in Haiti fighting insurgents together; Rosa's house; Quentin's hands framing the letter from Father in lamplight about Rosa's death.

The charged image, serving the conception, calls to mind all the other elements, artistic techniques, and characters.

Faulkner creates many patterns of *motifs*, including thematic ideas: gates, cabins, rooms, houses, doors, windows, flowers (mainly wisteria), rain, tears, hiding, dresses, blood, cannons and rifles, horses, dogs, tombstones, gardens, heat-cold contrast, fireflies, intense humidity in contrast to snow. Images of the two major settings contrast with each other: humid South, the college in Oxford, Mississippi, and cold North, Harvard in Cambridge, Massachusetts.

Faulkner makes full use of the technique of *objective correlative* (something in the objective world corresponding to something in the subjective world of a character). The Sutpen saga and its consequences, including the communal telling of stories about him, is a thematic objective correlative to Quentin's psyche, and Rosa's house is an objective correlative of her inner life.

Faulkner chose words and phrases to make images that are more often than not *surreal* or *expressionistic*, making language also often transcend the denotative and even the connotative to rise to levels of expression never before reached, causing readers sometimes to feel confused.

Some of the motifs are in the form of *simile and metaphor patterns*, often ironic or paradoxical. For instance, theater, photography, painting, and tableau figures of speech suggest the immobility, suspension, and transfixion of the characters. Some are related to character relationships: for instance, Rosa, the lifelong virgin; Sutpen, the demon with a design, seen and remembered.

For Faulkner's conception, *symbolism* of every type is essentially appropriate, even for the characters themselves, as Sutpen for instance regards his house as symbolic of the grand design, of himself, and the reader regards the two tombstones as general symbols of the same, and of what they have come to; one of them symbolizing the life of Ellen, the butterfly. Bon's name is symbolic: Bon = good, then Bond, bonded, bondage. Women as pure symbols have little other life in this story but to be symbolic. An instance of reciprocal irony is that the blacks who built the house symbolize the house, then the house symbolizes the blacks, especially Clytie living inside the house, who bars the front door, the back door, the stairs, the door to Henry's sickroom—all *tableaux*, symbolizing that blacks and whites, past and present, are transfixed between the dream of the ideal and the irony of reality. In various contexts, almost everything is symbolic.

Faulkner has imagined various uses for the device of *anticipation*. Faulkner has created a novel in which the characters experience simultaneously with the reader some of the techniques he employs, such as anticipation, somewhat akin, in this novel, to foreshadowing. The storytelling-listening process is such that characters and the reader often simultaneously anticipate what is to come.

Faulkner knows that readers become all the more enthralled when their expectations are reversed; the expectations of both reader and characters are reversed with unusual frequency in this novel. For example, Shreve and reader expect Sutpen's baby by Wash's granddaughter to be a boy, as Sutpen wanted so badly, but Faulkner uses the device of ironic *reversal*: the baby is a girl. Faulkner has imagined effective uses for the device of reversal. The reader's expectation that the next storyteller will be one of those introduced earlier is reversed when it is Shreve telling back the story Quentin told him, in which his attitude and his choice of words, not the story itself, are the main experience.

Faulkner is a master of the technique of *juxtaposition*, whereby one unit is juxtaposed to another in such a way as to arouse a third response in the reader's imagination. The technique is used in units as small as a sentence and as large as storytelling sessions, as when two characters in a certain time and place are unexpectedly juxtaposed, or when the ending of one chapter is juxtaposed to an unexpected, startling beginning of another.

The *pace* of the novel may seem very slow to readers who are still trying to get a fix on Faulkner's style and narrative structure. Actually, both in style and narrative the pace is deliberately slow, meditatively in some places, then speeded up in others—in both cases to express some facet of Faulkner's concept. The pace is faster throughout chapter 7, as befitting the tale of Sutpen's life, and in the short chapter 9, to enhance the climax.

Faulkner's *transitions* are deliberately unexpected. Scenes shift abruptly in time and space, in the midst of a storytelling session, and end abruptly, juxtaposed to a storytelling in a very different time and place.

We feel *tension* between the storyteller and the listener. How does that relate to Faulkner's concept? Tension among the characters in the stories being told and between the storytellers and their listeners is constant.

Each storyteller has a distinct *tone*: Faulkner slightly sardonic, Rosa angry and elegiac, Jason intellectual but sometimes lyrical, Quentin cool and matter-of-fact in retelling Sutpen's story, Shreve satirical but finally so sympathetic as to imagine and "become" with Quentin the two young men Henry and Bon riding through the night to the fatal gate.

Faulkner's concept is shot through with every type of *irony*. Out of violated innocence, Sutpen created a design, in the creation of which he is most guilty of violating the innocence of others, perhaps even Quentin, who has no desire to derive a design or even a concept out of listening to stories. A house slave barred the front door to Thomas and a house slave, Clytie, bars even the back door to white trash, Wash;

Sutpen rose above his lowly origin, admired by Wash, who slays him when he treats his granddaughter worse than he would a horse. Judith and Henry both loved a man who turned out to be black, an irony of one of the causes of the Civil War, slavery. Ideally, women were held up on a pedestal but in the real world they are confined to parentheses. Ironically, Bon's son is admitted to the house and allowed to live there, but he chooses to live in a cabin.

Faulkner's conception has guided him in his development of the *elements* of fiction: *character, conflict, setting,* and *theme.* In the setting of the past, conflicts among characters are primarily external but simultaneously internal; in the setting of the present, the conflict is mainly internal, focusing on Quentin.

The major *themes* are so enmeshed with the words as to frustrate extraction. An example is the major thematic focus on Quentin's listening to and retelling to his father and Shreve the Sutpen tale. He alone has heard everything, much of it all his life. The meaning of the novel lies in what that process expresses about Quentin as each reader interprets it. The story he has listened to far too many times expresses the theme that southerners want to be both civilized and wild, at least vicariously, or actually wild in war, but without consequences, which is all that follows through the years up until Quentin's final words.

After the South's defeat in the Civil War, southerners relived the past vicariously. Every character in the novel lives vicariously, except Quentin, who does not understand or care about the past, especially the Civil War, but who finally has a *vicarious experience* when he "becomes" Henry and Bon as one person, just as Henry and Judith experienced Bon vicariously through each other. Judith and Clytie variously relive their feelings for Bon by taking care of his son. Ironically, the seed of the Lost Cause is in poor whites, as when Wash worships Sutpen.

One psychological effect of living other people's lives is the enduring feeling of *missing life*, so that what one has missed dominates one's life. Many of the characters seldom saw Sutpen or Bon, but their vicariousness and sense of things missing resulted in affecting Father and Quentin as listeners, who in turn experienced vicariousness and a sense of the missing. Rosa missed it all, even her own courtship, and so did Judith.

All the artistic elements in the novel are extreme, on some super-hyper level of expressionism (reality distorted or exaggerated to express a traumatic subjective state). Proceeding from his conception, Faulkner has innovatively applied a wide range of artistic techniques to create a coherent, organic work of art that conveys to the reader a sense of *simultaneity* of all its parts as the reader moves through the novel and a sense of *inevitability* at the end, a sense that nothing could have been different without impairing the artistic whole. Anton Chekhov said, "Cut a story at any point and it will bleed." Characters feel a sense of inevitability about what has happened and will happen and even speak of that, and the reader feels that everything in the novel as it progresses and as it ends is inevitable.

More than a thousand articles and books have been written about this novel's meaning, but as the poet Archibald MacLeish said, "A poem should not mean but be," and *Absalom* is one of those novels that are first of all pure experiences.

Faulkner's uses of the art of fiction in *Absalom, Absalom!*, serving to realize his conception, may be seen almost page by page in the following list. (Page numbers referenced in this list are those in the 1990 Vintage International-Vintage Books corrected edition of the novel.)

Faulkner's Use of the Art of Fiction

Page

3	*Expressionistic effect.* Also 148, meditation
	Style: compound adjectives
7	*Question device*
9	*Photographs motif:* figurative and actual
15-21	*Pronoun ambiguity:* "he" "she" "it"
22	*Characters imagine:* implied regarding Rosa

Page

283 *Character revelation:* Henry learns from father that Bon is "part ne-
     gro."

284-85 *Juxtaposition:* of scene with Henry and Sutpen regarding Bon to
        Henry and Bon regarding Judith

286 *Gate motif:* Henry challenging Bon

     Parallel: Shreve challenges Quentin as Henry challenged Bon; see
     final page also

287 Quentin responses: he speaks only seven times in 65 pages, saying
     only a few words; speaks very little in final chapter

     Repetition: unity of effect, end of chapter 7, 234, and end of chapter
     8, 287, Shreve uses similar phrase

     Ironic question: Does Shreve feel more deeply about the story than
     Quentin?

288 *Chapter lengths:* 9 is shortest, style simple, 15 pages

     Omniscient narration: Faulkner's narration more sustained in this
     chapter

298 *Revelation, major:* Quentin discovers Henry lying sick in the house

     Juxtaposition: climactic scene in the hot bedroom in the house end-
     ing *"Henry Sutpen,"* next paragraph we are back in the cold bedroom
     at Harvard

298-99 *Literary allusion:* to Poe's "The Raven," "Nevermore."

299 *Surprise ending:* to Sutpen narrative—Clytie sets the house on fire,
     she and Henry perish, Rosa as witness

301 *Delay device:* Quentin finishes reading father's letter, which began
     160 pages before, about the death of Miss Rosa

303 *Climax:* of Quentin's experience of listening and telling and discov-
     ering—one of the most famous endings in literature

     Repetition: within a speech—Quentin: "I don't hate it!"

Works Cited

Faulkner, William. *Absalom, Absalom!: The Corrected Text.* 1936. New York:
     Vintage, 1990.

Langford, Gerald. *Faulkner's Revision of "Absalom, Absalom!": A Collation of
     the Manuscript and the Published Book.* Austin: University of Texas Press,
     1971.

Polk, Noel, and John D. Hart, eds. *"Absalom, Absalom!": A Concordance to the
     Novel.* West Point, NY: Faulkner Concordance Advisory Board, 1989.

Biography of William Faulkner _____

Lorie Watkins Fulton

Although William Faulkner claimed that his "ancestors came from Inverness, Scotland" and that the "principal family lines were Falconer, Murray, McAlpine, and Cameron," there "were more versions of the Falkner origins than the number of families Faulkner himself settled on" (Blotner 3, 4). Eventually, Faulkner's great-grandfather settled in what would later become Tippah County, Mississippi, and lived there for "the rest of his life, siring one of the most unusual southern families ever to be produced in that state and becoming, himself, the inspiration for one of the most extreme, most influential, most amazing legends to emerge from the nineteenth century South" (Duclos 16). This is the legend that William Faulkner inherited and, to be sure, incorporated into his fiction. More commonly referred to as "the Old Colonel," Faulkner's great-grandfather, William C. Falkner, serves as the prototype for Colonel John Sartoris in *Flags in the Dust* and *The Unvanquished*, and Donald Philip Duclos notes that "the entire Sartoris family have their counterparts in the Faulkner family with but little attempt made to disguise them" (6). The Old Colonel's Civil War exploits and literary successes influenced Faulkner from an early age: Duclos writes that like "Gail Hightower, in *Light in August*, William Faulkner too 'had grown up with a ghost'" (5). When asked what he wanted to be when he grew up, Faulkner told Miss Eades, his third-grade teacher, "I want to be a writer like my great-granddaddy" (Blotner 105). Become a writer he did. Faulkner went on to spend almost thirty years writing fiction set primarily in his native state.

Faulkner's success, however, did not always seem so assured. A high school dropout, he tried to enlist in the U.S. Army for service in World War I after his childhood sweetheart, Estelle Oldham, married another man. The army rejected Faulkner, but, determined to join the war effort, he finally enlisted as a cadet in the Canadian Royal Air

Force. The war ended before he saw active duty, although Faulkner sometimes allowed people to assume that he suffered injuries in combat that resulted in a limp and the placement of a steel plate in his head. In 1918, Faulkner returned to Oxford and soon enrolled in the University of Mississippi as a war veteran. On campus, Faulkner continued to write poetry, helped found a dramatic club called the Marionettes, wrote material for the club, and submitted artwork, fiction, and poetry to the school yearbook. Faulkner left Ole Miss after three terms and took a series of odd jobs, including becoming postmaster for the university post office and leading the local troop of Boy Scouts. With the help of friend Phil Stone, Faulkner did secure a contract with the Four Seas Company to publish a book of poetry, *The Marble Faun*, in 1924, but that same year the post office dismissed Faulkner because of charges of negligence brought by the postal inspector, and the Boy Scouts discharged him for "moral reasons," presumably related to alcohol. A failure by the standards of most Oxford citizens, Faulkner fortuitously left town for New Orleans with plans to sail for Europe in 1925. In New Orleans, Faulkner befriended Sherwood Anderson, a fellow modernist, who gave Faulkner entrée into the town's literary milieu and later changed the course of Faulkner's career by suggesting that Faulkner write about the material he knew best, the people of Oxford. During this period, Faulkner turned from poetry to fiction. He also began to write for the *New Orleans Times-Picayune*, and in 1926, after Faulkner returned from Europe, Boni and Liveright published his first two novels. *Soldiers' Pay* is a novel born of Faulkner's war experience, and *Mosquitoes* draws from his experience with the New Orleans literary scene. In his third novel, Faulkner took Anderson's advice and began writing tales of his apocryphal town of Jefferson, fictionally located in Yoknapatawpha County, Mississippi. Jefferson is a thinly veiled version of Faulkner's hometown, Oxford, located in Lafayette County. Faulkner said that in writing *Sartoris* he realized "my own little postage stamp of native soil was worth writing about and that I would never live long enough to exhaust it, and by sublimating the actual into apocryphal I would have complete liberty to use whatever talent I might have to its absolute top" (*Lion in the Garden* 255).

In 1929 Faulkner returned to Oxford and married his childhood sweetheart, Estelle, after she divorced Cornell Franklin. Faulkner, Estelle, and her children from the previous marriage (Malcolm and Victoria) lived in Oxford, and Faulkner continued to take jobs and write profitable short stories that allowed him time to work on his long (and still unprofitable) fiction. With a family to provide for, money was now of the utmost concern, especially given Faulkner's 1930 purchase of the dilapidated antebellum home that he later christened Rowan Oak. Moreover, the Faulkners attempted to begin a family of their own, but the couple's first child, Alabama, died shortly after her premature birth in January of 1931. Nevertheless, these years proved extraordinarily productive as Faulkner quickly published four volumes, including the Compson family saga titled *The Sound and the Fury* in 1929, the story of the Bundren family's tragicomic attempt to bury the family matriarch in *As I Lay Dying* in 1930, and the scandalous tale of violent crime and bootlegging in *Sanctuary* in 1931. Faulkner also published a collection of short stories, *These Thirteen*, in 1931, but his bills continued to outpace the proceeds of his literary production, so in 1932 he went to Hollywood to write for Metro-Goldwyn-Mayer (MGM).

During his several stints in Hollywood, Faulkner received on-screen credit for six screenplays, one of which, *Today We Live*, was based on his own short story "Turnabout." Although the work took time away from what Faulkner thought of as his serious work, these early years in Hollywood were extremely productive. Faulkner published his first novel dealing directly with race, *Light in August*, in 1932; his last volume of poetry, *A Green Bough*, in 1933; another collection of short stories, *Doctor Martino, and Other Stories*, in 1934; an aviation novel set primarily in New Orleans, *Pylon*, in 1935; and the novel that many critics consider his best, *Absalom, Absalom!*, in 1936. His personal life also changed significantly during these years. In June of 1933, Estelle gave birth to Faulkner's only surviving child, his daughter, Jill. Faulkner's familial financial obligations expanded again in 1936 when his brother Dean died in a plane crash. Faulkner took on the role of surrogate father to his niece, also named Dean. Faulkner's life also changed dramatically outside the realm of family during this period. In December of 1934, he met Howard Hawks's secretary, Meta Dougherty Carpenter, a young divorcée from Mississippi. Faulkner soon began the first of his several affairs with younger women when he became involved with Carpenter, and he also struggled with alcohol abuse during these stressful years. In January of 1936, he first checked in to Wright's Sanatorium, a nursing facility in Byhalia, Mississippi, and it proved to be the first of many stays he required to recover from alcoholic binges.

With the publication of *The Unvanquished*, a volume that contained many of Faulkner's stories about Bayard Sartoris reworked into novel form, and MGM's subsequent purchase of the screen rights, Faulkner finally secured much-needed revenue in 1938. The profits bought him time to write exclusively, and the next year, Faulkner published one of his most unusual works, *The Wild Palms* (later reissued with Faulkner's original title, *If I Forget Thee, Jerusalem*). The book interweaves two distinctly separate narratives in "The Wild Palms" and "Old Man" sections of the text. In *Faulkner in the University*, Faulkner says that he wrote "Old Man" as a thematic "counterpoint" to "The Wild Palms" (171). The first installment of the Snopes trilogy, *The Hamlet*, appeared in 1940, and in 1942 Faulkner published *Go Down, Moses, and Other Stories* (later versions dropped the phrase "and Other Stories" at Faulkner's insistence that the book was a novel). Faulkner dedicated *Go Down, Moses*, his second major exploration of race, to his former caretaker, Caroline Barr, who died in 1940. Deeply in debt by July of 1942, Faulkner headed back to Hollywood in the hope of becoming solvent.

In 1946 Viking Press published *The Portable Faulkner*, a representative collection of Faulkner's work, and Faulkner soon became more than merely solvent. Often credited with rescuing Faulkner's dwindling reputation, Malcolm Cowley, the volume's editor, helped bring the significant attention Faulkner already enjoyed abroad to bear in the author's home country. Financial stability followed critical recognition when, two years later, Faulkner published *Intruder in the Dust*, a coming-of-age mystery that features Chick Mallison's growing racial awareness via his relationship with Lucas Beauchamp. MGM quickly purchased the movie rights for $50,000, and Faulkner finally achieved some measure of financial independence. Faulkner followed *Intruder in the Dust* with a collection of mystery stories, *Knight's Gambit*, in 1949, and in 1950 his *Collected Stories* appeared. The pinnacle of this period of success came later that same year when he received the Nobel Prize in Literature.

After winning the Nobel Prize, Faulkner turned his attention to different venues. He went to New York to work on a stage version of *Requiem for a Nun* in 1951, and Random House published the novel that same year. Most significantly, though, the notoriously reclusive Faulkner embarked on a startlingly public period of political activity during this period, lecturing about race relations and civil rights at home and abroad as an ambassador for the State Department. In keeping with this political mind-set, in 1954 Faulkner finally published the book he had worked on for years, *A Fable*. Set during World War I, Easter week of 1918, the overtly political novel depicts a mutiny of sorts that results when a corporal in the French army and twelve of his men organize a cease-fire by convincing soldiers on both sides of the conflict to lay down their guns. The novel later won both a National Book Award and a Pulitzer Prize.

Although the early 1950s brought acclaim and an unprecedented measure of literary success, they were not happy years for Faulkner. He and Estelle both drank heavily, and Faulkner pursued additional affairs with younger women, including Jean Stein and Joan Williams. However, Faulkner entered into seemingly the most satisfying years of his life during the second half of this decade. A series of events were key to his peace: in 1954, his daughter, Jill, married Paul D. Summers, Jr., and moved to Charlottesville, Virginia. Jill soon gave birth to Faulkner's grandson, Paul D. Summers III, in 1956 (and two more sons in 1958 and 1961), and Faulkner took a position as writer-in-residence at the University of Virginia, in part to be closer to his daughter and her growing family. During the next two years Faulkner would appear before classes to talk about his fiction and various other topics. The record of these meetings, published as *Faulkner in the University*, shows that the classroom suited Faulkner. He settled into a routine of speaking and writing, and these years saw the publication of a volume of hunting stories, *Big Woods* (1955), and the second and third volumes of the Snopes trilogy, *The Town* (1957) and *The Mansion* (1959). Faulkner's planned move to Virginia, interrupted only by his death, is a testament to the happiness that he found there. That sentiment even permeated Faulkner's final work of fiction; *The Reivers* (1962), published only a month before Faulkner's death, is a remarkably hopeful coming-of-age story that features Lucius Priest's "reiving" or "stealing" of knowledge beyond his years. The novel won Faulkner's second (posthumous) Pulitzer.

In Virginia, Faulkner fueled his lifelong passion for horses by joining the Farmington Hunt Club, and in Mississippi, he continued to ride and train his own horses until just before his death. In January of 1962, he was thrown from a horse and never fully recovered from the injuries he sustained. He was thrown again on June 17 and drank increasingly as the pain worsened. Faulkner returned to Wright's Sanatorium on July 5 and suffered a massive heart attack at 1:30 A.M. on July 6. He was buried in St. Peter's Cemetery in Oxford the next day. Today, a sign on the street marking the easiest access to Faulkner's grave reads, "William Faulkner, The creator of Yoknapatawpha County." As Faulkner always insisted that the work was more important than the artist, he would have found the deceptively simple title quite fitting.

Works Cited and Consulted

Blotner, Joseph. *Faulkner: A Biography.* 2 vols. New York: Random House, 1974.

Duclos, Donald Philip. *Son of Sorrow: The Life, Works, and Influence of Colonel William C. Falkner, 1825-1889.* San Francisco: International Scholars, 1998.

Faulkner, William. *Faulkner in the University: Class Conferences at the University of Virginia, 1957-1958.* Ed. Frederick L. Gwynn and Joseph L. Blotner. Charlottesville: U of Virginia P, 1959.

_____. *Lion in the Garden: Interviews with William Faulkner, 1926-1962.* Ed. James B. Meriwether and Michael Millgate. New York: Random House, 1968.

Hamblin, Robert W., and Charles A. Peek, eds. *A William Faulkner Encyclopedia.* Westport, CT: Greenwood Press, 1999.

Padgett, John B. "William Faulkner Chronology." William Faulkner on the Web. http://www.mcsr.olemiss.edu/~egjbp/faulkner/chronology.html.

Bibliography

Bassett, John E. *William Faulkner: An Annotated Bibliography of Criticism Since 1988.* Lanham, MD: Scarecrow Press, 2009. An invaluable comprehensive collection of annotated criticism since 1988.

Blotner, Joseph. *Faulkner: A Biography.* 2 vols. New York: Random House, 1974. This work remains the standard biography on William Faulkner. A one-volume revised edition was published in 1984.

Faulkner, John. *My Brother Bill: An Affectionate Reminiscence.* New York: Trident, 1963. An engaging personal memoir by William Faulkner's brother.

The Faulkner Journal. Since 1985, this journal has published articles exclusively on Faulkner's work.

The Mississippi Quarterly. Each year, this journal typically devotes a special issue to William Faulkner.

The William Faulkner Email Discussion Group. This group is open to anyone interested in the author or his works. To subscribe via email, send the message "subscribe faulkner" to md@listserv.olemiss.edu.

 *the* PARIS REVIEW

The *Paris Review* Perspective _____

Nathaniel Rich for *The Paris Review*

INTERVIEWER: Some people say they can't understand your writing, even after they read it two or three times. What approach would you suggest for them?

WILLIAM FAULKNER: Read it four times.

—*The Paris Review* Writers at Work interview, 1956

There is a strong temptation when reading William Faulkner to proceed with caution. This is true of *Absalom, Absalom!* perhaps to a greater extent than any of his other novels. Each linguistic or logical impasse can send you back to the beginning of the sentence—or paragraph, or chapter, or, even, all the way back to the book's first line ("From a little after two oclock until almost sundown of the long still hot weary dead September afternoon . . . ")—to reread. Then reread again. Faulkner was not entirely kidding when he said that he had to be read four times in order to be understood. His beleaguered editors seem to agree. Modern editions of *Absalom, Absalom!* include a genealogy of the principal characters, a hand-drawn map of Jefferson and Yoknapatawpha County, and a chronology of events, accompanied by an apologetic editorial note explaining that actual dates of events "have been corrected in several instances to agree with the dates and facts of the novel." A reader who has not read the novel at least four times would do well to consult this index early and often, spoilers be damned.

Faulkner himself seems to be in on the joke. There is much about the novel that is willfully obfuscatory and complex. Two of my favorite examples rely on a dizzyingly repetitive sentence structure. I won't supply the context because it would only increase the confusion further:

> . . . and the people we lived among knew that we knew and we knew they knew we knew and we knew that they would have believed . . .
>
> . . . that Henry knew that Bon believed that Henry would know even from a disjointed word what Bon was talking about.

As it turns out, it is indeed possible to determine what Bon is talking about. I hope that one of the essays in this anthology will provide this service, since there is certainly not enough space here.

The novel's structure is also engineered for semicomprehension. It is composed of sections in which different characters relate, often second- or thirdhand, the story of Thomas Sutpen's accursed family. There are frequent interruptions from competing voices and inner monologues. Much of the novel's drama derives from misunderstandings between the characters and withheld information. Does Charles Bon realize that he's actually Thomas Sutpen's son? Does Sutpen realize that Bon is his son? Does Charles realize that he is the product of miscegenation? Does Judith really love Charles, despite having barely ever seen him? Does Henry Sutpen realize that Charles is his brother? And so on. The novel is assembled like a thousand-piece jigsaw puzzle: the border is put together first, and then the more colorful sections, in gradual and halting progress, until a coherent image finally emerges. Except, even at the end of the novel, not all of its mysteries are resolved. Why is Thomas Sutpen so determined to establish his family line, even to the point of committing murder? Why is Charles Bon so determined to marry Judith, his half sister? Why is Bon so determined to bring about his own death?

Just when Faulkner's characters seem to be on the verge of resolving these mysteries, Faulkner undermines their reliability. The voices of Quentin Compson and Shreve, the two chief narrators (who also appear in *The Sound and the Fury*), merge until they cannot be differentiated from each other: "It was Shreve speaking, though . . . it might have been either of them and was in a sense both: both thinking as one." The transformation continues until they become "people who perhaps had never existed at all anywhere," and finally "illusions" created by the mind of Sutpen himself. If the storytellers are shades, then it is not surprising that their tales cannot wholly be trusted. Faulkner points out that certain aspects of the story "Shreve had invented" but were "probably true enough"—a halfhearted claim at best.

So the impulse to go slowly is understandable—to make charts on a separate piece of paper and go back and forth from the novel to the index and then to the beginning of the novel again, feeling one's way like Quentin Compson stepping cautiously through the pitch dark Sutpen mansion, his hands outstretched before him: "He could not see, he knew that he could not see, yet he found that his eyelids and muscles were aching with strain while merging and dissolving red spots wheeled and vanished across the retinae."

But it's better to spare your retinae. I don't advocate reading the novel at an accelerated pace (impossible anyway), and some basic understanding of character and story is necessary (the index can be helpful here). But to go timidly through the novel's pages is to miss its chief pleasure, which is Faulkner's creation of a lush, dreamlike atmosphere in which fact and metaphor bleed together, and poetic sentiment trumps historical truth. The novel has the intensity of a high-grade fever. Whenever you put it down and try to think clearly about such pedestrian concerns as plot and narrative, the temperature cools and the dream vanishes. A wiser approach is to soldier ahead, hazard a small portion of comprehension, and surrender, reading in a state of frantic delirium straight through to the fiery finale. Only then should you go back and read again, and again, and again.

Miss Rosa at one point describes Sutpen reaching "some interval of sanity such as the mad know, just as the sane have intervals of madness to keep them aware that they are sane." *Absalom, Absalom!* is a mad novel. There are intervals of sanity, but it's best not to dwell too long in those moments. The madness is richer.

Copyright © 2012 by Nathaniel Rich.

Works Cited

Faulkner, William. *Absalom, Absalom!* 1936. New York: Modern Library, 1993.
_____. "The Art of Fiction No. 12." Interview with Jean Stein vanden Heuvel. *The Paris Review* 12 (Spring 1956).

CRITICAL
CONTEXTS

From Mapmaker to Geographer:
Faulkner's Sense of Space in *Absalom, Absalom!*____

Nicole Moulinoux

Mapping Yoknapatawpha

As readers, we all have childhood memories of wonderful maps, which adorned Robert Louis Stevenson's *Treasure Island*, J. R. R. Tolkien's *The Hobbit*, and Jonathan Swift's *Gulliver's Travels*, wishing that Miguel de Cervantes or Daniel Defoe had inserted maps into *Don Quixote* or *Robinson Crusoe*. As Faulknerian scholars, we all know that Sherwood Anderson's *Winesburg, Ohio* and Thomas Hardy's *Jude the Obscure* were familiar to Faulkner, and that they open with maps conceived as incentives to trigger off narratives. Quite obviously, William Faulkner had Hardy's Wessex in mind when he drew his own map of Yoknapatawpha, which he decided to place at the end of *Absalom, Absalom!* in the 1936 Random House edition.

The insertion of a map, its position in a novel, its legends, contents, and developments are often dismissed as marginal materials not worth considering, additional matter for appendices, just like chronologies or genealogies. I would argue that such paratext deserves closer examination: maps go beyond linguistic lines and permit another circulation and expression of artistic desire.

My purpose in this essay is not to follow the traditional academic canon that tries to equalize fact and fiction. I do not intend to examine Faulkner's Yoknapatawpha in the light of his "little postage stamp of native soil." The acceptance of a one-to-one correspondence between the fictional and the real does appear to me as a vain pursuit. (Readers interested in this perspective should see Gabriele Gutting's *Yoknapatawpha: The Function of Geographical and Historical Facts in Faulkner's Fictional Picture of the Deep South* or Charles S. Aiken's articles in the *Geographical Review.*)

My ambition is exactly the opposite, as I would like to play upon the apocryphal and measure William Faulkner against other literary

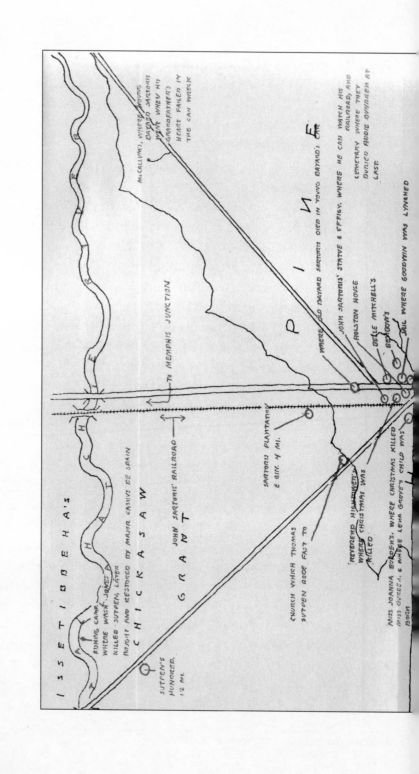

ISSETIBBEHA'S

FISHING CAMP,
WHERE WASH JONES
KILLED SUTPEN, LATER
BOUGHT AND RESIDED BY MAJOR CASSIUS DE SPAIN

CHICKASAW

JOHN SARTORIS' RAILROAD

GRANT

SUTPEN'S
HUNDRED.
12 MI.

CHURCH WHICH THOMAS
SUTPEN RODE FAST TO

MISS JOANNA BURDEN, WHERE CHRISTMAS KILLED
MISS BURDEN, & WHERE LENA GROVE'S CHILD WAS
BORN

'REVEREND HIGHTOWER',
WHERE CHRISTMAS WAS
KILLED

SARTORIS PLANTATION
& GIN. 4 MI.

TO MEMPHIS JUNCTION

McCALLUMS, WHERE YOUNG
BAYARD SARTORIS
WENT WHEN HIS
GRANDFATHER'S
HEART FAILED IN
THE CAR WRECK

P I N E

WHERE OLD BAYARD SARTORIS DIED IN YOUNG BAYARD'S

JOHN SARTORIS' STATUE & EFFIGY, WHERE WE CAN WATCH HIS
RAILROAD, AND
CEMETARY WHERE THEY
BURIED ADDIE BUNDREN AT
LAST.

ROLSTON HOUSE

BELLE MITCHELL'S

BEDGOW'S

JAIL WHERE GOODWIN WAS LYNCHED

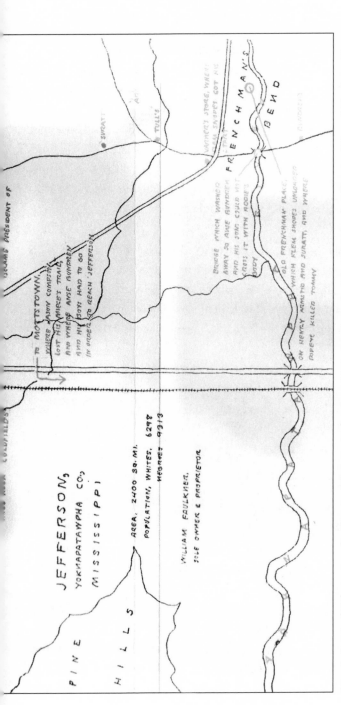

Map 1. Original Yoknapatawpha County, Mississippi, map as published at the end of the 1936 Random House edition of Absalom, Absalom! Copyright © the Literary Estate of William Faulkner. Reprinted by permission.

mapmakers to better establish his singularity. We have to admit that Faulkner himself does not encourage us to pay attention to his map, for he places it at the very end of *Absalom, Absalom!* together with his chronology and genealogy. If we believe Joseph Blotner, the writer was harassed by his editor, whose aim was to provide keys for what he considered to be a very hard novel. Finally, Faulkner complied with Hal Smith's desire to clear up some ambiguities and provide guideposts, which was indeed a clever strategy. He could thus leave his artistic construct as he had fashioned it and refuse other changes.

> A chronology of events and a genealogy of the characters would give the reader, in capsule form, information which he had not been able to extract from the text. But this material could go at the back of the book as a set of appendices; the reader who had tried to meet him on his own terms could consider it when he had finished, if he liked. (Blotner 937-38)

Faulkner was concerned enough to meet legitimate editorial objections through a series of safeguards. As mentioned by Blotner, James Joyce and T. S. Eliot had also been asked to provide keys for *Ulysses* and *The Waste Land*. It is this appendix I would like to question, as indeed it is too easily dismissed as a guide for incompetent readers.

The 1936 Random House Edition Map for *Absalom, Absalom!*

The very definition of the appendix as a reader's guide is first and foremost to be questioned, as the appendix does not fit editorial demand. The map drawn by Faulkner for this edition is obviously quite faulty (see Map 1), and I am not convinced that it can be considered a key to a better understanding of *Absalom, Absalom!*

Omissions are rife: many locations that are important for the unfolding of the story are left out. For example, the University of Mississippi attended by Charles Bon and Henry Sutpen in fictional Oxford, situated 40 miles from Jefferson, would have been a necessary landmark. The reader of *Absalom, Absalom!* would have been able to visualize Henry and Charles's numerous rides to and from Sutpen's Hundred. Meeting places, with the exception of Holston House, which does appear on the map, such as the drovers' tavern or Mr. Coldfield's crossroads store in Jefferson, should have been mentioned. Outside the city, the country store held by Wash Jones and later by Sutpen himself is also omitted.[1] What about essential directions for places such as New Orleans, which is one of the most frequented destinations in the novel? Its appearance would have been more interesting than those selected by the writer: Memphis, ignored by Henry but frequented by Ellen and Judith while on their shopping spree (marked as Memphis Junction), or the mention "to Mottstown," which actually refers more to *As I Lay Dying* or *Light in August*.

Readers could have been interested in a larger-scale project if *Absalom, Absalom!* was indeed the point: *continental*—either from Alberta, Canada, or from Harvard, Massachusetts (Shreve and Quentin), down to the Caribbean Islands with Haiti (Eulalia Bon) and Martinique (the French architect)—or *national*, a map of the United States showing the migration of the Sutpen family from West Virginia to the Tidewater in Virginia, Kentucky, Tennessee, and finally northern Mississippi. Another option for Faulkner could have been that of emphasizing southern history, showing the progression of Henry Sutpen and Charles Bon across Alabama, Georgia, the Carolinas, and Virginia with heroic landmarks, the *passages obligés* of the Civil War stressed in the novel: Sumpter, Corinth, Pittsburg Landing, Shiloh, Manassas, Gettysburg, and their way back home that way. Sutpen's trip could have been accounted for that way, as he took more than eight months to reach Sutpen's Hundred once the war was over.

Quite obviously, editorial demand was not Faulkner's preoccupation when he drew his own map, and he did not decide to concentrate on *Absalom, Absalom!* The map he drew out of his own impulse clearly had another ambition, as it encompasses the world of his previous fiction with special emphasis on *Sartoris*, *Sanctuary*, and *Light in August*. The lines of eventful peripeteia he wrote on this county-scale project indeed suggest a more complex circulation of the artist's own effects and reveal an intense work of symbolic reappropriation of the territory of which he still felt dispossessed, in spite of the label he had imposed upon it. Colliding forms of representation suggest a far more interesting project than that of a guide for the lower ranks of American readership.

Yet, in order to have a better understanding of what Faulkner authorized or not, what he mapped and/or surveyed, I would like to insist on the difficulties we meet when we try to analyze Faulkner's maps, as many composite drawings have been circulating without authorial consent.

Mapping and Remapping Yoknapatawpha

Scholars who did not have access to the original maps have made many errors. Critics such as Cleanth Brooks in his *William Faulkner: The Yoknapatawpha Country* (1963) or later in *William Faulkner: First Encounters* (1983), David Minter in *William Faulkner: His Life and Work* (1980), and the French authors writing for the prestigious collection *La Pléiade*, volume 2, used the wrong map, which was included in the Modern Library edition of 1951 and thus provided readers with an erroneous, recomposed construct. As underlined by Gabriele Gutting in *Yoknapatawpha: The Function of Geographical and Historical Facts in Faulkner's Fictional Picture of the Deep South*, a comparison of this reproduction with the original map published in the first edition of the 1936 novel reveals several notable differences: slightly smaller than the foldout map of the limited edition, it is printed in black with differently shaped indicators, with inversions (for instance, Mottstown is transferred from the right to the left side of the map), and the map legends, statistical data, and the legend "William Faulkner, Sole Owner and Proprietor" are dismissed at the bottom and no longer included in the lower-left section. Extra dots also appear with no reference (such as an extra spot in the southwest corner of Jefferson's Square, apparently the result of the redrawing and typesetting processes). This incorrectly redrawn map, owing to its smaller size, emphasizes the hub effect of Jefferson and explains why so many critics have regularly projected the myth of the wheel upon Yoknapatawpha, using their textual knowledge of Faulkner to impose this mythical figure upon the map itself. Now if we consider the original model, it is far more risky to straighten roads into spokes as they do not converge toward the center itself. Therefore, reassuring mythical grids are useless, unless we consider the wheel figure to be, like Addie's in *As I Lay Dying*, a faulty one.[2]

Yoknapatawpha was mapped once by Faulkner, apparently out of his own will and with pleasure for the 1936 Random House edition. It was included again as a two-color facsimile in the 1986 Random House reissue of *Absalom, Absalom!* It was revised and redrawn for *The Portable Faulkner*, with the writer's survey and consent, which is not the case for the map included in the 1951 Modern Library edition. Two incomplete drafts of the *Portable* project are also at our disposal, and the date inscribed (1945) authorizes us to think that they were designed for the volume edited by Malcolm Cowley; the incomplete draft, which appears on the front and end pages of the Garland volumes, was probably Faulkner's first attempt. The more elaborate draft is included in Louis Brodsky and Robert W. Hamblin' s *Faulkner: A Comprehensive Guide to the Brodsky Collection* (135). We can easily guess that it was no easy task for Faulkner to meet Cowley's editorial request and that he had difficulty fitting in all the capitalizations in the picture.

I would like to concentrate on the two pictorial portraits that received Faulkner's consent and to analyze the strategies implied by the literary mapmaker and those accepted by the surveyor of *The Portable Faulkner*.

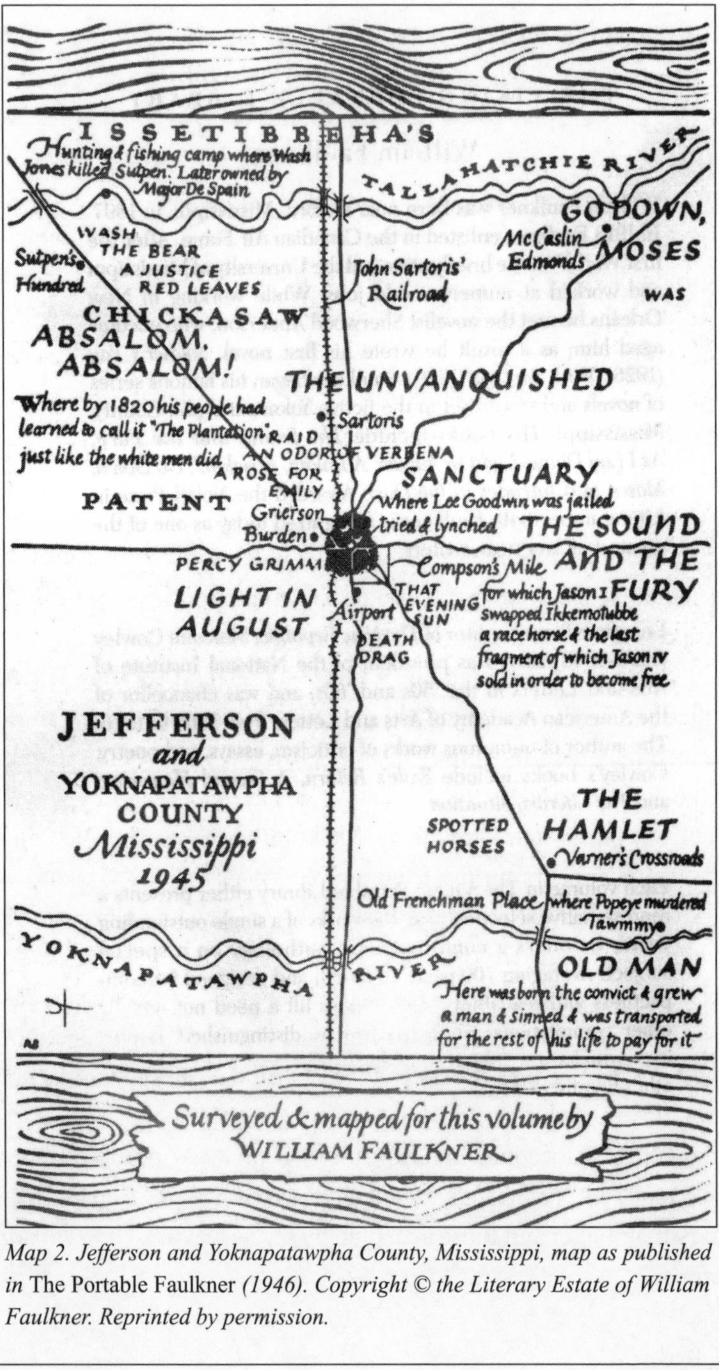
ISSETIBBEHA'S
Hunting & fishing camp where Wash Jones killed Sutpen. Later owned by Major De Spain
TALLAHATCHIE RIVER
GO DOWN, MOSES WAS
McCaslin Edmonds
WASH
THE BEAR
A JUSTICE
RED LEAVES
Sutpen's Hundred
John Sartoris' Railroad
CHICKASAW
ABSALOM, ABSALOM!
THE UNVANQUISHED
Where by 1820 his people had learned to call it "The Plantation" just like the white men did
Sartoris
RAID
AN ODOR OF VERBENA
A ROSE FOR EMILY
SANCTUARY
Where Lee Goodwin was jailed tried & lynched
PATENT
Grierson
Burden
THE SOUND AND THE FURY
PERCY GRIMM
Compson's Mile
LIGHT IN AUGUST
THAT EVENING SUN
Airport
for which Jason I swapped Ikkemotubbe a race horse & the last fragment of which Jason IV sold in order to become free
DEATH DRAG
JEFFERSON and YOKNAPATAWPHA COUNTY Mississippi 1945
THE HAMLET
SPOTTED HORSES
Varner's Crossroads
Old Frenchman Place
where Popeye murdered Tawmmy
YOKNAPATAWPHA RIVER
OLD MAN
Here was born the convict & grew a man & sinned & was transported for the rest of his life to pay for it
Surveyed & mapped for this volume by WILLIAM FAULKNER

Map 2. Jefferson and Yoknapatawpha County, Mississippi, map as published in The Portable Faulkner *(1946). Copyright © the Literary Estate of William Faulkner. Reprinted by permission.*

Faulkner as Literary Mapmaker

Though dealing with fictive territories, or *because of* dealing with fictive territories, novelistic maps respect a certain number of basic conventions for cartography: compass points, scales, boundaries. If we consider Stevenson's *Treasure Island*, the book Faulkner himself ordered for his grandsons, even if Jim Hawkins is reluctant to give the longitude and latitude, the compass rose is there. In Tolkien's *The Hobbit*, published in about the same period as *Absalom, Absalom!*, the compass points are marks in runes, with east at the top, as is customary for dwarf maps, and so read clockwise: east, south, west, north. According to the narrator, "Runes were old letters used for cutting or scratching on wood or stone. They were thin and only the dwarves made regular use of them, especially for private or secret records." Tolkien's model is quite in keeping with the pirates' mapping tradition close to the spirit of *Treasure Island*, which inspired Faulkner.[3]

The colors in Faulkner's red-and-black ink draft are quite similar to those mentioned by Tolkien in *The Hobbit*, yet it is difficult to ascribe meaning to what the colors symbolize. What is the logic behind them?

If we decide to put aside the overly simplistic draft of *Winesburg, Ohio* as closer to a cartoonist's sketch, yet a model Faulkner could not ignore, we may wonder why Faulkner decided to produce such anomalous maps. No compass rose, no scales, no boundaries. Was it so difficult to have a compass rose indicating north and south?

The absence of scale is also intriguing, as it completely subverts the meaning of a map. We recall Lewis Carroll's beautiful anecdote in *Sylvie and Bruno Concluded*, where the protagonist's ambition is to have the exact duplicate of a geographical setting and to make the map of the country on a mile-to-the-mile scale (Muehrcke and Muehrcke 319), thus refusing the mapping process, which is one of evaluation and selection.

"What do you consider the *largest* map that would be really useful?"

"About six inches to the mile."

"Only six *inches*!" exclaimed Mein Herr. "We very soon got to six *yards* to the mile. Then we tried a *hundred* yards to the mile. And then came the

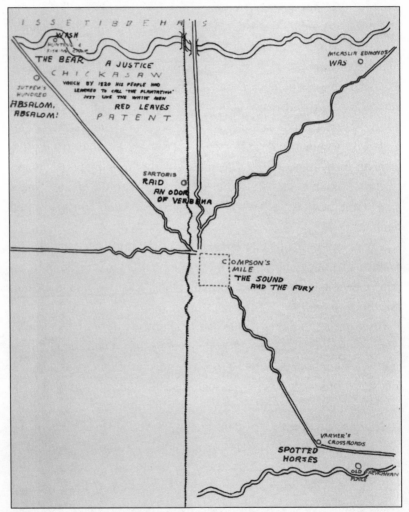

Map 3. Faulkner's second-draft map, originally designed for The Portable Faulkner *(1946), as published in Louis Brodsky and Robert W. Hamblin's* Faulkner: A Comprehensive Guide to the Brodsky Collection *(1982). Copyright © the Literary Estate of William Faulkner. Reprinted by permission.*

grandest idea of all! We actually made a map of the country on the scale of *a mile to the mile!*"

"Have you used it much?" I enquired.

"It has never been spread out yet," said Mein Herr: "the farmers objected: they said it would cover the whole country and shut out the sunlight! So we now use the country itself, as its own map, and I assure you it does nearly as well." (169)

The absence of scale is all the more surprising since Faulkner relies upon it when he indicates the distances on his 1936 map (see Map 1). For example, Sartoris is situated 4 miles from Jefferson and Sutpen's Hundred, 12 miles. The positioning of the Bundrens is the only problematic one as it does not appear to respect the implied scale. While the novel itself indicates a distance of 40 miles, it covers about 15 miles on the map and thus belittles the Bundrens' ordeal.[4] A more important distortion of distances appears on the *Portable Faulkner* map with the inclusion of "Old Man": "*Here was born the convict & grew a man & sinned & was transported for the rest of his life to pay for it.*" Such an intrusion baffles the storyline of the novel, located westward on the Mississippi and deftly integrated to comply with Malcolm Cowley's editorial request. Is it just in order to challenge cartographic codes just as he destabilized narrative ones that Faulkner decided to suppress scales?

The absence of borders has been generally understood as illustrating Faulkner's will to reach the universal by leaving the western and eastern sides open. Many critics have been prompt to notice that the map is quite close in shape to that of Mississippi with its capital Jackson, but the absence of vertical separations must be taken into consideration.

Here I would like to mention Malcolm Cowley's role in imposing the myth of "the essence of the Deep South" upon Yoknapatawpha and the pride he took in "inventing the miniature land" of Mr. Faulkner. In his introduction to *The Portable Faulkner*, Cowley notes:

I wrote this introduction in the autumn of 1945, at a time when Faulkner's books were little read and often disparaged. He had a few enthusiastic defenders, but no one, so it seemed to me then, had more than distantly suggested the scope and force and interdependence of his work as a whole. I was writing to overcome a general misconception, and that explains why, at various points, my emphasis was different from what it would be today. Yet I find it difficult to change what I said, except in the comparatively simple matter of bringing facts up to date. The original text was written with a good deal of advice from Faulkner. It has some historical value. (vii)

If we take into consideration Faulkner's first novels, we can easily see that it took many years for the writer to introduce the name of his county into his fiction (until *As I Lay Dying*, in fact) and that it was the city of Jefferson itself that was of paramount importance. Cowley's interpretation of Yoknapatawpha as a whole land in miniature became the way to read Faulkner and to entrap him into the regional (see Map 2). I think it is possible to challenge this reading in order to explain the absence of borders on Faulkner's maps. In "Shall Not Perish," originally published in *Story* in 1943, the concluding lines reveal Faulkner's awareness of the power of maps and his ambition to encapsulate America:

I had seen them too, who had never been further from Frenchman's Bend than I could return by night to sleep. It was like the wheel, like the sunset itself, hubbed at that little place that don't even show on a map, that not two hundred people out of all the earth know is named Frenchman's Bend or has any name at all, and spoking out in all the directions and touching them all, never a one too big for it to touch, never a one too little to be remembered: —the places that men and women have lived in and loved whether they had anything to paint pictures of them with or not, all the little places quiet enough to be lived in and loved and the names of them before they were quiet enough and the names of the deeds that made them quiet enough and the names of the men and the women who did the deeds, who lasted and endured and fought the battles and lost them and fought again because they didn't even know that they had been whipped, and tamed the wilderness and overpassed the mountains and deserts and died and still went on as the shape of the United States grew and went on. I knew them too: the men and women still powerful seventy-five years and twice that and twice that again afterward, still powerful and still dangerous and still coming, North and South and East and West, until the name of what they did and what they died for became just one single word, louder than any thunder. It was America, and it covered all the western earth. (*Collected Stories* 115)

Here we discover Faulkner's compass rose and the domain established, and we are in fact very close in spirit to Thomas Hardy's strategy. If we compare with Hardy's Wessex, which introduces most of Hardy's novels, "the Wessex of the Novels and Poems," we discover two maps within one, with the presence of a compass rose and scale, the left-hand section serving to position the county itself on the map of Great Britain. In contrast to Hardy's territorial setup, Faulkner decided to dismiss America as a reference frame. The absence of west and east borders leave in question not so much the area of the county, which is defined in the legend, but the circulation of frustration and desire with what should be metonymically contiguous: the Mississippi River and Natchez Trace, two founding myths evoked again and also dismissed in *Requiem for a Nun*.

Mark Twain's shadow reigns over the construction of Faulkner's maps. The writer could not separate his own domain from that of Twain and, as we see in *The Portable Faulkner*, did his best to draw the Mississippi into the picture with the inscription of "Old Man" (see Map 2). Faulkner was not ready to pay allegiance to his predecessors, nor was he, as a southerner, willing to integrate the national or, even worse, the continental frame. "The peremptory voice of the nation" was therefore not listened to but dismissed.

The absence of boundaries marks Faulkner's ambivalence toward his own nation and, when compared to Hardy's perspective, clearly reveals a rebellious response and a desire to be left out of it. "Jefferson, being neither on the Trace nor the River but lying about midway between" (*Requiem for a Nun* 477) could be an illustration of this in-betweenness selected by Faulkner for his maps.

The Portable Yoknapatawpha

Why do we have two maps? Why did Malcolm Cowley ask Faulkner to redraw his own map ten years after *Absalom, Absalom!*? New places to fix on the map? The publication of four new books—*The Unvanquished* (1938), *The Wild Palms* (1939), *The Hamlet* (1940), *Go Down, Moses* (1942)—more or less centered on Yoknapatawpha? Or was the transformation of a map into an index, a table of contents, meant to serve the anthological purpose Cowley had in mind: "spoon-rivering Faulkner's apocryphal county"?

In *The Faulkner-Cowley File*, a few letters enable us to better understand what was at stake. At a time when every one of Faulkner's books except *Sanctuary* was out of print,[5] Cowley wanted to make a Golden Book of Faulkner's apocryphal county, selecting the works that in about 200,000 words would give a sense of Yoknapatawpha County from Indian times to World War II, and, to quote Faulkner, "the whole thing would have fallen into pattern like a jigsaw puzzle when the magician's wand touched it" (Blotner 1187). Cowley would work on an introduction and the prefaces to the seven sections of *The Portable Faulkner* (he finally rejected the idea of the cycles: the Indians, the Compsons, etc.), and Faulkner would redraw a map "small enough to be reproduced inexpensively."

The two maps do not, in fact, have much in common, and the reader's emotional response to the foldout map inserted in the Random House edition cannot be compared with that provoked by the cheap reproduction included in *The Portable Faulkner*.

Faulkner's first map, with its creases and folds, conjures up the world of sea rovers with old parchments and sea chests and brings us back to its model: Stevenson's map in *Treasure Island*, not the printed one, but the map described in the narrative itself, a map found by Jim Hawkins and covered with carefully drawn hand-cramped characters in red ink:

The paper had been sealed in several places with a thimble by way of seal: the very thimble, perhaps, that I had found in the captain's pocket. The doctor opened the seals with great care, and there fell out the map of an island, with latitude and longitude, soundings, names of hills, and bays, and inlets, and every particular that would be needed to bring a ship to a safe anchorage upon its shores. It was about nine miles long and five across, shaped, you might say, like a fat dragon standing up, and had two fine land-locked harbors, and a hill in the center marked *The Spy-Glass*. There were several additions of a later date; but above, all three crosses of red ink—two on the north part of the island, one in the south-west, and, beside this last, in the same red ink, and in a small, neat hand, very different from the captain's tottery characters, these words: *Bulk of treasure here.* (39)

Now with that passage in mind, the indication in the right-hand corner of the *Absalom, Absalom!* map functions as an invitation to read Yoknapatawpha as Treasure Land: "Old Frenchman Place, which Flem Snopes unloaded on Henry Armstid and Suratt." Symptomatically, this indication with its underlying references to the treasure once buried in Old Frenchman's Place is suppressed in the *Portable Faulkner* map to emphasize "Spotted Horses," selected by Cowley in "The Peasants," section 4 of the anthology.

To meet editorial requirements, the *Portable Faulkner* map had to be reduced to a one-page format. The map was destined to the general public, anxious to "dip into regionalism" so as to make them forget the World War II context. The engraved wood effect used to frame the map as well as that of the rustic copper sign nailed to it emphasize the enticing, "souvenir-like" policy followed by the Viking Portable Library.

"Surveyed & mapped for this volume by William Faulkner," the legend, together with the date of 1945, marks the fall into marketing strategy and the very eviction of the writer who was once and supposedly—*ad vitam aeternam*—the sole owner and proprietor. Was Faulkner a negligent surveyor? We can imagine that he was not in a position to refuse Cowley's suggestions and that he approved for financial reasons. "A whole land in miniature" was conjured up indeed but with a difference.

The *Portable Faulkner* map privileges Indian lore, a back-to-nature and back-to-roots policy (the last wilderness and hunting stories) in a style reminiscent of *The Portable Hemingway*, which Malcolm Cowley had edited just before undertaking *The Portable Faulkner*. To emphasize local color, the presence of the dialectal is privileged (see the new spelling of Tawmmy, Map 2). The layout of the land, Pine Hills, landscapes, topographical elements, and directions are dismissed, and geographical markers are replaced by vague references to the history of the county. An effort is made to go back into the past and restore original names. Compson's becomes Compson's Mile to insist upon the origin of the land and its cession by Ikkemotubbe. Yet the reader is not given access to the first Indian name (Okatoba) at the time Jefferson was a trading post held by a Chickasaw agency (*Requiem for a Nun* 475), and the historical perspective is not consistent. Another noticeable change is the introduction of McCaslin Edmonds, who replaces MacCallum as a consequence of the selection of "Was," which discards the world of the yeomen farmers to admit another plantation, that of Uncle Buck and Buddy—Warwick—thus narrowing the sociological representation of the county and reinforcing the ideology of the plantation order. The farms of Surrat, Armstid, and Tull are also discarded together with the Bundrens' house, which signifies the disappearance of a whole community of southeastern farmers and the world of poor whites.

Faulkner's readers discover a very unusual and misleading selection of titles where it is impossible to distinguish novels from short stories, where even titles are erroneous: "A Rose for Emily Grierson" does not exist and is not the title that appears in the table of contents. As mentioned previously, locales are forced into the picture ("Death Drag" and its airport) or delocalized ("Old Man") to comply with the editorial project.

As many words are suppressed in the 1945 map (a 40 to 50 percent reduction due to the reduction in size and the capitalization of letters), not all the extracts selected by Cowley are marked, which reveals the complete lack of coherence contained in the project itself. Neophyte readers are therefore utterly at a loss if they want more than a dip into Faulkner's fiction.

Though the two maps represent the same symbolically constructed space, they are indeed to be opposed: the 1945 map puts forward an array of titles that appeal to the average reader. It leaves the reader free to discover the event itself, the character implied. By playing down topography, it dismisses geographical priorities and focuses on literary matter. The 1936 map is not conceived as an advertising poster but follows a more sophisticated logic of space. Faulkner's protagonists are not located at random but are linked to place in most intimate ways, respective of their own origins and social status. The map is first and foremost a key to understanding and experiencing place as destiny. Its ideological character, though reactionary in essence, is complex and full of contradictory forces.

From Map to Territory: Faulkner as Geographer

It is indeed tempting to follow the general trend imposed by Malcolm Cowley in *The Portable Faulkner* and reasserted by Cleanth Brooks in "History and the Sense of the Tragic"—that is, to reduce *Absalom, Absalom!* to "the best of the Old South which is dead." True enough, the presence of Rosa Coldfield's gothic paraphernalia as well as the tale told by General Compson's descendant emphasize the theme of the fall into history. What is more interesting, because constantly dismissed, is Faulkner's new awareness of space, a space organized by various societies that ambiguously and in the very margins of the successive tales question the validity of the link between the center and the periphery. Often evacuated or rapidly dismissed by the narrative voices, numerous questions concerning the control of space by the capital of the county are left unanswered. As shown on the 1936 map, with its crisscrossing of roads, waterways, and railways, the novel itself explores the in-between territory where conflicting interests are exposed to permit the emergence and circulation of new sets of rules resulting from the shock of cultures.

If we rely upon the core-periphery models theorized by American geographers in the twentieth century—for example, John Friedmann's—we can see that Faulkner as geographer follows the concepts developed in his time. Friedmann divides the world into four types of regions: the core regions, with a high potential for innovation and growth; the upward-transition regions, which come next to the core regions that benefit from their development; the resource-frontier regions, peripheral zones of virgin land open to settlement; and finally downward-transition regions, peripheral zones with declining rural economies, oriented toward the past and with no capacity for innovation. We can see that the four-stage model is at work in *Absalom, Absalom!* and we can measure Faulkner's originality with the superposition of two types of regions due to the telescoping of time: the resource frontier region of 1833 versus the downward-transition region of 1909, in which "the little town of Jefferson," to quote Miss Rosa, is already seen on the decline:

> "Because you are going away to attend the college at Harvard they tell me," she said. "So I dont imagine you will ever come back here and settle down as a country lawyer in a little town like Jefferson since Northern people have already seen to it that there is little left in the South for a young man." (7)

The core-periphery model used by Faulkner to characterize Jefferson in 1833 is that of the domination of a frontier village reigning over zones of virgin land, dictating its laws over the territory to be conquered in the American western tradition. "Jefferson was a village then: the Holston House, the courthouse, six stores, a blacksmith and a livery stable, a saloon frequented by drovers and peddlers, three churches and perhaps thirty residences" (25). As in any resource frontier region, the center-periphery model with the city of Jefferson as hub is not to be questioned as shown on the 1936 map until the arrival of Sutpen, who will deny the supremacy of Jefferson and select a different model, that of Sutpen's Hundred as an isolate.

Thomas Sutpen is more of a victim of "geographical haps" than of historical doom. The Tennessee Mountains, the Tidewater plantations, the Caribbean islands determine and condition his implantation into the South. Sutpen will perturb the ideology of the conquest by his decision to settle in a miasmic region with "a wild band of niggers." Sutpen denounces the validity of the core-periphery link just as he denounces his belonging to the county. The 1833 resource-frontier region rejects, on the edge of wilderness, a model that has the characteristics of an island, autonomous and alien, ruled over by a stranger who ignores the sovereignty of the nearby Anglo-Saxon puritan settlement. Sutpen, the outcast, introduces a replica of insurrectionary Haiti into Yoknapatawpha with its specific ways to negotiate class, race, and gender. If he dismantles social barriers, he erects new linguistic ones with the introduction of "a sort of broken French." Conceived as an island, Sutpen's Hundred respects the specificity of an unmoored territory, accessible only to adventurers who can approach it without penetrating its remote wilderness. Like the volcanic island of Haiti, it can be settled only on the periphery and never actually subdued. Sutpen's Hundred is therefore first defined as extraterritorial, barbarian, and alien, and the systemogenesis quite logically needs another time, that of the *illo tempore* of myth, to account for its creation and explain its otherness.

But if we pay closer attention to the relationships between the settlement itself and the isolate, it is fascinating to see the negotiations made along the roads and waterways that underline the interaction between the two systems, which question Mr. Compson's assertion that Sutpen forced Jefferson to accept him, while the text itself offers a more complex network of transactions to explain the emergence of a center-periphery relationship. The road from Jefferson to Sutpen's Hundred has been analyzed as a sort of Natchez Trace, which will finally bring civilization to the place. But the road from Sutpen's Hundred to Jefferson must not be underestimated, as it offers evidence not only of a certain form of resistance to civilization but also of the existence of contacts and compromises accepted by Jefferson itself. Such exchanges appear in the margins of the different tales, and they are never seriously questioned by narrative voices. The incorruptible puritan bastion with its law-abiding citizens is ready to condone the uncivilized and lawless along the country roads and thus establishes permeability between cultures. The reader will never know what happened between the vigilance committee and Sutpen when they met halfway between Jefferson and the plantation and why they all returned to the city after their confrontation.[6] Mr. Coldfield's decision to hire four wagons to be sent to the river to transport Sutpen's plunder also remains unexplained. The center-periphery links negotiated in *Absalom, Absalom!* question the foundations of cultures when dissociated from their original contexts and reveal that the isolate has a deeper impact upon the center than generally admitted by critics and permit a more complex treatment of the subversive at work in the novel.

The Inversion of the Model

Once rejected as alien and uncivilized, Sutpen's Hundred the isolate will be tamed into a southern country place, a traditional cotton plantation with its formal promenades and gardens tended by "niggers," which the county will also progressively assimilate. Sutpen even employs as overseer the son of "that same sheriff who had arrested him at his bride-to-be's gate on the day of his betrothal" (59). Though set in the periphery, Sutpen's Hundred will try to compete with the city itself, with the grandeur of the edifice compared to the courthouse itself. The display of colonial good taste and refinement exhibited in the profusion of mahogany and Limoges Haviland will contrast with what was once mere frontier rusticity. Yet quite paradoxically, when Sutpen's Hundred becomes acknowledged as an acceptable satellite, the center-periphery link will become loose. Sutpen will refuse to go to Jefferson and exchange with more distant cities such as Memphis or New Orleans, places related to slave and cotton economy and obviously more deeply implied in his family history.

During the Civil War, Sutpen's Hundred will be surprisingly turned into the model of the country plantation, puritan and provincial, close in spirit to what Jefferson once was and faced with the challenge of confronting the otherness of cosmopolitan cities. Strangely enough, the circulation of Latin culture with its Catholic exuberance once refused by the county of Yoknapatawpha will start anew while being denied by those (like Sutpen) who were the first to introduce it into the region. Once an isolate, then a satellite accepted by the county, Sutpen's Hundred becomes less of a territory and more of a locus of memory, the expression of the essence of southern culture with the stereotypical picture of its decline, the plantation set ablaze.

From Systemogenesis to Systemolysis

Absalom, Absalom! presents a unique and amazing case in Faulkner's fiction. From systemogenesis to systemolysis, the geographer describes the different stages of the creation, evolution, and utter destruction of a territory situated on the edge of wilderness. The core-periphery model at work with all its complexities and ambiguities points at the tyranny of topography over human destiny. It will be even more present in *Requiem for a Nun*, where Faulkner relates what he refused to do in *Absalom, Absalom!*—that is, the systemogenesis of the core of Yoknapatawpha itself—the city of Jefferson—and its progressive satellization by a new upward transition region. The opening of "The Golden Dome" illustrates the priority given to geography over history,[7] what was already at stake in the margins of *Absalom, Absalom!* and in its discarded appendix.

Notes

1. The text reads: "and so running his little crossroads store with a stock of plowshares and hame strings and calico and kerosene and cheap beads and ribbons and a clientele of freed niggers and (what is it? the word? White what—Yes, trash) with Jones for clerk and who knows maybe what delusions of making money out of the store to rebuild the plantation" (150).

2. "The titled lumber gleams dull yellow, water-soaked and heavy as lead, tilted at a steep angle into the ditch above the broken wheel; about the shattered spokes and about Jewel's ankles a runnel of yellow neither water nor earth swirls, curving with the yellow road neither of earth nor water, down the hill dissolving into a streaming mass of dark green neither of earth nor sky" (*As I Lay Dying* 33).

3. From *The Hobbit*:

> On the table in the light of a big lamp with a red shade he spread a piece of parchment rather like a map.
> "This was made by Thror, your grandfather, Thorin," he said in answer to the dwarves' excited questions. "It is a plan of the Mountain."
> "I don't see that this will help us much," said Thorin disappointedly after a glance. "I remember the Mountain well enough and the lands about it. And I know where Mirkwood is, and the Withered Heath where the great dragons bred."
> "There is a dragon marked in red on the Mountain," said Balin, "but it will be easy enough to find him without that, if ever we arrive there."
> "There is one point that you haven't noticed," said the wizard, "and that is the secret entrance. You see that rune on the West side, and the hand pointing to it from the other runes? That marks a hidden passage to the lower Halls." (Look at the map at the beginning of this book, and you will see the runes in red.) (20)

4. Faulkner's inconsistencies in the use of dates as well as distances are well known. If we take the example of *Absalom, Absalom!*, two successive pages (31 and 32) indicate different distances for Sutpen's Hundred neighborhood, 8 or 12 miles. The church to which Sutpen rode fast is either 8 or 12 miles from Sutpen's Hundred. The

new college attended by Henry Sutpen in the Mississippi hinterland is situated 300 miles from New Orleans (60) and 40 miles from Jefferson. Sutpen's Hundred, 12 miles from Jefferson, is 600 miles away from New Orleans, which means almost double the miles.

5. In his introduction to *The Portable Faulkner*, Cowley states that "in 1945 all his seventeen books were effectively out of print, with some of them unobtainable in the secondhand bookshops" (x).

6. "Doubtless something more than this transpired at the time, though none of the vigilance committee ever told it that I known of. All I ever heard is how the town, the men on the gallery of the Holston House saw Sutpen and the committee ride onto the square together, Sutpen a little in front and the others bunched behind him" (*Absalom, Absalom!* 36).

7. In *Requiem for a Nun*:

Jackson. Alt. 294 ft. Pop. (A.D. 1950) 201,092.

Located by an expedition of three Commissioners selected appointed and dispatched for that single purpose, on a high bluff above Pearl River at the approximate geographical center of the State, to be not a market nor industrial town, nor even as a place for men to live, but to be a capital, the Capital of a Commonwealth. (540)

Works Cited and Consulted

Aiken, Charles S. "Faulkner's Yoknapatawpha County: A Place in the American South." *Geographical Review* 69.3 (1979): 331-48.

_____. "Faulkner's Yoknapatawpha County: Geographical Fact into Fiction." *Geographical Review* 67.1 (1977): 1-21.

Atkinson, Ted. "The State." *A Companion to William Faulkner*. Ed. Richard C. V. Moreland. Malden, MA: Blackwell, 2007.

Blotner, Joseph. *Faulkner: A Biography*. 2 vols. New York: Random House, 1974.

Brodsky, Louis, and Robert W. Hamblin. *Faulkner: A Comprehensive Guide to the Brodsky Collection*. Vol.1. Jackson: UP of Mississippi, 1982.

Brooks, Cleanth. "History and the Sense of the Tragic." 1963. *William Faulkner's "Absalom, Absalom!"* Ed. Fred Hobson. New York: Oxford UP, 2003. 17-46.

_____. *William Faulkner: First Encounters*. New Haven, CT: Yale UP, 1983.

_____. *William Faulkner: The Yoknapatawpha Country*. New Haven, CT: Yale UP, 1963.

Carroll, Lewis. *Sylvie and Bruno Concluded*. London: Macmillan, 1893.

Faulkner, William. *Absalom, Absalom! Novels, 1936-1940*. Ed. Joseph Blotner and Noel Polk. New York: Library of America, 1990.

_____. *As I Lay Dying. Novels, 1930-1935*. Ed. Joseph Blotner and Noel Polk. New York: Library of America, 1985.

_____. *Collected Stories.* New York: Random House, 1950.

_____. *The Portable Faulkner.* 1946. Ed. Malcolm Cowley. New York: Random House, 1977.

_____. *Requiem for a Nun. Novels, 1942-1954.* Ed. Joseph Blotner and Noel Polk. New York: Library of America, 1994.

Gutting, Gabriele. *Yoknapatawpha: The Function of Geographical and Historical Facts in Faulkner's Fictional Picture of the Deep South.* Frankfurt: Peter Lang, 1992.

Minter, David. *William Faulkner: His Life and Work.* 1980. Baltimore: Johns Hopkins UP, 1997.

Muehrcke, Philip C., and Juliana O. Muehrcke. "Maps in Literature." *Geographical Review* 64.3 (1974): 317-38.

Stevenson, Robert Louis. *Treasure Island.* Paris: Rainbow Library, 1952.

Tolkien, J. R. R. *The Hobbit.* 1937. London: HarperCollins, 1999.

Cultural Context:
Absalom, Absalom!

Ted Atkinson

In the assessment of the quality of novels, rankings are notoriously unreliable aids for drawing valid conclusions. The results usually beg more questions than they answer about where a given novel belongs in relation to others and in the larger scheme of literary history. Nevertheless, rankings can be useful for measuring general cultural perceptions, as in the case of William Faulkner's *Absalom, Absalom!*—a novel that has met with mixed yet telling results. Consider, for example, that *Absalom* ranked first in a survey of academics and southern writers conducted by the *Oxford American* magazine in 2009 to determine "The Best Southern Novels." By contrast, *Absalom* did not make the list of top books when PBS polled experts in 2007 as part of its *American Masters* feature on the American novel. In the Modern Library's 1998 series of surveys, *Absalom* failed to register in the board's list of the one hundred greatest novels, though it made the top forty in the readers' list. (Incidentally, *The Sound and the Fury*, *As I Lay Dying*, and *Light in August* did earn prime spots in the board's list.) One conclusion to draw from these surveys is that *Absalom* still carries the weight (or the baggage, some would say) in American culture of being a—if not *the*—quintessential southern novel. Ever since Faulkner's rise from obscurity in the 1940s, the novel has served scholars and general readers alike as a case study in the historical, cultural, and psychological effects of southern regional identity commonly perceived to be at odds with the preconceptions of outsiders assured of the South's supposedly essential and distinctive qualities. While *Absalom, Absalom!* is most certainly indicative of Faulkner's personal experiences and literary engagement with the history and culture of the U.S. South, it also exposes "the South" as a concept formed in a process of cultural construction. On a broader spectrum, *Absalom* bears visible marks of its production during the turbulent 1930s, when the Great Depression indelibly shaped American cultural production while simultaneously conveying themes that ensure its timelessness. These factors and others enable the novel's remarkable adaptability to a range of cultural contexts and critical perspectives and its seemingly inexhaustible capacity for remaining relevant.

The long-standing perception of *Absalom, Absalom!* as a novel of the South has its roots in the appropriation of Faulkner for the promotion of southern literature as vibrant force in modern American culture. Traditional narratives of southern literary history point to the formation of the Fugitives, a cadre of poet-scholars at Vanderbilt University in the 1920s, as the seminal moment in the Southern Renaissance—a flowering of arts and letters in the South that would eventually find its paragon in William Faulkner. Out of the Fugitives emerged the Southern Agrarians, whose *I'll Take My Stand* (1930) served as a manifesto that fiercely defended the South from attacks by critics such as H. L. Mencken by arguing that the region's agrarian values and deeply rooted traditions made it a crucial ballast to guard against the dehumanizing and homogenizing effects of modernity. By the 1940s the Southern Agrarians were integral to the formation of the New Criticism—a mode of scholarly inquiry that concentrated on the formal properties of literature and the appreciation of its humanistic values to lend more rigor and structure to the discipline of literary studies. For proponents of southern literature as a distinctive body of work and a valid academic discipline, Faulkner's fiction served as a means to the end of accruing cultural capital by reasserting traditional values associated with the humanities. Cleanth Brooks's influential essay on *Absalom, Absalom!* titled "History and the Sense of the Tragic" exemplifies the strategy of accentuating Faulkner's southern heritage while aligning him with enduring literary traditions to elevate him from the realm of cultural subgenres to which critics of the 1930s had relegated him. Toward this end Brooks argues that *Absalom* is "more than a bottle of Gothic sauce to be used to spice up our own preconceptions about the history of American society" and thus should be viewed as a southern-inflected modern tragedy with roots in the classical and Renaissance traditions of Sophocles and Shakespeare (in Hobson 17, 19). As Lawrence H. Schwartz convincingly argues, such readings underwrote Faulkner's recovery from literary obscurity and his elevation to the pantheon of great American writers. Consequently, the recognition of Faulkner's genius was in many ways a product of a post-World War II cultural politics in which the New Criticism and the study of modern southern literature were able to flourish.

In spite of the insistence by Brooks and others that Faulkner's worth should be measured primarily in terms of a virtuosic rendering of what Faulkner described in his 1950 Nobel Prize acceptance speech as "the old verities and truths of the heart, the universal truths lacking which any story is ephemeral and doomed—love and honor and pity and pride and compassion and sacrifice," the enthusiastic endorsements by southern intellectuals with axes to grind and turf to defend contributed in large part to the persistent labeling of Faulkner as first and foremost a "Southern writer" (Meriwether 120). Arguably no other factor was more influential in this perception than the interpretation of Quentin Compson in *Absalom, Absalom!* as the embodiment of an essential southern identity born of tormented historical consciousness. Michael Kreyling cogently analyzes the central role that Quentin Compson played in validating fundamental assumptions about the South and southern literature that charted the course of southern studies and remain influential in American culture to this day. Referencing the defensive, dichotomous approach to the South that Quentin exhibits in response to the probing questions of his Harvard roommate, Shreve McCannon, Kreyling notes that devotees of southern literature find in Quentin "our central, agonistic, split-personality model. Quentin swings from sacred memory to profane present, consistently failing to imagine a community save one riven by miscegenation, incest, racial guilt, and shame" (5). Less conflicted and more savvy than Quentin, Kreyling argues, the "literary nucleus of the Fugitive-Agrarian brotherhood" projected him in American culture as an ideal image of the modern southerner compelled to aim a "backward glance," as Allen Tate famously put it, while standing precariously on the border between the traditional past and an uncertain future shaped by modernity (5). Quentin's love-"I don't hate it" relationship with the South was perfectly in keeping with the critical spirit that southern intellectuals identified as the driving force of the historical consciousness active in the modern South and, by extension, in the literature of the Southern Renaissance. Faulkner's characterization of Quentin as a son of the South traumatized by the region's tragic history to the point of feeling a paradoxical blend of fidelity and angst has been so influential that critics refer to this brand of southern identity and historical consciousness as the "Quentin thesis" (Kreyling 113). As Kreyling rightly points out, C. Vann Woodward was as adept as any literary critic in bolstering the notion of the conflicted historical consciousness that the "Quentin thesis" posits in assuming a fixed southern identity distinctive from national affiliation. In Woodward's influential book *The Burden of Southern History*, he writes, "The experience of evil and the experience of tragedy are parts of the southern heritage that are as difficult to reconcile with the American legend of innocence and social felicity as the experience of poverty and defeat are to reconcile with the legends of abundance and success" (21). In addition to tragic historical consciousness, a bevy of traits distinguishing the South as a unique region accumulated over time in works of history, sociology, and literary criticism: religious sensibility; familial devotion and dysfunction; a culture of violence, racial and class conflict among the planter/merchant elite, poor whites, and African Americans; and landmarks such as the remnants or ruins of plantation houses, general stores, and the ramshackle quarters inhabited by slaves and later sharecroppers dotting and distinguishing the southern landscape. Tellingly, readers of *Absalom* can find each of these woven into the textual fabric of the novel, thus compounding its value for those heavily invested in the "Quentin thesis."

Also a central figure in *The Sound and the Fury*, Faulkner's first bona fide masterpiece, Quentin Compson finds himself in *Absalom, Absalom!* confronting the demons of the past and the sins of the fathers in microcosmic narrative form. For Quentin, the rags-to-riches-to-rags saga of ruthless planter Thomas Sutpen assumes mythic proportions. Summoned by Rosa Coldfield to bear witness to her account of Sutpen, Quentin unwittingly assumes the role of confessor as he listens to Rosa's scathing narrative assault on Sutpen as "a demon" and "not a gentleman" (9). Sutpen's story functions as a myth of personal revelation that explains the origins of Rosa's existence as an embittered spinster with a seething hatred for the man who offered her a demeaning marriage "proposal" after the death of Ellen, Rosa's sister and Sutpen's wife. Increasingly, however, Sutpen's story undergoes revision and expansion, primarily in response to the famous prompt issued by Shreve to Quentin: *"Tell about the South. What's it like there. What do they do there. Why do they live there. Why do they live at all"* (142). The more Quentin tells, and the more Quentin and Shreve tell together one cold night in their dorm room as they transform the Sutpen saga along the lines of a Walter Scott historical romance, the more Quentin feels implicated in the material—or, better yet, the material history that the storytelling evokes. Now Sutpen's saga functions as a myth that explains the origins of the South, implicating Quentin by revealing to him a legacy of brutal exploitation in the service of insatiable greed. Rendered steadily more traumatized as Shreve relentlessly drives the narrative forward, Quentin brings a culmination to the collaboration with his famous response to Shreve's query, "Why do you hate the South?" *"I don't. I don't! I don't hate it! I don't hate it!"* Quentin says in an obvious attempt, as numerous critics have noted, to convince not Shreve but himself that he doesn't despise where he comes from and, as a result of this native influence, who he is (303). Over the years Quentin's response to Shreve has become a mantra of sorts—a convenient reference to denote the unsettling ambivalence felt by southerners when confronted with the shameful burden of history and the compulsion to defend the South against the slings and arrows of external preconceptions. This response to history, as Quentin's characterization demonstrates, can result in a loss of individual identity to the overwhelming force of collective memory: "His childhood was full of them; his very body was an empty hall echoing with sonorous defeated names; he was not a being, an entity, he was a commonwealth" (7).

Not surprisingly, the heavy influence of *Absalom* in general and the "Quentin thesis" in particular in shaping traditional conceptions of southern identity, literature, and history has served as a focal point in postmodern American culture for those intent on challenging fundamental assumptions about the South. In most instances these challenges aim to redirect understanding of southern culture away from the influence of the Fugitives-Agrarians-New Critics who "determined the currents followed for most of [the twentieth] century by demarcating before/after, neo/post-, renaissance/other" (Kreyling 5). With the advent of multiculturalism, readings of Faulkner steeped in feminism, African American studies, and new directions in American and southern studies, for example, have critiqued the monolithic view of "the South." Such readings question the process of privileged white males casting a privileged white male character as the embodiment of "essential" southern qualities such as a tragic view of history and the compulsion to defend the South out of a mixture of shame and devotion.

For some feminist critics, Quentin's defensiveness is actually offensiveness in disguise. As Minrose C. Gwin notes in a groundbreaking essay on *Absalom* informed by feminist and psychoanalytic theory, Quentin's tragic persona and the appropriation of Sutpen's narrative by Quentin, Mr. Compson, and Shreve is part of a broader patriarchal collusion that silences Rosa by casting her narrative as the "mad" ravings of a scorned, "hysterical" woman. Gwin recovers Rosa's narrative from the force of male authority by arguing that Rosa "insists on the possibility of female desire and female symbolization . . . within a patriarchal culture that turns on the male fear of deprivation of power" (in Hobson 153). From the standpoint of African American studies, Thadious M. Davis concentrates on Faulkner's representation of black characters to yield fresh insights into his complex treatment of race as a major theme, demonstrating Faulkner's relevance to national conversations about the history of racism in America. In one frequently cited essay, Davis draws on the concept of "signifying" developed by Henry Louis Gates, Jr., to examine how black characters in *Absalom* figure as abstractions that nonetheless influence narrative formation. Like Gwin and in the spirit of multiculturalism, Davis seeks to bring marginalized voices from the background into the foreground to show that they are crucial to *Absalom*'s intricate form. Accordingly, Davis contends, "The addition of the Negro lifts the Sutpen legend from a flat canvas and transforms it into a powerful vehicle of individual will, of complex human motives and emotions, of personal, social, historical interactions" (in Hobson 71).

Such reassessments of *Absalom* pave the way for more recent efforts to challenge monolithic thinking by exposing "the South" as an imagined community, a monoculture conceived from a limited point of view that obscures the multicultural reality of many Souths. In the current context of globalization, diverse models of the South derive from remapping or removing boundaries to promote understanding of connections among the U.S. South, the postplantation regions of Latin America, and the global South. When promoting these models, many scholars come to bury Quentin Compson, not to praise him, asserting the need to move once and for all beyond the long shadow of cultural influence cast by the "Quentin thesis." In spite of such attempts to decenter Faulkner and *Absalom*, however, both remain central to evolving discourses about the nature and validity of regional identity in the context of globalism, demonstrating further *Absalom*'s remarkable staying power. From the academic circles of southern studies to scores of college syllabi to the vast and influential cultural sphere of Oprah's Book Club, *Absalom, Absalom!* continues to attract critics and general readers interested in its compelling, labyrinthine plot and still resonant themes.

Ironically, the deployment of Quentin Compson to support a definition of southern identity rooted in essentialism and the backlash against this long-standing cultural practice at times share the same flaw: not sufficiently accounting for the ways that Faulkner's rendering of Quentin in *Absalom* calls into question claims of fixed identity. The passage cited most frequently to illustrate Quentin's belief in an essential southern identity is his response to Shreve during an interrogation that Shreve conducts in the manner of an attorney badgering his witness. After a flurry of questions posed by Shreve about southern preoccupation with the past, especially the destruction and defeat of the South during the Civil War, Quentin answers, "You can't understand it. You would have to be born there" (289). For many readers Quentin's claim that southerners acquire a fundamental understanding of the region by birthright is a prime example of reductive thinking about the South. Moreover, it contributes to the proliferation of derivative responses in American culture by those who view Quentin as the ideal role model for representing or cultivating the identity of the tormented southerner. Though such interpretations have some standing, they can make the mistake of reading Quentin's comment in isolation. After all, Quentin follows up his statement about birthright by undercutting his claim, saying "I don't know" twice when Shreve presses him on the question of understanding the South (289).

It is intriguing to explore the possibility that Quentin's "I don't know" might reveal as much as his "*I don't hate it*" when it comes to assessing his and, by extension, Faulkner's response to influential ideas about southern identity. While not knowing is far less dramatic than cloaking self-loathing in willful denial and much less handy for performing the role of conflicted southerner or capturing the "essence" of "the South," Quentin's uncertainty is useful for considering how *Absalom* defies what can be called the cultural logic of southern exceptionalism. Rather than joining cultural representations that reinforce the notion that the South's inherent difference from the rest of the nation is a naturally occurring phenomenon, *Absalom* exposes this view of the South as imagined in "the rag-tag and bob-ends of old tales talking," as the narrator describes Quentin and Shreve's creative collaboration in adapting the tale of Thomas Sutpen (243).

Regardless of the motivation, the pervasive tendency to treat *Absalom, Absalom!* as a prime example of southern literature is a factor that has led critics and popular audiences to diminish or overlook influences in the broader historical and cultural context informing the novel's production. Adding to this oversight has been the reluctance in traditional strains of Faulkner scholarship to make tangible connections between Faulkner's texts and their historical, cultural, and social contexts. Unlike the unapologetically political writers and critics who dominated the literary scene in the 1930s from the Left, the reasoning goes, Faulkner produced fiction that was timeless and universal—not bound to one time but aesthetically crafted for all time. Subsequently, the development of a wider, more nuanced spectrum of interpretation has allowed for comprehending Faulkner's novels and stories as both impressive literary achievements with extensive appeal and texts immediately responsive to the contexts in which they were produced. Employing this critical approach reveals *Absalom, Absalom!* to be a novel that emerged in many respects from its engagement with issues and concerns prevalent in American culture during the mid-1930s—a decade encompassing the national and global crises of the Great Depression and the onset of World War II.

When *Absalom, Absalom!* appeared in 1936, it was part of a Depression trend toward producing cultural works set completely or in part during the U.S. Civil War. In fact, critics often cite *Absalom* as a great Civil War novel, primarily for encompassing in its sweeping and intricate narrative vista the antebellum drive toward the war, its destructive and volatile aftermath in the Reconstruction period, and the modern formation of the Lost Cause—a post-Confederate mythology cultivated to redeem the South's defeat and to affirm values favorable to restoration of the old order. Arguably, the trend began with Evelyn Scott's *The Wave* (1929), a text that arrived virtually in lockstep with the collapse of the stock market that ushered in the Depression. The novelist Stark Young, whom Faulkner counted among his friends, published *So Red the Rose* in 1934, and Paramount released the film adaptation the following year to capitalize on the novel's popularity. Other notable Hollywood films set during the Civil War included a tale of espionage called *Operator 13* (1934), a Shirley Temple vehicle titled *The Littlest Rebel* (1935), and *Jezebel* (1938), with Bette Davis in the leading role. Southern Agrarian Andrew Lytle published his Civil War novel *The Long Night* in 1936. Of course, towering above all these examples were Margaret Mitchell's *Gone with the Wind*, also published in 1936, and David O. Selznick's MGM film adaptation of the novel released in 1939.

For the most part, Faulkner scholars have responded to the fact that *Absalom, Absalom!* and *Gone with the Wind* entered the cultural sphere in the same year by noting the minimal similarities between the two novels and novelists and then emphasizing the pronounced differences. One readily apparent difference is the gulf that separates the two works in terms of popularity. Whereas Mitchell's novel was a runaway best seller, Faulkner's had a first run of only roughly six thousand copies. On one hand, Mitchell's novel inspired an acclaimed film adaptation that ensured *Gone with the Wind* achievement of iconic status. On the other hand, Faulkner's novel, which he composed in large part during one of his stints in Hollywood, failed to make it onto the big screen in spite of his best efforts to sell the movie rights. This failure is all the more ironic when one considers that, as Joseph R. Urgo argues, *Absalom*'s alignment with the cinematic process offers strong evidence of Hollywood's influence on Faulkner: "*Absalom, Absalom!* is a celebration of *collaboration* as a fruitful human exercise toward creating new works of art and reaching new levels of comprehension. Faulkner learned this in Hollywood" (58). Like all of Faulkner's other novels produced to that point, *Absalom* wound up out of print until the author's resurrection from obscurity in the 1940s. Unlike Mitchell's epic historical romance, with its clear-cut narration, linear plotting, and popularization of Old South mythology, Faulkner's novel offers frequent shifts among storytellers, varying and uncertain accounts of the same characters and events, and an unflinching view of history that exposes how the idealized narrative of the American Dream, with the "self-made man" as its protagonist, masks the nightmares of those who fall prey to his insatiable greed, unscrupulous manipulation and exploitation, and destructive violence.

Though the differences between Mitchell and Faulkner and their 1936 novels are indeed pronounced and profound, the two works have affinities that qualify as more than superficial or incidental in the context of the Great Depression. Consider, for example, how Mitchell's protagonist, the inimitable Scarlett O'Hara, compares to Faulkner's enigmatic Thomas Sutpen. Both characters possess a desire for power and privilege that intensifies in response to hardship and deprivation. The devastating effects of the Civil War force Scarlett into dire straits and call for ingenuity derived from her survival instinct. Determined to save her beloved Tara, the family plantation, in a state of ruin as Reconstruction ensues, Scarlett engages in self-reconstruction. This process is evident in the novel and film when Scarlett dons a makeshift dress made from the salvageable remnants of plush curtains to fashion herself as virtually unfazed by the catastrophic war and its aftermath. Without a material foundation for support, though, Scarlett must rely solely on social performance if she is to convince Rhett Butler that she is still the proverbial belle of the ball. Eventually Scarlett is able to restore the balance between material means and the outward appearance of social status, but only by using her guile and selling her already compromised soul to the "devil" of industrialism.

In a similar vein, Thomas Sutpen realized in his formative years, according to Mr. Compson, that the trappings of wealth and privilege would be crucial to his assuming the social role of the planter-gentleman in a convincing manner. Sent to deliver a message to a planter in Tidewater, Virginia, the young Sutpen learned from a house slave that the front door was off-limits to those of the Sutpens' inferior class. The incident, in Mr. Compson's view, gave rise to Sutpen's design on power, for Sutpen realized the connection between material possessions and social status. Sutpen recounted to Quentin's grandfather how the experience of being denied entrance via the front door brought a revelation about the planter class: "So to combat them you have got to have what they have that made them do what he did. You got to have land and niggers and a fine house to combat them with" (192).

For both Scarlett and Sutpen the most important asset is landownership because it provides literal and symbolic grounds for social identity and economic stability. Both characters show a fierce determination to restore their plantations to former glory as a means of reclaiming their identities and reasserting the old order. From Mitchell's perspective, Tara serves as a symbol of agrarian harmony—a plantation cast in the aura of a romanticized Old South to beckon Scarlett's return to "purity" after she has overtly pursued profit in the manner supposedly confined to crass northern industrialists. Sutpen's Hundred is the flip side of the "moonlight and magnolias" coin, as it were. Rather than serving as an object of desire promising to restore wholeness, as in the case of Scarlett's longing for Tara, Sutpen's Hundred symbolizes the perpetually unfulfilled desire that stems from the ambitious pursuit of material gain and the obsessive drive to preserve the "purity" of the familial bloodline exemplified in Sutpen's determination to sire a suitable male heir. Unlike Mitchell, Faulkner draws on elements of Old South mythology only insofar as he subjects them to interrogation and exposes their flaws.

Though Faulkner's and Mitchell's novels are quite different in most respects, they do share a common interest in exploring how means, or the lack thereof, shape individual subjectivity and affect the stability and viability of American social order. In this regard *Absalom, Absalom!* and *Gone with the Wind* constructed the Civil War setting as a usable past for Depression audiences all too aware, whether consciously or unconsciously, of the parallels between the historical national crisis and the contemporary one. Not surprisingly, popular audiences found in Scarlett's mix of ambition and determination, expressed in her famous declaration in the novel and film, "I'll never be hungry again," an inspirational model of resilience in the face of hard times. Thomas Sutpen, whose ruthlessness is not tempered by Old South sentimentality, was too strong a dose of reality for a Depression public longing to believe in the American Dream as a romantic ideal even in the face of substantial evidence to the contrary.

While the usable past in *Absalom, Absalom!* revealed harsh realities about the capacity for brutality and exploitation in pursuit of the American Dream at a time when that pursuit seemed in jeopardy, it also engaged issues beyond the domestic front in the realm of geopolitics. Many of the same elements rendering Faulkner's characterization of Thomas Sutpen a scathing critique of the "self-made man" as an ideological concept made it a timely and probing exploration of the ego-driven design on power most vividly on display in the dictators fueling the rise of fascism on the world stage. As I have argued elsewhere, Sutpen's design on power resembles in key respects that of the dictator intent on achieving absolute authority (Atkinson 162). A pronounced aspect of Sutpen's character is his preoccupation with infrastructure as both a means and a measure of his power, as well as a determinant of his identity.

The various narratives of Sutpen's rise to power have in common an emphasis on his drive to realize his vision of Sutpen's Hundred. The plantation, with its impressive "big house" supported by the requisite white columns, is Sutpen's domain—the main source and resonant symbol of his claim to planter status. As the alternating narrators suggest, though, the validity of this claim was not a matter of course but a result of Sutpen's design: acquiring and displaying material wealth, gaining some semblance of credibility through his marriage to the respectable Ellen Coldfield, and assuming the role of planter while demanding that he be accepted as such. The people of Yoknapatawpha, at least in Mr. Compson's account, acquiesce to Sutpen not because they recognize him as a "true" aristocrat according to conventional standards but because he has acquired the trappings—the same ones as the

Tidewater planter—necessary for assuming the social role he desires. The notion of Sutpen as a "self-made" man thus resonates with broader implications. Sutpen makes himself in the way of a Hitler, Mussolini, or Franco: he amplifies his ego through material and symbolic means, forcing the acquiescence of the masses that allows him to seize power and come closer to realizing his ambitions. In light of the interpretation of Sutpen as a proto-fascist, it is fitting that Faulkner, in a gesture foreshadowing his role as vocal opponent of totalitarianism on the post-World War II international stage, offered to donate proceeds from the sale of the original manuscript of *Absalom* to the cause of defeating the fascist Franco in the Spanish Civil War (Blotner 1020).

An additional element of *Absalom* that suggests its response to the rise of fascism in the 1930s is the chronic anxiety about racial "purity" exhibited in the Sutpen saga, especially the theme of miscegenation that figures centrally in Quentin and Shreve's narrative collaboration. According to Shreve, the specter of racial impurity took precedence in Henry Sutpen's mind when he decided that he had no other choice but to murder his mixed-race half brother, Charles Bon, to prevent Charles from marrying Henry's sister and Bon's half sister, Judith Sutpen. "*So it's the miscegenation, not the incest, which you cant bear,*" Shreve imagines Charles saying to Henry before the murder. At the end of the novel, Shreve returns to the issue, surmising that the attempt to rid the Sutpen line of miscegenation failed in a final stroke of tragic irony: the fact that the crazed, howling, and elusive Jim Bond, the grandson of Charles Bon, wound up as the sole "remainder" of Sutpen's design (302).

Shreve's meditation on Bond as precursor to a future of racial mixing that brings the demise of supposedly untainted whiteness punctuates the novel's chronic preoccupation with the ideology of racial purity. Not only does this preoccupation call to mind the racial theories that shaped Hitler's "final solution," but it also exposes the ideological underpinnings of the eugenics movement—a set of quasi-scientific theories that placed Caucasians at the pinnacle of racial hierarchy, assigned essential qualities to different races, and asserted the necessity for preventing racial mixing. This phenomenon emerged in the United States and, as historians have documented, heavily influenced Hitler's fantasies of Aryan racial superiority that fueled the rise of Nazism. With a nuanced complexity and frankness uncharacteristic of southern—or, for that matter, American—novels of the period, *Absalom, Absalom!* questions the "logic" of white supremacy, revealing it to be a flawed system built on the shaky foundation of fantasies inspired by chronic anxieties and fears of inadequacy. Faulkner reveals that Sutpen's lingering doubts about his own self-worth and, in turn, about the validity of his claim to elevated social status drive his ambitious design at the same time that they produce destabilizing questions about its integrity expressed in terms of imperiled whiteness.

Appropriately, a novel featuring myriad accounts of the same subject now is itself the subject of multiple and diverse readings. Notwithstanding successful attempts to expand the critical scope for examining *Absalom, Absalom!*, the work will likely retain its distinction as a "southern novel" for some time to come. Even as scholars in southern, American, and now New World studies continue efforts to move beyond the "Quentin thesis" and to advance readings of *Absalom* that eschew traditional regionalism, purveyors of a distinctive southern identity in American culture at large still invoke Faulkner's novel to signify ambivalence toward the South supposedly inherent in its denizens. This gesture now usually comes with the requisite ironic twist of postmodernism. Once played in earnest self-fashioning, the role of Quentin Compson, tormented southerner, is assumed in contemporary American culture with mocking self-awareness. Conceived in high modernism, Quentin Compson was in many respects an ideal agent for southern intellectuals who recognized the potential for shaping elements of this transatlantic cultural movement to the purpose of expressing the alienation and anxieties attending the individual life in a region under transformation by the forces of modernity. But *Absalom, Absalom!* as a whole was conceived during the tumult of the Great Depression—a factor that left lasting impressions on the novel's production and broadened the scope of its cultural influence, as the saga of Thomas Sutpen most vividly demonstrates. A key indicator of Faulkner's impressive achievement is that *Absalom, Absalom!* adapts to changing historical and cultural conditions, and in the hands of readers attuned to the multiple ways of finding meaning, those conditions would appear to adapt to it. For this reason among others, *Absalom, Absalom!* will likely remain a fixture in American culture, a continual presence "always reminding us to never forget" that it has important things to say (Faulkner 289).

Works Cited

Atkinson, Ted. *Faulkner and the Great Depression: Aesthetics, Ideology, and Cultural Politics*. Athens: U of Georgia P, 2006.

Blotner, Joseph. *Faulkner: A Biography*. 2 vols. New York: Random House, 1974.

Faulkner, William. *Absalom, Absalom!: The Corrected Text*. 1936. New York: Vintage, 1986.

Hobson, Fred, ed. *William Faulkner's "Absalom, Absalom!": A Casebook*. New York: Oxford UP, 2003.

Kreyling, Michael. *Inventing Southern Literature*. Jackson: UP of Mississippi, 1998.

Meriwether, James B., ed. *William Faulkner: Essays, Speeches, and Public Letters*. New York: Modern Library, 2004.

Mitchell, Margaret. *Gone with the Wind*. 1936. New York: Charles Scribner's Sons, 2007.

Schwartz, Lawrence H. *Creating Faulkner's Reputation: The Politics of Modern Literary Criticism*. Knoxville: U of Tennessee P, 1990.

Urgo, Joseph R. "*Absalom, Absalom!*: The Movie." *American Literature* 62.1 (1990): 56-73.

Woodward, C. Vann. *The Burden of Southern History*. New York: Vintage, 1961.

Tragedy and the Modern American Novel:
The Great Gatsby, Absalom, Absalom!, and *All the King's Men*_____

Randy Hendricks

> Sin and suffering and shame there must always be in the world, I suppose, but I believe that in this new world of ours it is still mainly from one to another one, and oftener still from one to one's self. We have death too in America, and a great deal of disagreeable and painful disease, which the multiplicity of our patent medicines does not seem to cure; but this is tragedy that comes in the very nature of things, and is not peculiarly American, as the large, cheerful average of health and success and happy life is. It will not do to boast, but it is well to be true to the facts, and to see that, apart from these purely mortal troubles, the race here has enjoyed conditions in which most of the ills that have darkened its annals might be averted by honest work and unselfish behavior.
>
> —William Dean Howells, *Criticism and Fiction* (62)

Howells uses the word *tragedy* in the common modern way to mean simply bad things that happen to people in the ordinary course of life. He also implies that tragedy as a formal literary genre would be inappropriate for treating American subjects. His is an American take on an assumption that reaches back at least to the eighteenth century, when reason and science, including an emerging faith in social science, became associated with the rise of the novel, part of an evolution of culture and letters that displaced older genres such as tragedy and epic. By 1925 Theodore Dreiser could publish a novel with the title *An American Tragedy*, as if he were directly challenging Howells's interpretation of American experience. Dreiser's novel signals an important impulse in twentieth-century American fiction. If we think only of three famous American novels from the 1920s to the 1940s—F. Scott Fitzgerald's *The Great Gatsby* (1925), William Faulkner's *Absalom, Absalom!* (1936), and Robert Penn Warren's *All the King's Men* (1946)—we see in critically acclaimed fiction the use of tragedy to tell an American story, or counter-American story, though each is stamped with the individual vision of its gifted creator.

Tragedy is not a term to be oversimplified. For the most part, we think of tragedy as a dramatic form that flourished particularly in ancient Greece and again in Elizabethan England. To this day we enjoy the works of Aeschylus, Euripides, and Sophocles. Shakespeare is, of course, the playwright we associate most with Elizabethan England, though he was by no means the only playwright and certainly not the only popular one. Shakespeare might have been as distanced in cultural perspective from Sophocles as we are from both. For that matter, because technology seems to accelerate the pace at which we become distanced from the past, Fitzgerald, Faulkner, and Warren might also seem to be figures from a distant culture. It is useful then to consider the assumptions behind tragedy, whether Greek, Elizabethan, or modern. Originally tragedy involved the fall of a gifted man or woman, a member of a noble family, from a high station to destruction. The tragic sense assumes an inevitable failure in life through some combination of fate and human flaw. Yet tragedy values life for the courage, dignity, and, perhaps most important of all, knowledge human beings might gain in the face of the fact that their actions are doomed to fail. The tragic hero is generally one who recognizes at last the role of his or her own character in the destruction. In later tragedy the central figure might well come from a lower class but still shares with the classic and Elizabethan hero the characteristics of dignity and, sometimes at least, self-knowledge in the face of ruin.

The chief assumption for Greek and Elizabethan tragedy, however different the two cultures, may have been the *closed* nature of the universe. It was a universe presided over by deities remarkable precisely for their irrational and arbitrary natures, yet one certainty in that universe was the *secondary* role humanity played in it. The basic conflict in tragedy has to do with the exorbitant human will running headlong into a moral order that, in the end, demands humility. The movement of tragedy is the movement through a disruption of that order and through the violence that attends that disruption to the restoration of that order. The tragedian's assumption of such an order makes oracles, soothsayers, and prophesying witches not only possible but even practical dramatic devices in tragedy; even these intermediaries seem to maximize the ironic structure. The Oracle at Delphi tells the young Oedipus only about half of what he really needs to know. The caldron-stirring witches seem deliberately to tease Macbeth into his terrible fate with their half-truths. Even when the blind prophet Tiresias tries to tell Oedipus the whole truth, it is too late—Oedipus had long before fulfilled the Oracle's prophecy that he would kill his own father and lie with his own mother—and Oedipus is so locked in the blind rage of his own ego by that point that he dismisses the long-trusted seer.

What use could a modern novelist possibly make of such an antiquated vision of life? The eighteenth century reimagined God as the perfectly reasonable Creator whose universe was embedded almost mechanistically with laws that could be understood through science. The drive toward modernism was largely the movement through ever-advancing technologies. We take for granted such miraculous human achievements as vaccines, flight, nuclear power, and the World Wide Web—except when such technologies fail or go horribly wrong. The growing faith in technologies since the eighteenth century made faith in God seem antiquated or, more accurately, to make God secondary to or even complicit in human progress. Yet, as Paul Fussell has pointed out, with World War I, the word *machine*, which had previously been linked with hope for human kind, became "invariably coupled" with the word *gun* (24). In other words, however much the modern world might have outgrown the older tragic sense of life, human action still seemed to entail violence and destruction. Even if the moral order necessary for the tragedian was no longer available to the modern writer, Fussell's observation makes clear that one essential element of tragedy clearly still was available, even necessary—a special sense of *irony*.

The early twentieth century witnessed a galvanizing of artistic response to the combination of destruction and complacent faith in technology. Realism, especially Howellsian realism, seemed to many people inadequate to meet the writer's task of telling the truth. In his novel *Ulysses*, James Joyce used the *Odyssey* as an overlay to tell the story of his ordinary modern Dubliner Leopold Bloom. Reviewing the book, the poet T. S. Eliot wrote that Joyce had given writers a new "mythical method," comparing its significance to an important "scientific discovery" (177-78). Eliot adapted the method himself for one of the twentieth century's most famous and influential poems, *The Waste Land*. The "mythical method," cubism, expressionism, surrealism, and stream-of-consciousness narrative were all developments artists took advantage of, often in combination, to bend artistic representation away from realistic verisimilitude for what many believed was a deeper penetration of social and psychological reality. In light of such developments, it should come as no surprise that some writers would make use of a presumably antiquated tragic vision to tell their truths.

If we take the term *myth* to mean a narrative by which a group identifies itself, each of the three novels is concerned with the American myth of self-making. If that myth has a literary origin, it is Benjamin Franklin's *Autobiography*. On his first page Franklin makes explicit his purpose for writing about his rise from "Poverty and Obscurity" to a "State of Affluence and some Degree of Reputation in the World": others might find his "means" of doing so "fit to be imitated" (1). Many since have indeed found Franklin's story of hard work, self-education, good manners and morals, public service, and, above all, the careful cultivation of a public image "fit to be imitated." The celebrity autobiography offered as self-help guide remains a perennial best seller today. Naturally, the story of the rise from humble beginnings requires an emphasis on those beginnings. Franklin's description of his arrival in Philadelphia, the city that would be closely associated with his name and success, provides an origin for this important element in the myth. He arrives dirty, without luggage (his pockets stuffed with spare socks), with little money (and since there is as yet no national currency, no knowledge of the actual value of his coins in this strange new place), and hungry. When he sees a boy with bread, he tells us, "I had made many a meal on bread" (20). The sentence registers immediately with anyone schooled in the myth. It is the equivalent of being born in a log cabin on the frontier. It signals not only humble origins but also the can-do-ness, the toughness, one carries through life after transcending one's origins. We value Abraham Lincoln largely on these terms, even if we do roll our eyes when members of our own families talk about "hard times." In the 1979 film *The Jerk*, the very white Steve Martin opens the story of his character's life with the claim, "I was born a poor black child." Schooled in the myth, we know why the line is funny. But Fitzgerald, Faulkner, and Warren all evoke the myth in their novels very seriously as each is deeply interested in the psychology of the myth and its impact on individuals and society.

Consider the youthful confidence of Faulkner's Thomas Sutpen in *Absalom, Absalom!* as he describes his first steps to escape the poverty into which he had been born:

> "What I learned was that there was a place called the West Indies to which poor men went in ships and became rich, it didn't matter how, so long as that man was clever and courageous: the latter of which I believed that I possessed, the former of which I believed that, if it were to be learned by energy and will in the school of endeavor and experience, I should learn." (242)

While Franklin recalls his humble beginnings with nostalgia and achieves a specific rhetorical purpose, Sutpen's need to rise from his station is a psychological necessity precipitated by the shocking discovery of his place in the Tidewater society into which he enters when his shiftless father moves the family from the mountains of western Virginia to take a vaguely defined job for a Virginia planter. Sent to the main house on some errand by his father, young Sutpen is met at the front door by a slave in full livery who instructs the boy to go to the back to deliver his message. Struck by this treatment, Sutpen takes to the woods, much as Huck Finn often does, to think through what has happened to him and what it means. By the end of this tortured thinking session, he has concluded that the only way to combat his enemy—the planter, not the slave—is to imitate him; that is, he must have land and slaves himself. He leaves home that very night to seek his fortune.

The improbability of Sutpen's action is part of the larger-than-life image the multiple narrators of the novel have to contend with. Fitzgerald's Jay Gatsby and Warren's Willie Stark undergo similar kinds of shocks in discovering their places in society; in Willie's case, his place in the political machinery that runs the society. While Gatsby had long been dissatisfied with the shiftlessness and poverty of his North Dakota farm life, his goal is galvanized for him early on when as a poor young army lieutenant he is prevented from pursuing a relationship with Daisy Fay, the most popular young girl in Louisville society. He sets out to regain her with action as large and in some ways as improbable as Sutpen's. Willie Stark's early shock occurs when he discovers that the political backers who urge him to run for governor do so only to split the vote to ensure the win for their actual favorite. Out of this experience Cousin Willie from the country begins the transformation into the ruthless Boss, who in time becomes the most powerful man in the state. Like those of Gatsby and Sutpen, his transformation involves beginning to behave like his "enemies." (Willie does, of course, take full Franklinesque advantage of his humble origins for political purposes.) In each case a sudden shock initiates the need to rise in social status, a rise necessary for the tragic fall to come. From an achieved position of power, each of the main characters exercises his determined and even ruthless will, and the result is tremendous destruction, but even the ruthlessness proceeds from an innocent, even idealistic, belief in the rightness of will.

All three novels are remarkable for their narrative structures. Both *The Great Gatsby* and *All the King's Men* use a first-person narrator who, while seeming to report the story of the central character—Jay

Gatsby or Willie Stark—in fact reveals his own story through his involvement with the central character. Each story for the narrator is a story of resignation, of the feeling of invulnerability through non-involvement that in the end turns out to be false. Nick Carraway's decision to return to the Midwest after Gatsby's death and his total disgust with Daisy and Tom is Fitzgerald's equivalent of Warren's having Jack Burden leave Burden's Landing after the deaths of Willie and Adam, the idealistic doctor who kills Willie, and return to life and a necessary commitment to "the awful responsibility of Time" (531). What we get through both Nick and Jack is a modern, cynical, and seemingly aloof view of the man of action, more specifically the man of idealized action, who asserts his will in order to change his destiny. What both Nick and Jack come to in the end is a discovery of their own involvement in that action.

It is easy to forget that *Absalom, Absalom!* is not also a first-person novel. It is in fact a third-person novel in which the narrative is rendered through the visions of four distinct characters—Rosa Coldfield; Jason Compson II; his son, Quentin; and Quentin's Harvard roommate, Shreve McCannon. The novel opens on a late summer afternoon with Quentin sitting in the parlor of the home of old and outraged Rosa Coldfield, who sees Thomas Sutpen as the demon who came upon the land and created its ruin, dooming her family and his own children to outrage and destruction. As a survivor of the Sutpen destruction, she tells again the story that Quentin already feels is part of his inheritance. But she wants Quentin to do more than listen to her; she needs him to accompany her to the old Sutpen mansion because she believes something is out there. Later that same day, as Quentin waits for the time to collect Rosa and fulfill his commitment to her, he talks further of the story with his father as they sit on their porch. Mr. Compson knows a good deal, primarily because his own father had been a friend and something of a confidant of Thomas Sutpen, but Mr. Compson also has an intellectual interest in the story and offers some possible interpretations. Mr. Compson thinks of the people involved as remote, as people "of a dead time" (89); his relation to the story is something like a modern man going to the theater to watch an ancient tragedy. But Mr. Compson does not hold the key. What he knows—that Charles Bon kept and had a child by an octoroon mistress in New Orleans—does not adequately explain in that culture why Henry Sutpen would shoot Bon to prevent his marriage to Judith.

In chapter 6, the scene of the telling shifts to some time later and from Mississippi to the Harvard dorm room Quentin shares with Shreve. We quickly learn that the story has already taken on a heavy presence even here as Quentin has repeatedly been asked since coming to the North to "tell about the South" (174). While Quentin feels rather oppressed by the story, Shreve—detached by both his age and his birthplace, Canada—finds it fascinating, "better than Ben-Hur" (227), and he treats it as something of a game as the two boys use the scant facts they know and their imaginations to fill it in. "Let me play," Shreve says, wanting a turn at the narrative (280). All the while, Quentin has the key. He got the final answer to the central question when he took Rosa to Sutpen's Hundred and they discovered the dying Henry Sutpen there. Presumably Quentin learned Henry's motive for killing Bon from Henry himself, even though only a small segment of the conversation they had is recorded.[1] Henry had killed Bon not because of the mistress, not even to prevent incest—as we have now discovered that Bon is Thomas Sutpen's son by his first wife—but to prevent miscegenation, as we further learn that Thomas Sutpen had abandoned that wife when he learned of her black ancestry. As Sutpen had put it to Quentin's grandfather: "I found that she was not and could never be, through no fault of her own, adjunctive or incremental to the design which I had in mind, so I provided for her and put her aside" (240). Quentin's grandfather is shocked by the act, but even more by the innocence Sutpen displays in believing such matters can be settled by fair monetary adjustments.

By decentering the narrative as he has, Faulkner achieves a suspense through the slow, incremental revelation of the motive for the

Critical Insights

novel's central action. But he also suggests—through the fact that imagination is required to flesh out the story, through such speculations as Mr. Compson's, and through the completely different responses to the story we see in Quentin and in Shreve—a pluralizing that suggests a modern disintegration of a single interpretive strategy, the lack of a common set of values by which action may be seen clearly and judged.

It would be a mistake, however, to leave the matter just here: to say that all three novelists have adopted the modern disintegration of a common point of view simply to give the lie to the American Dream. If all three novelists represent a thoroughly modern consciousness through their inventive narrative techniques, they also offer an alternative to both the innocence of the American myth and the cynicism of a modern detachment. While we see a great deal of human manipulation that brings about the tragic ends in each case, there is also operating in each novel an interpretation of experience that strongly resembles the sense of order necessary for tragedy. This is achieved largely through specific patterns of imagery. In *All the King's Men* and *Absalom, Absalom!*, in fact, we see some strikingly similar patterns.

After suspending the story of Willie Stark to tell the story of his supposed nineteenth-century ancestor Cass Mastern, Jack Burden reflects on the meaning of the pattern of Mastern's tragic life. Cass betrays his best friend by taking his wife as a lover. When the friend discovers the affair, he commits suicide. The adulterers are guilt-stricken, and the wife compounds the sin by selling the slave Phebe, who knows all, to a trader headed for the New Orleans slave market. After a violent but futile attempt to rescue Phebe, Cass leaves Kentucky and returns to his Mississippi plantation and frees his own slaves. After he tries for a year to work the land with freedmen and -women, tensions with surrounding plantations force him to admit the futility of this effort as well, and he pays passage for his former slaves to go North. When the Civil War begins, Cass joins the Confederate Army as a private and passively waits to die in battle. Lying in an Atlanta hospital fatally wounded, he writes in his journal: "I have lived to do no man good, and have seen others suffer for my sin. I do not question the Justice of God, that others have suffered from my sin, for it may be that only by the suffering of the innocent does God affirm that men are brothers, and brothers in His Holy Name" (226).

Readers have sometimes questioned the presence of this story in the novel. The action takes place almost seventy years before the Stark story, and there is no direct connection between the two. But we can probably see well enough the thematic relation of the two stories if we consider Jack's even more frightening idea about a brotherhood dependent on suffering:

> Cass Mastern . . . learned that the world is all of one piece. He learned that the world is like an enormous spider web and if you touch it, however lightly, at any point, the vibration ripples to the remotest perimeter and the drowsy spider feels the tingle and is drowsy no more but springs out to fling the gossamer coils about you who have touched the web and then inject the black numbing poison. It does not matter whether or not you meant to brush the web of things. . . . what happens always happens and there is the spider, bearded black and with his great faceted eyes glittering like mirrors in the sun, or like God's eye, and the fangs dripping. (227)

Jack Burden can come to this conclusion, however, only after he himself has lived through the Stark story, after he has lived through the deaths of his actual father, Judge Irwin, his friend Adam Stanton, and his friend and "boss" Willie Stark, all of whom die violently in a string of connected actions that may well be likened to the vibrations of a spider's web. Also Jack has to face his own responsibility for the Judge's suicide because it was Jack who used his historian's/detective's skills to uncover the old scandal in the Judge's past that Willie, his political rival, could use against him. In short, Jack has to confront his own place in the spider web. Withdrawal and detachment and finally even cynicism are not options. The *order* of the web will not allow them.

Readers may also be puzzled by how profoundly the story of the House of Sutpen affects young Quentin Compson. After all, by the late summer and fall of 1909, most of the action of the Sutpen story is long over. But Faulkner has his own images to suggest the kind of interconnectedness that Warren delineates. Judith Sutpen provides one such image not long after her brother shoots and kills her fiancé, Charles Bon. Judith had given a letter she received from Bon late in the Civil War to Quentin's grandmother. The letter is one of the scarce artifacts available for the later generation to piece the story together, but there is also what Judith supposedly said to Quentin's grandmother at the time:

"You are born at the same time with a lot of other people, all mixed up with them, like trying to, having to, move your and arms and legs with strings only the same strings are hitched to all the other arms and legs and the others all trying and they don't know why either except that the strings are all in one another's way like five or six people all trying to make a rug on the same loom only each one wants to weave his own pattern into the rug." (127)

The loom world Judith discovers seems very similar to Jack's spider web. Similar images abound in *Absalom, Absalom!* Quentin, to provide just one more example, describes the impact of the past upon the present by imagining the past as one pool and the present as another, but the two are connected by a "narrow umbilical water-cord," and the ripples made by the pebbles dropped in the pool of the past make waves through this water-cord on into the pool of the present so that "nothing ever happens once and is finished" (261). There is, in other words, a temporal as well as a spatial or social dimension of the interconnected world. Even the style of the novel often suggests the interconnectedness of the loom and the water imagery. Consider, for example, how much time and action are encompassed in just the first couple of paragraphs of the first chapter. As Quentin listens to Rosa, he is aware that he has grown up with the story to the point that "the mere names were interchangeable and almost myriad. His childhood was full of them; his very body was an empty hall echoing with sonorous defeated names; he was not a being, an entity, he was a common-wealth" (12). Toward the end of the novel Quentin says to Shreve, "I am older at twenty than a lot of people who have died" (377).

Small wonder Quentin is shaking by the end. The point to be stressed, though, is that by depicting the world as being "all of one piece" in its temporal and spatial dimensions, Faulkner and Warren have created worlds that resemble the world of tragedy sufficiently for a collision course with the American myth of self-making, which of course depends on individualism and separateness, not on a concep-tion of the individual as a "commonwealth." The tragic end in each case is effected in part by the innocence of the protagonist bent on re-making himself meeting the reality of the loom and the web.

Through somewhat different means, Fitzgerald comes to a similar end. Fitzgerald has immersed the characters in his novel in the popular culture of the 1920s. The action takes place in an atmosphere of popu-lar songs and dances, advertising, radio, and speakeasies. Much of the atmosphere is represented through Gatsby's elaborate parties—night-long affairs of heavy drinking, blurred identities, and even violence, with artificial light (even the moon seems ordered for the occasions), ice sculptures, multiple suppers, and a paid band to complete the pic-ture. All of this is staged by Gatsby to create a certain impression, and he stages himself to create a similar impression. His speech, character-ized by his addressing men as "Old Sport," can be like thumbing through the pages of a dozen magazines (71). Gatsby calls attention to his house, car, and airplane as signs of his success. He depicts himself as a war hero—a claim that may well have some validity—yet when he points out that "even Montenegro, little Montenegro down on the Adriatic sea" (70) awarded him a medal, he is borrowing directly from the life of Alvin York, who became famous for his daring in the Argonne during World War I (Lee 39). Later when Daisy tells Gatsby, "You always look so cool. . . . you resemble the advertisement of the man" (125), we learn even more about the sources of Gatsby's self-staging. Today's readers might call up an image of a more recent iconic figure, but Fitzgerald's contemporaries would have known exactly the figure Daisy meant—the Arrow Shirt man, the center of one of the most successful advertising campaigns in history and an icon for much of the twentieth century, whose handsome features, air of mystery, obvious sophistication, and appeal to and power over women created a desirable image of manhood. Even Daisy's wording suggests that the ad was for a type of man, to which the quality and fashion of the collars and shirts he wore became inevitably attached. These are the sources of the public identity that Gatsby has rather literally put on to achieve his goal of impressing and winning Daisy Fay, now Daisy Buchanan.

But Fitzgerald, too, has his own kind of counterimagery to suggest the problem with making oneself up whole through a powerful will. There are the eyes on the billboard advertisement of Dr. T. J. Eckleburg, like God's eyes, watching out over all in the Valley of Ashes through which the characters must pass on the way from West and East Egg into the city—a dumping ground for the fires of industrial civilization—through which men move like shadows, ill defined, and indistinct (27). There is above all the lyrical and elegiac conclusion of the novel in which Nick glosses Gatsby's story with the past, as both Faulkner and Warren gloss their stories in their own fashions. Nick wonders how the eastern shore must have appeared to the eyes of the first Dutch sailors who saw it, before the trees gave way for the houses:

> a fresh, green breast of the new world. Its vanished trees . . . had once pandered in whispers to the last and greatest of all human dreams; for a transitory enchanted moment man must have held his breath in the presence of this continent, compelled into an aesthetic contemplation he neither understood nor desired, face to face for the last time in history with something commensurate to his capacity for wonder. (189)

Nick goes on to compare Gatsby's desire for Daisy with what the Dutch sailors experienced, but by doing so he casts the American experience as a futile resistance to history:

> Gatsby believed in the green light, the orgastic future that year by year recedes before us. It eluded us then, but that's no matter—tomorrow we will run faster, stretch out our arms farther. . . . And one fine morning—
>
> So we beat on, boats against the current, borne back ceaselessly into the past. (189)

A combination of cynicism and lyricism, Nick's notion resembles Judith Sutpen's description of the loom. The very motion of the novel, with its pattern of reverse migration from West to East, may well suggest the cyclical nature of the return captured in the final sentence. The point is that, as in the other two novels, an older, more universal sense of the world is brought to bear on the present.

Robert B. Heilman has written that some early reviewers and critics of *All the King's Men* missed the point of the novel very badly because they simply did not know how to read tragedy: "The artist proceeds from the region [the South] to the civilization, and from the civilization to the dangers of disintegration implicit in human life; this is tragedy; but they cannot read it, and in their confusion they are as complacent as if they were protecting Humpty down there under the covers" (23). A failure to see the tragic sensibility at work in all three novels considered here means missing a large element of their artistic power. The tragedy modifies the American myth of the rise and subjects it to irony, without merely mocking it out of its human dimension. At the same time the tragedy pulls the cynic off the sidelines and back into the world of action. Even Shreve McCannon moves from irreverence to awe in regard to the Sutpen story. So the tensions among the three— American myth, modern consciousness, tragic sense—are not resolved once and for all. We do not leave the novels cheered up and with a program for going forward. We find nothing "fit to be imitated" in them, except perhaps the dignity of having faced with the artists the *real* in several of its multiple and contradictory dimensions.

Note

1. For a more detailed discussion of how Quentin learned the truth, see Cleanth Brooks's chapter on the novel in his *William Faulkner: The Yoknapatawpha Country*, 295-324.

Works Cited

Brooks, Cleanth. *William Faulkner: The Yoknapatawpha Country*. 1963. Baton Rouge: Louisiana State UP, 1990.

Dreiser, Theodore. *An American Tragedy*. 1925. Cleveland, OH: World, 1946.

Eliot, T. S. "*Ulysses*, Order, and Myth." *The Dial* (November 1923). Rpt. in *Selected Prose of T. S. Eliot*. Ed. Frank Kermode. New York: Harcourt Brace Jovanovich, 1975. 175-78.

Faulkner, William. *Absalom, Absalom!* 1936. New York: Random House-Vintage, 1972.

Fitzgerald, F. Scott. *The Great Gatsby*. 1925. New York: Simon & Schuster, 1995.

Franklin, Benjamin. *Autobiography*. Norton Critical Edition. Ed. J. A. Leo Lemay and P. M. Zall. New York: W. W. Norton, 1986.

Fussell, Paul. *The Great War and Modern Memory*. New York: Oxford UP, 1975.

Heilman, Robert B. "Melpomene as Wallflower; or, the Reading of Tragedy." *Sewanee Review* 55 (1947): 154-66. Rpt. in *Twentieth Century Interpretations of "All the King's Men."* Ed. Robert H. Chambers. Englewood Cliffs, NJ: Prentice Hall, 1977. 17-28.

Howells, William Dean. *Criticism and Fiction*. 1891. *Criticism and Fiction and Other Essays*. Ed. Clara Marburg Kirk and Rudolf Kirk. New York: New York UP, 1959.

Lee, David D. *Sergeant York: An American Hero*. Lexington: UP of Kentucky, 1985.

Warren, Robert Penn. *All the King's Men*. 1946. New York: Harcourt Brace Jovanovich, 1974.

The Critical Reception of *Absalom, Absalom!* _____

Kevin Eyster

Dividing time between Rowan Oak, his home in Oxford, Mississippi, and Hollywood, California, where he was writing screenplays for various film studios, William Faulkner completed the manuscript of *Absalom, Absalom!* in January of 1936. Handing it to a fellow screenwriter, he said, "I think it's the best novel yet written by an American" (qtd. in Blotner 364). While many readers eventually would consider the novel to be the Nobel laureate's finest, initial reviews of *Absalom* were mixed.

Writing in *The New Yorker*, Clifton Fadiman described *Absalom* as "the most consistently boring novel by a reputable writer to come my way during the last decade" (62). Mary Colum, in the *Forum*, dismissed the novel as "too incoherent" and ultimately "unsuccessful" (35). Bernard DeVoto both praised and condemned "Mr. Faulkner's new fantasia," suggesting the novel showed "a magnificent technical dexterity" but also "a style in the process of disintegration" (3-4). Herschel Brickell predicted *Absalom* would "rank as one of its author's major works" (15). Malcolm Cowley, who felt the novel left readers "confused" at times, still saw it as Faulkner's "strongest" and "most unified" ("Poe" 22). In the 1940s Cowley would be instrumental in establishing Faulkner as "the most studied American author," with "his ninth novel, *Absalom, Absalom!* [receiving] more critical attention than any other, with the possible exception of *The Sound and the Fury*" (Muhlenfeld xi).

According to John E. Bassett, studies of the novel have fallen into

> two major categories, one focusing on the nineteenth-century story of Thomas Sutpen and the other the twentieth-century dilemma of Quentin Compson. The first is concerned with social themes, myth and legend, tragic form and character; the second deals with narrative techniques, epistemological issues, and the novel's connection, through Quentin . . . to *The Sound and the Fury*. (276)

Bassett's two categories suggest the range of topics that critics have written about in discussing *Absalom, Absalom!* over seven decades.

In 1945 Cowley's *The Portable Faulkner* was published, when "Faulkner's books were little read and often disparaged" (vii). This collection of Faulkner's writing included a chapter from *Absalom*. In his introduction, Cowley summarized the plot and referred to the novel as a "Gothic romance" and a "tragic fable of Southern history" (xviii). Cowley saw *Absalom* as "structurally the soundest of all the novels in the Yoknapatawpha series," with the principal theme being "Colonel Sutpen's design" and the secondary themes being those of "incest and miscegenation" (xxiii). When *The Portable Faulkner* was revised and expanded in 1967, Cowley added Faulkner's 1950 "Address upon Receiving the Nobel Prize for Literature" (vi) and an afterword in which he acknowledged "a Mississippi flood of critical studies" occurring in the 1950s and 1960s (xxviii).

Ilse Dusoir Lind, for example, compared the novel to classical mythology and the Bible:

> A synopsis of the Sutpen legend would read like one of the summaries of Greek myths conveniently placed as prologue to modern translations of Greek plays. The continuing . . . analogies which exist between Sutpen and Oedipus, Sutpen's sons [Charles Bon and Henry Sutpen] and Eteocles and Polyneices, Judith and Antigone, suggest the Oedipus trilogy might have served as a general guide in the drafting of the plot. At the same time, Sutpen's fall and the obliteration of his house bring to mind the great myth of man's original fall from innocence and the visitations of divine justice upon third and fourth generations. Old Testament violence evoking God's wrath is recaptured here in a legend of a father [Thomas Sutpen] turning against son [Bon], son [Henry] against father [Sutpen], and brother [Henry] against brother [Bon]. (889)

Lind also addressed how the thematic relationship between past and present and the events of the Sutpen family story are conceived: "The

Sutpen tragedy as communicated in the novel has no 'objective' existence. It is the collective product of the workings of the minds of three story tellers, abetted by the collaboration of a fourth. The Sutpen tragedy is the novel's center of . . . interest, but the narrators are the center of the novel" (890). Echoing Lind but shifting the emphasis from the novel's mythic and tragic to its legendary stratum, Olga Vickery explained:

> All the narrators are sincerely trying to be truthful, correcting and contradicting themselves as they reconstruct the past, and all have certain unique qualifications for the task. Miss Rosa obviously has the advantage of having lived through the events and of a close personal knowledge of Sutpen, while Mr. Compson has his carefully guarded objectivity, and Quentin and Shreve the uncluttered perspective afforded the passage of time. Yet it is plain that the result of their efforts is not the truth about Sutpen but rather three quite distinct legends which reveal as much about the narrators as about Sutpen. (86)

As writer-in-residence in 1958 at the University of Virginia, Faulkner himself said that each narrator in *Absalom* does see a part of the truth, but each one's endeavor to tell the story of Thomas Sutpen is also another attempt to explain her or his own life experience (*University* 273-74). He acknowledged that readers would play a key role in the making of meaning: "When the reader has read all these thirteen ways of looking at the blackbird, the reader has his own fourteenth image of that blackbird which I would like to think is the truth" (274). The reader must piece together the interrelated versions of the legend of Thomas Sutpen by an "external narrator" and four "character narrators" (Ruppersburg 11) to determine what is being told, how it is being told, and why it is being told.

Notably, Cleanth Brooks addressed the what, how, and why. As a practitioner of the New Criticism, in 1963 Brooks explored the novel's central themes, characterization, structure, and narrative technique.

Declaring *Absalom* "the most brilliantly written of all of Faulkner's novels," Brooks asserted there "are actually few instances in modern fiction of a more perfect adaptation of form to matter and of an intricacy that justifies itself at every point through the significance and intensity which it makes possible" ("History" 46). Seeing the novel as a "wonderful detective story," Brooks emphasized how it serves as "persuasive commentary upon the thesis that much of 'history' is really a kind of imaginative construction. . . . The novel then has to do not merely with the meaning of Sutpen's career but with the nature of historical truth and with the problem of how we can 'know' the past" (34, 31). To support his position he added "notes" to his analysis, comparing verifiable facts with the narrators' conjectures. His notes assist readers in understanding the plot and complement the chronology, genealogy, and map of Yoknapatawpha County that Faulkner had included when the novel was originally published in October of 1936. Brooks was also one of the first critics to discuss the "story of Judith," Thomas and Ellen Coldfield Sutpen's daughter and Henry's older sister, describing her as "one of Faulkner's finest characters of endurance . . . and not merely through numb, bleak stoicism but also through compassion and love" (41). The works of Lind, Vickery, and Brooks are representative of the critical studies of *Absalom* that were published in the 1950s and 1960s.

The 1970s saw topics revisited and expanded as well as the advent of more formal theoretical interpretations. In her study of time in relation to history and myth, Patricia Tobin utilized a structuralist approach. "Within the novel," Tobin wrote, "Faulkner articulates an inquiry into the interplay of historical time and mythic timelessness" (252). She concluded: "The ultimate failure of [the] narrators to integrate myth [the synchronic] with history [the diachronic], linear with nonlinear time, the past with the present, is at once Faulkner's vision of man's misfortune and his justification of the esthetic form of his novel" (254). Reiterating that "all Faulkner's narrators exhibit a crucial need to know Sutpen so that they might know themselves" (260), Tobin envisioned "the Sutpen family" as "*the* genealogical family of the South" (268), with the consequences felt generationally, leading to "the disintegration of a family, a social order, and an entire culture" (257). The receptacle of this legacy of course is Quentin, who intimates, through the behavior of Sutpen toward Charles Bon and Henry, "the fragility of the father-son relationship, and the tragic absurdity that makes Henry's four choices—bigamy, incest, fratricide, and miscegenation—all sins against the family" (269). Tobin's structuralist reading anticipated the psychoanalytic approach to the novel developed by John T. Irwin.

Extending earlier thematic readings of *Absalom*, Irwin asserted in 1987 that of "the many levels of meaning" in the novel, "the deepest . . . is to be found in the symbolic identification of incest and miscegenation" (10), which spring from the "archetype of the brother who must kill to protect or avenge the honor of his sister" (9). He related this deepest level to the Judith-Bon-Henry triangle, manifested in the narcissistic "doubling" (12, 14) between Henry and Bon, and in the repetition of "Sutpen's revenge for the affront that he suffered as a boy in Bon's revenge for the affront that he and his mother [Eulalia Bon] suffered at Sutpen's hands during Sutpen's quest for revenge" (17). But he also related it to Quentin, whom Irwin described as "the central narrator" and the "principal narrative consciousness in *Absalom*" (10). Irwin explored how "Quentin projects his own unacceptable impulses" (13) onto the story he helps shape and create, and in so doing reveals a great deal about himself and his family. He linked Quentin's suicide in *The Sound and the Fury* (1929) to the "murder of Bon by Henry": "This whole repetitive structure is made even more problematic by the fact that the explanation which Quentin gives for Bon's murder (that Bon is black, i.e., the shadow self) may well be simply the return of the repressed—simply an unconscious projection of Quentin's own psychic history" (16) based on his feelings for his sister, Caddy, and conflicts with his father.

Repeating the father-son relationship, according to Irwin, "Quentin's act of narration . . . is an attempt to seize his father's authority by gaining temporal priority. In the struggle with his father, Quentin will prove that he is a better man by being a better narrator," with "the basis" being the son's "authority to tell" parts of the Sutpen story "to his father" and by extension to Shreve, having made "a journey into the dark, womblike Sutpen mansion, a journey back into the past," where Quentin "has learned more about events that occurred before he was born than either his father or grandfather knew" (31). However, this narrative "mastery" (28) is short-lived for Quentin because "his narrative struggle with Shreve" (33), as the Nietzschean "'revenge against time'" (18), is a "circular labyrinth" (33) that Quentin can escape only by taking his own life. Irwin's Freudian approach laid the groundwork for Doreen Fowler's "Lacanian interpretation" of the novel in the 1990s.

Yet another level of the novel considered by critics is the intertextuality between *Absalom* and the King James Version of the Bible, specifically the title in relation to the Old Testament and II Samuel. Two studies in 1974 reached different conclusions. Ralph Behrens emphasized similarities between the house of David and the house of Sutpen: "David's rise to kingship in many ways parallels Sutpen's rise, and David's unhappy later days suggest many of the horrifying events that bring Sutpen's dynasty to an end" (29). In contrast, John V. Hagopian acknowledged that "the title of [Faulkner's] greatest novel comes from David's lament, 'O my son Absalom, O Absalom, my son, my son!' (II Samuel, 19:4)," and "although the novel is full of Biblical allusions, there is not a single reference to David or to Absalom" (131). Hagopian noted several differences between the two stories and suggested that if *"Absalom, Absalom!* is related to the Old Testament, it is by ironic inversion," because "Sutpen is simply incapable" of the "degree of love and compassion" shown by David (134). Behrens's and Hagopian's interpretations of this substruct anticipated such readings as Glenn Meeter's, who focused on Faulkner's "handling of the David analogy" and Quentin's role as "redactor" (116, 118), as the character narrator who absorbs the other versions and retells the Sutpen legend in its fullest form.

At the end of the 1970s, Donald M. Kartiganer took a critical position distinct from Cowley's and subsequent views "as the source of a body of criticism that interprets all the books [of the Faulkner canon] as one book, the whole corpus as the author's 'postage stamp of native soil'" (xiv), and from the New Critics, who "[reject] the necessity of synthesizing the canon and instead . . . bind up the wounds of fragmentation from within the individual works" to accentuate "aesthetic unity" (xv). For Kartiganer, Faulkner is "a modern novelist who must begin by dislocating the possibilities of form," so that *Absalom*'s "design . . . never denies its dubious status, its origins in contingency" (xvii).

In his "high modernist" reading of *Absalom*, which along with *Light in August* (1932) Kartiganer called Faulkner's "best . . . examples of achieved design" (xviii), he reconsidered how the character narrators invest themselves in the Sutpen story. "In presenting the story through these personal and necessarily distorting perspectives," he determined, "Faulkner dramatizes the creativity of the interpretive act, the process by which meaning emerges from the meeting of history with the most private and vested interests" (74). Differentiating the "strategies for self-exoneration" in the "narratives of Rosa [Coldfield] and [Mr.] Compson" (74) from "the images of imaginatively realized truth" (84) embodied in Quentin and Shreve's version, Kartiganer saw in the latter's collaborative discourse "a supreme fiction": "In terms of form, this part of [*Absalom*] is the climactic moment in Faulkner's career, for it is here that his essential style of fragmentation, of isolated narrators and actors placed at odd intervals on the rim of a single event, moves toward its most profound meaning" (77). Going on to ask the question, "How do Quentin and Shreve discover the blackness in Charles Bon?" (94), Kartiganer inferred that for "Quentin, trying to imagine truth in 1910, blackness rather than incest is the only adequate motive for" Henry to "murder" Bon (101). Such a question and answer took on added meaning when explored by Thadious M. Davis in 1983, during a decade when theoretical approaches to the novel continued.

In her book-length study of race relations, Davis explained how "'the Negro,' the white man's own creation . . . is a central imaginative force in Faulkner's fiction," functioning "both as concept and as character" by becoming "an integral component of the structural and thematic patterns in much of Faulkner's art" (2). "A synopsis of the Sutpen legend without the inclusion of the Negro," Davis asserted, "is a story without motivation or . . . meaning" (182). She saw a necessary, reciprocal relationship in the novel's "narrative development" (187), so that the character narrators are dependent on their inventions from the past to understand Sutpen and his legacy:

> Each of the narrators invents his [or her] own "Negro" in defining himself [or herself] and in expressing the limits of his [or her] imagination, personality, and humanity. Miss Rosa creates Clytie, Sutpen's slave daughter, and the "wild niggers" who build Sutpen's Hundred. Mr. Compson draws the New Orleans octoroon and her son Charles Etienne St. Valerie Bon. Quentin and Shreve imagine Charles Bon and his mother Eulalia [and Jim Bond]. (190-91)

Two of the many racially motivated confrontations that Davis examined are crucial. Calling the first "one of the most starkly honest scenes in the Faulkner canon," Davis noted that Rosa's meeting with Clytie on the steps leading to the upstairs of the Sutpen mansion "probes the psychological and cultural realities of race and kinship" (207). The second "reiterates the ultimate tragedy of the Sutpen legend: the son's [Henry's] meeting with the father [during the Civil War] is reduced to a racial confrontation; kinship, whether physical or spiritual, may be denied when one party is 'Negro'" (209). Davis's study proved foundational for future readings of the Faulkner canon in general and *Absalom* in particular through the lens of African American criticism, exemplified in the 1990s by Doreen Fowler and Kevin Railey, who show how Faulkner was "challenging and exposing racial censorship" (Fowler, "Reading" 137) by depicting "racial identity" as "a social construction" (Railey 41).

Concurring that *Absalom* "is Faulkner's most accomplished, moving, and sustained meditation on the act of fabricating meaning" (115), John T. Matthews in 1982 applied French poststructuralist Jacques Derrida's "meditation on the nature of language" to Faulkner's "homespun tale-telling" (23). Matthews observed that "a principle that . . . governs" the novel is that Faulkner's "language always escapes the simple dichotomy of presence and absence" (61). Since the character narrators exist only in the language they create, according to Matthews, readers can "account both for the shades of sorrow and despair among the narrators of Sutpen's story . . . and for the moments of gleeful, intoxicating invention" (61). As readers, we understand both "Sutpen's failure" (161) and the character narrators' investment in recreating his design and its consequences as existing solely in language, in story: "Telling the Sutpen story demands loving, violent play; the moments of significance arise out of the repetition and revision of the story" (150). "More broadly," Matthews argued, "the novel poses a view of identity as language; no character lives beyond the moment of his or her voice since all thought and consciousness appear to Faulkner as kinds of talk" (151). Faulkner "celebrates the narrators' marriages of speaking and hearing . . . because they complicate, trouble, and challenge the offenses of Sutpen's tragic innocence" (161).

Faulkner critics in the 1980s moved the discussion of narrative technique into the theoretical realm of narratology. For example, Karen McPherson utilized the theories of French scholars Roland Barthes and Gerard Genette, and Stephen M. Ross those of the Russian scholar Mikhail Bakhtin. Reading *Absalom* as "a struggle between restraint and insistence" (438), where "outrage and bafflement haunt the telling . . . bursting with narrative voices" (439), McPherson contended that there are "essentially two *narrators*—equally subject to the tyranny of the tale: Quentin and Rosa. The tale imposed itself upon these two because it needs telling, and those who were directly involved in the history—Clytie, Jim Bond, and Henry—do not narrate" (439). For McPherson, the novel's "narrative experimentation . . . undermin[es] the self-reflection of the telling . . . to produce . . . the delineation of the unspoken, and a silence that *tells*" (431-32). The focal point of the novel's "temporal manipulation," its "incongruities," and its "sequential problem[s]" (434), is Quentin:

> Suspended between having to *listen* and having to *be (telling)*, Quentin slips from thought into the "long silence of notpeople, in notlanguage," where one no longer hears the language of Quentin recounting, one hears the language of Quentin *hearing*—and this language is occupied by other discourses, those of Miss Rosa in Chapter One and Mr. Compson in Chapter Seven. (435)

Suggesting that "Quentin is a narrator *narrated*" (441), McPherson aptly noted, "What he attempts, in the narrative, to delay and suppress, forces itself upon him and upon the telling, through the discourse of his *listener* [Shreve and, by extension, the reader], in a narration that is neither clearly Quentin's nor Shreve's but a narrative voice that forces itself upon both of them" (440).

This third-person, "narrative voice" Stephen Ross labeled "an oratorical Overvoice pervading the entire text" (220). The "function of the Overvoice is to evoke the past" (221). Through Faulkner's use of "Southern rhetoric" (217) and application of "the South's oratorical discursive practices" (218), the novel "instructs us [on] how to read it by imaging its own discourse" (222). While McPherson referred to the act of reading *Absalom* as the "reader as writer'" (438), Ross insisted that the novel "is a listener's more than a teller's story, a reader's text more than a writer's" (228). He reasoned: "*Absalom* presumes an energetics of oratorical voice through which language can be transcended and the past rescued. Through the elaborate recapitulation of past events the novel accumulates what seem to be versions of the imaginative real and the imaginative true, and thereby creates a textual monument to its own endeavor" (222), making the novel—and, by extension, the reading experience—self-referential.

Such analyses as McPherson's and Ross's pushed the critical envelope further, opening the novel's intricate layering and incremental unfolding to levels that take into account not only the imagined and envisioned but also the spoken and the unspoken. The impingement of the past on the present becomes even more compelling through these studies of Faulkner's complex narrative technique and the demands placed on active, participatory readers.

Anticipating the Faulkner centennial in 1997, scholars in the 1990s were prolific in their production of critical studies of the Faulkner canon, especially of *Absalom*. At the beginning of the decade, two book-length studies of the novel offered fruitful detailed readings with differing points of emphasis. Dirk Kuyk, Jr., took the concept of "design" and showed how it functions in a variety of ways in the novel, be it Sutpen's, other characters', the narrators', or readers' designs. Recalling Cleanth Brooks's notion that Faulkner creates in Sutpen "a character of heroic proportions" (30), Kuyk stated that "once we have grasped what Sutpen's design was, we will see in it less self-serving ambition and more of an aspiration that might actually deserve the word *heroic*" (5). Kuyk observed in Sutpen "not merely" the desire "to acquire a dynasty, but to acquire it so that he could turn it against dynastic society itself" (17).

Robert Dale Parker delineated a detailed reading of the novel's nine chapters, organizing his book "so that people can read the novel two or three chapters at a time and then read the corresponding section of this book in the way a student might attend a class after being asked to read each quarter or so of a long novel" (vii). Seeing *Absalom* as a novel with "no simple answers but configurations of contending questions and answers" (viii), Parker utilized "a wide range of critical methods," including "structuralism, poststructuralism, feminism, psychoanalysis, and cultural . . . criticism" (vii). Whereas Kuyk detailed *Absalom*'s "*fabula*—a chronological outline of the major acts of the book" (29) in "chronological order" (45-60), Parker illustrated its "narrative structure" (167-69).

Discussing Faulkner's experiences in Hollywood, Joseph R. Urgo explored the novel's cinematic qualities and screenplay characteristics. Urgo ascertained that *Absalom* "is about movie-making, and the production of images and moving pictures" (294). Returning to the novel's final chapters and Quentin and Shreve's narrative collaboration, Urgo determined: "In the same way a director, in collaboration with writers and producers and technical assistants, makes a film from various scenes, shots and file footage at his disposal, Quentin and Shreve make a Sutpen story from materials which Quentin produces and Shreve ultimately shapes, or directs, into a coherent pattern" (296). He concluded by suggesting that, although *Absalom* "contains filmic elements—montage, collision, suspended time—what is most filmic . . . are not specific, cinematic techniques but the presentation of the creative [writing] process in a reified manner" (303-4).

Minrose C. Gwin's 1990 analysis of Rosa Coldfield began "at the interstices of deconstruction, psychoanalysis, and feminism" (69). Determining that "Miss Rosa's message" in the novel's first and fifth chapters is both "terrifying and tantalizing" (70), Gwin asserted that Rosa inevitably "becomes the feminine space that male narrative writes itself upon" (71). Gwin asked, "Does Faulkner want Rosa silenced, or is he writing her silence as the hysterical symptom of the Old South's patriarchal narrative of mastery?" (71). In order "to read the feminine in Faulkner," Gwin argued, "we must acknowledge its strangeness . . . the mystery of its textuality" (77). Her interpretation reveals how feminist readers "may have much to fear from Rosa Coldfield's narrative desire to say the madness of her culture, for what happens in *Absalom* is that Rosa disappears into the text of madness which she herself creates and which generates the force of the narrative" (64). "Much of the narrative force," Gwin reasoned, "derives from Mr. Compson's, Shreve's, even Quentin's efforts to master Rosa's text by distancing and diminishing her as a subject" (68). For Gwin, the reader ultimately must embody Rosa's situation: "To experience the madness of Rosa's text we must allow ourselves to be inscribed by it. We must acknowledge our complicity in its otherness" (71). In the end, Gwin concluded, the "space between Faulkner and Rosa . . . may be less than we think; for he, like the feminine of his own creation, tells us that history can never be over, that 'was' can never be 'was,' and that cultural madness writes itself . . . upon us all" (92).

J. Hillis Miller based his poststructuralist reading of the novel, published in 1995, on the interrelationship between the ideological and the topographical. Summarizing the theories of Karl Marx, Louis Althusser, and Paul de Man, Miller defined "ideology" as "an erroneous relation between consciousness and material reality" (256). Drawing on the "Three Fates of contemporary cultural studies: race, gender, and class" (262), he determined that "everything that happens in *Absalom, Absalom!*" is contingent on these ideologies "and would be impossible without them" (267). He contemplated how *Absalom* both critiques and reinforces southern ideology. "On the one hand, the novel may give knowledge about ideology that might help liberate us from it. On the other hand, the novel may have an irresistible performative effect that goes against that knowledge" (269). "A possible means of liberation" from the ideologies of the South is the "topographical," because "Faulkner has a strong topographical imagination. The events of his novels take place within elaborately mapped mental or textual landscapes in which characters are associated with places" (272). Using Judith's letter from Bon and her giving of the letter to Quentin's grandmother as a primary example, Miller "links this passage with the topographical motifs in the novel" (272). Recalling Quentin and Shreve's "overpass to love" (Faulkner, *Absalom* 253), Miller noted that it is the discernible geography of Faulkner's imagination and sense of place that develops "our relation as readers to the characters in the novel [as] a kind of love" (275). Miller deduced that, although "an incommensurability between knowledge and action remains the human condition" (276), "love here" through the act of reading *Absalom* "is the name for a relation to history and to other people that may transform ideology and provide the glimpse of an escape from it"

(275). In essence, though the characters cannot escape the ideological, readers perhaps can.

The progression of historical readings of the novel, especially of Sutpen's innocence and his design—what Arthur F. Kinney refers to as "genealogy as dynasty" (1) and Eric Sundquist explains in light of Abraham Lincoln's "most famous speech on the House Divided" (110)—reached fruition in 1994 in Barbara Ladd's new historical interpretation. By "tracing the history of colonization and miscegenation in the Deep South" (221) as it was manifested by means of the phenomenon of passing and the classification of "quadroons" and "octoroons" (219), Ladd showed how the "assumptions about race, culture, and politics under the new American government" (224) created a "segregationist ideology of the United States" (223), ultimately undercutting "the dream of U.S. national unity" (220). Within this historical context, Ladd showed how the "issue of race mixing and the effort to keep the mixed blood out of the white family (or nation) in *Absalom, Absalom!* is a return, through the medium of psychological family drama, to the issue of assimilation versus segregation of the Creole" (232). "One of the most profound achievements" of the novel, Ladd formulated, "is its power of commentary on this . . . use of the Creole of color" (221). Specifically, as "Quentin's story unfolds, Bon is transformed from colonialist Creole into Thomas Sutpen's eldest son into 'the nigger that's going to sleep with your sister'" (241). Bon's apparent "'taint' of African ancestry" is based on a "conversation that supposedly reveals Bon as black," but this conversation "is not included in the text," so that the "reason for the murder of Charles Bon by Henry Sutpen in 1865 becomes one of the novel's central mysteries," an "obsession for each speaker" to explain, and the "means by which Faulkner might explore the implications of his own generation's imperialist designs" (232, 235). The latter is a topic considered further by cultural critics Richard Godden, Charles Hannon, and Sara Gerend, who have focused on "labor trauma particular to a southern system of production" (Godden 4), "storytelling . . . as a kind of labor that masks other, more exploitative forms of labor" (Hannon 76), and "early twentieth-century U.S. imperialist representations of Haiti in *Absalom*" (Gerend 18).

Along with such historical and cultural studies, Bon's identity and the implications of Sutpen's design remained focal points among critics. Drawing on the work of reader-response theorist Wolfgang Iser, Nancy Batty, for example, described the "assumption that Henry Sutpen actually murdered Charles Bon" as prescriptive and asked the central question, "Are contemporary critics of the novel willing to extend the notion of indeterminacy in the text to what has always been assumed to be its very bedrock, the alleged murder of Bon by Henry?" Batty's 1994 study focused on "ambiguities in the text," exemplified by her rereading of Rosa's narrative in chapter 5 and Quentin and Shreve's in chapter 6 to question who was buried next to Ellen: "The fact that Bon's grave is located next to that of Ellen . . . and that, in this position, it usurps the final resting place of Henry . . . , raises even more suspicion about what or who is buried there." Declaring that the novel embodies a "public version" of "private truth," Batty encouraged her readers to "reread" *Absalom* "with a mind equally open to the wonder of its radical indeterminacy."

"Design" took on added meaning when Judith Bryant Wittenberg related the concept to Faulkner's career as a writer. "Numerous attempts by critics in recent decades to articulate the nature of Faulkner's 'grand design,' his overarching metatext," led Wittenberg to reconsider the "tensions" in Faulkner's experience "as a writer," which in *Absalom*, the author's "culminating text, coalesce quite distinctively around the issue of career" (100). Parallels within the novel and its place in the Faulkner canon point to "what is . . . notable about *Absalom* [in] the way . . . it . . . both celebrates and profoundly questions the feasibility of a career that," be it Sutpen's or Faulkner's, "proceeds by conscious design" (102).

Criticism of *Absalom* during the first decade of the new millennium continued to reshape the critical canon and returned to the fundamentals of close reading. Matthew R. Vaughn, for example, applied the queer theories of Eve Kosofsky Sedgwick and Michael Moon to understand better "the expression of gay male identity" in *Absalom* (520). Focusing on Mr. Compson's narration in chapter 4 and Quentin and Shreve's in the later chapters, Vaughn explained how the "tragic erotic triangle" of Henry, Judith, and Bon functions as "the triangulation of desire" and "the process of queer initiation" (520). He explored how "Henry's position within the erotic triangle is characterized by a precarious negotiation between the demands of Southern masculinity and his own homosexual desires" (520). Though "triangulation becomes an acceptable means of expressing gay identity indirectly," Henry's "obsessive adherence to the conventions of Southern morality will ultimately thwart even this vicarious strategy" (521) Vaughn concluded, "Ultimately, the dominant Southern ideology works not only to suppress gay identity, but to become in Henry's hands the gunshot that results in his exile, Bon's death, and Judith's spinsterhood," as well as "the story . . . through which" Quentin and Shreve "explore their repressed desires" (521, 526).

A significant addition to Faulkner studies resulted from comparisons of Faulkner's fiction to that of Toni Morrison. Augmenting one of the most fruitful book-length studies of Faulkner's fiction from the previous decade, *Unflinching Gaze: Faulkner and Morrison Re-Envisioned* (1997; edited by Carol A. Kolmerten, Stephen M. Ross, and Judith Bryant Wittenberg), Peter Ramos in 2008 explored how the Nobel laureates' two greatest novels, *Absalom, Absalom!* and *Beloved* (1987), "employ the tropes and literary techniques traditionally aligned with tales of the supernatural. . . . These are ghost stories, except they are meant to be taken seriously" (48). Ramos considered how, for Faulkner and Morrison, the "dilemma of how to address slavery and its legacy results in a specific crisis of repression. . . . each novel employs the trope of the image of a ghost in order to attempt to explain the history in question" (48-49). While the ghost in *Beloved* is the return of the murdered infant as a young adult, in *Absalom* the character narrators and their subjects are referred to as ghosts, with Quentin being "ghost-like, victim of hauntings, and tragically alive all at once" (51). For Sutpen and his family in *Absalom* and Sethe and her family in *Beloved*, "a personal crisis speaks to and reflects a larger, social crisis," which is "the tragedy of slavery—its practices, consequences and unfinished history" (53). The embodiment of Sutpen's feigned innocence, his denial of Charles Bon, and his willingness to sacrifice Henry to preserve his design is Sutpen's grandson, Jim Bond. As Ramos aptly noted, "Jim Bond's indecipherable howling may be the nearest Faulkner ever comes to articulating the tragedy, not only of Sutpen, but of the antebellum South and its legacies" (59).

Coming full circle in 2010, Joseph Urgo and Noel Polk added to the *Reading Faulkner* series a "Glossary and Commentary" on *Absalom* to help readers "unpack the meaning of Faulkner's language" by asking and answering "basic questions: What do these words mean? What else might they mean, in the context of what precedes and follows their appearance on the page? How might we usefully connect them to other parts of the novel?" (xii). Urgo and Polk fittingly suggested how the novel initially should be read in relation to their detailed analysis: "We insist that you *not* attempt to use this guide during your first encounters with *Absalom, Absalom!* We would not deny, or in any way intervene in, your own original reactions to the deliberate complexities and confusions of one of Faulkner's, and therefore literature's, most magnificent achievements" (xv). Like the many other critical studies, Urgo and Polk's "guide" is not a substitute for reading the primary work; rather, it is part of the supplemental, secondary material available to be put to use by those rereading the novel.

As readers consider the critical canon over seven decades, Cowley's observations ring true; into the twenty-first century, the number of published essays, book chapters, and books devoted to *Absalom* alone will surpass one thousand. With the Faulkner and Yoknapatawpha Conference held each summer in Oxford, Mississippi, the ongoing publication of *The Faulkner Journal* and a yearly "special issue" of

The Mississippi Quarterly devoted to Faulkner criticism, as well as scholarly Web sites focusing on the author's life and literature, the study of William Faulkner continues unabated.

Works Cited

Bassett, John E. *"Absalom, Absalom!*: The Limits of Narrative Form." *Modern Language Quarterly* 46 (1985): 276-92.

Batty, Nancy. "The Riddle of *Absalom, Absalom!*: Looking at the Wrong Blackbird?" *Mississippi Quarterly* 47.3 (Summer 1994): 461-88.

Behrens, Ralph. "Collapse of Dynasty: The Thematic Center of *Absalom, Absalom!*" *PMLA* 89 (1974): 24-33.

Blotner, Joseph. *Faulkner: A Biography*. 1974. New York: Vintage, 1991.

Brickell, Herschel. *"Absalom, Absalom!" Review of Reviews* Dec. 1936.

Brooks, Cleanth. "History and the Sense of the Tragic." 1963. *William Faulkner's "Absalom, Absalom!": A Casebook*. Ed. Fred Hobson. New York: Oxford UP, 2003. 17-46.

———. "Notes to *Absalom, Absalom!*" *William Faulkner: The Yoknapatawpha Country*. New Haven, CT: Yale UP, 1963. 429-36.

Colum, Mary. "Faulkner's Struggle with Technique." *Forum* 97 (January 1937): 35-36.

Cowley, Malcolm. "Poe in Mississippi." *The New Republic* 4 Nov. 1936.

———, ed. *The Portable Faulkner*. 1946. New York: Penguin, 2003.

Davis, Thadious M. *Faulkner's "Negro": Art and the Southern Context*. Baton Rouge: Louisiana State UP, 1983.

DeVoto, Bernard. "Witchcraft in Mississippi." *Saturday Review of Literature* 31 Oct. 1936. Rpt. in *Critical Essays on William Faulkner: The Sutpen Family*. Ed. Arthur F. Kinney. New York: G. K. Hall, 1996. 107-13.

Fadiman, Clifton. "Faulkner, Extra-Special, Double-Distilled." *The New Yorker* 31 Oct. 1936.

Faulkner, William. *Absalom, Absalom!* 1936. New York: Vintage, 1990.

———. *Faulkner in the University: Class Conferences at the University of Virginia, 1957-1958*. Ed. Frederick L. Gwynn and Joseph L. Blotner. Charlottesville: U of Virginia P, 1959.

Fowler, Doreen. *Faulkner: The Return of the Repressed*. 1997. Charlottesville: UP of Virginia, 2000.

———. "Reading the Absences: Race and Narration in Faulkner's *Absalom, Absalom!*" *Faulkner at 100: Retrospect and Prospect*. Ed. Donald M. Kartiganer and Ann J. Abadie. Jackson: UP of Mississippi, 2000. 132-39.

Gerend, Sara. "'My Son, My Son!': Paternalism, Haiti, and Early Twentieth-Century American Imperialism in William Faulkner's *Absalom, Absalom!*" *Southern Literary Journal* 42.1 (Fall 2009): 17-31.

Godden, Richard. *Fictions of Labor: William Faulkner and the South's Long Revolution*. New York: Cambridge UP, 1997.

Gwin, Minrose C. *The Feminine and Faulkner: Reading (Beyond) Sexual Difference*. Knoxville: U of Tennessee P, 1990.

Hagopian, John V. "The Biblical Background of Faulkner's *Absalom, Absalom!*" *The CEA Critic* 36 (1974): 22-24. Rpt. in *William Faulkner's "Absalom, Absalom!": A Critical Casebook*. Ed. Elisabeth Muhlenfeld. New York: Garland, 1984. 131-34.

Hannon, Charles. *Faulkner and the Discourses of Culture*. Baton Rouge: Louisiana State UP, 2005.

Irwin, John T. "Doubling and Incest/Repetition and Revenge." *William Faulkner's "Absalom, Absalom!"* Ed. Harold Bloom. New York: Chelsea House, 1987. 9-34.

Kartiganer, Donald M. *The Fragile Thread: The Meaning of Form in Faulkner's Novels*. Amherst: U of Massachusetts P, 1979.

Kinney, Arthur F. Introduction. *Critical Essays on William Faulkner: The Sutpen Family*. Ed. Arthur F. Kinney. New York: G. K. Hall, 1996. 1-46.

Kolmerten, Carol A., Stephen M. Ross, and Judith Bryant Wittenberg, eds. *Unflinching Gaze: Morrison and Faulkner Re-Envisioned*. Jackson: UP of Mississippi, 1997.

Kuyk, Dirk, Jr. *Sutpen's Design: Interpreting Faulkner's "Absalom, Absalom!"* Charlottesville: UP of Virginia, 1990.

Ladd, Barbara. "'The Direction of the Howling': Nationalism and the Color Line in *Absalom, Absalom!*" *American Literature* 66.3 (Sept. 1994): 525-51. Rpt. in *William Faulkner's "Absalom, Absalom!": A Casebook*. Ed. Fred Hobson. New York: Oxford UP, 2003. 219-50.

Lind, Ilse Dusoir. "The Design and Meaning of *Absalom, Absalom!*" *PMLA* 70 (1955): 887-912.

McPherson, Karen. "*Absalom, Absalom!* Telling Scratches." *Modern Fiction Studies* 33.3 (Autumn 1987): 431-50.

Matthews, John T. *The Play of Faulkner's Language*. Ithaca, NY: Cornell UP, 1982.

Meeter, Glenn. "Quentin as Redactor: Biblical Analogy in Faulkner's *Absalom, Absalom!*" *Faulkner and Religion*. Ed. Doreen Fowler and Ann J. Abadie. Jackson: UP of Mississippi, 1991. 103-26.

Miller, J. Hillis. "Ideology and Topography in Faulkner's *Absalom, Absalom!*" *Faulkner and Ideology*. Ed. Donald M. Kartiganer and Ann J. Abadie. Jackson: UP of Mississippi, 1995. 253-76.

Muhlenfeld, Elisabeth. Introduction. *William Faulkner's "Absalom, Absalom!": A Critical Casebook*. Ed. Elisabeth Muhlenfeld. New York: Garland, 1984. xi-xxxix.

Parker, Robert Dale. *"Absalom, Absalom!": The Questioning of Fictions*. Boston: Twayne, 1991.

Railey, Kevin. "*Absalom, Absalom!* and the Southern Ideology of Race." *The Faulkner Journal* 14.2 (Spring 1999): 41-55.

Ramos, Peter. "Beyond Silence and Realism: Trauma and the Function of Ghosts in *Absalom, Absalom!* and *Beloved*." *The Faulkner Journal* 23.2 (Spring 2008): 47-66.

Ross, Stephen M. *Fiction's Inexhaustible Voice: Speech and Writing in Faulkner*. Athens: U of Georgia P, 1989.

Ruppersburg, Hugh M. *Voice and Eye in Faulkner's Fiction*. Athens: U of Georgia P, 1983.

Sundquist, Eric. "*Absalom, Absalom!* and the House Divided." *William Faulkner's "Absalom, Absalom!": A Casebook*. Ed. Fred Hobson. New York: Oxford UP, 2003. 107-49.

Tobin, Patricia. "The Time of Myth and History in *Absalom, Absalom!*" *American Literature* 45 (1973): 252-70.

Urgo, Joseph R. "*Absalom, Absalom!*: The Movie." *American Literature* 62.1 (Mar. 1990): 56-73. Rpt. in *William Faulkner: Six Decades of Criticism*. Ed. Linda Wagner-Martin. East Lansing: Michigan State UP, 2002. 293-310.

Urgo, Joseph R., and Noel Polk. *Reading Faulkner: "Absalom, Absalom!"* Jackson: UP of Mississippi, 2010.

Vaughn, Matthew R. "'Other Souths': The Expression of Gay Identity in *Absalom, Absalom!*" *Mississippi Quarterly* 60.3 (Summer 2007): 519-28.

Vickery, Olga. *The Novels of William Faulkner*. 1959. Baton Rouge: Louisiana State UP, 1964.

Wittenberg, Judith Bryant. "*Absalom, Absalom!* and the Challenges of Career Design." *Faulkner at 100: Retrospect and Prospect*. Ed. Donald M. Kartiganer and Ann J. Abadie. Jackson: UP of Mississippi, 2000. 100-108.

Gates and Doors and Metaphors:
Materiality and (Dis)Embodied Sexuality in *Absalom, Absalom!*_____

Aimee E. Berger

It may be, as T. S. Eliot wrote, that the property of a great work is its ability to communicate before it is understood. In his 1963 study *William Faulkner: The Yoknapatawpha Country*, Cleanth Brooks reminds us of Eliot's definition and then goes on to say: "*Absalom, Absalom!* passes this test triumphantly. It has meant something very powerful and important to all sorts of people and who is to say that, under the circumstances, this something was not the thing to be said to that particular reader?" (295). This is not to say that the reader is everything and the text only a mirror for what the reader wants to see in it, but rather, that is Brooks's way (and mine) of acknowledging the difficulties in arriving at anything like a static or definitive analysis of the book. It is also a way of acknowledging that this book can speak to you long before you really understand what it is saying. Maybe, too, Brooks is confirming what I have come to believe about the book, which is that it communicates many things all at once, but as readers (and writers), we understand it differently at different times.

Writing about *Absalom, Absalom!*, like reading it, is a difficult task, which is not to say it is not worthwhile. But it helps, I think, to acknowledge that there are complexities here that confound even careful readers and seasoned writers. This is in part because *Absalom, Absalom!* is a book of loose ends, built around absent people with unknowable feelings and motives, in which ongoing conjecture masquerades as narrative reality. Elliptical and fragmentary, told by many voices in a confusing chronology, it leaves the careful reader with more questions than answers.

The starting point for this essay was the question "Why Quentin?" I was in good company for asking this; Quentin asks it himself, wondering why in the world he should have been "summoned" by Rosa

Coldfield to be the recipient of this story (6). Later, in conversation with his father, he twice demands, "Why tell me about it?" (7). Though Rosa and Mr. Compson offer explanations, Quentin disputes them both. But it's a good question: Why *did* Faulkner raise Quentin from his grave and send him back in time to the summer before his suicide in order to collect the pieces of the Sutpen story? The question seemed especially pertinent given that one of the main pre-texts of the novel was a short story, "Evangeline," that is plotted around the same main event (the murder of Charles Bon by Henry Sutpen in order to prevent Bon's marriage to Judith) and contains many of the same characters but is narrated by a reporter named Don. It bears mentioning, perhaps, that in "Evangeline" there is no possibility that Charles Bon is *either* black *or* the brother of Judith and Henry.

Quentin's involvement with the Sutpen story closely precedes his suicide in *The Sound and the Fury*, a fact that has led many critics to raise questions: What is the connection? Why would Quentin be so devastated by the events of Sutpen's story that he is robbed of all hope and kills himself shortly after? Starting the process of thinking about this novel, I outlined the parallels between Quentin Compson and Thomas Sutpen: their "tragic innocence," their (self)destruction, and the demands of "the South" on both, or rather the demands made by their internalized interpretations of "the South," which compelled each to create and live within rigid codes or "designs" that ultimately, tragically, failed them. As an aside, I noted that for each man, his design or code was one in which women figured prominently, but as abstractions or passive objects, never as fully human subjects with stories and hopes and designs of their own. Shreve pretty much sums up the view taken of women by the male narrators of the text when he says, without the irony that is so often characteristic of his speech, "a woman . . . didn't need to want or hope or expect anything" (303).

Initially, I also accepted the interpretation of Sutpen's story as "the" story of "the" South and therefore imagined that Quentin was brought back in order to show us what it was about the South that was so destructive that it essentially swamped poor Quentin and left him foundering: speechless on the stairs in Sutpen's Hundred in the fall of 1909 and dead the next year in the Charles River, drowned for good and all. And I accepted that the central problem of the South had to do with race, so I focused on analyses of the novel that foregrounded racial themes, even though I sensed that something was lacking in many of these explanations. Something that the story had communicated to me lingered beyond my understanding, and I sensed that whatever it was, it had not pressed itself strongly on other readers either and therefore had eluded analysis.

If we take "race as the cardinal theme of *Absalom* (the motor of its tragedy)," as some critics do (Weinstein 51), we can safely conflate the stories of Thomas and Henry (father and son share the same concern: to protect the House of Sutpen from a black intruder) and even conclude that the story of the South being examined is the story of its racial legacy, but we cannot answer my question, "Why Quentin?" Nothing in Quentin's story predisposes him to feel *personally* implicated in racialized conflict—so if race is the motor of this story, why bring Quentin back to crank it up?

As I continued to ponder the relationship between Quentin's and Thomas Sutpen's stories, I began to feel, uncomfortably, a growing sense of kinship with Mr. Compson, a character who has never much moved me and one who has certainly never before inspired any such fellow feeling. But I shared his frustration over the failure of "the ragtag and bob-ends of old tales and talking" (303) and of "letters without signature or salutation" (80) to explain the events of this story. His frustration leads him to utter his memorable summary of the entire (surface) narrative, "It just does not explain!" Still, I wasn't so discouraged that I could go along with him to his conclusion that "perhaps that's it: they don't explain and we are not supposed to know" (80). Instead, I took up another question: What exactly did Quentin learn from this story? And then I wondered, How, or from which Sutpen, had he learned it?

Many critics have focused on Thomas Sutpen as the central character of this text, no doubt because, as Irving Howe notes, "no other Faulkner character rules a book so completely as does Sutpen in *Absalom, Absalom!*" (222). It is fitting that Thomas Sutpen should rule the book in much the same way that he rules his House (I'm using this word in its older and broader sense to mean both his plantation and his progeny) and fitting, too, that he should capture the imagination of the novel's critics in the same way he captures the imaginations of the book's narrators, including those like Quentin and Shreve who never even met him. But just because he is a dominant character doesn't mean that he is the singular catalyst for the actions of the plot or the singular expression of its themes. In other words, Thomas Sutpen does not *explain*. And he doesn't answer my question.

Of course, not all Faulkner critics take Thomas Sutpen as the central figure or infer from Sutpen's significance in the narrative that the "Sutpen story" that most interests Quentin and accounts for Faulkner's resurrection of him is Thomas's. The parallels between Henry and Quentin are often the subject of analysis. But one assumption that most critics share along these lines is that primary among the commonalities between Henry and Quentin is the centrality of the father figure to the inner and outer lives of both boys. In these readings, the fathers are seen to exercise tremendous and constant influence over the lives of their sons, and it is to the father that each boy feels the greatest allegiance, striving to live within the code or design bequeathed to him. Moreover, each is shaped, doomed even, by that striving, his actions guided and governed by the shadowy father figure, his flawed blueprints architecting the son's (or sons') destruction.

Along with Quentin and Henry's common fascination with their fathers, an interest in what Brooks delicately refers to as "the problem of incest" (318) is also seen by many to unite them (though only a few linger over what this might really mean or acknowledge that this might not be an abstract interest having to do with notions of honor so much as an actual, corporeal/sexual interest). The problem of incest to which Brooks is referring could be either the proposed incest between Charles Bon and Judith Sutpen or Henry's own incestuous feelings, but the nature of the problem is always discussed in abstract terms, having to do more with codes of honor than with sex. Later critics take up this line of reasoning and similarly avoid discussing the desire for the sister as a sexual, corporeal one.

The true object of desire is seen by some to be the other boy, and by others to be the father. André Bleikasten, for example, argues that "the point about the incest with Caddy is that it is conceived as *confessed* to the father" (87) as part of an attempt to provoke paternal retaliation and thereby move on through the Oedipal drama. Similar arguments are raised about Charles Bon and whose love he is really after, as when Philip Weinstein writes that the Bon constructed by Quentin and Shreve is "apparently in love with Judith, more credibly in love with Henry, but ultimately in love with his father, Sutpen" (146). Other critical interpretations focus on the "homoerotic tension between Quentin and Shreve" (Polk 142) as parallel to suggestions raised in *Absalom* about the homoerotic or at least homosocial bond between Charles and Henry. Mr. Compson seems especially keen on this possibility, envisioning a Charles Bon who "loved Judith after his fashion but he loved Henry, too . . . perhaps . . . he loved Henry the better of the two, seeing perhaps in the sister merely the shadow, the woman vessel with which to consummate the love whose actual object was the youth" (86). He returns to this theory more forcefully soon after, saying, "It was not Judith who was the object of Bon's love or of Henry's solicitude. She was just the blank shape, the empty vessel in which each of them strove to preserve . . . what each conceived the other to believe him to be" (95). Note that his later iteration of the idea is far more abstract, losing the word "consummate" and its undeniable sexual connotation, replacing the sense of Judith as conduit for the boys' love with the notion that she is a mirror for their illusions. As Quentin will later show himself to be, Mr. Compson is a narrator concerned with questions of the body and of desire, but ultimately so uncomfortable with the issues they raise that he must replace corporeal desires with abstractions or withdraw into silence.

Yet, the novel is littered with references to actual sexual desire as part of Henry's interest in his sister. Note the way in which Mr. Compson's analysis tries to focus on Henry's abstract interest in Judith (her sexual purity tied to his provincial sense of honor) but slips into the corporeal images he just can't seem to avoid:

> [Henry] may have been conscious that his fierce provincial's pride in his sister's virginity was a false quantity.... perhaps this is the pure and perfect incest, the brother realizing that the sister's virginity must be destroyed in order to have existed at all, taking that virginity in the person of the brother-in-law, the man whom he would be if he could become, metamorphose into, the lover, the husband. (76-77)

That is, metaphorically at least, exactly what happens on the day of Charles Bon and Judith's wedding, when the man who bursts through the bedroom door to see her half dressed in her wedding gown is not Bon but Henry.

Critical assumptions about the centrality of the father and each other to the lives of these fictional boys are analytical frameworks that turn Judith into a passive object, despite Faulkner's vivid descriptions of her and the persistent intrusion of sexual imagery and metaphor. The male narrators (and most critics) disqualify Judith Sutpen from consideration as one of the novel's forces to be reckoned with. But common sense, or at least my sense of the world, suggests to me that where men fight over a woman, the woman does, in fact, matter; she is, in fact, the force over whom the reckoning is taking place. I write "Ockum's razor?" in the margin of my notebook. I later forget what I meant by this and have to Google the phrase to jog my memory. Matters are complicated by my misspelling, and I keep coming back to blogs and review sites for a band out of St. Louis with a new four-song EP, but I follow the bread crumbs, realize my mistake, correct my spelling, and remind myself that "Ockham's (or Occum's) razor" refers to the idea that, when faced with multiple explanations or theories for a phenomenon, the simplest one, the one based on the fewest assumptions, is likely the most credible.

So, I decide that Judith Sutpen *does* matter, that perhaps she more than matters: perhaps Judith Sutpen *explains*. Though the men's narratives move consistently away from acknowledging Judith's embodiment and the sexual nature of the union to which she and Bon aspire, and therefore away from the sexual motive behind Henry's crime, these aspects of the story's central action are made visible through Faulkner's focus on materiality (objects) and corporeality (bodies), a focus that is at times direct and therefore available to us through close reading and at other times rendered metaphorically through the letter Judith receives, the gate, and the bedroom door, all of which can be read as metaphors of the body.

But to get to such a reading will require an almost archaeological approach, as the details that support this reading are buried by the relentless theorizing of Mr. Compson and the runaway narrative imaginings of Quentin and Shreve, three of the four dominant narrators. Through them, women's bodies become "blank shapes," "empty vessels," and "substanceless shells," and the story threatens to come unmoored from economies of sexual desire. But the narratives offered by Rosa and Shreve, when he forces the issue despite Quentin's refusal to engage with him at such times, provide an anchor.

Through the imaginings of Quentin and Shreve, bodies take on substance and are vividly imagined in physical settings; affected by weather, hunger, and exhaustion; materially situated, and interactive, though it is most often male bodies they are imagining. Through their narration, corporeality is restored to the text, but not desire, at least not often the desire of the man, Bon, for the woman, Judith, and certainly not of Judith for Bon. It begins to seem that Mr. Compson is correct in saying, "You cannot even imagine [Bon] and Judith alone together. Try to do it and the nearest you can come is a projection of them . . . two shades pacing, serene and untroubled by flesh . . . two serene phantoms who seem to watch, hover, impartial attentive and quiet" (77); but then, in the middle of chapter 8, Shreve hijacks the narrative and tries to get Quentin to join him in just such an imagining. Shreve's talk becomes more pointedly sexual as he goes on, his description of the North Mississippi landscape includes alder and Judas trees with "hard, tight, sticky buds like young girls' nipples" (258) and moves on rapidly to contemplation of the "vain evanescence of the fleshly encounter . . . when the brief all is done [and] you must retreat from both love and pleasure, gather up your own rubbish and refuse—the hats and pants and shoes which you drag through the world—and retreat" (259), clearly a reference to the aftermath of sex.

Faulkner takes pains to show Quentin's extreme discomfort during all such talk. Quentin not only becomes silent but also seems to be trying to disappear physically. He is a "laxed and hunched figure" as Shreve imagines the intensifying feelings within the Henry-Judith-Bon triangle (257). After Shreve's description of the buds-like-nipples and the aftermath of the fleshly encounter, we see Quentin with "his shoulders hugged inward and hunched, his face lowered and he looking somehow curiously smaller than he actually was" (259). He speaks only once through all of it, and then it is to object to Shreve's conflation of sexual desire with love when Shreve offers the metaphor of the woman as lemon sherbet, easy and enticing and "there for you to take" (258). Shreve tries to draw Quentin into the conversation by asking him a series of questions about love, to which Quentin consistently responds, "I don't know," until Shreve finally changes tack and moves on to a different sort of imagining, away from the sexual and back to a more courtly vision of love, at which point Quentin reenters their dialogue.

Eventually they do come to an imagining of the physical relationship between Bon and Judith—a kiss, his hand momentarily on her behind, and Judith's memory of these physical exchanges. But these moments of imagining Judith and Bon together are brief. Despite Shreve's efforts to return the narrative to talk of love and sex, at Quentin's sullen insistence, contemplation of the relationship between Judith and Bon repeatedly returns them to contemplation of the relationship between Henry and Bon, and the privileging of that relationship posits Judith as nothing more than the (ultimately fatal) link between them.

So it is to Rosa's narrative, the artifact of the letter and the metaphorical significance of it alongside the gate and door to which we will have to turn to complete our analysis. Though we will see Judith as a fully corporeal figure in Rosa's narrative, she is consistently disembodied and, importantly, desexualized by the men's, which also, not coincidentally, represent her as bounded spatially, protected behind the gates and doors of her father's house. Though we are told that she ventures away from Sutpen's Hundred on occasion, we readers are invited to accompany her only once. Also not coincidentally, this is the only occasion in the text where she gives a speech of any length or significance, the scene in which she delivers Bon's letter to our Mr. Compson's mother.

The letter Judith gives to Mrs. Compson is one of the few actual artifacts/facts in the novel and a crucial catalyst in the plot. Announcing, "We have waited long enough" (101), it ends the stasis that has held them all in place, moves Charles and Henry toward their fatal appointment at the gate and Judith toward her destiny as a widow-who-was-never-a-bride, an eternal virgin who will spend the remainder of her days laboring and impoverished in a shapeless gingham dress. This dress will be referred to well over a dozen times, and one cannot help but be reminded of the similarity between these descriptions and those of Sutpen's sisters earlier in the narrative. The attention paid to Judith's clothing is part of a pattern that foregrounds material, specifically corporeal, images and therefore is a matter of some concern to us as we attempt to read bodies back into this text.

Though critical attention has turned away from a reading of *Absalom* that would focus on sexual desire as a governing or motivating factor in the novel, the references to bodies and metaphors that point to the body are many. In particular, Faulkner demonstrates acute concern with women's bodies. He writes in detail about how they smell; for example, the novel begins in Miss Rosa's room, which fills with "the rank smell of female flesh long embattled in virginity" (6). He details the labor they perform and its consequences—"girls with sweating bodies" (87), for example, are mentioned several times—as well as the changes that time wreaks on them (witness the lengthy description of Ellen's body as she ages toward death on pages 50-51). There are many references to flesh (the word appears dozens of times) and bone, such as this description of Judith: "not thin now, but gaunt, the Sutpen skull showing indeed now through the worn, the Coldfield, flesh" (100). And Faulkner even goes into detail about what they wear—as only one example, Judith's clothing is mentioned more than two dozen times within one hundred pages. At one point, Charles Bon is even described as "a garment which Judith might wear" (59).

Despite Mr. Compson's antiseptic vision of the South as a place where "we . . . made our women into ladies. Then the war came and made the ladies into ghosts" (7), the constant attention to women's physical bodies, often in distinctly unladylike terms, indicates their importance not as abstractions or ghosts but as *bodies*, operating as bodies operate and producing what bodies produce. Among the operations and productions of the body, of course, are sexual desire and sexual action.

It is Rosa's narrative that gives us Judith as an embodied presence and therefore runs strongly counter to the male narrators' depiction of her as disembodied and desexualized. Rosa insists, often explicitly, on the embodied nature of desire, speaking in both sensuous and romantic terms, as when she refers to the "moment only virgins know: when the entire delicate spirit's bent is one anonymous, climaxless epicene and unravished nuptial" (116), but also in more frank language of "a virgin's itching discontent" (117). Her narration, whether flowery or frank, insists on women's sexuality and physical desire, insists that love is not only words but also "suspirations of the twinning souls" and "best of all, better far than this, the actual living and the dreamy flesh" (119).

She also reminds us of the potential violence, both emotional and physical, that bodies can do to one another, "because there is something in the touch of flesh with flesh which abrogates, cuts sharp and straight across the devious channels of decorous ordering" (112). This statement is significant on its own, but its significance is amplified by reference to touch in a key scene of violence in the novel, the scene in which Wash Jones kills Thomas Sutpen. Sutpen demands, "Don't you touch me, Wash—'I'm going to tech you Kernel'" (151), at which point Sutpen slashes him with the whip, and Wash cuts down his fallen hero with a rusty scythe.

But in this novel, pain can come even from the threat of that "touch of flesh with flesh," which is, after all, the actual aim of marriage, as Shreve and Quentin imagine that Henry knows and therefore defines Judith's would-be husband as a "man . . . whose every move and action and speech would say to me, I have seen and touched parts of your sister's body that you will never see and touch" (262). Apparently, even an imagined touch can cut sharp and straight through the heart of a brother whose relationship to his sister is so "curious and unusual" (79).

Perhaps so long as Judith and Bon's love was suspended by distance and conducted in letters, Henry felt no such cut, and therefore it took the long ride to Sutpen's Hundred, a ride described in highly physical and sexualized language, to remind him that the courtly stage of Bon's relationship to Judith was coming to a rapid and predictable end behind a closed bedroom door. But if Henry had understood the significance of letters in this novel, he might have been spurred to action much earlier, as letters in *Absalom* are clearly metaphors of the body as well as material artifacts that both speak and create desire.

Letters perform all sorts of magic here, conjuring for the reader sensate images of the sender or the place from which they were sent, seducing a young country girl and enabling her brother, when he reads one, to "metamorphosis into the body which was to become his sister's lover" (79). They also function as metaphors of the body. Note that when you encounter the word "letter" in this novel, the word "hand" will always be close by. Letters are "in [the writer's] hand," delivered or passed by hand, described as "notes in hand" (12), and lying on desks or tables between the hands of the receiver or held in the receiver's hand. They are not only stand-ins for the absent senders, as we see most clearly in the Christmas visit scene, after Henry and Bon have ridden off and Judith "waked and they were gone, and only the letter, the note, remaining" (73), but also, in crucial ways, they *are* the senders. Quentin opens his father's letter "so that his [father's] hand could lie on the strange, lamplit table in Cambridge" (141). Bon's letter is his "dead tongue speaking" (102). Quentin and Shreve imagine Bon longing for a letter from Sutpen, or just "a word, Charles, *in his hand* . . . or a lock of his hair or a paring from his fingernails" (261; emphasis added), a catalog that clearly connects the letter to other by-products of the body. Letters in *Absalom* not only open up another world or time and allow the reader to become one with the writer imaginatively but also function materially in that the letter is a point of contact, something real that forms a connection, "passing from one hand to another, one mind to another . . . something, something that might make a mark on something that *was* once" (101). Passing Bon's letter to Mrs. Compson with these words is Judith's way of leaving a mark, a sign of her having been alive and real, a body upon the earth, not just a ghost haunting the periphery of others' lives, a woman like her mother, so ethereal and invisible it was "as if she had never lived at all" (9).

While certainly a significant metaphor, the particular status of this letter as a material artifact is pronounced (even the details of its material production are meticulously described), and it seems to invite us to read it as such. It is a letter that speaks distinctly and directly of bodies, inviting the reader to contemplate the embodied reality of the writer, the desire of that body for "soap and clean linen," and then, too, the desire of that body for another's: "We have waited long enough" (101). The letter not only speaks but also creates desire. Judith's response is to make ready her wedding dress, a project that demonstrates her own desire. The dress will not be completed; the desire it signifies will not be fulfilled.

But Judith's transmission of the letter to Mrs. Compson, her stated intention to have it "pass from one hand to another," speaks of her understanding of the letter as more than just words, and so serves to return us to contemplate the embodied reality of Judith Sutpen. Her understanding of the letter is that it is real, a material artifact that passes from the hand of one person into the hand of another and so serves as a bond between bodies, which were themselves once real and animated by desire, which was also real. Recognizing the possibilities in reading the Judith-Bon story as a story of desiring bodies, we can logically read the gate and the bedroom door as metaphors of the body and see clearly that Judith and her sexuality are much more significant to this story than Mr. Compson or Quentin are willing to have us believe.

The purpose of a gate or fence is to act as a boundary, demonstrating ownership of what lies behind it. In the case of Sutpen's Hundred, beyond the gate is not just the "Dominion" of Thomas Sutpen but also the actual physical person of his daughter, Judith, who is perceived by the men in the text as part of what is protected or at least bounded and claimed by the men who surround her. In the imaginings of Quentin and Shreve—and no doubt this would have been close to the view of Henry and Bon and all men of their time—Henry's descriptions of Judith cause Bon to think, "I am not hearing about a young girl, a virgin; I am hearing about a narrow delicate fenced virgin field already furrowed and bedded so that all I shall need to do is drop the seeds in, caress it smooth again" (261). Henry, though, does not want Bon's seed anywhere near Judith (and there will be no caressing, either). By killing Bon before he can pass through the gate, Henry accomplishes the very task that Quentin, whose own sister's sexuality was his constant preoccupation in *The Sound and the Fury*, most wished to have accomplished himself; Henry ensures his sister's perpetual virginity and thereby maintains control of her sexuality and sexual body.

Not only does Henry manage to ensure that Bon will never enter Judith's bedroom or engage in any of the acts that entry would imply, but he also claims the right to enter it himself. Awaiting the arrival of her would-be husband/lover, Judith, behind the closed door of her bedroom, that most private and intimate of domestic spaces furnished with "nuptial couch" and "marriage bed" (108), hears footsteps running in the hall, and there is "just time to snatch up the unfinished dress and hold it before her as the door burst open upon her brother" (108). This scene is imagined several times, first by Rosa and then by Quentin. The image of the brother and sister, he in the doorway, she beside the bed, "looking at one another across the up-raised and unfinished dress" (108) becomes "something which [Quentin] could not pass" (138, 142), an image already highly charged that becomes elaborated and further eroticized in his imaginings of it. Twice he will be rendered mute and unable to listen to someone speaking to him, captivated by the scene that plays out in his mind of

> that door . . . the white girl in her underthings (made of flour sacking when there had been flour, of window curtains when not) pausing, looking at the door, the yellowed creamy mass of old intricate satin and lace spread carefully on the bed and then caught swiftly up by the girl and held before her as the door crashed in and the brother stood there. (139)

Henry's acts of violence, first to protect the "virgin field" that is his sister's body with a gun (that trusty phallic symbol) and then to "burst through" her bedroom door himself, become acts of sexualized violence through which he gains access to the private interior space that represents the private body of his sister. As Richard C. Moreland writes in "Compulsive and Revisionary Repetition," in this scene we see Henry "coming face to face with his own incestuous erotic desire and the violence it has done to Judith" (57). Perhaps this is what Ellen foresaw, or some semblance of it, that moved her to ask Rosa repeatedly to "protect her. Protect Judith at least" (10, 15, 68). Quentin's fixation on the scene is, as Moreland observes, indeed ironic, as well as significant for an understanding of why this Sutpen story compels Quentin's resurrection.

Recognizing the centrality of Judith, and of sex, to this story enables a reading that explains both Henry's actions and perhaps Quentin's and explains why Quentin was brought back to tell, as best he can, this story, which is his story as well. In this reading, it is not the social aspect of the marriage (the tainting of the House of Sutpen) that Henry objects to, as many critics have stated or inferred, but the sexual aspect. It isn't his father's dynasty or a code of familial honor that resides in his sister's virginity but that virginity itself that he wants to protect and claim. It is not his sister's body as conduit to Bon or proxy for his father that motivates the murder at the gate but rather her body itself. The body of his sister, in its corporeal, sexual reality, is what Henry guards, and it is this, of course, that is the "repetition forward" of Quentin's story in *The Sound and the Fury*. Given that Henry manages to accomplish precisely what Quentin fails to accomplish, his knowledge of the Sutpen story may in fact help explain his despair and suicide. But certainly it answers my question: "Why Quentin?"

Works Cited

Bleikasten, André. *The Ink of Melancholy: Faulkner's Novels from "The Sound and the Fury" to "Light in August."* Bloomington: Indiana UP, 1990.

Brooks, Cleanth. *William Faulkner: The Yoknapatawpha Country*. Baton Rouge: Louisiana State UP, 1963.

Faulkner, William. *Absalom, Absalom!: The Corrected Text*. 1936. New York: Vintage, 1990.

Howe, Irving. *William Faulkner: A Critical Study*. 4th ed. Chicago: Elephant Paperbacks, 1975.

Moreland, Richard C. "Compulsive and Revisionary Repetition: Faulkner's 'Barn Burning' and the Craft of Writing Difference." *Faulkner and the Craft of Fiction*. Ed. Doreen Fowler and Ann J. Abadie. Jackson: UP of Mississippi, 1989.

Polk, Noel. *Children of the Dark House: Text and Context in Faulkner*. Jackson: UP of Mississippi, 1996.

Weinstein, Philip M. *What Else but Love? The Ordeal of Race in Faulkner and Morrison*. New York: Columbia UP, 1996.

CRITICAL READINGS

Past as Present:
Absalom, Absalom!

Absalom, Absalom! has no close precedent, even in Faulkner's own works. Hindsight suggests now that much in modern fiction, and in modern opinion, should have prepared us for it, but it is not really surprising that most of the early reviewers were bewildered. Like *The Waste Land*, *Absalom* has many voices but no official, sanctioned Voice. The voices in it speak from many points of view, none of them removed from the criticism of irony. *Absalom* demonstrated once more Faulkner's artistic courage.

Compared with *Absalom*, *The Sound and the Fury* seems almost traditional. It shocks us at first by asking us to see the Compson world through the mind of an idiot for whom the present has reality chiefly as it reminds him of the past, and it takes us through two subsequent limited views of many of the same events before, in the last section, we come back again to the present to stay. Yet everything in the first three sections prepares us for the last, which corrects and completes them by centering on Dilsey. Nothing in what has preceded the last section, and nothing within it, undermines Dilsey's authority. Aesthetically, we are compelled to accept her and the criticism of the others which her character and actions imply.

In *Absalom* there is no Dilsey, or anything corresponding to her. There is only Quentin, who speaks with no special authority, mostly in the words of others, and who does not act at all; and Shreve, who speaks as one amazed, even outraged, by a tale hard to credit and almost impossible to understand, and who, when he is not repeating what Quentin has told him, invents a version based on no uniquely privileged knowledge of the facts. Quentin and Shreve together finally imagine a version of Sutpen's story that has both plausibility and meaning, but the plausibility rests upon our willingness to accept as correct certain speculations of theirs for which they can offer no solid

Past as Present: *Absalom, Absalom!* **131**

proof, and the meaning is left implicit, without even such partial dramatic statement as Dilsey gives to the meaning of the Compson story in her section of *The Sound and the Fury*.

Quentin has grown up with the Sutpen legend. He does not have to listen very closely to Miss Rosa Coldfield's retelling: he already knows not only the main plot but many of the sub-climaxes and lesser actors:

> His childhood was full of them; his very body was an empty hall echoing with sonorous defeated names; he was not a being, an entity, he was a commonwealth. He was a barracks filled with stubborn back-looking ghosts. . . .

Quentin has heard it before—and he will hear it again, from his father later on this same afternoon and later still from Shreve. He lacks only the sense of reality and meaning that neither Miss Rosa, with the bias created by her hatred of Sutpen, nor his father, with his surmises that are sometimes shrewd but sometimes wide of the mark, can give him. The fact about Sutpen's story that will not let Quentin rest is that everything is known about it except what is most important to know.

As Quentin tells his college roommate what he has been told and what he discovered for himself the night a few months before when he went to the ruined house with Miss Rosa, the two of them imaginatively recreate and relive Sutpen's story. The novel that emerges from their cooperative retelling has seemed to many readers best defined as a lyric evocation of the Southern past: the novel as poem. Quentin and Shreve retell the facts about Sutpen and his children in order to discover the feelings that can make the facts credible, rehearsing the deeds to discover the motives. The result is a kind of poem on time and death and the presentness of the past which seems so remote when we know only the "facts," a poem on the failure of the old order in the South, created by an evocation of the "ghosts" that have haunted Quentin's life. Quentin and Shreve are young, imaginative, easily moved to sympathetic identification. The joint product of their efforts, as they work with memory and imagination, evokes, in a style of sustained intensity of pitch, a feeling of the mystery and a sense of the pain and defeat of human life. It conveys its impressions through some of the most sharply realized images in modern writing in a rhetoric strained almost to the breaking point by an agony of identification with the suffering of the characters.

But *Absalom* cannot be completely understood in terms of this analogy with a lyric poem. The insight is useful in its pointing to pure evocation achieved through a strategy of indirection, but it leaves the central fact of the form of *Absalom*—its multiple retellings of what is in one sense already known and in another sense eludes knowing—unrelated to the feelings evoked and the meanings created by the form. Much of Faulkner's fiction may be called lyrical, and criticism today forces on us a recognition of the fact that all successful novels are in some sense like poems. The uniqueness of *Absalom* is not to be found here, so much as in the fact that it takes its form from its search for the truth about human life as that truth may be discovered by understanding the past, in which actions are complete, whole, so that we may put motive, deed, and consequence all into one picture.

Early in the book, as Quentin listens to Miss Coldfield, there is a passage which takes us some distance toward a recognition of the central theme and intent of the novel and suggests its strategy:

> Quentin seemed to see them, the four of them arranged into the conventional family group of the period, with formal and lifeless decorum, and seen now as the fading and ancient photograph itself would have been seen enlarged and of whose presence there the voice's owner was not even aware, as if she (Miss Coldfield) had never seen this room before—a picture, a group which even to Quentin had a quality strange, contradictory and bizarre; not quite comprehensible. . . .

The whole effort of Quentin and Shreve, who end by becoming twin narrators, is to comprehend what is "not quite comprehensible." There is something in the picture "not (even to twenty) quite right": they try to get it right, correcting each other's "faultings," sometimes supplying alternative explanations, imagining alternative motives and actions, sometimes agreeing, as on Bon. What was true for Quentin's father as he talked on the porch on that September evening before Quentin went out to the old house with Miss Rosa is only a little less true for Quentin and Shreve:

> It's just incredible. It does not explain. Or perhaps that's it: they don't explain and we are not supposed to know. We have a few old mouth-to-mouth tales; we exhume from trunks and boxes and drawers letters without salutation or signature, in which men and women who once lived and breathed are now merely initials or nicknames out of some now incomprehensible affection which sound to us like Sanskrit or Chocktaw; we see dimly people, the people in whose living blood and seed we ourselves lay dormant and waiting, in this shadowy attenuation of time possessing now heroic proportions, performing their acts of simple passion and simple violence, impervious to time and inexplicable. . . .

Quentin and Shreve think they know the answer to the question that baffled Quentin's father at this point in his narration, but other questions remain for them to speculate on. Their difficulty is not in any paucity of "evidence"—of massed anecdote, belief, interpretation, even "facts," such as the letter Quentin has before him as they talk and his memory of what he saw and heard on his trip with Miss Rosa. Their difficulty lies in making the leap from facts, or what they or someone else can only suppose to be facts, to understanding, to insight, to meaning.

The story they finally put together is a product of their imagination working as best it can toward truth with the over-abundant, conflicting, and enigmatic material at hand. As bias is balanced against bias and distorted views give way to views with different distortions, fragmented and overlapping pictures of people and actions emerge from the multiple mirrors and screens of the telling. Then the fragments begin to fall into place for us and at last they cohere in a story possessing an immediacy, a distinctness of outline, and an evocativeness almost unparalleled in modern fiction. The dim ghosts evoked by Miss Rosa out of the distant past take on flesh and their actions finally take on meaning as we move from Miss Rosa's memories to Shreve's and Quentin's imaginings. A story is told, and a meaning expressed, despite a technique seemingly designed to delay the telling and withhold meaning.

There is a curious and significant relation between immediacy and meaning, on the one hand, and the number and complexity of the reflectors and screens, the "difficulties," on the other. "Then he thought *No. If I had been there I could not have seen it this plain.*" Quentin and Shreve are both troubled by the impossibility of checking in some incontrovertible way the correctness of their interpretations. All their reconstructions are prefaced by "as if," spoken or unspoken. Yet for the reader there is more lifelikeness in what Quentin and Shreve partly imagine than in what is "known"—as a comparison of Chapter Eight, presenting Bon from his own point of view as imagined by Shreve and Quentin, with Quentin's retelling of Miss Rosa's initial presentation of Sutpen, whom she had "known" very well indeed, will show. The implication is clear. An act of imagination is needed if we are to get at lifelike, humanly meaningful, truth; but to gain the lifelikeness we sacrifice the certainty of the publicly demonstrable. "'Wait. You don't know whether what you see is what you are looking at or what you believe. Wait.'"

In the language of science, the experimenter is not passive in his experiment, his nature and purposes not irrelevant to his results. Shreve and Quentin supplement and correct each other; and Shreve, Quentin, and the reader join with Miss Rosa and Quentin's father and grandfather in a joint effort to understand Sutpen and search out what is hidden. Sutpen cannot be questioned, and Quentin's experience in the house has to be understood in relation to matters that cannot be known with certainty; and then it becomes hardly distinguishable from what has been posited, imagined. The tale that finally takes shape in the mind of the reader of *Absalom* is in several senses a cooperative construct—not a figment or a fantasy but something creatively discovered.

As it may be said of the naturalistic novel that it attempted to probe behind conventional interpretations and values to get at "fact," so it may be said of *Absalom* that it tries to get behind not only received interpretations but the public facts themselves to get at what Faulkner has called in the introduction to "Monk" in *Knight's Gambit*, "credibility and verisimilitude." One of the meanings of *Absalom* is that the central effort of the naturalistic novel, to transfer a "slice of life" onto the printed page without any shaping act of imagination, interpretation, and judgment, is impossible. It is impossible not because the sacrifice of art to truth is too great a price to pay but because without the kind of imaginative effort and creation we find always at the center of art, there is not only no art but no truth.

2

The complications of the telling can be clarified somewhat if we think of the basic story—Sutpen, from his early youth through the death of his remaining son and half-Negro daughter—as having not one but several narrative frames. The telling of the story by Quentin to Shreve—and partly later by Shreve to Quentin—makes the frame which encloses all the others. But this telling and retelling is based on versions of the same story, or of parts of it, given to Quentin by Miss Rosa and father; and father's version is based in large part on a version given him by his father, who got it in part from Sutpen himself. Since in Quentin's version each of these people speaks in his own voice, often at great length and circumstantially, with unintended revelation of himself in the process, what we have in effect is a series of frames, one within the other, like the picture of a picture containing a picture, and so on.

The outer frame, the telling of the story within the present of the novel—not the present of the first chapter, which is a memory of a day some four months before—takes place in Quentin's college room at Harvard in January, 1910. At first Quentin is alone, reliving in memory that afternoon in Miss Rosa's house and the later talk of Sutpen by his father. Then Shreve comes in and together they go over the story once more, with Shreve doing much of the talking, basing his version on what Quentin has already told him and using his imagination to fill the gaps. When they come to Bon's part of the story they are in perfect agreement, though about Bon and his motives and character they know less than about anyone else. Finally they go to bed and Quentin relives in memory once more the evening with Miss Rosa at the Sutpen house of which he has already told Shreve. This Shreve-Quentin frame is the largest and most distant of the frames.

In the first chapter then we begin where memory intersects the past at a point very close to the present, with Quentin becoming actively involved in the story whose general outline he has known for as long as be can remember. Almost at once we move back into the more distant past with Miss Rosa, without however being allowed to forget the present (now already past) in which Quentin sits in the stifling room and listens. Then this frame, this telling, is replaced by a frame supplied by father's account of Sutpen and his speculations on the meaning of the letter he gives Quentin. Again we move back and forth between past and present—the present of the telling, which is already past by the time we are able to identify it. Then the absoluteness of this frame too is destroyed and we see father's telling of the story as only another version, and not without its distortions. Shreve and Quentin talking in their college dormitory room now supply the frame to replace Miss Rosa in her "office" and father on the gallery. Miss Rosa's inadequacy as interpreter—her bias—has been apparent all along, and now it becomes clear that some of father's interpretations and speculations too are unacceptable: ". . . neither Shreve nor Quentin believed that the visit affected Henry as Mr. Compson seemed to think. . . ." But on another matter, "'maybe this was one place where your old man was right.'" As the frames are shifted and the implicit distortions discovered, we see the motive for the continual retelling. Each new version is a part of the search in which Quentin and Shreve involve the reader, the search for a truth beyond and behind distortion.

So the past has to be continually reinterpreted; and each reinterpretation becomes a part of the accumulating past; a part even of the past which it attempts to interpret. A knowledge of the end supplies the motive for the search for the beginning: the earliest part of the story—Sutpen's boyhood and young manhood before he came to Jefferson—is retold by Quentin, as his father had told him, in response to Shreve's reaction to Miss Rosa's completed story of the "demon." Perhaps the demon could be understood if we knew what made him as he was. So the telling circles in on the story from a different angle—Sutpen's own account, multiply filtered, of his past and his intentions. The motive for the retellings, the reinterpretations, each of which adds new facts as well as a new perspective and makes necessary a reinterpretation of the facts already known, is constant, and it supplies the organizing principle of the novel.

3

Shreve's role as interpretive listener and finally as partial narrator is crucial. By the time we discover his presence we are more than half-way through the book and we realize now that both Miss Rosa's telling and father's retelling are part of the past which Shreve and Quentin have rehearsed. Now a new frame, more distant from Sutpen, comes into focus. As father had been less intimately involved in the Sutpen story than Miss Rosa, so Shreve the Canadian is less involved than father. The movement is one of progressive disengagement, a moving outward from the center. Yet the parts of the story that Shreve retells are among the most vivid and circumstantial in the whole book. Shreve's imagination moves freely. His presence in the story makes possible the widest of the circling movements through which the subject is approached.

In one of his recapitulations, Shreve calls Sutpen, in a caricature of Miss Rosa's own words, "this Faustus, this demon, this Beelzebub . . . who appeared suddenly one Sunday with two pistols and twenty subsidiary demons," thus reducing Sutpen to ordinary size by his humorous exaggeration and offering an implicit comment on Miss Rosa's "demonizing." His humorous summary follows immediately after a recital calculated to make us feel the weight and at least the partial justice of Miss Rosa's terms. Shreve's presence in the book is one of the ways in which the tone is controlled.

Shreve puts Sutpen's whole story in another kind of perspective when he says, toward the end, "'So he just wanted a grandson. . . . That was all he was after. Jesus, the South is fine, isn't it. It's better than the theater, isn't it. It's better than Ben Hur, isn't it.'" *Absalom* has been called Gothic and obsessive, but true Gothic cannot survive irony, and obsession does not admit criticism. Here the irony and the criticism are central. When Shreve speaks of "the money, the jack, that he (the demon) has voluntarily surrendered" his very language, even when he is not offering any explicit comment, provides a perspective that can come only with distance and that could not come from Quentin, who is part and product of what he is telling.

As Quentin and Shreve sit "in the now tomblike air,"

the two of them creating between them, out of the rag-tag and bob-ends of old tales and talking, people who perhaps had never existed at all anywhere. . . .

what emerges is substantially different from what would have emerged had there been no Shreve for Quentin to talk and listen to. In the context of the passage I have just quoted we don't know for sure that there *was* a dishonest lawyer who had private reasons for wanting Bon to come in contact with his father, Sutpen, much less that the reasons

Shreve is giving for the posited lawyer's actions are the true ones. But we are ready now, prepared by the interchange between Quentin and Shreve, to speculate with them, to invent probable characters and fill in details to make the story, the given incomprehensible facts, plausible. This is one of the most extreme examples of the conjectural method of the whole search that Quentin and Shreve are engaged in; and it is made to seem natural, right, because Shreve, who cannot be accused of excessive closeness to the material, offers the speculation.

In the last chapter Shreve's presence becomes decisive. He speaks for most readers when he says

> We don't live among defeated grandfathers and freed slaves . . . and bullets in the dining room table and such, to be always reminding us to never forget . . . a kind of entailed birthright father and son and father and son of never forgiving General Sherman. . . .

This would be a peculiar sort of comment for one of the two narrators to make at a climactic point if there were as little aesthetic distance in *Absalom* as some have said. In Shreve's definition of the difference between his own Canadian background and Quentin's Southern one there is an implied comment on Sutpen's story that Quentin would have been incapable of making. Not that Shreve is right and Quentin wrong, but that Shreve's is another, and clarifying, point of view. "You cant understand it," Quentin tells Shreve. "You would have to be born there." To which a comment Shreve makes later, on another matter, could serve as a partial reply: "The South. Jesus. No wonder you folks all outlive yourselves by years and years and years."

And it is Shreve who at the end offers the prediction that "the Jim Bonds are going to conquer the western hemisphere" and asks Quentin why he hates the South. Shreve adds distance, controlling irony, to a story that otherwise might be obsessive or too shrill. If his final question to Quentin is, perhaps, somewhat unprepared for, so that we may find the ironic effect a little forced at this point, nevertheless he discharges his crucial function in the story with wonderful economy. His point of view is not the final one because there is no final one explicitly stated anywhere in the book. There are only other points of view and the implications of the form of the whole.

4

In the absence of chronologically related plot as the controlling factor, the relations of points of view govern the order of the chapters. Chapter One is Miss Rosa's. Miss Rosa lives in the past, in the cherishing of her hatred and her frustration. Quentin is restive as he listens, not only because of the heat, and partly discounts what she tells him. Her view of the past is simple, moralistic, and, to Quentin, quite incredible. For her Sutpen was an evil man, satanic, with no redeeming qualities.

The next three chapters are Quentin's father's. His point of view is that of the interested but emotionally uninvolved rational observer. Unlike Miss Rosa, father is impressed by the mystery of human action and frequently confesses himself baffled in his search for understanding. If he is biased in any way it is slightly in Sutpen's favor, partly because the town condemned Sutpen and father is an iconoclast who has little respect for conventional opinion, partly because much of his information he got from his father, who was Sutpen's one friend in the community, the only one willing to defend him against outraged public opinion.

Chapter Five is Miss Rosa's again. We are now prepared for a verbatim report of a part of what she said to Quentin that afternoon. Miss Rosa, it is clearer now, not only hates Sutpen but judges him from a point of view not wholly distinct from his own. Sutpen's actions destroyed not only his "design"—his plan for his life, his purpose—but hers. She shares, it begins to appear, both his racial and his class prejudices, and she hates him chiefly because he destroyed for her that social eminence, respectability, and security which it was the aim of his design to secure for himself and his posterity. Yet though we recognize and allow for her obsessive hatred, we learn much from her account that we should not otherwise know, and we cannot entirely discount her judgment.

Chapter Six is Shreve's retelling of what Quentin has told him of what Quentin's father has told Quentin. Shreve keeps calling Miss Rosa "Aunt Rosa": he does not quite understand, and he is not concerned to try to master, the details of Southern kinship ties and class etiquette. He sees "this old dame," Miss Rosa, and her tale without any of Quentin's painfully mixed feelings, simply with astonishment verging on incredulity. The snow on Shreve's overcoat sleeve suggests the distance from which he views this tale which began for us in the "long still hot weary" afternoon when Quentin sat with Miss Rosa. And Shreve himself, with his ruddy vitality, contrasts sharply with the other narrators—with the passive Quentin, and with Miss Rosa herself, whose very existence seems a mere "disturbance" of the dust of that "dead September afternoon."

Parts of Sutpen's story have been told and retold now from points of view both hostile and friendly or neutral, by narrators within his own culture, and again from a point of view entirely external. How did he view himself? What would be added to our knowledge of him and his motivations if we could share his own self-awareness? Chapter Seven gives us Sutpen's story, the first part of it largely in a paraphrase of his own statements and some of it in his own words, as he told it to Quentin's grandfather—and as grandfather told it to father and father told it to Quentin and Quentin told it to Shreve: there is no certainty even in *ipsissima verba*, no possibility of getting back to "the thing in itself" of Sutpen's consciousness.

Sutpen saw himself alternately in the role of innocence betrayed and the role of a man who had made some mistake in adding a row of figures. Grandfather does not question his self-evaluation, simply passes it on. We are given almost no reason and very little opportunity, within the early part of this chapter, to question Sutpen or to step outside his frame of reference. The poor child who had been turned away from the door of the rich man's house conceived a design for his life calculated to put him in a position where he could never again be humiliated by anyone. Since he could see that the rewards in life went to the "courageous and shrewd" and since, though he felt sure he had courage, he had failed in his design, he must have made a mistake, a miscalculation somewhere. What could it be?

Toward the end of the chapter there is, not negative moral judgment and certainly not Miss Rosa's hatred of Sutpen, but a kind of neutral clarification of Sutpen's own story offered in the comments of Quentin prompted by the interruptions of Shreve. Quentin interprets the "design" as essentially "getting richer and richer" and the innocence as a kind of moral obtuseness:

> that innocence which believed that the ingredients of morality were like the ingredients of pie or cake and once you had measured them and balanced them and mixed them and put them into the oven it was all finished and nothing but pie or cake could come out.

Quentin's father, on whose report Quentin is drawing here, sees Sutpen as "fogbound by his own private embattlement of personal morality" but he seems to accept Sutpen's idea that his design was created solely for the "vindication" of "that little boy who approached that door fifty years ago and was turned away." He gives us Sutpen's climactic question to grandfather without indicating that he thinks we should have to redesign it to make it ask another question, with different assumptions in it, before we could answer it:

> 'You see, I had a design in my mind. Whether it was a good or a bad design is beside the point; the question is, Where did I make the mistake in it. . . .'

Most of the material of this chapter comes ultimately from grandfather, who was not only Sutpen's "advocate" but the only one in Jefferson who knew about the past which had shaped him to be what he was. Since this report of Sutpen's history has the additional advantage, if "inside knowledge" is an advantage, of resting on Sutpen's own self-awareness, it constitutes an effective foil to the "demonizing" of Miss Rosa, through whom we first met Sutpen.

Chapter Eight is Bon's chapter, his story (and Henry's, but chiefly his) as interpreted sympathetically by Shreve and Quentin. Shreve is no longer amused, ironic. He has been drawn into the tale now: this is a part he can feel, thinks he can understand. And for the first time he and Quentin are in complete agreement in their interpretive reconstructions. It no longer matters who is speaking: each is capable of taking up where the other left off, completing the other's thought. This is the most direct and circumstantial segment of the whole tale. It might be called interpretation by immersion, or by empathy. It penetrates Bon's consciousness to discover his point of view, reporting his experiences in detail, complete with imaginary conversations for which there is no warrant in the literally known facts. In place of Miss Rosa's bald summaries of Sutpen's whole career, mingled with moral judgments, we have here a detailed "realistic" rendering of the qualitative aspects of a few of Bon's experiences. There is no certainty, of course, that Shreve and Quentin are right in the details of their reconstruction. They are biased, for one thing, being young like Bon and easily aroused to sympathy by the spectacle which the idea of him presents. And they are relatively uninformed, for another thing; there are some very crucial facts that they cannot know for sure, such as when Bon told Henry, if in fact he did tell him, that he was not only his half brother but was part Negro. Yet the reader is led by the circumstantial solidity of this chapter to feel more certain that this sympathetic account of Bon is correct than he is of any other interpretation he has encountered so far in the book.

Chapter Nine presents what might be called a general perspective on the whole tale. We are beyond the uniquely biased views of those who were closest to Sutpen. Two things happen at this point. First, Quentin and Shreve come into the foreground of the picture explicitly as narrators. No longer merely voices speaking to us in the words of the past, chiefly through direct and indirect quotation, they now appear as preservers of a past which must in some degree be created in order to be preserved. We are told more of Quentin's immediate sensations than we have been told before. The afternoon in Miss Rosa's house when she talked to Quentin in the office seems far away, as though it were as remote in time as in space. Miss Rosa is dead, and we recall from her tale chiefly a sense of the "victorious dust" that her recital made Quentin think of at the time. All those able to speak from direct knowledge of Sutpen are now gone; all that remains is the mutual creative remembering of Quentin and Shreve.

The second thing that happens is that as the appearance of objectivity evaporates the "facts" come back into focus and we move out again from subjective to objective. We learn for the first time in this last chapter what Quentin experienced that night when he went with Miss Rosa to Sutpen's decaying mansion. Everything before this has been hearsay, rumor, conjecture, hypothesis, or, at best, biased accounts of matters of fact. Here we are in the presence of something that we know "really happened," the terrible culmination of the Sutpen story. We are in a position to understand and to respond emotionally and imaginatively. Quentin does not need to theorize, or even create an atmosphere. The bare, elliptical, subjective record, the fragmentary memory, of what happened that night is enough. Without what has preceded the record would be meaningless. We now see that Quentin had to prepare Shreve for this direct confrontation with the living past; that any literal-minded insistence on "sticking to the facts," would have made it impossible for these facts, the only ones connected with Sutpen that Quentin can be absolutely sure of from personal experience, to convey any meaning.

Though Quentin's meeting with Henry is the one thing in the novel which may conceivably justify a charge of pointless mystification—why are we not told what Quentin learns from Henry?—yet I think the bareness of this climactic episode suggests its own justification. This meeting was a confrontation with a flesh-and-blood ghost. Here is proof that the past is "real" (though not yet, for Quentin at the time, explicable). This is the shock that motivates the search for understanding. In giving us the incident only in the barest outline, Faulkner is following the Jamesian formula of making the reader imagine. By the time we come to the episode in the book we have plenty of material for the imagination to work with. We discover, better than if we were told, that the past is still alive, still with us, demanding to be understood.

We end, in this last chapter, sharing Quentin's and Shreve's certainty about just two other matters of the first importance: that Sutpen brought his destruction upon himself, and that Bon asked only for recognition. But the first of these certainties rests upon the second, and the second is itself "certain" only if we either decide to trust Quentin and Shreve to be right or if we have so far shared their imaginative adventure as to arrive with them at the same conclusion. It is, at any rate, beyond proof. The whole meaning of Sutpen's history hangs on this leap of the imagination.

5

But *Absalom, Absalom!* is not an exercise in perspectivist history, it is a novel; it tells a story. Each chapter contributes something to our knowledge of the action. It is true that we know something of the end of the story before we know the beginning, but what we know of the end is tantalizingly incomplete until we get to the end of the book; and what we know of the beginning of Sutpen's story, by the end of the book, could not have been understood earlier. If tricks are being played with time here, if the form is less conspicuously temporal than spatial or conceptual, it is not in the interest of obscuring the story but of making possible an existential understanding of it.

The versions of the Southern past that Quentin has grown up with he recognizes as inadequate, but he is not interested in adding to them one more subjective version, his own. What he is interested in is "the truth." But the truth, he discovers, and we discover with him, is no rabbit to be pulled out of the hat by some sleight of hand. The traditional novelist's pretense of omniscience could be kept up only so long as Miss Rosa's view of life obtained. Just because Quentin is interested in truth he must reject too simple a view of it. The "spatial" form of the novel *is*, from one point of view, *symbolizes*, from another, Quentin's probing beyond and behind appearances to get at reality. *Absalom* is conspicuously an orderly book, but the order in it springs from within, from the human need and effort to understand, not from anything external to itself. It substitutes an aesthetic and human order for temporal order. The result is a story inseparable from its meanings.

But the screens, the baffles that keep us from getting directly at the facts, are not only thematically expressive, they serve a more elementary, but indispensable, need of fiction. They do not lessen but increase the suspense. We learn in the first chapter, for instance, that Sutpen must have said or done something outrageously shocking to Miss Rosa to precipitate her departure from his house. We do not learn what it was until much later, but meanwhile we have never been allowed entirely to forget it. Again, we hear of Wash Jones early as an ill-mannered "poor white" who brought Miss Rosa the news of Bon's death. We learn later that he was responsible for Sutpen's death, but not how. We find out later still something of the manner of the death, hearing of the rusty scythe. But only toward the end do we witness the death itself, one of the great scenes in literature. Meanwhile our conception of Jones has been growing so that by the time we see him kill Sutpen we are prepared to see the action of this grim and silent avenger as both psychologically motivated and far-reaching in its symbolic implications. Our knowing ahead of time something of what would happen— as though we had a premonition at once certain and indistinct—has not lessened but actually increased the impact of the scene.

The characters of *Absalom* grow, emerge and develop, as we catch glimpses of them from different angles. When we finally confront Judith directly, after we already know the outline of her life, we are prepared to feel her few words and actions reverberating in areas that would have been closed to us without the preparation. She has become a figure of tragic proportions. The fluid and subjective quality of *Absalom*'s sifting of memory implies no diminution or beclouding of the world of significant action.

6

If Shreve and Quentin are right in their sympathetic estimate of Bon, then the immediate cause of the tragic events that resulted in the failure of Sutpen's design was his refusal to recognize his part-Negro son. Bon, Shreve and Quentin both believe, would have given up Judith and gone away if he had had any sign at all from his father, even the most private and minimal acknowledgment of their relationship. Shreve and Quentin cannot be sure that they are right. If they are wrong and Bon was a conscienceless extortioner, then the failure of Sutpen's design was caused, not by moral failure but as he himself thought, by ignorance, by the simple fact of his not knowing when he married her that Bon's mother was part Negro.

The title of the book, with its Biblical allusion, supports the hypothesis of Shreve and Quentin. Sutpen would not say "My son" to Bon as David said it to Absalom even after Absalom's rebellion. And different as he was from his father, Henry acted in the end on the same racist principle, killing Bon finally to prevent not incest but miscegenation. One meaning of *Absalom* then is that when the Old South was faced with a choice it could not avoid, it chose to destroy itself rather than admit brotherhood across racial lines.

But the theme is broader and deeper than the race problem which serves as its vehicle and embodiment. Sutpen was a cold and ruthless man motivated by a driving ambition to be his own god. His intelligence and courage won him a measure of success, but his pride destroyed him. In Martin Buber's contemporary terminology, for Sutpen other people were objects to be manipulated, related to him in an "I-it" relation. He not only never achieves, he never once even approaches, an "I-Thou" relation. Sutpen was the new man, the post-Machiavellian man consciously living by power-knowledge alone, refusing to acknowledge the validity of principles that he cannot or will not live by and granting reality to nothing that cannot be known with abstract rational clarity. He lives by a calculated expediency.

Sutpen the rationalist and positivist would have agreed with a pronouncement in a recent book-length attack on the Christianity of Eliot and other modern writers, that "Progress for the whole human race would be, if not inevitable, at least highly probable, if a sufficient majority of people were trained to use their reasoning power on their general experience, as a scientist is trained to use his reasoning power on his special experience."[1] Sutpen of course was not so much interested in the progress of "the whole human race" as he was in the progress of Sutpen, but there the difference ends. When he came to grandfather to review his life he was concerned to discover not which of his actions had been morally right and which wrong but where he had made the mistake which kept them from being, as modern scienteers would say, "effective." "Whether it was a good or a bad design is beside the point." When he put away Bon's mother, his first wife, on discovering her taint of Negro blood, he did so, he told grandfather later, because he found her "unsuitable to his purpose"—that is, ineffective for the forwarding of his intelligently conceived plan. Later he could calculate no advantage to be gained by recognizing Bon as his son, and he was not one to be moved by the incalculable. There is point as well as humor in Shreve's characterization of him as Faustus. He is also related to Ahab and Ethan Brand.

The total form of the novel implies the ultimate reason for the failure of Sutpen's design.[2] Considered as an integral symbol the form of *Absalom* says that reality is unknowable in Sutpen's way, by weighing, measuring, and calculating. It says that without an "unscientific" act of imagination and even of faith—like Shreve's and Quentin's faith in Bon—we cannot know the things which are most worth knowing. Naturally Sutpen failed in his design, and naturally he could not imagine where his error had been. His error had been ultimately, of course, in the moral sense, that he had always treated people as things. Even Bon falls into the same error when he tries to use Judith as a lever to move Sutpen, to get recognition.

Absalom also has implications about the nature and role of history that are worthy of further thought. Quentin's effort to understand Sutpen is an attempt to interpret all history, man's history. Quentin encounters two conflicting modes of interpretation, is satisfied by neither, and creates, with Shreve, a third that has some of the features of both.

Miss Rosa's interpretation epitomizes the traditional views with which Quentin has grown up. This "demonizing," this interpretation in terms of inflexible moral judgment, does not, to his mind, explain: the past remains incredible and unreal. Nor is he satisfied by his father's view that there is no meaning at all in history, that the only proper response is to call it a mystery that we are "not meant to understand." Father is as close to nihilism here as he was in *The Sound and the Fury*. Between Miss Rosa's belief that Southern history was God's punishment of the South, and of herself in particular—precisely for what she is unable to imagine—and father's denial of any intelligibility, Quentin is unable to choose.

The view that he and Shreve together work out has in common with these two views more than its tragic cast. Implicitly—and unlike Miss Rosa's and father's views the final one in the book is wholly implicit— they find room for moral judgment: Sutpen's *hubris*, his narrow rationalism, his lack of love, all these are descriptions that imply the relevance of moral judgment. But Quentin and Shreve do not categorize Sutpen as simply a "bad" man: they know that to do so is to substitute judgment for explanation. With father they feel the mystery of human life, but they are not satisfied cynically to give up the effort to understand. The view in terms of which they operate is that of classical-Christian tragedy, at once Greek and Biblical: history contains both

God's judgment and man's decision, both necessity and freedom, and it has sufficient intelligibility for our human purposes. But its meaning is neither given nor entirely withheld. It must be achieved, created by imagination and faith. Historical meaning is a construct.

Such a view of history contrasts sharply with Marxist and "scientific" theories of history, but it has much in common with the best historiography of the thirties and of our own time. It has in it something of the historical relativism of the school of Beard and Becker. Becker's presidential address to the American Historical Association in 1931 criticized simplistic notions of historical "fact." Robinson's "new history," more than a decade older than *Absalom*, had been an attack on "scientific" history. More recently, Herbert Butterfield's essays on the philosophy of history, in *History and Human Relations* and *Christianity and History*, are written in terms of assumptions perfectly consistent with those that are operative in *Absalom*. Oscar Handlin's recent *Chance or Destiny: Turning Points in American History* brilliantly displays the interpretive possibilities which a creative search like that of Quentin and Shreve may offer. As a novel built from the clash of conflicting views of history, *Absalom* seems to me as relevant now as when it was written.

No doubt *Absalom* gets its chief effect as a novel from our sense that we are participating in its search for the truth. *Absalom* draws us in, makes us share its creative discovery, as few novels do. The lack of an authoritative voice puts a greater burden on us as readers than we may want to bear. Faulkner ran this risk when he wrote it. He has had to wait long for a just appreciation of its greatness. Few readers were ready for it in the thirties. But if we can and will bear our proper burden as readers we shall find the rewards correspondingly great.

Absalom is the novel not denying its status as fiction but positively enlarging and capitalizing upon it. It appropriately closes Faulkner's period of most rapid and successful productivity with a full-scale thematic exploration of what had been implied in all the major works so far: that fiction is neither lie nor document but a kind of knowledge which has no substitute and to which there is no unimaginative short-cut. Adding to this the implication that fiction is not unique in its dependence upon imagination and the necessary deviousness of its strategy, it suggests a view of life that Faulkner was to make increasingly explicit in later works.

From *William Faulkner: From Jefferson to the World* (1959), pp. 149-169. Copyright © 1959 by The University Press of Kentucky. Reprinted with permission of The University Press of Kentucky.

Notes

1. Kathleen Nott, *The Emperor's Clothes*, Indiana University Press, 1955, p. 5.
2. For a discussion of the way in which the style (i.e., grammar and rhetoric) is functional, see Robert H. Zoellner, "Faulkner's Prose Style in *Absalom, Absalom!*," *American Literature*, 30 (January, 1959), 486-502.

Quentin! Listen!

David Madden

Ernest Hemingway once declared that "All modern American literature comes from Huckleberry Finn," and there is some truth in that pompous pronouncement.[1]

Risking pomposity, I wish to make not one but several declarations: that all Southern literature *comes out* of the Civil War and Reconstruction, that all Southern novels are *about* the Civil War and Reconstruction, that *Absalom, Absalom!* is the best example of that phenomenon, not only in the Faulkner canon, but in all Southern literature, that *Absalom, Absalom!* is my choice as the greatest Civil War novel, that Colonel Thomas Sutpen, man of action in the Antebellum, Civil War, and Reconstruction eras, is *not*, as he is often held up to be, the protagonist of *Absalom, Absalom!*, that Quentin Compson, the most passive of Sutpen's vicarious witnesses, *is* the protagonist, that the most pertinent way to show that Quentin is the protagonist is to examine the techniques of the art of fiction that Faulkner employs in this novel, that Quentin Compson's consciousness is the most trenchant expression of the legacy of the Civil War at the deepest existential level.

How is it that all Southern literature *comes out* of the Civil War and Reconstruction, and that all Southern novels are *about* the Civil War and Reconstruction? The effect of the war and Reconstruction has so permeated Southern history and consciousness that anything a Southerner writes derives from that prolonged effect process, and that process itself is delineated in *Absalom, Absalom!* more deliberately and clearly than in any other Southern novel. By contrast, there is no such thing as a Northern novel, nor a true Civil War novel by a Northerner–*The Red Badge of Courage*, for instance, is about war per se—because there is no such thing as a Northerner, except in the minds of Southerners, who are, however, both very real and very surreal to Northerners.

A catalytic experience for civilizations throughout history, *war*, especially the Civil War, is a catalyst for Faulkner personally and for his characters, especially Quentin Compson, whose consciousness is at the center of Faulkner's creative consciousness. Every force seeks a form. I use "Civil War" as an all-embracive term for Antebellum, Civil War, Reconstruction force and legacy eras because the Civil War is a catalyst for all lines of trajectory. The lines of trajectory of Antebellum forces converge and explode in the Civil War, the lines of trajectory in the Civil War are tangled, the lines of trajectory in Reconstruction spread out and hang like a web until Quentin's last year, 1910, four years before World War I; the web was reshaped by Jim Crow, World War I, the Depression, and the civil rights movement, and it hangs still over us all. Obsessive talk of the myriad trajectories of those external forces ignites forces of emotion, imagination, and intellect in Quentin's consciousness and unconsciousness.

Absalom, Absalom! is my choice as the greatest Civil War novel, *not even though* it does not directly depict war, but *because* of the ways in which the war is more alluded to and its effects implied than dramatized. Faulkner implies ways in which life in the South led up to the war, was profoundly traumatized by it, and, more emphatically, by Reconstruction; and we may infer that it permeated, in myriad ways, Faulkner's own life. In *not* dealing directly with battles, Faulkner evokes, in his pervasive use of the technique of context and implication, what is more important—the war's effect on Americans, especially Southerners, right on up to you and me today.

In the works in which he figures, Quentin so seldom acts upon or interacts with other characters that readers are enabled to respond only to his consciousness as he passively reacts to and reluctantly but in anguish meditates upon the actions of others. Quentin is Faulkner's expressionistic embodiment of the process that makes all Southern literature about the Civil War. There is no character quite like Quentin in Southern fiction, not in Carson McCullers's *The Heart Is a Lonely Hunter,* all of whose four major characters are locked in the isolation of their own psyches, but do, at least, tell their personal stories, even if only to a mute, who is himself somewhat like Quentin; not in William

Styron's *Lie Down in Darkness*, although that novel resembles *The Sound and the Fury*; not in Thomas Wolfe's four epic novels, even though they feature the same hero; not in any Civil War novels by Southerners, although the hero of *The History of Rome Hanks and Kindred Matters*, by Northerner Joseph Pennell, faintly resembles Quentin-as-listener. Having found nothing in all fiction as fascinatingly complex as Quentin's shifting role in the works of Faulkner, I would claim for Quentin a significant uniqueness in all world literature, while lamenting that he is one of its most neglected characters, even though several critics, especially John Irwin in *Doubling and Incest/Repetition and Revenge* (1975), Estella Schoenberg in *Old Tales and Talking* (1977), and Noel Polk in *Children of the Dark House* (1996), have made us more aware of him.

That, compared with his other characters, Quentin was always a vital, sharply focused presence in Faulkner's consciousness is demonstrated by the fact that when he discussed his characters in public he referred to the males as "the boy" and often had lapses of memory about them, but he almost always called Quentin by name, and about *him*, his memory was always clear. Several major and numerous minor characters reappear in Faulkner's work but Quentin has the distinction of being a major character in two of Faulkner's major works and in four short stories, "That Evening Sun," "A Justice," "A Bear Hunt," and "Lion." That Horace Benbow resembles Quentin, especially in the early versions of *Sartoris* and *Sanctuary*, that Faulkner "rehearsed" Quentin and Sutpen in the short story "Evangeline," and that one *might* imagine Quentin as the anonymous "we" narrator of "A Rose for Emily" emphasize Quentin's centrality in the Faulkner canon.

The other three narrators of *The Sound and the Fury*, Benjy, Jason, and Faulkner himself, seldom refer to Quentin. Benjy's stream of consciousness expresses pure being in timelessness. Had Faulkner allowed Caddy (his "heart's darling"), to whom all the narrators relentlessly refer, to speak, would she have spoken of Quentin? I think not. Caddy's naming her daughter Quentin seems an ironic dismissal of

Quentin and his incestuous longing for her.[2] Quentin's obsession with Caddy is so strong that his confession is that of a man whose life flashes before him as he drowns. Jason's tough guy narration is realistic self-justification. But to whom do these brothers speak? Isolated within their very different egos, none of the three brothers have listeners. Faulkner presents their narrations as pure literary artifice. But Faulkner narrates the fourth section of *The Sound and the Fury* in full awareness that *he* has what his characters, especially Quentin, his alterego, *lack*, but do not crave, a community of readers, of listeners.

I am now proposing to publishers that the two novels and four short stories in which Quentin is either the protagonist or a major character be brought together in a single volume of about 600 pages. My study of those works and their effect on me personally and as a fiction writer has led me to the conviction that if they are gathered into a single volume, with an introduction explaining why, the average Faulkner reader may grasp the essence of this elusive character.

Colonel Thomas Sutpen, man of action in the Antebellum, Civil War, and Reconstruction eras, is not the protagonist of *Absalom, Absalom!*[3] I am convinced that the repeated focus on Sutpen by many readers and critics distorts the novel, and turns Quentin into a mere narrative device at best and makes him gratuitous at worst.[4]

On the surface, *Absalom, Absalom!* is a dramatic rendering of the ways in which Thomas Sutpen the legend becomes the creation of the Southern oral storytelling tradition, a tradition nurtured in Antebellum wilderness, magnified in Civil War defeat, and transmuted in humiliation, resentment, and self-loathing through Reconstruction on into 1910, Quentin's twentieth year.

As a little boy, Sutpen, who sprang from poor white trash, was commanded by a black servant to enter a mansion by the back door. This wound to Thomas Sutpen's very identity inspired his dream of becoming the owner of a mansion and slaves. He obsessively and savagely pursued a grand design to force that dream into reality, a dream that became a nightmare for everyone around him, especially his wives, white and black, and his sons and daughters, white and black, his sister-in-law, Miss Rosa, the children of his black son, the poor white trash man who worshipfully served him, and that man's granddaughter and great-granddaughter. Sutpen himself was satisfied only with the image of himself that the design was created to produce, the image of a man above all other men, who were to be merely witnesses to his rise and to the perpetuation of his blood, while he seemed to take little pleasure in the land, the mansion, the women, the children, or in the many other men and women who figured in his operatic design.

From the moment the townspeople set eyes upon the wild stranger who would become known as Thomas Sutpen, the demon, the ogre, leading his gang of wild slaves through the town, the exaggerated and conflicting stories began, stories that told how he bought a hundred square miles of wilderness, tamed the wilderness, built a mansion, amassed a fortune, married the daughter of a prominent citizen, on whom he begat a son and daughter, Henry and Judith, how he went off to war to protect those products of that design, how during Reconstruction, his fortunes so declined that he became the keeper of a store and how Wash Jones, his poor white trash Sancho Panza in this Quixotic epic slew Sutpen with the scythe he had borrowed from Sutpen.

That is far more than enough for storytellers—that is, *everybody*—in any impoverished Deep South small town to thrive on. Faulkner thrived on such stories until he could become a writer and reimagine and expand upon them, until he could imagine what is missing, the answers to the many mysteries and secrets that always germinate behind the façade of such legends. So Faulkner creates the keepers of the secret answers to the mysteries that seem to constitute the very identities of the later storytellers and their children. They are motivated, in that later era, a time of no grand actions such as the Civil War, in that long, trance-like era of "old tales and talking" (243), to bring the dark mysteries out into the daylight. They discover finally: that Charles Bon, Henry Sutpen's roommate, at the University of Mississippi, who followed a design of his own, schemed to go with Henry to Sutpen's Hundred to confront Sutpen for abandoning his mother and to reveal that he is Sutpen's son, but that he meets Judith, who falls in love with him; that the confrontation with Sutpen was delayed by the war; that when his father revealed to him that Bon was his half-brother and part Negro, Henry shot Bon to defend his sister's honor, then fled; that when Sutpen's wife Ellen died, he proposed that her sister, Rosa, become a mere body out of which he could produce a male heir, and that he was refused; that the Negro house servant Clytie was also Sutpen's daughter, and that Sutpen had not only begotten children of his slaves but had turned at last to a poor white trash girl and begot a child by her, all three of whom the grandfather, Wash Jones, slaughtered; that Charles Bon's child, too, came to Sutpen's mansion and was taken in by Judith and Clytie; and finally that Henry returned from exile almost forty years later and hid in the now-derelict "dark house," until discovered by his Aunt Rosa and Quentin, and that it was Clytie the slave daughter who applied a scorched earth climax to the Sutpen epic by setting the mansion on fire, perishing with her white brother Henry.

Although the long postwar era of the Lost Cause produced few men of action like Colonel Sutpen, it produced a legion of storytellers and multitudes of listeners, and this backward marching, backward looking parade of storytellers and listeners comes finally to a dead end in Quentin Compson.

Given the obvious fact that lives like Colonel Thomas Sutpen's have been the stuff of fiction, both very good and very bad, from Homer and Sophocles to the present, why do I feel compelled, almost messianically, to urge, along with several scholars, that greater attention must be paid to Quentin, whose affinities are all with the palest of postmodern antiheroes?

Sutpen's story expresses the desire of Southerners to be both civilized, as in Jefferson, and wild, as in the Civil War. Quentin can be neither nor does he even aspire to be either. Both the South and Quentin are transfixed between the nightmare of the past and its legacy in the present. Jason gives his son the same name Sir Walter Scott gave his man of action, *Quentin Durward*, the young Scot who fought for a foreign king in 1468, an ironic contrast to Quentin Compson. Quentin's grandfather's storytelling does not inspire Quentin's father, Jason, to a life of action, and Jason's storytelling fails to inspire Quentin to a life of action; Jason's only act is to pass on the story, imbued with his own character and personality. Quentin's only acts are the passive ones of reluctant listening, anguished retelling, of going along with his father to the Sutpen cemetery and going along with Miss Rosa into Sutpen's house, of staring at his father's letter in his room at Harvard.

Unlike his father, Jason, Quentin does not want to know, understand, become involved in the story of Sutpen and others, and tell it to future kin, to a community of listeners. Part of Quentin's problem is that he knows that, like people, like Sutpen himself, civilizations, such as Greece and Rome, come and go, so why not the South and its Sutpens? Quentin knows that he cannot forge an identity out of a heroic past as precarious as common everyday life, even if he could or desired to do it.

Quentin's negativity, both stated and implied, pervades the novel. In early chapters, Quentin responds to questions with a "yes" that conceals a diffident "no" and later with a "no" that conceals a panicked "yes." "Better that he were dead," Grandfather said of Charles Bon's son, "better that he had never lived."[5] Quentin, Faulkner implies, would apply that comment to himself, the Quentin who says of himself, "I am older than many people who have died" (301). Miss Rosa will not "reconcile herself to letting him [Sutpen's son] lie dead in peace" (289), Shreve says to Quentin, who, the reader may infer, has already "become" Henry, wanting to lie dead in peace himself. "So now I shall have to go in" (294), thinks Quentin, invading Henry Sutpen's hiding place to satisfy Miss Rosa's craving for an answer to the mystery of "a ghost" in the old mansion, Miss Rosa who has refused to remain a ghost herself, and so Quentin moves out of storytelling into reality, to witness the suicide by fire of Clytie and Henry (and to commit his own suicide by water in *The Sound and the Fury*). The reader might wonder whether Charles Bon, recently revealed to be Thomas Sutpen's mixed blood son, forced Henry to kill him to avoid marrying their sister and fathering another mixed breed child, but the context of Quentin's listening might well imply that Quentin would conclude that he did, because, unable to respond to any positives intended by the storytellers, Quentin is deeply affected by all the suicides and suicidal behavior in the novel.

Faulkner implies that as each storyteller tells a story, earlier storytellers are remembered, so that Quentin's grandfather is a dominant figure hovering over Jason's telling about how his father helped Judith, and the reader feels his presence also, and so does Quentin, even more intensely. The reader must imagine, then, that as he listens specifically to Rosa, then to his father, then to Shreve, Quentin feels the urgent speaking presence of many other storytellers. Quentin is never of one mind. As early as the first few pages, Faulkner tells the reader that there are "two separate Quentins now talking to one another in the long silence of notpeople in notlanguage" (4-5), and that a third Quentin is listening to those two voices. "The eagerness of the listener," says Jane Eyre, in Brontë's novel, "quickens the tongue of a narrator," but unlike his father and Shreve, Quentin is not an eager listener, so the storytellers strive harder to capture and keep his attention and stimulate his interest, with the effect that he is all the more tormented, giving rise to the relentlessly implied questions, "Why *me*? What do you want me to *do*?" Early in the novel and then again halfway through, Quentin thinks, "Yes, I have had to listen too long" (102, 157). To what? To the implied pleas that he forge his identity out of these stories, but even more to the implications of the stories as they apply to who he really is, a potential suicide. Near the end, when Shreve's telling the story back to Quentin reaches a high pitch of intensity, Quentin yells, "Wait!" and thinks, "I am going to have to hear it all over again. . . . I shall have to never listen to anything else but this again forever" (222). Influenced by the vigor and pace of Shreve's own enthralled retelling, Quentin takes up parts of the tale yet again, compulsive, obsessed, manic (225).

Sutpen's saga is unimaginative, in itself uninteresting; it is simple, operatic melodrama (not tragedy, as some have argued, not even near-tragedy), and, as such, it is *one* major expression of the South's and the world's conception of life in the South before, during, and after the Civil War. Sutpen's motive for telling his story to Grandfather Compson is self-justification and self-aggrandizement, a simple continuation of all his other actions. The men, women, and children, white and slave, who witness Sutpen's life, create his legend by telling his story in fragments that promote mystery and suspense, fragments embellished by imagination and repeated from generation to generation until they torment Quentin's ears. Exhorted to listen, Quentin is the principal listener in the novel. As Nick Carraway, not Gatsby, is the protagonist of *The Great Gatsby*, as Jack Burden, not Willie Stark, is the protagonist of *All the King's Men*, as the narrator, not Roderick Usher, is the protagonist of "The Fall of the House of Usher," an even more apt example—because the true protagonist of all first person narratives is the narrator—so Quentin, not Sutpen, is the protagonist of *Absalom*. The major difference is that Quentin the listener is not the sole storyteller in the novel. That some critics mistakenly identify Quentin as the sole narrator (as opposed to storyteller) testifies to the strength of the impression one gets of the pervasiveness of his consciousness, an effect toward which all Faulkner's techniques are deliberately working.[6]

Had he intended Sutpen to be the protagonist, Faulkner was in command of an array of techniques that he could have adroitly employed to tell Sutpen's simple, melodramatic story, to delineate its complex implications about the South, much more effectively. For instance, he could have used the omniscient point of view, getting into the perspectives of all the major characters; or he could have used third person, central intelligence point of view technique from Judith's or Henry's perspective; or he could have imagined a first person narration, with Judith or Henry as narrator, with one of Bon's descendants as listener.

Who *does* tell the story and to whom? Faulkner uses the omniscient point of view, from which he tells the reader that Miss Rosa and

Quentin's father told Sutpen's story to Quentin, who tells it to Shreve, who tells it back to Quentin. Why does Faulkner create Rosa and Quentin's father as storytellers, since neither knows enough to tell the whole story? And why is Quentin necessary as a listener-storyteller since he knows only what they tell him and especially since his verbal responses seldom exceed "yes" and "no" and his mental responses do not directly express the effects of their storytelling upon his consciousness? The blunt question Faulkner deliberately poses for readers is this: *What is Quentin doing in this novel?*

We know that Faulkner had already told Sutpen's story with two narrators like Quentin and Shreve in the short story "Evangeline," written five years before *Absalom*. Both the basic "I" narrator and his friend who tells him parts of the story are keenly interested listeners who are motivated to seek answers to mysteries. Very little narrative evidence in the novel but all of the fiction techniques point to Quentin as Faulkner's primary interest. There are two Faulkners in this novel, one the artist at work, the other Faulkner's alter ego, given the name "Quentin."

Faulkner implies that before chapter 2 begins, Quentin has told his father the story Miss Rosa told him, and he implies that before chapter 6, Quentin has told Shreve the story of Miss Rosa. Faulkner renders Quentin's telling a story only once, when he and Shreve are retelling Sutpen's story together. The effect of this use of context and implication is to *suggest* that Quentin is ostensibly the major storyteller, while providing the reader's basic experience with Quentin as the Quentin who listens to stories.

The most pertinent way to show not only *that* Quentin is the protagonist but *how* he is the protagonist is to examine the techniques of the art of fiction that Faulkner employs in this novel and their effect on the reader. The techniques fiction writers use are in themselves expressions of meaning and conveyors to the reader of experience; that is true especially of innovative writers, and truest of Faulkner the innovator in this novel. One may see in Faulkner's careful and full revisions the stress he placed on the use of innovative techniques that in themselves would express the emotional, imaginative, and intellectual meaning of the novel.[7] This novel is a veritable encyclopedia of innovative techniques and innovative use of conventional techniques. Gathering all the Quentin fiction around *Absalom, Absalom!* will enable readers not only to understand Quentin and the works in which he figures, but to understand Faulkner's innovative techniques as well, and that understanding would most probably make all his works far more accessible.

Faulkner's overall technique is to combine innovative literary techniques with the dynamics of oral storytelling techniques to achieve the overall effect of a complex meditation, which the reader responding to implication must attribute to Quentin. The unique passiveness in Quentin's character enables, perhaps forces Faulkner to achieve technical effects not otherwise possible, effects that constitute much of his greatness as an innovative literary artist.

The ideal reader for this novel will examine Faulkner's use of the techniques of fiction to express his intentions. Just as readers may be aware of Faulkner's literary techniques, even Quentin and the storytellers themselves are conscious of the techniques of storytelling that they use to affect their listeners. Quentin tells Shreve, "I reckon Grandfather was saying [to Sutpen] 'Wait wait for God's sake wait' about like you are until he [Sutpen] finally did stop and back up and start over again with at least some regard for cause and effect even if none for logical sequence and continuity . . . telling it all over and still it was not absolutely clear" (199). By his use of techniques, such as metaphor, Faulkner teaches the reader how to read *Absalom*. "Maybe nothing ever happens once and is finished," meditates Quentin. "Maybe happen is never once but like ripples maybe on water after the pebble sinks, the ripples moving on, spreading . . ." (210). Quentin's metaphor alerts the reader to expect that the narrative events and other elements in this novel will not happen only once, but will be repeated in other forms, enhanced by Faulkner's patterned and controlled repetition of motifs, metaphors, and phrases.

Only through an awareness of Faulkner's artistry can the general reader feel the full impact and respond to the myriad implications of Quentin's drama of consciousness. Faulkner's ideal reader for this novel will become aware not just of narrative strategy but of his use of the technique of point of view, a complicated mixture of omniscient, third person central intelligence, to use Henry James's term, interior monologue, and *four* quoted first person narrations, with variations in style; his manipulation of shifting contexts to make simultaneous implications about Sutpen's story and Quentin's responses; his use of allusions to enrich the contexts; his use of transitions and lack of transitions in time and space, to disorient and reorient the reader and Quentin; his deliberately ambiguous and tormenting use of pronouns, especially "he," "they," and "it"; his use of the devices of incremental repetition, questions, digressions, interruptions, odd punctuation, long, complex parentheticals, long convoluted sentences, paragraphs as long as eight pages, juxtapositions, expressionistic effects, irony, parallels, symbolism, and startling imagery.

All those techniques achieve a sense of simultaneity and inevitability that result in a unity so complex many readers and some critics do not fully comprehend it, partly because the techniques I have listed cause disorientation and dismay, as his first vital reader, his editor, lamented to Faulkner.[8] While all of his techniques serve the Sutpen story, they simultaneously serve the more important characterization, created mostly by context and implication, of Quentin, whose responses are often similar to the frustrated, irritated, gasping reader's. Readers have asked, Why does Faulkner use such a vast array of techniques? Faulkner strives to create shifting, complex contexts within which to stimulate the reader's mind with implications that express what cannot be directly expressed—as he knew from the limited effect of Quentin's first person testimony in *The Sound and the Fury* and in "That Evening Sun," published two years later—and simultaneously to explore, perhaps subconsciously, his own (Faulkner's) psyche indirectly through Quentin's implied psyche.

The ostensible Antebellum, Civil War, Reconstruction generic narrative of the stock character Sutpen becomes meaningful as a paradigm of the decline of the South not in itself, but mainly as fragmented and embedded in the neurotic, probably psychotic consciousness of Quentin. Sutpen's story is an objective correlative of Quentin's ineffable state of consciousness.

Faulkner's achievement in this novel, as in all his best work, lies not in his having imagined the story of Thomas Sutpen but in his having imagined the techniques that innovatively render that story and its implications; and a unique achievement of this novel alone is that it is not mainly Faulkner's character-narrative based imagination but his techniques that create Quentin Compson. The medium *is* the message.

Faulkner is interested in each of the characters, especially in listeners who become storytellers, but his identification with Quentin was essential to his being. Faulkner is Quentin, but he takes a major step further than focus on Quentin by delineating each of three other character's immersion in Sutpen's story, with the effect that the novel is more about each of the characters and about the process of their storytelling than it is about Sutpen himself.[9] But when we compare the centrality of Quentin as listener and storyteller with the other characters, we find that no potential for further development is active at the heart of Rosa's story, because it is static and always was; Mr. Compson's narrative is impersonal—he has no motive beyond a pure compulsion to tell stories, except for the weak inference that he aims to affect and teach Quentin; Shreve's involvement is transitory. Southerners tell stories to teach and to create identity, especially as a postwar, Lost Cause ritual. Rosa and Quentin's father say, in effect, "Quentin! Listen! So you can transmit it to our own kind, to your children!" But Quentin will have no children. Staring at his father's letter about Rosa's death, as if in a trance, he tells the story to a sardonic, Northern foreigner, Shreve, as if to be overheard telling it to himself, a dramatic monologue that is simultaneously a soliloquy. He tells it to take possession of the story, to give himself a sense that he exists, that he is not himself a ghost born of the ghosts of the past, but finally, he tells it to rid himself of the burden of Southern history, which as one of the last of the Compson line, he feels, but by mere torpor does not accept. Nor does he accept the implied obligation to pass it on through the representative story of Sutpen. Quentin starts with no ostensible motive to tell, and ends with none, but the reader must infer his existential dilemma from the innovative techniques Faulkner employs.

As omniscient narrator unusual in the infrequency of his speaking, Faulkner meshes his own narration with all the storytellers, who also have a kind of omniscience through overreaching imaginations, and Faulkner's complex consciousness finally meshes with Quentin's. Faulkner, a master of point of view technique, creates the most complex pattern in this novel. There are three elements: Faulkner's omniscient voices, voices telling "old tales and talking" (243), and Quentin's meditation voice. Within Faulkner's omniscient point of view, the various storytellers tell their stories. As Faulkner moves from one to another, sometimes within only a few sentences, the very juxtaposition of one storyteller to another expresses some aspect of Quentin's consciousness of storytellers and of times and places. Near the end of chapter 8, for instance, three storytellers intersect and interact on a single page: Clytie, like a messenger in a Greek tragedy, describing Wash Jones's slaughter of his granddaughter and his great granddaughter, and Sutpen, as retold by Quentin's father, who imagines the missing parts, retold again by Quentin to Shreve, who interrupts, as told by Faulkner (233-34). Faulkner's own infrequent narration almost always relates to Quentin, with the effect that the reader is always aware of the presence of the Faulkner-Quentin consciousness even as Miss Rosa, Jason, and Shreve are telling stories. The precept that the protagonist of every first person narrative is the narrator applies to each storyteller in this novel. Faulkner modifies that aesthetic so that the novel becomes essentially more about Quentin as the major listener than as storyteller.

"So they will have told you doubtless already" (107) is a kind of phrase repeated to Quentin often. Subconsciously, Quentin is acutely aware of not just the listener-tellers Faulkner quotes, but of those people who are listeners only and even of tellers and listeners who are only implied in the novel: Charles Bon has told stories to his roommate Henry, Clytie has told Grandfather Compson a story, Grandfather Compson has told his son Jason a story—all those tellings are paraphrased by Miss Rosa and Jason, who tell the stories to Quentin, the all-encompassing listener. The reader must pay attention to Quentin and imagine the conscious and subconscious effects on Quentin of Shreve's sardonic retelling of the Sutpen story. As these listener-story-tellers talk, readers should be ever mindful, as Quentin is, of the always-hovering presence of those characters to whom Faulkner does not give a storytelling voice: Sutpen's children, Judith and Henry, and those with black blood, Clytie and Bon, and that ever-present representative of the poor white trash from which Sutpen also sprang—Wash Jones. Faulkner does not directly give them storytelling voices because the technique of context and implication enables him to evoke their voices without quoting them.

Faulkner stresses the fact that each of the tellers of the Sutpen tale dwells upon fragments that reflect needs in their own lives: Rosa's love for Sutpen, Quentin's grandfather's friendship with Sutpen, Sutpen's own egocentric story of himself as told to Grandfather Compson, Jason Compson's desire to exhibit to his son Quentin his intellectual analysis of the Sutpen-Rosa story, and even the wise-cracking Northerner Shreve's exhilaration in retelling to Quentin the saga Quentin has just told him. The narrative logic of the Sutpen story as told by Rosa and Quentin's father calls for a listener who can and does respond fully, interactively, and meaningfully as the telling progresses. But Quentin is as far from being that kind of listener as any Southern twenty year old could be. Through Quentin's responses, and lack of responses, to the telling and the tale, Faulkner suggests to the reader the negative nature of the values of the world Sutpen and his witnesses represent. At no time does Quentin even hint that he derives any value on an exemplary level from what is being transmitted to him; he responds on a personal, subjective level to the stories he is told, affected most by parallels in his own life, mainly the relationship between himself and his sister Caddy, as seen in the brother-sister relationship of Henry Sutpen and Judith Sutpen, and, far less important, by parallels between the friendship of Henry and Charles Bon and the roommate relationship of Quentin and Shreve. Faulkner was once asked, "how much can a reader feel that this is the Quentin, the same Quentin, who appeared in *The Sound and the Fury*—that is, a man thinking about his own Compson family, his own sister?" Faulkner replied, "To me he's consistent. That he approached the Sutpen family with the same ophthalmia that he appreciated his own troubles."[10]

The legacy of the Civil War and Reconstruction in the South today is expressed in the varied responses of individuals. Quentin Compson, the most passive of Sutpen's vicarious witnesses, *is* the protagonist. The consciousness of Quentin Compson is the most trenchant expression of the legacy of the Civil War at the deepest existential level. The vigor of the transmission of the values of the Southern way of life, symbolized in Faulkner by high potency sexuality, mostly perverse in various ways, from generation to generation ends in Quentin's implied impotence, which is not only sexual but intellectual. Faulkner dramatizes the fact that while the conventional Southern values, which coalesced in the issues and the warrior mentality of the Civil War, fail to produce creative acts in the lives of individual descendants, the legends do stimulate each individual listener's imaginative participation, a value that transcends the ritual teaching function of the South's past. For them the unvicarious life is not worth living; at least they have *that* much of a life.

Storytelling inflames the imagination of the listener. Jason demonstrates that effect, saying often, "I imagine" (82, 85-87). But Quentin goes further and imaginatively becomes one of the characters with whom he most unconsciously identifies: Henry Sutpen. The image of Henry and Charles Bon "facing one another at the gate" triggers

Quentin's own vicarious response: "It seemed to Quentin that he could actually see them" (105). A paradox in the power of the imagination is suggested when Faulkner as author says that Quentin "could see it; he might even have been there," as Henry kissed his sister Judith before returning to war, but Quentin contradicts his creator, thinking, "*No. If I had been there I could not have seen it this plain*" (155). Even though he knows he has listened too long and too much, until he is not listening anymore, and has no desire to be a storyteller (280), Quentin responds to his Canadian roommate, Shreve, when he exhorts him to "tell about the South" (142). Quentin infects Shreve with "the virus of suggestion" (Henry James's phrase). Shreve's imagination is so activated that he reimagines the story of Henry and Charles Bon, exploring possibilities, rendering the story even more ironic, that, for instance, Charles Bon saves the life of his brother Henry who later kills Charles Bon *because* he is his brother and Judith's (237-38, 254, 275). Quentin tells the story to Shreve only to get rid of it by telling it as an act of betrayal to a cynical listener, who tells it back to him, ironically, in an empathy so profound, Quentin and Shreve together not only retell it in two voices as one voice, but imagine their counterparts, Henry Sutpen and Charles Bon, so vividly that Quentin and Shreve feel they have become one, then they become Henry and Bon, "in the cold room . . . there was now not two of them but four," so that Quentin and Shreve and Henry and *his* roommate Bon are "riding the two horses through the iron darkness" (236-37).

The inflamed imagination leaps into vicarious experience. Sutpen, Bon, and Henry enact a story—and Wash Jones violently ends it. Rosa, Jason, Quentin, Shreve, and Faulkner do not act—they listen to the story and retell it. Vicarious experience is a major motif in the novel. All the storytellers to whom he listens are people whose lives are intensely vicarious, so that Quentin the listener is a captive of the vicariousness of others. The South that Quentin knows through storytellers has, ever since defeat in the Civil War, been living vicariously at a level that threatens sanity, and Quentin symbolizes the product of that quality in the South—the inflamed imagination in an action vacuum. "But you were not listening," Quentin tells himself, in one of his meditation passages, "because you knew it all already, had . . . absorbed it already without the medium of speech somehow from having been born and living beside it, with it" (172). But in the telling, the lives of others seem, compared with his own, very compelling: the lives of Henry and Judith, especially, but even Miss Rosa's and his father's. Jason tells Quentin that Judith and Henry were a "single personality with two bodies both of which had been seduced almost simultaneously by a man [Charles Bon] whom at the time Judith had never even seen" (73), only heard her brother tell stories about. Judith communes with her dead lover Bon through his son by another woman, taking care of him, and when Judith dies, Clytie lives vicariously through the same boy, raising him. From the same class as Sutpen, Wash Jones vicariously lives the dream of wealth through Sutpen. After the war, Wash meets the returning hero at the gate, "Well, Kernel, they kilt us but they aint whupped us yit, air they?" (150). Unlike Quentin and the others, Wash Jones, who has lived vicariously through his hero Sutpen, finally commits a real act, but out of the kind of past he has vicariously lived, he can act only in violence.

Every non-reality quality in the other nonactive characters is paralleled in Quentin, usually to a greater degree: meditation, imagination, passivity, accede (torpor, inaction). As he listens to stories about Sutpen and other men of action all his life told by numerous people, Quentin becomes aware that he has no life of action. The kind of story-telling and listening process Faulkner presents is a form of meditation, but the only literal mediation to which he gives the reader access is Quentin's.[11] Faulkner is interested less in the drama of action than in the drama of human consciousness. By the end, Quentin has turned even more inward (and will finally turn against himself). Even his imagination and his meditations are limited, narrow in scope, and fail to result in a compulsion to tell stories as a means of perpetuating the past and maintaining a sense of community.

Myriad voices speak obsessively to Quentin about his legacy, the epic story of the settling of his home region, and the lingering effects of the war fought to preserve that way of life. But Quentin brings to his reluctant listening to those voices his own private sexual feelings about Caddy, delineated in *The Sound and the Fury* and, as a submerged psychological process, in "That Evening Sun," in which again Quentin, not Nancy, is the protagonist. Joseph Blotner quotes Faulkner as saying that Quentin in *Absalom, Absalom!* listens to the story of the brother and sister, Henry and Judith Sutpen, as a bitter parallel to his own incestuous longings for his sister Caddy and his own bitter failure to protect his sister's honor.[12] Similarly, in "That Evening Sun," Quentin, who does not act, who only listens, is listening most attentively to Caddy's questions that relate to sex. The effect of Faulkner's technique of implication from shifting contexts in the various works featuring Quentin may culminate in the general implication that Quentin kills himself in *The Sound and the Fury* not so much out of guilt for merely desiring his own sister as out of a profound apprehending of the fact that he exists intensely only when he responds in amazement and bewilderment to the tales people tell him about people who are, compared with himself, very much alive. His is a purely existential dilemma, as posed by Kierkegaard in *The Sickness unto Death*, Martin Heidegger in *Existence and Being*, Rollo May in *The Meaning of Anxiety*, Jean-Paul Sartre in *Being and Nothingness* and in *Nausea*, Albert Camus in *The Stranger*, and Katherine Ann Porter in "Flowering Judas." Quentin is far less active, less questing than even the narrators in the Sartre and Camus novels and his accede, a mortal sin in the Catholic Church, is more severe than Laura's in Katherine Anne Porter's "Flowering Judas."

We know that the storyteller's need to identify a personal parallel among the characters in the stories is most acute in Quentin (who "becomes" Henry) because Faulkner *implies* the need, rather than letting Quentin directly state it, but his need is so great that the vicarious imagination can not save him. Quentin's need is the basic need to *be*, and his basic dilemma the anxiety that emanates from the inability to *be*. If existence precedes essence, Quentin's sense of his own existence is such that essence can hardly flow from it. Existential psychologist Rollo May defines anxiety as "the experience of the threat of imminent nonbeing. Anxiety is the subjective state of the individual's becoming aware that his existence can become destroyed, that he can lose himself and his world, that he can become 'nothing' . . . anxiety overwhelms the person's awareness of existence, blots out the sense of time, dulls the memory of the past, and erases the future . . . it attacks the center of one's being. . . . Anxiety is ontological, fear is not. Anxiety always involves inner conflict. . . . Ontological guilt 'arises' from forfeiting one's own potentialities."[13] Miss Rosa, his father, and others fervently tell Quentin stories about people who have lived fervently on a level of action; Quentin, even considering that he is young, has no life of action himself about which anybody could fervently tell a story. Even fervently telling a story is an action, but Quentin himself tells the Rosa-Sutpen story to Shreve in a kind of bewildered, impotent, static voice that Faulkner gives us in a controlled series of fragments. Far from motivating him to live a life of action that might embody the values of the Old South, both the tellers and the tales only make Quentin aware of how empty his own life and consciousness are. Quentin is passionate only in the last line, as Meursault is passionate, yelling at the priest, only at the end of *The Stranger*. When Shreve asks Quentin, "Why do you hate the South?" Quentin's hysterically anguished denial, "I dont hate it!" is true. His existential dilemma is that, having a self so famished, he doesn't even hate himself.

In *Absalom*, his father, Miss Rosa, and others offer family and public history for their own varied reasons, but they provide a way for Quentin to transcend his subjective sexual impotence and his emotional, imaginative, and intellectual paralysis. Given Quentin's inability to respond as an active receiver of the legacy, Faulkner implies that Quentin's dilemma is deeper than incestuous longing, that it is the existential dilemma of being and nothingness. Quentin is now and always has been a shadow verging on nothingness, amazed and anguished at the spectacle of richer lives of action or of active preservers of the lives of more active people. Quentin, who ends in suicide, helps us see why Faulkner himself, who in life merely posed as a warrior and man of action, who *may* have considered suicide, turned to creative recreation, with war and its aftermath as the human action with the greatest range of possibilities in life and in literature. Meditating on Quentin, my student Melissa Wilkinson, in a moment of intellectual ecstasy, exclaimed, "It's wonderful that Faulkner could make so much out of nothing."

Many critics see Quentin as Faulkner's alter ego, his most autobiographical character.[14] Quentin was one of his favorite characters. He might have said, "*Quentin c'est moi!*" If a writer's life is most truly expressed in the act of creation, rather than in a recital of actual events, *Absalom, Absalom!* is Faulkner's autobiography as a person via Quentin and as an artist at work creating Quentin. Paradoxically, Quentin's narrow, single-minded consciousness is at the center of Faulkner's myriad-minded consciousness.

Quentin is listening, subconsciously, on the deepest level, deeper than the Henry-Judith incest implication, listening to the basic meaning of Sutpen's design, which is a calculated effort by the boy Sutpen to exist by having the mansion and all that went with a plantation way of life, because turned away from the front door of the mansion, the boy had an intuition of existential anxiety, the fear of nonbeing. Sutpen's design ends in catastrophe, maybe a suicidal overreaching. As both reader and Quentin listen to the Sutpen stories, Faulkner enables us to imagine Quentin's thoughts and emotions.

Faulkner, I imagine, and Sutpen felt the same anxiety but Sutpen distracted himself by building an empire, which failed him and his community; Faulkner distracted himself from anxiety by creating his Yoknapawtapha saga which, as a work of art that triumphs like Keats's urn, did not fail him and will not fail his readers, if they work with him as his collaborators by responding not only to the surface complications but to the implications that the shifting contexts generate. Faulkner's ideal reader will then feel unbearable pathos for Quentin in ways no other novel can stimulate.

Poem X in Faulkner's *A Green Bough* has been referred to as "Twilight," an apt title for Faulkner's meditation on the Quentin beneath the line by line surface of the novel:

> A terrific figure on an urn—
> . . . caught between his two horizons,
> Forgetting that he cant return.[15]

This an allusion to the town emptied of its folk in Keats's "Ode on a Grecian Urn."

And Edgar Allan Poe's poem "Alone" evokes a sense of Quentin's life:

> From childhood's hour I have not been
> As others were:
> I have not seen as others saw:
> I could not bring
> My passion from a common spring . . .
> And all I loved, I loved alone.
> Then—in my childhood . . . was drawn
> The mystery which binds me still . . .
> From the cloud that took the form
> Of a demon in my view.[16]

For Quentin, the demon is not Sutpen, whom others called demon, but the spot of grease on the road where Quentin merely wished he could have more fully existed.

From *Faulkner and War* (2004) edited by Noel Polk and Ann J. Abadie. Copyright © 2004 by David Madden. Reprinted with permission of David Madden.

Notes

1. Ernest Hemingway, *Green Hills of Africa* (New York: Charles Scribner's Sons, 1935), 22.

2. *Faulkner in the University*, ed. Frederick L. Gwynn and Joseph L. Blotner (Charlottesville: University Press of Virginia, 1959), 6, 263. Faulkner describes Caddy and her relationship with Quentin.

3. Faulkner disagrees, while stressing Quentin's importance. The argument may proceed not only from the author's intent in the novel but from its effect. *Faulkner in the University*, 71, 274-75.

4. One of the most recent examples is Dirk Kuyk, Jr., *Sutpen's Design: Interpreting Faulkner's "Absalom, Absalom!"* (Charlottesville: University Press of Virginia, 1990). Cleanth Brooks is an earlier, salient example, even though he understood, as a New Critic, how point of view expresses essence in a work of fiction: *William Faulkner: The Yoknapatawpha Country* (New Haven: Yale University Press, 1963), 295-324. See also his "Appendix B: Notes to *Absalom, Absalom!*" in *Twentieth Century Interpretations of "Absalom, Absalom!,"* ed. Arnold Goldman (Englewood Cliffs, N.J.: Prentice-Hall, Inc., 1971), 107-13. In most of the essays in that collection, the emphasis is upon the importance of the Sutpen story, with no stress on its effect upon Quentin.

5. William Faulkner, *Absalom, Absalom!* (1936; New York: Vintage International, 1986), 166. All page numbers hereafter are in parentheses, referencing the latest edition, Vintage International-Vintage Books, 1990, which is the corrected text of the 1936 edition, ed. Noel Polk, which first appeared in an edition in 1986 with different pagination.

6. Cleanth Brooks is again a major example: "All the information the reader has comes through Quentin directly or through Quentin's conversations." Brooks fails to call attention to the omniscient narrator of the entire novel, Faulkner himself. *Twentieth Century Interpretations of "Absalom, Absalom!,"* 107. In the same volume, Thomas E. Connolly instructs us that "Quentin" is "the principal narrator." Also in that volume, Richard Poirier says much the same thing (12-13). This misunderstanding is frequently repeated elsewhere. Ambiguity may be the culprit. To distinguish between Faulkner as authorial narrator and the characters he quotes telling old tales and talking, one should use the term "storyteller" for Quentin and others.

7. Gerald Langford, *Faulkner's Revision of "Absalom, Absalom!"* (Austin: University of Texas Press, 1971). See his introduction.

8. Joseph Blotner, *Faulkner: A Biography*, 1 vol. (New York: Random House, 1984), 348.

9. Langford, 3.

10. *Faulkner in the University*, 274.

11. *Absalom, Absalom!* A good example begins on 148.

12. Blotner, 348-49.

13. *Existence: A New Dimension in Psychiatry and Psychology* (New York: Basic Books, 1958), ed. Rollo May, Ernest Angel, and Henri F. Ellenberger, 50-54.

14. Among those critics who deal extensively with this question are John T. Irwin,

Doubling and Incest/Repetition and Revenge: A Speculative Reading of Faulkner (Baltimore: Johns Hopkins University Press, 1975); Estella Schoenberg, *Old Tales and Talking: Quentin Compson in William Faulkner's* Absalom, Absalom! *and Related Works* (Jackson: University Press of Mississippi, 1977); Michael Grimwood, *Heart in Conflict: Faulkner's Struggles with Vocation* (Athens: University of Georgia Press, 1987). In *Critical Essays on William Faulkner: The Compson Family* (Boston: G.K. Hall and Company, 1982), ed. Arthur F. Kinney, several of the contributors take up the question. An interesting revelation of Faulkner's identification with Quentin is the fact that "he told Joan [Williams] to send her letters to Quentin Compson, General Delivery, in Oxford." Blotner, 520.

15. *The Marble Faun and A Green Bough* (New York: Random House, nd.) facsimile reprint, 30.

16. *The Portable Poe* (New York: The Viking Press, 1945), 637-38.

Subverting History:
Women, Narrative, and Patriarchy
in *Absalom, Absalom!*

Susan V. Donaldson

William Faulkner's portrayal of women has attracted heated debate ever since Maxwell Geismar charged the Mississippi writer with misogyny more than forty years ago.[1] Albert Guerard, for one, has observed that Faulkner's reputed hostility to women presents special problems precisely because "it is unrepressed and even undisguised" (109). Even critics predisposed to defend Faulkner's characterization of women, like Cleanth Brooks, unwittingly find themselves resorting to a paternalistic vocabulary of "active" men and "fostering and sustaining" women, as John Duvall pointed out in a fine article a few years ago (qtd. 44). Indeed, from Duvall's perspective, such readers rely on terms and precepts inherited from a good many of Faulkner's male narrators—a disturbing reminder indeed for readers concerned with characterization of women in the Yoknapatawpha saga (45).

Nowhere would Faulkner's own paternalism and unease with women *appear* to be more embedded in his fiction than in the history of Thomas Sutpen as it is told and retold in *Absalom, Absalom!* From the very beginning of Rosa Coldfield's narrative, it would seem, Sutpen's intent is clear: to establish a plantation dynasty in Mississippi, the very nature of which is interchangeable with patriarchy, the passing of power and property from father to son. In this history, as it is made by Sutpen and constructed by the novel's four narrators, women appear to serve only as the means of perpetuating that dynasty—as mothers, wives and sisters—figures standing in the shadows and margins of the narrative.

What happens, though, if we consciously resist the stories told by and about Thomas Sutpen, if we direct our attention not to Sutpen, the center of those stories, but to their margins and shadows? In short, what happens if we read as feminist readers and refuse to accept the making of history in *Absalom, Absalom!* as inevitable or "natural"? I would argue that such a "resistance to codification," in Judith Fetterley's words, reveals a very different novel, one that, like Penelope, unravels as quickly as it weaves a tapestry of words, history and paternalistic myths (viii). We might discover, in fact, not one but two stories, one about the making of historical narrative and patriarchy and one about their unmaking.

Such a reading requires a self-conscious determination to resist the various entanglements offered by a text as compelling as *Absalom, Absalom!* and by earlier readings as well. Students of reading and gender, like Elizabeth Flynn, Patrocinio Schweickart, Elizabeth Meese and Jonathan Culler, suggest that such resistance essentially involves "reading the text as it was *not* meant to be read, in fact, reading it against itself" (Schweickart 50). As Schweickart observes, one must "identify the choices proffered by the text and, equally important, what the text precludes—namely, the possibility of reading as a woman *without* putting one's self in the position of the other, of reading so as to affirm womanhood as another, equally valid, paradigm of human existence" (50). And by focusing on what the text and its interpreters preclude as well as include, we can uncover what we might call the "otherness" of storytelling and story-making, as Elizabeth Meese might suggest: all those aspects of the text that have been repressed in earlier readings to accommodate interpretive conventions required by cultural priorities (xi).

In the case of *Absalom, Absalom!* interpretive conventions have led us to focus our energy as readers on the hypnotic story of Thomas Sutpen.[2] His determination to wrest a plantation and an aristocratic dynasty from the wilderness of North Mississippi also attracts the full attention of the text's narrators—Rosa Coldfield, Mr. Compson, Quentin Compson and Shreve McCannon. For them and for students of the South as well, Sutpen's story seems to evoke the tragic dimensions of the region's history, in which property, race, family and hubris are inextricably intertwined.

But by listening to those "garrulous outraged baffled ghosts" (5) who populate the novel and who endlessly recite Sutpen's story, we neglect those characters in *Absalom, Absalom!* who retreat to the silent regions of the novel—Sutpen's second wife Ellen, who takes to her bed and slowly withers away; Judith, Sutpen's daughter, who puzzles the narrators with her impenetrable calm and silence; Sutpen's mysterious and elusive first wife, who may or may not be pondering revenge; and Clytie, Sutpen's mulatto daughter, who eventually burns down the House of Sutpen.

These are characters who seem to live in the breaks and empty spaces of the narrative, who threaten to disrupt and even destroy the continuities of history woven by the narrators. As such, they form their own narrative of sorts, a muted story underlying Sutpen's dominant history (to borrow Elaine Showalter's terms), a muted story, moreover, of gaps, disruptions, discontinuities and even precipitous endings. If the story told by the four main narrators, then, suggests the making of history, this muted story hints at its unmaking.

This is not to say, however, that the story of Thomas Sutpen's rise and fall does not compel considerable attention. By the lights of the Compson family, Sutpen might be a vulgar, ill-bred man masquerading as an aristocrat, but he is still vital enough to attract the storytelling efforts of three generations of Compsons, from Sutpen's only friend General Compson to Quentin Compson huddled with his roommate Shreve in a cold Harvard dormitory. And even Rosa Coldfield, who considers herself Sutpen's sworn enemy and who pronounces him a demon "*not articulated in this world*" (214), insists that her brother-in-law's story must be told so that, as Quentin Compson, her reluctant audience, wryly thinks, people will "*know at last why God let us lose the War: that only through the blood of our men and the tears of our women could He stay this demon and efface his name and lineage from the earth*" (8).

Above all, what attracts the attention of these four narrators is the need to place Sutpen's story in some sort of understandable sequence.

For they are all concerned with the making of history, with devising explanations for the curious and the uncertain and with imposing coherence on separate events by seeking cause-and-effect relationships establishing connections. There are, after all, a good many connections that need to be established to understand the fragmented pictures of Thomas Sutpen's story handed down by the community—his abrupt appearance in Jefferson, the way he makes his money to buy and design Sutpen's Hundred, his decision to marry Ellen Coldfield, the friendship between Charles Bon and Henry Sutpen, Thomas Sutpen's mysterious trip to New Orleans, Judith Sutpen's broken engagement, Henry Sutpen's murder of Bon, Sutpen's courtship of Rosa and Judith's decision to raise Charles Bon's son. As Mr. Compson reminds us, "we have a few old mouth-to-mouth tales; we exhume from old trunks and boxes and drawers letters without salutation or signature, in which men and women who once lived and breathed are now merely initials or nicknames out of some now incomprehensible affection which sound to us like Sanskrit or Chocktaw . . ." (124).

Hence the need to establish sequence and plot in those old mouth-to-mouth tales becomes all the more pressing, especially in regard to the puzzling decline and fall of the Sutpen family's history. For Rosa the explanation lies with her definition of Sutpen as a demon unarticulated in this world whom only civil war can eventually destroy. For Compson the answers lie with the impassioned friendship of Henry and Charles Bon and the octoroon mistress that Henry discovers. For Shreve and Quentin the plot goes back even further, to Thomas Sutpen's first marriage and its legacy of miscegenation and the possibility of incest.

However different the conclusions reached by the storytellers are, their concerns and their very language remain remarkably the same. They are determined to impose order and sequence on the story of Thomas Sutpen, to bridge the breaks between the pieces they have inherited, and the effort to find connections is underscored by the hypotactic style eventually appropriating the stories of each and every one of the narrators. The length and complexity of their very sentences, as one subordinate clause inevitably follows another, reflect both their determination to make connections and the storytelling antecedents uniting them. Not without reason, then, do Quentin and Shreve make frequent mention of the stories' underlying similarities. *"Yes, we are both Father,"* Quentin thinks. *"Or maybe Father and I are both Shreve; maybe it took Father and me both to make Shreve or Shreve and me both to make Father or maybe Thomas Sutpen to make all of us"* (326-27).

This last remark is particularly revealing because it suggests just how dependent all these storytellers, with the possible exception of Rosa Coldfield, are on the fragmented stories that Thomas Sutpen tells General Compson on two occasions: once during Sutpen's chase of the runaway French architect brought in to help build the plantation manor and once during the Civil War when Sutpen tries to puzzle out where his grand design has gone wrong. For like the storytellers who follow him, Sutpen deliberately seeks out causes, effects and connections. "'You see, I had a design in my mind,'" he says, reflecting on his daughter's shattered engagement, his son's disappearance and the imminent loss of his great wealth. "'Whether it was a good or a bad design is beside the point; the question is, Where did I make the mistake in it, what did I do or misdo in it, whom or what injure by it to the extent which this would indicate'" (329). And it is this same casting about for reasons and causes that distinguishes the storytellers who later reconstruct his life and the story of his family.

Indeed, in a manner of speaking the novel's narrators are all heirs to Sutpen's own storytelling and design-making. By accepting that legacy and by passing stories of the ambitious planter to the next storyteller, they re-enact the line of succession that Sutpen himself yearns to establish—the passing of grand design from father to son. The fragments of old tales and the compelling urge to establish continuity are handed down from General Compson to Mr. Compson, who in turn bequeaths the tales to Quentin, who finally passes the stories on to Shreve, just as Rosa Coldfield, herself an heir of sorts, passes on the legacy of storytelling to Quentin and tells him that "maybe some day you will remember this and write about it" (6). Successors to Thomas Sutpen as storyteller, they are themselves fathers of their own tales to be passed on to storytelling sons.

In this respect, feminist critics like Teresa de Lauretis might recognize the narratives Faulkner's storytellers weave and re-weave as essentially oedipal, stories of fathers and sons leaving little room for sisters, wives or daughters except as adjuncts to that central bond between father and son. Essentially, de Lauretis builds her definition of oedipal narrative on Roland Barthes's characterization of "the pleasure of the text" as "a staging of the (absent, hidden or hypostatized) father" (10). Even more emphatically than Barthes, though, de Lauretis argues that narrative in general as defined in Western culture constitutes patriarchy and is constitutive thereby. The very movement of narrative, by her lights, "specifies and even produces the masculine position as that of mythical subject, and the feminine position as mythical obstacle or, simply, the space in which that movement occurs" (143). Hence in storytelling patterns established by tales of ancient heroes like Oedipus and Perseus, even "major" female characters, like Medusa and the Sphinx, survive "inscribed in hero narratives, in someone else's story, not their own" (109).

It is, in fact, as figures in someone else's story, marginal characters at best, that women exist in tales told by Sutpen to General Compson and in the stories to follow. As the planter himself bluntly remarks, they are simply "incremental to the design which I had in mind" (300). Sutpen's great design of establishing a plantation—and, implicitly, a patriarchy—that can be passed down his male line offers no other possible place for women than that of making the continuity of his plantation dynasty possible. They are adjuncts to the tale but not tellers or even voices in their own right. Thinking back on the story that Sutpen passes on to General Compson, Mr. Compson notes briefly, "So it was no tale about women, and certainly not about love" (310). If there is any room at all for women in the few stories that Sutpen himself tells, it is in the corners and shadows of the narrative. Even in his tale of the slave uprising on Haiti, the girl who becomes his first wife is only "a shadow that almost emerged for a moment and then faded again but not completely away" (308).

Women are relegated to the same dim corners and shadows in all those stories following Sutpen's tale. All the women in Sutpen's family, from his first wife to Clytie, are regarded by the narrators, even Rosa, as mere adjuncts to Sutpen's design, helpless pawns who readily succumb to Sutpen's manipulations, ambitions and bombast. In a novel about talking and about a driven man whose very shoulders are described as "forensic" and "oratorical," the Sutpen women are remarkably silent and remote (344). Even when narrative attention focuses on them, as in stories of Judith's adolescence and courtship, Ellen, Judith, Clytie and Sutpen's mysterious first wife slip into the more distant regions of the tale. In adolescence, for instance, Judith is so inaccessible that she seems to be beyond even the reach of her grandfather Coldfield's voice. From the perspective of Mr. Compson, unwittingly repeating Sutpen's narrative strategy of expelling women to the margin, Judith appears to move in a "complete detachment and imperviousness to actuality almost like physical deafness" (84). Similarly remote is Ellen, who has been "corrupted," according to Mr. Compson, by Sutpen's ambition to manufacture at Sutpen's Hundred a ready-made aristocratic family and dynasty (86). Acquiescing to Sutpen's design, she escapes, Mr. Compson asserts, into "a world of pure illusion in which, safe from any harm, she moved, lived, from attitude to attitude against her background of chatelaine to the largest, wife to the wealthiest, mother of the most fortunate" (83). From this perspective, stamped by Sutpen's own design and narrative, women do *appear* to lead lives "not only divorced from, but irrevocably excommunicated from, all reality" (240). They are indeed divorced from the reality deliberately woven by storytelling and the making of history in *Absalom,*

Absalom! Ellen herself suggests something of that retreat from history when she takes to her bed on the eve of the Civil War.

If there is any role in history for the novel's women, it would seem to be the one suggested by Rosa Coldfield, the only woman in the dominant story who is permitted a voice. For even Rosa, who is described as *"the chief disciple and advocate of that cult of demon-harrying of which . . . [Sutpen] was the chief object,"* accepts the role as servant to the making of Thomas Sutpen's history (347). Although she considers herself the town's poet laureate fiercely guarding the heroism of the past, she is ultimately no less an adjunct to Thomas Sutpen's design than Ellen is. Her very voice serves not so much her own purposes and desires as those of Sutpen's looming ghost, "as if it were the voice which he haunted where a more fortunate one would have had a house" (4). And like the other women in the making of this history, even her voice retreats to the margins of the narrative. We are told that her voice "would not cease, it would just vanish" as it gave life and breath to the shadow of Thomas Sutpen (4). Indeed, Rosa herself seems to vanish as the making of Sutpen's story attracts the storytelling efforts of Mr. Compson, Quentin and Shreve. Once she refuses Sutpen's pragmatic proposition that she bear a son before the two commit themselves to marriage, Rosa no longer has any place in the narrative. She is eventually reduced to a reference in Mr. Compson's letter about her funeral, herself an adjunct to Mr. Compson's own storytelling design.[3]

Such retreats into the margin, though, whether by Rosa's voice or by Ellen in the last two years of her life, suggest the possibility of severing the connections and disrupting the history so carefully constructed by the narrators in the dominant story. Like Ellen, who retreats to a darkened room in "baffled incomprehension" (97), these withdrawals remind us of the breaks, inconsistencies and absences that the narrators seek to repair in order to establish order, sequence and connections, in short, to make history (see Brooks 286). They remind us that these connections are tentative, speculative and ultimately uncertain, comparable to General Compson's definition of language as "that meagre and fragile thread . . . by which the little surface corners and edges of men's secret and solitary lives may be joined for an instant now and then before sinking back into the darkness" (313).

They also repeatedly remind us of the uneasiness of narrators confronted with the difficult task of imposing order on the separate fragments of Sutpen's life. Too many times the narrators must recount events that seem to take place, in Rosa's words, "without rhyme or reason or shadow of excuse" (17). Too many times they must confront the breaks in the plots they reconstruct—their lack of knowledge about Sutpen's interview with Henry on the Christmas Eve before the war, Sutpen's trip to New Orleans, Bon's feelings for Judith, the years Henry and Bon spent during the war and Henry's reasons for murdering Bon at the very gates of the Sutpen manor. "It's just incredible," Mr. Compson admits. "It just does not explain. Or perhaps that's it: they dont explain and we are not supposed to know" (124).

Hence the narrators frequently reveal fears that such breaks will bring their storytelling efforts to an abrupt and precipitous end. They are forever telling each other to wait so that they can carefully establish narrative sequence and even forestall hasty conclusions. As Quentin tells Shreve, Sutpen's first story told to General Compson is so hastily narrated and abrupt that the general is forced to cry, "'Wait wait for God's sake wait' about like you are until he finally did stop and back up and start over again with at least some regard for cause and effect even if none for logical sequence and continuity" (308). It is a plea that is echoed time and time again by both Quentin and Shreve in particular whenever the narrative they fabricate between them threatens to come to a rapid conclusion—in speculation about Sutpen's final meeting with Henry in a Confederate camp, in reconstructions of Wash Jones's murder of Sutpen, in the fictions they weave of Charles Bon's motives. We even hear this plea for prolonging the narrative in the cries for extra time uttered by Bon and Henry as imagined by Shreve and Quentin in the last section. Like their narrators, Henry and Charles are apparently trying to stave off the final confrontation. As such, characters and narrators suggest that Peter Brooks's definition of the motives propelling narrative is all too apt. Narrative desire, he notes in *Reading for the Plot*, "is the wish for the end, for fulfillment, but fulfillment must be delayed so that we can understand it in relation to origin and to desire itself" (111).

It is this desire, I would suggest, that the muted story of *Absalom, Absalom!* threatens to thwart. This second story seems all the more subversive because it follows none of the narrative patterns of sequence, order and cause and effect characterizing the dominant story. Indeed, it is not even properly told. If it exists at all, it is in the margins, breaks, contradictions and silences inhabited by the women who supposedly serve as tools in Thomas Sutpen's design and implicitly in the telling of history. And as a story that is not told, it undermines the plots and connections so carefully constructed by the dominant narrators and even threatens to bring their plots to an abrupt end altogether.

Indeed, instead of offering answers, solutions and connections, as the dominant story does, this untold story simply poses questions, and, more often than not, the silent women in Thomas Sutpen's story who retreat to the far regions of the narrative serve as emblems of those questions, empty spaces that can never quite be filled by the endless words that weave Sutpen's tale. They are women who all give pause to the carefully constructed narratives of history. Judith's very existence, for instance, seems to slow down the fevered calculations of the Bons' lawyer conjured up by Quentin and Shreve. As the two young men themselves speculate, "you could maybe even have seen the question mark after it and the other words even: *daughter? daughter? daughter?* trailing off not because thinking trailed off, but on the contrary thinking stopped right still then . . ." (376). Like Judith, in fact, Ellen, Clytie and Sutpen's first wife all seem to fall "into the space where the *daughter? daughter? daughter?* never had quite showed" (385-86).

It is in that space that we are reminded of the tenuous connections required by the making of history and patriarchy. Early in Mr. Compson's story, for instance, we are told that Ellen retreats to her room in

"bewildered and uncomprehending amazement" after Henry's mysterious interview with his father and his abrupt disappearance from
Sutpen's Hundred (103). And even though Mr. Compson seeks an explanation for that disappearance in the existence of Charles Bon's octoroon mistress, the tentative nature of that conclusion is made clear by
the repeated coupling of Ellen's baffled retreat with Henry's furious
departure from Sutpen's domain. Even more resistant to explanation
are Judith and Clytie, whose elusiveness defeats the best storytelling
efforts of both Mr. Compson and Rosa Coldfield. For both narrators,
Judith and Clytie resist the categories that fit so easily into the narrative of patriarchal history-making—dutiful daughter, eager betrothed,
faithful servant, obedient retainer. Rather, they are women whose most
characteristic traits are their contradictions. To Mr. Compson Judith is
"absolutely impenetrable, absolutely serene: no mourning, not even
grief" (157). So elusive is she that she seems to subvert the very order
of narrative sequence, for Mr. Compson tells us that she is a "*daughter
doomed to spinsterhood who had chosen spinsterhood already before
there was anyone named Charles Bon since the aunt who came to suc-
cor her in bereavement and sorrow found neither but instead that calm
absolutely impenetrable face*" (228). Similarly, Clytie is anything but a
mere servant, especially to Rosa Coldfield, to whom the black woman
is "*perverse inscrutable and paradox: free, yet incapable of freedom
who had never once called herself a slave . . .*" (195).

More to the point, the sudden entry of these women into the narratives of the dominant story often undermines the best efforts of the narrators to establish sequence and continuity. In the early part of Compson's story, for instance, Judith serves primarily as "the blank shape,
the empty vessel" in which Charles Bon and Henry seek each other and
themselves (148). But when Compson recounts the episode in which
Judith bestows Charles Bon's letter upon General Compson's wife—
the first time, incidentally, that Judith moves to the narrative center—
the storytelling abruptly breaks, and we as readers are returned to the
year 1909 and the Compson porch, where Quentin and his father are

talking. Similarly disruptive is Clytie in Rosa's second round of story-telling. It is Clytie who stands between Rosa and Judith on the stairs of Sutpen's Hundred the day Charles Bon is killed, and it is her presence, described by Rosa as "*that furious yet absolutely rocklike and immobile antagonism*," which stops Rosa in her headlong rush up the stairs and even shifts her narrative back to the days of the courtship of Judith and Charles Bon (170). And as if Clytie's interruption were not enough, Judith appears at the stairs and utters a single word, "Clytie," the sound of which once again shifts Rosa's story back into the past to that early "summer of wistaria," when she silently dogs Judith's and Bon's footsteps. Even that brief recovery of memory is checked by Judith's second response on the stairs, "*Yes, Rosa?*"—a question that returns Rosa to the moment on the stairs and, as she observes herself, enters "*calmly into the midstride of my running*" (186).

Equally striking are the unexpected breaks preceded by brief mention of that elusive first wife in the stories told by Sutpen of his early days on the Haitian plantation. For as Quentin tells Shreve, Sutpen's story, told to General Compson during the hunt for the escaped French architect, suddenly stops with the young entrepreneur's engagement to the daughter of his Haitian employer. It is at this stage of the narrative, Quentin says, that Sutpen "stopped talking, telling it" (318). It would be thirty years before Sutpen would pick up the narrative thread and continue the telling of the story to General Compson. And when the latter finally relates his decision to put aside his wife, not just Sutpen's story is broken off. Quentin's narration is interrupted as well; we return to the scene of storytelling at Harvard in 1909. The story that Quentin and Shreve then tell together jumps ahead twenty-eight years.

Indeed, both that first wife and Clytie threaten to bring these stories—and, implicitly, the making of history—to a precipitous end. It is "the old Sabine," after all, who is pictured by Quentin and Shreve as brooding on vengeance and Sutpen's eventual downfall (378). According to the history they construct, she may—or may not—be plotting the meeting of Sutpen and Charles Bon that promises to reveal the secrets of Sutpen's past and to destroy his dynasty—in short, to bring his history to an abrupt halt by cutting through delays, hesitations and pleas for time to prolong history's making. So subversive is her presence (or nonpresence, as the case may be) that we cannot even be certain she actually exists. As the third-person narrator of *Absalom, Absalom!* notes, she and her calculating lawyer are fabrications created by Quentin and Shreve, "people who perhaps had never existed at all anywhere, who, shadows, were shadows not of flesh and blood which had lived and died but shadows in turn of what were . . . shades too" (379). Indeed, the "old Sabine" is one of the most conspicuous empty spaces in the narrative, a character whose very name occupies no place in the round of stories. Only in the third-person narrator's "Genealogy" is her name given as "Eulalia Bon" (475). If she lives at all, it is in the shifting frontier between history and its making, and as such, the shadow she casts upon Sutpen's story reminds us of its fictionality, of the arbitrary connections and order it seeks to make.

Most subversive of all, though, is Clytie, who brings an end to the history of the House of Sutpen by setting fire to the manor. She does so in part to keep the dying Henry Sutpen, now sequestered in the house, from being arrested for the long-ago murder of Charles Bon, but her action also succeeds in preventing Henry from telling and retelling the story of the Sutpens. For it is a story that seems to beg to be told and retold as suggested in that hypnotic encounter between Henry and Quentin the night that Rosa and Quentin travel to Sutpen's Hundred. Thinking back on the night, Quentin fears that "waking or sleeping it was the same and would be the same forever as long as he lived" (464). Again and again he hears himself ask Henry who he is, how long he has been there and why he has returned home, and repeatedly the troubled young man hears Henry's answers. Clytie's action, though, brings an end to the telling and retelling of stories and the making of history, as Rosa, one of those makers of history, recognizes as she desperately fights off the men pulling her out of the burning house.

Not for nothing, then, does Mr. Compson early on suggest that perhaps Clytie's name should really be Cassandra, "to designate the presiding augur of . . . [Sutpen's] disaster" (74). One of the most silent characters in the text as a whole, her very presence serves to contradict the "forensic" and "oratorical" swaggering upon which Thomas Sutpen relies to define himself and his patriarchal design. She is, in fact, nearly the opposite of her progenitor Raby in "Evangeline," a short story predating the writing of *Absalom, Absalom!* and offering an early version of the Sutpen saga.[4] Unlike Raby, who tells the story of Judith, Charles Bon and Henry Sutpen to an irreverent first-person narrator, Clytie has no words to offer to the making of Sutpen's story. She is, rather, one of the contradictions and anomalies inadvertently left over by Sutpen's patriarchal design and by the making of history. Ultimately, she is, like the other Sutpen women, the empty space providing not just the tools for making patriarchy and narrative but also the breaks, discontinuities and precipitous endings bringing that effort to a close.

Therefore, we would do well to remember that what is *not* told in a story like Thomas Sutpen's may be as important as what *is* told. For if, as de Lauretis suggests, an oedipal or patriarchal narrative conceives of the subject and movement of the tale as masculine and of the space and setting as feminine, the space may hold just as much portent for the movement of the masculine subject. By paying attention to those empty spaces, breaks and margins in *Absalom, Absalom!* and by resisting earlier characterizations of the text as a story primarily about Sutpen and his narrators, we discover a narrative that unravels almost as quickly as it is woven and history that is unmade nearly as soon as it is made. We also discover that those women characters who have been the subject of so much anguished commentary may indeed be more subversive than they appear through the eyes of earlier critics. For what we learn in the end from such a double reading, one that concentrates both on what *is* told and *not* told, is not just the seductions of patriarchy but its limits and weaknesses as well.

From *Southern Quarterly* 26 (Summer 1988): 19-32. Copyright © 1988 by University of Southern Mississippi. Reprinted with permission of University of Southern Mississippi.

Notes

1. A summary of the conference paper on which this article is based appeared as "Subverting History: Women and Narrative in *Absalom, Absalom!*" in *Commemorating the Past: Celebrations and Retrospection*, Southeastern American Studies Conference Proceedings 1987, ed. Don Harkness (Tampa, FL: American Studies Press. 1987): 37-40. I should also note here my thanks to Professor Noel Polk of the University of Southern Mississippi and Professor Walter Wenska of the College of William and Mary, both of whom took time out to read and comment on an earlier version of the essay.

2. See, for example, the essays in *William Faulkner's* Absalom, Absalom! *A Critical Casebook* (Muhlenfeld, ed.). A notable exception in this respect is Deborah L. Clarke's fine article, "Familiar and Fantastic: Women in *Absalom, Absalom!*"

3. I am indebted to Professor Wenska for this insight.

4. For background on the writing of "Evangeline" and *Absalom, Absalom!* in general, see Muhlenfeld (xi-xxxix) and Joseph Blotner's note on "Evangeline" in Faulkner's *Uncollected Stories* (709).

Works Cited

Barthes, Roland. *The Pleasure of the Text*. Trans. Richard Miller. New York: Hill and Wang, 1975.

Brooks, Peter. *Reading for the Plot: Desire and Intention in Narrative*. 1984. New York: Vintage. 1985.

Clarke, Deborah L. "Familiar and Fantastic: Women in *Absalom, Absalom!*" *Faulkner Journal* 2 (1986): 62-72.

Culler, Jonathan. *On Deconstruction: Theory and Criticism after Structuralism*. Ithaca: Cornell UP. 1982,

De Lauretis, Teresa. *Alice Doesn't: Feminism, Semiotics, Cinema*. Bloomington: Indiana UP. 1984.

Duvall, John N. "Faulkner's Critics and Women: The Voice of the Community." *Faulkner and Women: Faulkner and Yoknapatawpha, 1985*. Ed. Doreen Fowler and Ann J. Abadie. Jackson: UP of Mississippi, 1986.

Faulkner, William. *Absalom, Absalom!* Corrected text. 1986. New York: Vintage, 1987.

_____. *Uncollected Stories*. Ed. Joseph Blotner. New York: Vintage. 1981.

Fetterley, Judith. *The Resisting Reader: A Feminist Approach to American Fiction*. Bloomington: Indiana UP 1978.

Flynn, Elizabeth A., and Patrocinio P. Schweickart, eds. *Gender and Reading: Essays on Readers, Texts, and Contexts*. Baltimore: Johns Hopkins UP, 1986.

Geismar, Maxwell. *Writers in Crisis: The American Novel between Two Wars*. Boston: Houghton Mifflin. 1942.

Guerard, Albert J. *The Triumph of the Novel: Dickens, Dostoevsky, Faulkner*. New York: Oxford UP, 1976.

Meese, Elizabeth. *Crossing the Double-Cross: The Practice of Feminist Criticism*. Chapel Hill: U of North Carolina P, 1986.

Muhlenfeld, Elisabeth, ed. *William Faulkner's* Absalom, Absalom! *Critical Casebook*. New York: Garland, 1984.

Schweickart, Patrocinio P. "Reading Ourselves: Toward a Feminist Theory of Reading." Flynn and Schweickart 31-62.

Showalter, Elaine. "Feminist Criticism in the Wilderness." *The New Feminist Criticism: Essays on Women, Literature, and Theory*. Ed. Elaine Showalter. New York: Pantheon, 1985. 243-70.

Absalom, Absalom!:
Story-Telling as a Mode of Transcendence _____

Richard Forrer

"The past is never dead. It's not even past," says Gavin Stevens in *Requiem for a Nun*, and therewith summarizes the basic dilemma that confronts many of William Faulkner's characters, especially those in *Absalom, Absalom!* In this novel, the Southern narrators—Mr. Compson, his son Quentin, and Rosa Coldfield—relive a past which they believe has irreparably ruined their lives. This belief shapes their imaginative re-creations of the Sutpen saga. As a consequence these accounts of the past often resemble chanted lamentations for a hopeless future. The reality of the past in *Absalom, Absalom!* is determined no less by the narrators' state of consciousness than by the known "facts" about the past. Herein lies one of the novel's major problems as well as one of its principal themes: the relationship between the present and past. Are there such things as pure "facts"—unconditioned by imaginative interpretation—which "speak for themselves" to thereby disclose the reality of the past, or is the reality of the past ultimately the imaginative creation of our present concerns?

Faulkner's treatment of this problem in *Absalom, Absalom!* is ambiguous.[1] On the one hand, the people in the novel seem able to gain access to the reality of the past only through the imaginative re-creation of events. On the other hand, there are several "facts" about the Sutpens which the narrators use to guide their reconstructions of the past. These facts include Sutpen's scheme to rise above his impoverished circumstances, Wash Jones's murder of Sutpen, Etienne Bon's public fights with whites and blacks, Henry's murder of Charles Bon, and a letter that has neither salutation nor signature.[2] However, like the letter, none of these facts speaks for itself. Each retains an aura of mystery that invites—even necessitates—imaginative conjecture for understanding it. These ambiguities in Faulkner's treatment of the relationship between the present and past in *Absalom, Absalom!* are clearly demonstrated in Quentin's unexpected encounter with Henry Sutpen at the Sutpen mansion.

This episode is given to us only in part. Quentin enters a tomb-like room and sees Henry on his deathbed, "the wasted yellow face with closed, almost transparent eyelids on the pillow, the wasted hands crossed on the breast as if he were already a corpse" (373).[3] It is as though Quentin were seeing in Henry the condensed residue of the past offering itself for Quentin's careful inspection, but finally stunning Quentin with its utter incomprehensibility.

> *And you are———?*
> *Henry Sutpen.*
> *And you have been here———?*
> *Four years.*
> *And you came home———?*
> *To die. Yes.*
> *To die?*
> *Yes. To die.*
> *And you have been here———?*
> *Four years.*
> *And you are———?*
> *Henry Sutpen.* (373)

In this brief scene, "fact" and "reality," "past" and "present" are incarnated in the person of Henry Sutpen. Faulkner clearly presents Henry's emaciation as a living image of the gradual and inexorable wastage of life that is perhaps, for Faulkner, the ultimately discoverable "fact" of Southern history. Certainly this fact finally leads Quentin to join others in their efforts to imaginatively re-create the reality of the past. In this novel, the past becomes a series of often conflicting imaginative constructs which the narrators themselves accept as truthful visions of reality. Fact and interpretation are virtually one for these narrators. Hence it is difficult—if not impossible at many points—for either the narrators or reader to distinguish the past as it actually was from the past that is an imaginative creation. But important as this difficulty is, it points further to the fundamental problem that forms the real dramatic center of interest in the narrative careers of Mr. Compson, Quentin, and Rosa Coldfield: namely, do these imaginative constructs provide them any means at all for transcending their paralyzing obsession with the failures of the past? This, then, is the problem proposed for examination in this essay. However, no reading of *Absalom, Absalom!* can ignore its structural complexities. It is important to demonstrate first how such elements in the novel as its involuted language, fragmented narrational structure, disjointed chronological framework, superimposed times, oral traditions, and diffused "omniscient narrator" complicate Faulkner's treatment of his characters, their plights, and the relationships among them.

I

One of the most striking structural elements in this novel is the language itself.[4] Communication between the narrators is difficult, if only because they use a dense, involuted language which strains and batters at discovering meaning in human actions. The harder these people struggle to communicate with each other, the more isolated they become, miring themselves in a quicksand of sentences. General Compson gives memorable expression to his sense of isolation when he describes language as "that meager and fragile thread . . . by which the little surface corners and edges of men's secret and solitary lives may be joined for an instant now and then before sinking back into the darkness . . ." (251). A brief scene involving two of the story's (now dead) figures dramatizes this seemingly unbridgeable gap. Thomas Sutpen and Wash Jones (who has murdered Sutpen) are lounging and talking in the great scuppernong arbor in the sky when a shadow disturbs their otherwise shadowless paradise. The creator of this humorous scene, Shreve McCannon, imagines how Sutpen *"would stop talk-*

ing and Jones would stop guffawing and they would look at one another, groping, grave, intent, and [Sutpen] would say, 'What was it, Wash? Something happened. What was it?' and Jones . . . groping too, sober too, saying, 'I dont know, Kernel. Whut?' each watching the other" (186).

A second element, the novel's fragmented narrative structure, reinforces this sense of people unable to communicate with one another. Faulkner's method of "multiple narrators,"[5] with its continuous shifting of narrative viewpoint, presents a busy ethos of minds swaying, grasping, bumping in hydra-like fashion as they together seek to mold the Sutpen saga into a rationally comprehensible story about the past. At the outset, this labyrinth of narratives appears to reflect a community of people knit together by their common interest in understanding the rise and fall of the Sutpen family, but it soon becomes apparent that the narrators are unable to sustain any positive sense of community among themselves. *Absalom, Absalom!* dramatizes the increasingly divisive and disintegrating impact the Sutpen saga—itself a mirror of Southern history[6]—has upon narrators who are already alienated from each other.

Furthermore, these narrators are unreliable, as Faulkner himself admits.[7] Their narratives consequently give rise to distorted, sometimes conflicting, portraits of Sutpen and his family.[8] These interpretations not only disclose each narrator's character and different aspects of Sutpen, but also directly involve the reader in the narrators' efforts to make sense of the Sutpen saga. The reader experiences the plight of the narrators and must himself seek his own solution for it. Faulkner suggests his artistic intention in this regard when he describes Sutpen as being

> a little too big for people no greater in stature than Quentin and Miss Rosa and Mr. Compson to see all at once. It would have taken perhaps a wiser or more tolerant or more sensitive or more thoughtful person to see him as he was. It was . . . thirteen ways of looking at a blackbird. But the truth, I

would like to think, comes out . . . when the reader has read all these thirteen different ways of looking at the blackbird, [and then] the reader has his own fourteenth image of that blackbird which I would like to think is the truth.[9]

The reader himself is saddled with the narrators' unfinished task of learning the truth about Sutpen. To achieve this end, however, he must first seek to understand the narrators—their values, shaping concerns, and limitations—in order to compare and contrast their various interpretations and finally synthesize them into his own imaginative vision of Sutpen. This strongly reinforces what the novel itself suggests: that, for Faulkner, only our imaginative grasp of those obsessive concerns which shape our present lives enables us to repossess the truth about the past.

However, the reader's effort to formulate an accurate, or truthful, picture of Sutpen encounters a further difficulty in a third structural element: the novel's disjointed chronological framework. The reader, like Jefferson, first sees Sutpen in mid-career, and, in chapters 2-4, Mr. Compson narrates how a community increasingly hostile to Sutpen generates rumors and stories—which later become legends—to explain his mysterious appearance and unconventional behavior. Not until late in the novel—chapter 7—does the reader learn of Sutpen's origins, and this account comes from Sutpen himself. The chronological line of narration is further jumbled when each of the narrators, in accordance with his own preoccupations, selectively focuses his attention on isolated episodes. Faulkner complicates this general scrambling of events by dividing the novel into nearly equal halves—chapters 1-5 and chapters 6-9—which comprise two widely separated days in the life of Quentin Compson. In chapters 1-5, the actual present is a Sunday afternoon in Jefferson during September, 1909. Quentin, who already knows Sutpen's story in its general outlines, unwillingly hears it again, first from Rosa Coldfield, then from his father, as each seeks to understand the past failures of their tradition. These older narrators gradually abandon any concern for sequential time—indeed they gradually discard all distinctions between present and past time—as they increasingly articulate their belief that the present is nothing more than an image of the ruined past. However, it is not until the second half of the novel that the chronological framework completely collapses, and events—and people—typically appear before the narrators' eyes like uncontrollable apparitions. The setting in chapters 6-9 is Quentin's Harvard room during a winter's night in January, 1910, as Quentin tries to shape the Sutpen saga into a comprehensible picture of the South for Shreve. But Sutpen's story is like a string of knotted mysteries, and Quentin's mind simultaneously flits against all of them, seeking to unravel them together at one time, thereby creating a jagged, involuted line of narration. It is as though this effort to explain his Southern heritage to an outsider destroys all logical connections, all rational categories, and moves him (with Shreve) into a timeless oneiric realm where truth reveals itself through the dramatic form of symbolic enactments. In this realm, the narrators experience a simultaneity of past and present which often makes them and the characters they re-create virtually indistinguishable, so that the reader finds it increasingly hard to determine whether the novel actually renders a factual picture of the past, or whether, for Faulkner, the importance of the Sutpen saga resides in the various ways it mirrors the inner landscape of the narrators.

Moreover, the meager supply of known facts hampers any effort to distinguish between fact and hearsay, between true and false conjectures.[10] By and large, the narrators must rely upon the extensive oral tradition handed down through the Compson family. This tradition includes Rosa's outraged account of her past relationship to Sutpen (which she repeats to Quentin) and the conjectures of both General Compson and Mr. Compson. Quentin and Shreve later use these materials, and sometimes alter them in accordance with new conjectures based on their own adolescent concerns. However, all the narrators also have access to Sutpen's own brief account of himself which he tells General Compson, his only friend in Jefferson. Sutpen describes his upbringing in the West Virginia mountains, his family's migration to the Tidewater region where they live in poverty on the plantation of his father's employer, his first exposure to slavery, his sense of insult when a Negro servant tells him that he must always go to the back door of the plantation house, his consequent plan—his "vast kingly dream"—to rectify this insult, his life and marriage in Haiti, his abandonment of his first wife and mulatto son, and his perplexity regarding the mysterious appearance of Charles Bon, whose presence—according to the aging Sutpen—threatens to collapse his otherwise successfully realized plan.[11] These, then, are some major facts about Sutpen's own inner life which the reader—if he accepts the reliability of General Compson's account of them—can use to evaluate the plausibility of some reconstructed portions of Sutpen's career. Nevertheless, very little, if anything, so definite is known about other events in the Sutpen saga. For information regarding these events, the reader, like the narrators, must turn to "the rag-tag and bob-ends of old tales and talking" (303)—that pastiche of gossip, legends, and surmises which emerges as the residents of Jefferson seek to explain Sutpen and his family's tragedy.

However, the reader has some valuable help in this regard. For among the many narrators, there is an almost unnoticeable presiding presence—a special kind of omniscient narrator—who makes many important distinctions between reality and the various distortions of it.[12] Although this narrator typically appears in disconnected patches throughout the story, he does sustain a stable presence in chapter 1, the first half of chapter 2, and the last chapter. The narrative maze is thus sandwiched between two sections marked by this narrator's stabilizing and clarifying sense of reality. Since the importance of this narrator has virtually gone unnoticed in the critical literature, a brief treatment of his complex role is in order.[13]

The omniscient narrator has traditionally always told a story as though he already knew the characters prior to the act of telling itself.

This narrator, however, typically presents the characters in *Absalom, Absalom!* as though he were seeing them for the first time, and he often seeks to learn more about them by imaginatively becoming their way of seeing and experiencing life. Like Ishmael in *Moby Dick*, this narrator assumes various guises in order to imaginatively feel—or "to see feelingly"[14]—human possibilities other than his own. Unlike Ishmael, however, this narrator takes on no definite outline in the story itself. Rather, he remains a kind of free-floating sensibility, a fluctuating tone of voice, which periodically deflates, directly or indirectly, various exaggerations by the narrators. For example, after Rosa gives her first hectic account of Sutpen, in which she portrays the people of the antebellum South as heroic figures (14-30), the narrator parodies this notion of an heroic past (31). Moreover, his own account of Sutpen (31-43) is marked by a restrained tone and balanced perspective which Rosa lacks. And his description of Sutpen's heroic qualities, unlike Rosa's, renders neither a positive nor negative judgment.

Quite often, however, this narrator evaluates the viewpoints of others in a more explicit way. Sometimes he simply contradicts another narrator; at other times he immediately affirms that what a narrator has just said is true—or essentially true—or else, by way of corroboration, he sometimes later repeats what another has earlier said; on other occasions, most notably during the extended guesswork of Quentin and Shreve, he only says of their conjectures that "maybe," or "perhaps," or "probably" they are true, or else he altogether discounts them. This procedure cautions the reader against a too ready acceptance of their account. Occasionally this narrator also warns the reader about important flaws or limitations in another narrator's sense of reality. He pictures Quentin, for example, as being too young to be an astute observer of others—as possessing "that state of virginity which is neither boy's nor girl's" (324)—and he describes the note Rosa sends Quentin "as revealing a character cold, implacable, and even ruthless" (10). (There are many such instances in which the narrator looks to externals—for example, houses, furniture, clothes, postures, handwriting—for revelations of character.) But Rosa's family has also victimized her, according to the narrator, whose sympathetic description of her childhood as a criminal choking of the spirit leads him to call her "a crucified child" (8). He typically makes simplistic moral judgments—even about Sutpen—impossible, and it is to him the reader must look to discover any reliable spiritual norms in the fictional world of *Absalom, Absalom!*

But another noteworthy feature of this novel is that the narrator's normative status in no way exempts him from the plight of the other narrators. He too experiences the corrosive impact of the Sutpen saga, which fragments his presence throughout the middle portion of the novel. However, the narrator's periodic appearances do help in various ways to restore the reader's bearings in a world of slanted perceptions, thereby creating the impression that he is slowly unwinding a reality from its corkscrewed encasement in distorted perceptions.[15] Sometimes the narrator separates the conflicting views of Sutpen and notes significant omissions. Such clarifications not only alert the reader to the possibility of other unmentioned omissions; they also encourage, even require, the reader's interpretive activity. As Conrad Aiken puts it: "The reader must simply make up his mind to go to work, and in a sense to cooperate."[16] Occasionally this narrator also offers his own interpretation of a character or event, as is exemplified in his statement that the South lost the Civil War because of its rigid adherence to aristocratic values in military matters (345-46). At other times he comments on the nature of the relationships between the various narrators, between each narrator and the Sutpens, and between the Sutpens themselves. A memorable example of such commentary is the narrator's description of Sutpen's homecoming after the Civil War: the starkness of gesture and word has the ring of Greek tragedy. Judith

met [Sutpen] on his return, not with the fury and despair perhaps which he might have expected even though knowing as little, having learned as little, about women as Mr. Compson said he had, yet certainly with something

---

other than the icy calm with which, according to Miss Coldfield, she met him—the kiss again after almost two years, on the brow; the voices, the speeches, quiet, contained, almost impersonal: 'And ——?' 'Yes. Henry killed him' followed by the brief tears which ceased on the instant when they began, as if the moisture consisted of a single sheet or layer thin as a cigarette paper and in the shape of a human face; the 'Ah, Clytie. Ah, Rosa. —— Well, Wash. I was unable to penetrate far enough behind the Yankee lines to cut a piece from that coat tail as I promised you' . . . and that was all. He had returned. (277-78)

The narrator here repeats a scene previously described by Rosa Coldfield (159), thereby creating a corrective, normative account of this past episode—but without clarifying for us the enigmatic relationships among Sutpen, Judith, Henry, and Charles Bon.[17] He stands with the other narrators before the sphinx-like reality of the Sutpen family, which also resists his own efforts to understand it. It is as though Sutpen's story surrounds him, absorbs him, and so thoroughly disperses his own outward-pushing interpretation that it finally appears only as a fabric of unlinked patches. His own narrative career dramatizes the extreme difficulties which, in spite of his omniscience, the Sutpen tragedy poses for any effort—no matter how insistent—to transcend its divisive and corrosive impact upon the present. In this novel, the ultimately discoverable fact about Southern history is its paralyzing capacity for trapping people within ritual-like recitations of the past. Mr. Compson, Quentin, and Rosa are locked into viewing the present through their image of the past and the problem facing them is whether their obsessive focus on this image can create a mode of understanding that would finally enable them to transcend this debilitating image.

Such a possibility is in fact realized in three imagined episodes: Mr. Compson's sympathetic rendering of Etienne Bon's tragic career, his moving account of Wash Jones's disillusionment and death, and Quentin's (and Shreve's) reliving of Henry Sutpen's decision to kill

Charles Bon. In these scenes, as nowhere else in the novel, the past is so clearly evoked, and so quivers with life, that the reality portrayed seems unquestionably true. And yet it is worth noting that these are scenes wherein historical fact and reality are supremely the creations of the embittered imagination—creations of that outrage and impotence that hamstring the lives of Quentin and his father.

II

Throughout his narrative, Mr. Compson variously expresses his bitter sense of being buried alive within an unwanted fate. He considers himself the unjust victim of the Civil War, which reduced his aristocratic family to middle-class status. Life no longer holds together for him; it is "full of sound and fury, signifying nothing"—a phrase he often quotes, or amply echoes, in his meditations on the Sutpen family. He gives this sense of meaninglessness striking expression in his complaint that before the Civil War men had an heroic stature which the complexities of modern life now deny him: "Yes . . . [they were] people too as we are, and victims too as we are, but victims of a different circumstance, simpler and therefore, integer for integer, larger, more heroic and the figures therefore more heroic too, not dwarfed and involved but distinct, uncomplex who had the gift of loving once or dying once instead of being diffused and scattered creatures drawn blindly limb from limb from a grab bag and assembled . . ." (89). The belief that he is a malformed puppet of fate is Mr. Compson's nemesis. The only redeeming feature of this belief is that it enables him to sympathetically render the outrage and hurt of persons like Wash Jones and Charles Bon's mulatto son, Etienne Bon, who are the social and economic victims of a discriminatory society. Mr. Compson in fact creates two of the novel's most memorable episodes when—like the narrator himself—he imaginatively relives another's way of seeing and feeling life.

In his account of Etienne Bon, Mr. Compson dramatizes a life irreparably ruined by Etienne's youthful discovery "that he [is], must be, a negro" (198). Etienne lives a sheltered life in New Orleans until the age of twelve (the year is 1871), when Clytie brings him to Sutpen's Hundred. Although the boy could have passed for white, Clytie and Judith nevertheless raise him as a Negro. Mr. Compson imaginatively renders the boy experiencing this reversal of fate as a fall from paradise—where he was exposed to racial hatred—into a world which, "*through no fault nor willing of [his] own*," dooms him to a disprized existence (198). The "shard of broken mirror" which Judith found beneath his mattress leads Mr. Compson further to imagine Etienne spending "hours of amazed and tearless grief . . . before it, examining himself . . . with quiet and incredulous incomprehension" (199). Disbelief and bewilderment—these later turn into anger and fatalistic desperation, according to Mr. Compson, who movingly describes Etienne's pathetic efforts to regain his lost sense of dignity: his teenage fights with the Negroes at Sutpen's Hundred, his marriage to a "coal black" woman whom he flaunts before Negroes and whites alike, his painful ritual of provoking severe beatings from both whites and Negroes, and his refusal of Judith's (presumed) offer to take care of his wife and child, Jim Bond, so that he can move elsewhere and pass for white.[18] Mr. Compson here creates a picture of hopeless striving surpassed only by his portrayal of Wash Jones, which exhibits a similar sensitivity to the struggles of others against an unwanted fate.

Wash Jones, the drinking companion of Thomas Sutpen, is an ill-mannered, ignorant, guffawing, malaria-ridden "poor white" who, in Mr. Compson's account, views Sutpen as the model of perfect manhood. Sutpen is, to borrow Mr. Compson's words, Wash's "own lonely apotheosis" (282)—the embodiment of those aspirations Wash can never realize within the Southern caste system. Mr. Compson even imagines Wash casting Sutpen on horseback into an image of deity: "*If God Himself was to come down and ride the natural earth, that's what He would aim to look like*" (282). By means of these words, Mr. Compson simultaneously posits in Wash's character both a deep awareness of the unbridgeable distance between himself and Sutpen, who is at the top of the social order, and an unqualified trust in Sutpen's integrity, which Wash expresses in response to Sutpen's courtship of his thirteen-year-old granddaughter, Milly. "'I know that whatever your hands tech,'" he tells Sutpen (in a conversation which General Compson overhears), "'whether hit's a regiment of men or a ignorant gal or just a hound dog, that you will make hit right'" (284). One year later, Milly and Sutpen's mare give birth on the same day; Sutpen first checks the mare, then visits Milly; and, upon learning that Milly's child is not the male heir he wants, Sutpen tells her: "'Well, Milly; too bad you're not a mare too. Then I could give you a decent stall in the stable'" (286). The midwife later reports that Wash overhears these words while waiting outside Milly's cabin. Mr. Compson imagines their impact: ". . . for a second Wash must not have felt the very earth under his feet while he watched Sutpen emerge from the house, the riding whip in his hand, thinking quietly, like in a dream: *I kaint have heard what I know I heard. I just know I kaint* thinking *That was what got him up. It was that colt. It aint me or mine either. It wasn't even his own that got him out of bed*" (288). Overwhelmed by anger, hurt, and disillusionment, Wash kills Sutpen with Sutpen's own rusty scythe. Like Mr. Compson, Wash is now past sixty—"old, too old," Mr. Compson says, "to run far even if he were to run who could never escape" the "men of Sutpen's own kind" (289-90). Mr. Compson's moving portrayal of Wash—sitting alone in the cabin window waiting for the sheriff, realizing the impossibility of escape, and finally rising above his circumstances by choosing his manner of death—resembles a vicarious effort on Mr. Compson's part to imaginatively express a protest against his own fatalistic sense that uncontrollable forces have doomed him to a meaningless life. Indeed he so deeply resonates with Wash's predicament that at several points in his narrative Mr. Compson virtually becomes Wash Jones, as, for example, in the following soliloquy addressed to Sutpen's body.

Old Wash Jones come a tumble at last. He thought he had Sutpen, but Sutpen fooled him. . . . 'But I never expected that, Kernel! You know I never! . . . You know I never expected or asked or wanted nothing from arra living man but what I expected from you. And I never asked that. I didn't think hit would need' . . . thinking *Better if his kind and mine too had never drawn the breath of life on this earth. Better that all who remain of us be blasted from the face of it than that another Wash Jones should see his whole life shredded from him and shrivel away like a dried shuck thrown onto the fire.* (290-91)

Mr. Compson here imaginatively expresses a common bond with Wash in his betrayal by that cultural ideal he fully trusts—a betrayal which, as Mr. Compson renders it, empties his life of all meaning and thereby evokes Wash's uncompromising defiance: a terrifying and indiscriminate unleashing of his fury. When the posse arrives, Wash decapitates the child and Milly, rushes out of the cabin to where the scythe lies, and, arms uplifted, runs toward the gathered knot of men:

> "running into the lanterns so that now they could see the scythe raised above his head; they could see his face, his eyes too, as he ran with the scythe above his head, straight into the lanterns and the gun barrels, making no sound, no outcry while [sheriff] de Spain ran backward before hint, saying, 'Jones! Stop! Stop, or I'll kill you. Jones! Jones! *Jones!*'" (292)

In one grand tragic image, Wash—the mute, unanswerable apotheosis of the South's lower classes—vents an impotent outrage against social betrayals for which there seems no redress but choosing an acceptable death. The careers of Wash Jones and Etienne Bon dramatize the wastage of life made inevitable by a caste system that forecloses, or destroys, all possibilities for communication between Negroes and whites and between upper- and lower-class whites.

Mr. Compson's narrative suggests, however, a constructive way for making such communication possible in the present (i.e., 1909). There can be no gainsaying that Mr. Compson occasionally expresses an oblique, if not direct, commitment to those class distinctions inherited from his aristocratic upbringing. He nevertheless hurdles these distinctions when his sympathetic rendering of socially defined inferiors makes their responses to society seem both logical and justifiable. In the cruel fates that others suffer, he sees bleaker and more pitiable visions of his own unwanted destiny, and he envisions Etienne and Wash as the irreparably injured victims of society who suffer the tragic price of struggling against forces beyond their control. His tragic fatalism thus becomes a spiritual bond with others that enables him to realize a common humanity that transcends all racial and social distinctions. In this sense, Mr. Compson's narrative career gives credence to the narrator's claim—which directly contravenes Mr. Compson's fatalism—that self-transcendence is possible because men have within themselves a spiritual reality that transcends—and requires their transcending—all social and cultural barriers (258). Mr. Compson never recognizes his accomplishment for what it is; rather, he views his imaginative renderings of Etienne and Wash as proofs that further substantiate his paralyzing belief that history inevitably deposits men into unacceptable fates where they remain stranded without any means of transcendence, except death.

No less than his father, Quentin Compson also experiences life as an unscalable grave. Quentin is less a person than a severely disoriented state of consciousness evoked by relatives and neighbors who constantly impose upon him, willy-nilly, haunting images of the past. The narrator likens Quentin to "an empty hall echoing with sonorous defeated names; he was not a being, an entity, he was a commonwealth. He was a barracks filled with stubborn back-looking ghosts still recovering" from the Civil War (12). Quentin seeks to escape this inherited past by enrolling at Harvard, only to discover that Northerners like Shreve will not let him forget his Southern heritage. "*Tell* [me] *about the South*," Shreve demands. "*What's it like there. What do they do there. Why do they live there. Why do they live at all*" (174). The "burden of southern history" here becomes for Quentin a curse upon his own life, and throughout his narrative, Quentin increasingly despairs of having any other future except the dreary prospect of "forever" hearing—and answering—such demands that he justify his existence (277, 373). His ritualistic retelling of Sutpen's story mirrors his search for anything trustworthy that would promise him release, now or later, from this curse. But this quest only issues in his bleak vision of an endless cycle of repeated events—what he calls *"the old ineradicable rhythm"* of history (261)—that denies him any means of spiritual transcendence.[19] The model of ultimate reality for Quentin is an insurmountable history that buries him alive in the crypt of the past.

The failure of Quentin's quest derives in part from his reliance on language itself. He must use words to define, or locate, the reality he seeks; but this reality, as the narrator himself indicates with his metaphor of the Mississippi River (258), beggars description. Quentin finds it difficult enough, if not impossible, to make his words even yield a somewhat comprehensible image of the deepest human realities in his Southern heritage. Like many of Faulkner's characters, Quentin struggles with the realization—to borrow Addie Bundren's words from *As I Lay Dying*—that "words dont ever fit even what they are trying to say at."[20] Language becomes for Quentin the symbol of man's hopelessness, which he explicitly affirms by twice quoting his grandfather's definition of language as "that meager and fragile thread . . . by which the little surface corners and edges of men's secret and solitary lives may be joined for an instant now and then before sinking back into the darkness. . . ."

But an equally important factor for understanding Quentin's failure is that his heritage itself remains a stumbling-block to any sympathetic relationship between himself and Shreve. Shreve initially views the Civil War as the theatrical embodiment of a farcical way of life. The South's history is an incomprehensible three-ring circus to Shreve, who eventually reduces Sutpen's entire career to the quest for a grandson, and then quips: "'Jesus the South is fine, isn't it. It's better than the theatre, isn't it. It's better than Ben Hur, isn't it'" (217). Their differing cultural backgrounds hinder any mutuality of response. Nevertheless, Shreve at times genuinely seeks to bridge the gulf between them. "I . . . want to understand [the South's history] if I can. . . . Because it's something my people haven't got. Or if we have got it, it all happened long ago across the water and so now there aint anything to look at every day to remind us of it" (361). Although they grope at overcoming the distances between themselves, the past tragedy they re-create, in which social distinctions destroy any possible reconciliation between Henry Sutpen and Charles Bon, ultimately recapitulates—indeed becomes identical with—the relationship between Quentin and Shreve wherein cultural barriers keep them at loggerheads.

Quentin and Shreve discover and pursue their mutual interest in the presumed love affair between Judith Sutpen and Charles Bon. Mr. Compson's account is their main source of information about Judith and Bon, but they substantially alter it in order to create a romantic story that expresses the way they want things to have been between Judith and Bon. For Mr. Compson, the picture he creates of Bon struggling against Sutpen's implacable refusal to acknowledge him as his son is only an unproven conjecture, but the boys accept and movingly render it as an established fact.[21] Moreover, Quentin and Shreve simply reject Mr. Compson's conjecture that Bon uses his (presumably) forthcoming marriage to Judith as a tool for wresting from Henry and Sutpen their acceptance of him as a brother and son. Rather, they re-create Bon in the image of a concerned lover who sacrifices his love for Judith's sake, thereby exonerating him of the charge that he cruelly abuses Judith's love. The remainder of their narrative, which unfolds with growing intensity in its portrayal of the racial conflict between Henry and Bon as it moves toward its tragic consummation, is thus an effort to show that Bon is true to his love for Judith. This interpretation is based upon Mr. Compson's report that on the day of Bon's murder Judith finds a picture of Bon's octoroon wife in the locket she (assumedly) gave him with her own picture in it, and Shreve presents

Judith's apparent lack of grief (which Rosa reports) as the result Bon seeks through a deliberate strategy. Bon switched the pictures, Shreve says, "because he said to himself, 'If Henry dont mean what he said, it will be all right; I can take it out and destroy it. But if he does mean what he said, it will be the only way I will have to say to her, *I was no good; do not grieve for me*'" (359).[22] Quentin agrees, as though he expects such self-deprecation toward a white woman from a Negro.[23] This interpretation, in which Bon honorably resolves his conflicting interests, becomes for Quentin and Shreve the means for salvaging something good from that tragic struggle between two races which finally dooms the Sutpen family to virtual extinction: the sole survivor is Jim Bond, Charles Bon's idiot grandson.

One important consequence of this salvaging process is the unusually intense intimacy it creates between Quentin and Shreve. The narrator describes them as two virgin lovers whose mode of telling the Sutpen saga becomes a "happy marriage of speaking and hearing wherein each before the demand, the requirement, forgave condoned and forgot the faulting of the other—faultings both in the creating of this shade whom they discussed (rather, existed in) and in the hearing and sifting and discarding the false and conserving what seemed true, or fit the preconceived—in order to overpass to love, where there might be paradox and inconsistency but nothing fault nor false" (316). However, this initial interest in love finally gives way to a more intense re-creation of Bon's relationship with Henry which enables Quentin and Shreve to realize a spiritual unity far more profound in implication. According to the narrator, Quentin and Shreve experience not only a oneness of blood, but also a mutual identity with Henry and Bon in which they are "transmogrified into the spirits' travail" of Bon and Henry (345), and thereby lose their pre-selected identities (Charles-Shreve and Henry-Quentin) (351). All distinctions between the present and past virtually disappear, all barriers of culture, race, and class are temporarily suspended—or hurdled—while they imaginatively act out the inevitable collision between two unyielding wills.[24] It is a most memorable episode which, in its starkness and dramatic economy, rivals the best scenes in Sophoclean tragedy wherein the characters, fully aware of the consequences to themselves, irrevocably affirm conflicting values.

The boys base their account on the well-established fact that Sutpen visited Henry at his camp during the final months of the Civil War. Otherwise most of their narrative is pure conjecture, since very little, if anything, is known about this portion of the Sutpen saga. They first speculate that Sutpen visits Henry in order to tell him that Bon is a mulatto,[25] and then imagine the crushing impact this disclosure must have had on Henry, who, according to their account, has long known that Bon is his brother without proscribing Bon's marriage to Judith. But Henry's fear of miscegenation creates a crisis of conscience which he finally resolves with the decision to kill Bon if he still seeks to marry Judith. The die is cast when Bon discovers Sutpen's final denial of him through Henry. Bon's sense of insult leads him to use the threat of miscegenation—*"I'm the nigger that's going to sleep with your sister"*—to test the depth of Henry's prior acceptance of him as an incestuous brother. When Henry forbids Bon to marry Judith, Bon lays his insulted humanity on the line: *"You will have to stop me, Henry"* (358). (This portrayal of Bon as the outraged defender of his human worth contradicts their portrayal of Bon as Judith's self-deprecating lover.)

The issue here, pushed to the breaking point, is the tragic refusal of Southerners, black and white alike, to create a new and unifying vision of a common humanity—even after the prolonged suffering of a Civil War. Henry asserts the supremacy of white blood over Negro blood, and in response Bon similarly defines himself according to the moral terms of the antebellum social order by affirming his blackness against whiteness. This episode dramatizes what for Faulkner is the discoverable truth about the Civil War: that racial attitudes were not—nor ever can be—altered "by mere force of law or economic threat."[26] The consequences of this uncompromising allegiance to the Southern caste-system are horrifyingly incarnated in the corpse-like figure of Henry

Sutpen, who is reduced to nothing more than the desire to die. His fleshly apparition projects in one summarizing image the possible future of those who, like Mr. Compson, Rosa, and Quentin, keep their vision fastened on past failures. In short, the drama of Henry's wasted life ultimately reveals the incontrovertible "fact" that if these narrators are to avoid his destiny, they must make the failures of their past yield a new and revitalizing image of their humanity.

The preceding episodes demonstrate that such self-transcendence becomes possible—is in fact realized—when the narrator imaginatively repossesses the values of others as expressions of his own deepest self. The upper-class narrators of these episodes dramatize their possibilities in terms of the price they exact from socially defined inferiors who realize and suffer them in their own lives. However, despite the great moments in which all social and cultural distinctions are momentarily abolished, *Absalom, Absalom!* still remains a bleak, a very bleak, novel. This bleakness derives in part from the failure of the narrators to make their quite remarkable artistic creations yield any deeper understanding of themselves or the past.

Certainly the entire artistic endeavor of Quentin and Shreve finally collapses as Shreve needlessly goads Quentin with satirical remarks about how "'the Jim Bonds are going to conquer the western hemisphere'" (378). Everything salutary, all sense of cultural barriers transcended, each insight gained during the sympathetic suspension of their alienation while re-creating the tragic relationship between Henry and Bon—all these are suddenly lost when Shreve asks his last and churlish question: "'Why do you hate the South?'" (378). Southern history here becomes, in Faulkner's treatment of it, a paradigm for the destructive realities in all human relationships, since the relationship between Quentin and Shreve mirrors that failure of imagination which is the very ground of the Sutpen tragedy. The reader could indeed justifiably draw the conclusion that Faulkner presents these analogous failures of the past and present as legitimation for Quentin's belief that life is an inescapable series of endlessly repeated events, had the narrative of Quentin and Shreve contained no moments of self-transcendence. Such moments do exist, however, for Quentin and Shreve, but their import is lost on narrators who have no models of transcendence for defining these moments as expressions of trustworthy values that would enable them to build a new relationship on the foundation of the past. Like Mr. Compson's career, their narrative careers dramatize the process whereby disbelief in any form of transcendence generates a seemingly irreversible alienation, futility, and despair in human relationships. These negative consequences—so forcefully exemplified by the narrators' crippled lives and the wastage of truly great imaginative creations that lead nowhere—point to the conclusion that, for Faulkner, man must ultimately approach the past through reliance on a model of transcendence that transforms his imaginative encounter with the past into a means whereby he can repossess his humanity anew in the present. At least this is the stance of the narrator, who, in describing the relationship between Quentin and Shreve, affirms a model of transcendence that undercuts the fatalism of Mr. Compson and Quentin.[27] Although "born half a continent apart," the narrator says, Quentin and Shreve are nevertheless "joined, connected after a fashion in a sort of geographical transubstantiation by that Continental Trough, that River which runs not only through the physical land of which it is the geologic umbilical, not only runs through the spiritual lives of the beings within its scope, but is very Environment itself which laughs at degrees of latitude and temperature, though some of these beings, like Shreve, have never seen it" (258). The narrator here presents the Mississippi River as a model that visualizes an unseen, but existing spiritual reality—both within and without man—that makes possible transcendence of all differences among men. The fact that the narrators realize this possibility in the greatest moments of the novel gives dramatic plausibility to this model of transcendence, which thereby becomes the novel's one source of hope, though human flaws hedge it in on all sides.

Absalom, Absalom! ultimately suggests that any artistic effort put into the accurate portrayal of the past remains fruitless and inert unless through it man demonstrates his present possibility for recovering a new image of his humanity. The artistic rendering of history in the narratives of Mr. Compson, Quentin, and Shreve is not enough for Faulkner. The artistry must also humanize the artist.

From *The Southern Literary Journal*, Volume 9, no. 1. Copyright © 1976 by the Department of English and Comparative Literature of the University of North Carolina at Chapel Hill. Published by the University of North Carolina Press. Used by permission of the publisher. www.uncpress.unc.edu

Notes

1. This novel (published in 1936) can thus be seen within the context of the debate on this problem which has claimed the attention of both historians and philosophers of history since the early 1930's. See *The Philosophy of History in Our Time: An Anthology*, ed. Hans Meyerhoff (Garden City, New York: Doubleday, 1959), pp. 85-224, for selected readings that treat this problem.

2. This letter (pp. 129-32), which the narrators assume is a love letter from Charles Bon to Judith Sutpen, is the sole document that survives the Sutpens' tragedy. If Bon did in fact send this letter to Judith as Mr. Compson assumes (the novel nowhere establishes the validity of this assumption), then it constitutes first-hand evidence about Bon and his relationship to Judith, and can therefore be used to test the probable truth of Shreve's and Quentin's imaginative reconstruction of his later career. However, Shreve and Quentin—and most critics—ignore this letter. To be sure, the letter itself poses problems. Both its contents and careful construction are teasingly enigmatic and thus evoke conjecture. Moreover, its purpose is not readily apparent, so that, if used, it requires prior interpretation of the intention shaping the letter.

3. All page citations in this essay refer to William Faulkner, *Absalom, Absalom!* (New York: Modern Library, 1936).

4. For concise discussions of how linguistic style becomes functional in this novel, or in Faulkner's works in general, see Robert H. Zoellner, "Faulkner's Prose Style in *Absalom, Absalom!*," *American Literature*, 30 (Jan. 1959), 486-502, and Conrad Aiken, "William Faulkner: The Novel as Form" in Frederick J. Hoffman and Olga Vickery, eds., *William Faulkner: Three Decades of Criticism* (New York: Harcourt, Brace and World, 1963), pp. 135-42.

5. Edmond Volpe, *A Reader's Guide to William Faulkner* (New York: Farrar, Straus and Co., 1964), p. 189.

6. For opposing views as to how closely Sutpen's career is to be linked with the Southern tradition, see Cleanth Brooks, *William Faulkner: The Yoknapatawpha Coun-*

try (New Haven: Yale Univ. Press, 1964), pp. 426 ff., and Olga W. Vickery, *The Novels of William Faulkner* (Baton Rouge: Louisiana State Univ. Press, 1964), pp. 93 ff. Certainly Brooks's view on this matter comports with that of both General Compson and Mr. Compson. Both men view Sutpen as a ruthless businessman who functions something like a plantation owner, but who displays neither the virtues, nor any understanding, of the Southern planter's communal role. To them, Sutpen represents an impersonal acceptance of a life-style that leaves him untouched as a person.

7. Frederick L. Gwynn and Joseph L. Blotner, eds., *Faulkner in the University* (New York: Vintage Books, 1959), p. 273. See also Walter J. Slatoff, *Quest for Failure: A Study of William Faulkner* (Ithaca: Cornell Univ. Press, 1960), p. 198.

8. See Ilse Dusoir Lind, "The Design and Meaning of *Absalom, Absalom!*" in *Three Decades*, pp. 278-304, for an analysis which identifies these various interpretations.

9. Gwynn and Blotner, *Faulkner in the University*, p. 274.

10. See Brooks, *William Faulkner*, pp. 429-36, for a convenient list of these known facts and events and the main conjectures used to explain them.

11. It is difficult to determine from whom Quentin learns that Bon is Sutpen's mulatto son—General Compson (who may have learned it from Sutpen), Henry Sutpen, or Rosa Coldfield. See Gerald Langford, ed., *Faulkner's Revision of* Absalom, Absalom!: *A Collation of the Manuscript and the Published Book* (Austin: Univ. of Texas Press, 1971), pp. 5 ff., and Brooks, *William Faulkner*, pp. 436 ff., for differing views on this matter. But this debate about who knows of Bon's Negro blood—a debate in which Brooks follows his materials with a sure eye—has an aspect that so far has gone unnoticed. If, as Quentin indicates (226), Sutpen himself did not tell General Compson that Bon was his mulatto son, it is at least clear that General Compson has guessed it to be so, although he never tells this to Mr. Compson. In this regard, Quentin makes a noteworthy response to Shreve's observation that when General Compson relates Sutpen's story to Mr. Compson, the General seems to know nothing about Bon's Negro blood: "'Yes,' Quentin said. 'Grandfather was the only friend [Sutpen] had'" (p. 274).

12. Hereafter the omniscient narrator will be referred to simply as the "narrator." All other narrators, when mentioned, are always named so as to avoid possible confusion. The omniscient narrator's substantive remarks appear on the following pages of the Modern Library edition: 7-14, 21-22, 31-43, 88-89, 128-29, 132-33, 172-76, 181, 187-91, 208-209, 217-18, 238, 255-56, 258, 265, 274-75, 277-78, 280, 293-95, 299, 303, 311, 314, 316, 321, 324-25, 334-36, 344-46, 351, and nearly every page of chapter 9. These pages constitute the basis for my subsequent remarks on the complex role of this narrator.

13. However, see John W. Hunt, *William Faulkner: Art in Theological Tension* (Syracuse: Syracuse Univ. Press, 1965), p. 103, and Volpe, *A Reader's Guide*, p. 189.

14. Giles B. Gunn, "Reflections on My Ideal Critic," *Criterion*, 11 (Spring 1972), 21.

15. Conrad Aiken describes this particular quality as an "elaborate method of *deliberately withheld meaning*, of progressive and partial and delayed disclosure. . . ." Hoffman and Vickery, *Three Decades*, p. 138.

16. Ibid.

17. For example, whose "human face"—Henry's or Charles Bon's—makes Judith momentarily cry? Did Sutpen deliberately force Henry's hand? If so, does Judith know this? Moreover, does she know that Bon is her half-brother, and that he is a mulatto?

18. This last episode has no factual basis, unless Judith relates it to General Compson (but the novel nowhere substantiates this).

19. William Poirier writes that Quentin "cannot be divorced from the spiritual dead end which his mother represents and which his father pathetically articulates. . . . The father has slowly undermined for Quentin the myth of any spiritual transcendence by what seems to be the mechanism of historical fact." Frederick J. Hoffman and Olga W. Vickery, eds., *William Faulkner: Two Decades of Criticism* (East Lansing: Michigan State College Press, 1954), p. 218. See also p. 308 of *Absalom, Absalom!*

20. William Faulkner, *As I Lay Dying* (New York: Vintage Books, 1957), p. 163.

21. After Quentin tells his father that Bon was Sutpen's son (266), Mr. Compson then assumes that Bon probably knew that Sutpen was his father. But it is only conjecture, since, as Mr. Compson says, nobody ever knew whether Bon knew that Sutpen was his father or, if he did, whether he was seeking revenge (269).

22. Shreve creates this episode involving the switching of pictures, which he wrongly attributes to Mr. Compson's account. Hence this notion that Bon switched pictures for this purpose is a conjecture which, for Shreve and Quentin, expresses their image of Bon's nobility.

23. See p. 208 of *Absalom, Absalom!* where Quentin calls Etienne Bon both an "animal" and an "it."

24. At one point the narrative runs thus: "*Suddenly Henry grasps the pistol, jerks it free of Bon's hand* stands so, *the pistol in his hand, panting and panting*" [my omission of italics] (358).

25. However, Sutpen's own words—". . . if I am forced to play my last trump card" (274)—give plausibility to this speculation.

26. In his "Letter to a Northern Editor," Faulkner writes: "The Northerner is not even aware yet of what that war really proved. He assumes that it merely proved to the Southerner that he was wrong. It didn't do that because the Southerner already knew he was wrong and accepted that gambit even when he knew it was the fatal one. What that war should have done, but failed to do, was to prove to the North that the South will go to any length, even that fatal and already doomed one, before it will accept alteration of its racial condition by mere force of law or economic threat." James B. Meriwether, ed., *Essays, Speeches, and Public Letters by William Faulkner* (New York: Random House, 1965), p. 89. See also C. Vann Woodward, *The Burden of Southern History* (Baton Rouge: Louisiana State Univ. Press, 1960), pp. 20-21, 62.

27. The narrator further rejects Mr. Compson's fatalism by describing Etienne Bon as one who "decreed and created" his own "Gethsemane" (208-209).

Black Feminism and the Canon:
Faulkner's *Absalom, Absalom!* and Morrison's *Beloved* as Gothic Romances_____

Philip Goldstein

In the 1940s, when the New Critics first established the canonical status of William Faulkner's work, they claimed that it reveals what Robert Penn Warren called the "moral confusion" of the "modern world," which can "look back nostalgically upon the old world of traditional values and feel loss and perhaps despair" (112). In the 1990s, when the success of the black feminist Toni Morrison has generated important new studies of her work and Faulkner's, scholars suggest that, as Carol A. Kolmerten says, "Read together, the fiction of Faulkner and Morrison offers a richly varied and profoundly moving meditation on racial, cultural, and gender issues in twentieth-century America."[1] Although such rereadings of Faulkner have appeared before, the new studies of Faulkner and Morrison pose more acutely a troublesome contradiction in his reception—how can his work "look back nostalgically" upon the Old South's "world of traditional values" and still offer a "richly varied and profoundly moving meditation on racial, cultural, and gender issues"?

What such contradictory accounts of Faulkner and Morrison's work show is that the cultural politics of the New Criticism, which first established Faulkner's reputation in the 1940s, and that of Black Studies, especially black feminism, which recognized Morrison's value in the 1980s, differ markedly. That is, the New Criticism supported the Southern Agrarian movement and the modernist avant-garde and condemned the "progress," industry, liberalism, science, wealth, bureaucracy, and democratic equality of the Yankee North (see Jancovich 71-101), whereas black feminism describes the history of African American women, including their experience of oppression and liberation, and their neglect and misconstruction by established black and white scholars or critics. To explain the impact of this historical transformation, I will suggest that to read Morrison as a great artist is to revise or revalue Faulkner and her other precursors; at the same time, to revise her precursors is to underwrite her status as an original artist. Gothic romances like Bram Stoker's *Dracula* and Emily Brontë's *Wuthering Heights* provide the intertextual conventions in terms of which I will explain the revaluation of Morrison's *Beloved* and in particular Faulkner's *Absalom, Absalom!* Although *Absalom, Absalom!* has been lauded as the greatest American novel (see Kuyk 2), I will suggest that *Beloved* is a more profound romance than *Absalom, Absalom!* is because *Beloved* depicts a more significant horror and because it repudiates *Absalom, Absalom!*'s modernist pessimism and affirms the African American community and its traditions. Traditional critics repudiate such generic interpretations on the grounds that Faulkner and Morrison transcend what Philip Weinstein calls their "distinctive racial and gender positioning" and, far from failing "their potential, . . . achieve it, becoming Faulkner and Morrison" (162). My revaluation opposes such conventional notions of literature's formal autonomy and acknowledges the changing conditions of modern literary study.

The conventions of gothic romances include multiple narrators, tormented lovers, dominating figures, spiritual exorcisms, and haunted houses. More importantly, insofar as the conventions herald the triumph of good over evil or the victory of divine providence, the gothic romance assumes that history or providence, not the romantic imagination, improves social life. An epistolary novel, *Dracula*, which includes the diverse narratives of Lucy, Mina, Jonathan Harker, Van Helsing, and others, produces a remarkably coherent account in which the vampire finds peace, and western civilization is saved, when Lord Godalming or Quincy Morris drive a stake through a vampire's heart. In *Wuthering Heights*, the narrators, who include Lockwood, the London resident, and Nelly Dean, the practical servant, also produce a remarkable coherent account. In it the frustrated passion of Heathcliff and Catherine, whose death ends her torment but not Heathcliff's; the

degradation and revenge of Heathcliff, who gradually comes to dominate the Grange and the Heights; and the triumphs of Cathy and
Hareton, the second generation, show that in a providential sense the
history of the Linton and Earnshaw families, not the romantic imagination, explains their improvement.

Absalom, Absalom! and *Beloved* also include multiple narrators,
tormented lovers, dominating figures, and haunted houses but do not
share this providential view of history. Rather, *Absalom, Absalom!* and
Beloved adopt the Aristotelian belief that the artistic imagination characterizes social life more profoundly than the mundane study of historical fact or providential design does. The conflicting multiple narratives of *Absalom, Absalom!* emphasize the speculative character of its
history, whereas *Beloved* retells the true story of Margaret Garner, an
escaped slave who killed her daughter rather than allow a slaveowner
to claim her under the fugitive slave law; however, the multiple narratives of both novels imply that the artistic imagination recreates the living reality of the dead past more profoundly than factual or providential histories do.[2]

To explain the dramatic rise and tragic fall of Sutpen and his family
and heirs, the narratives of *Absalom, Absalom!* provide alternative visions or competing views, rather than a coherent account. Raised in a
devout Protestant household, Rosa Coldfield tells a gothic horror story
in which Sutpen arises from nowhere, builds Sutpen's Hundred, dominates the town, and destroys her, her sister Ellen, and her sister's children. Rosa considers Sutpen a demon because of his unknown origins,
his status as an independent outsider, and his motive in marrying her
sister Ellen and having children—he wished to establish a dynasty in
patriarchal fashion. Moreover, Rosa never understands why Sutpen
gets Henry to kill Bon, since the murder sends Henry, his only male
heir, into hiding and destroys the dynasty Sutpen hoped to establish.
Nor does she understand why, with his design in ruins and the South in
defeat, he offers to marry her; rather, she condemns herself and her fate
and excoriates his demonic character because, as Mr. Compson tells

us, Sutpen stipulates that, before the ceremony can take place, she must produce a male heir.

Mr. Compson retells Sutpen's story in a more realistic fashion but voices a fin-de-siècle decadence. For instance, to explain what destroys Sutpen and his family, Mr. Compson blames his fear of incest. Sutpen got Henry to destroy Bon because Sutpen could not tolerate Bon's marrying his half sister. In a similar fashion, Mr. Compson takes Rosa's repudiation of Sutpen to show how women make an absolute ideal of virginity. Like Rosa, Mr. Compson admits, however, that the facts of Sutpen's life and family just do not add up.

Quentin/Shreve put together a liberal exposé in which Southern fears of miscegenation explain Sutpen's demise and perhaps the South's as well. Recounting the story Sutpen told General Compson while they pursued Sutpen's escaping French architect, Quentin and Shreve say that Sutpen, born into a poor mountain family, turns himself into a rich, powerful plantation owner because he suffered degradation: a black slave with a "balloon" face would not allow him to enter the front door of a plantation. After debating whether or not to avenge himself on the plantation owner, Sutpen commits himself to a grand design: he travels to the Caribbean, where he acquires substantial wealth, marries and then disavows Eulalia Bon and his son, buys Indian land in Mississippi, builds Sutpen's Hundred, and marries Ellen Coldfield, daughter of the respectable and pious Goodhue Coldfield. To explain why Sutpen forces his son Henry to kill Charles Bon, Quentin and Shreve surmise that Charles Bon is the son whom Sutpen disavowed when he learned that Eulalia Bon, his first wife, was part black. They say that, even though Sutpen, who engages his slaves in hand-to-hand combat, is egalitarian, he cannot accept Eulalia Bon as his wife, admit that Charles Bon is his son or permit him to marry Judith because, if Sutpen allows the Bons' black blood to mingle with Sutpen's white blood, he would violate the Old South's code of honor. To explain why his loyal servant Wash Jones kills him with a scythe, Quentin and Shreve also blame his patriarchal design. Because of it, he enrages Jones when he rejects Wash's daughter, whom he has impregnated, after she gives birth to a baby girl.

Quentin and Shreve also suggest that, while the second generation of *Wuthering Heights* overcomes the limitations of the first, Sutpen's family degenerates after the Civil War. Sutpen's Hundred is haunted by Henry, who returns to live his last days in the wrecked mansion hidden like a ghost, and by Charles Etienne Bon and Jim Bond, the descendants of Charles Bon. More loving than Sutpen was, Judith and Clytie, Sutpen's black daughter, retrieve Charles Etienne Bon from New Orleans and raise him like a son, but, just as the mansion is boarded up and left to decay, so he flaunts his mixed blood and dies of disease, while his son Jim Bond degenerates into idiocy, yowling insanely when Clytie, to save Henry from Rosa, burns down the mansion.

Since Faulkner's revisions of *Absalom, Absalom!* emphasize the narratives of Quentin and Shreve, who have the uncanny clairvoyance of Darl in *As I Lay Dying* (Langford 3), readers usually credit Quentin and Shreve's account the most—Cleanth Brooks even argues that Henry told Quentin the truth during the night in which Quentin drove Rosa to Sutpen's Hundred; still, Shreve, who comes from Canada, not Mississippi, shares enough of Quentin's narrative to remind the reader that, like Rosa's gothic and Mr. Compson's naturalistic narrative, Quentin and Shreve's liberal narrative is also speculative.

Beloved's narrators, who recount their painful experience of plantation slavery and its aftermath, also produce indeterminacy, but, in keeping with the novel's theme of "rememory," the narrators try not to remember what they end up remembering most fully. For instance, Paul D kept his painful memories at the Sweet Home plantation and on a chain gang locked up in what the novel calls "a tin cup" until he got together with Sethe, who brought them out. Sethe tries unsuccessfully to forget her sexual abuse and subsequent escape from Sweet Home, her mother's neglect of her and death by hanging, the difficult birth of Denver, and her murder of her daughter; but the advent of Paul D and of Beloved move her to remember these painful events. Beloved remembers little at first but eventually expresses traumatic feelings of abandonment and isolation. Terrified by Sethe, Denver initially goes deaf but eventually saves the family when Sethe's and Beloved's destructive relationship drives her to despair. Less one-sided than Faulkner, who does not allow Charles Bon or Clytie much of a narrative, Morrison also gives narratives to Edward Bodwin, who remembers what fun he had fighting slavery and where in 124 Bluestone he buried his toys, and Schoolteacher, who regrets his nephews' unscientific manner of training slaves.

Moreover, like Sutpen's Hundred, 124 Bluestone is haunted. The ghost of Beloved, the baby whom Sethe murdered when Schoolteacher came to reclaim her and her children, torments Denver and drives away her two brothers. Paul D, who arrives at 124 eighteen years after the murder of the baby, exorcises the ghost and gives the family a future together; nonetheless, a lost teenage girl who calls herself Beloved reincarnates the ghost and dominates 124. Unlike Dracula, Heathcliff, or Sutpen, this girl owns little besides her clothes and her scars; still, she forces Paul D to have sex with her even though the sexual intercourse humiliates him and drives him away from Sethe. With Paul D gone, she moves Sethe to give up the "outside world" and to assume she reincarnates the murdered baby. Overcome with guilt, Sethe stops working and ministers to Beloved's unrestrained desires, so much so that Beloved, pregnant with Paul D's child, grows big, while Sethe gets thin and wasted.

This demonic or supernatural conception of Beloved has led some critics to call her a succubus, incubus, or vampire (see Plasa 93-94 and Barnett 193-94). Not only the ghost of the murdered baby but also Sethe's experience in the clearing, where unknown hands nearly strangle her, validate this view. So do the mythical footprints that people find in the forest after Beloved has run off, footprints that anticipate the wild woman of *Jazz*. This view is qualified, at the same time, by the male perspective of Paul D and Stamp Paid, a former slave devoted to the community. They say, as Sethe did at first, that Beloved does not reincarnate the child whom Sethe killed; rather, a slaveowner kept her in his home and sexually abused her until she killed him and escaped.

The demonic conception is also qualified by Beloved's narrative, which does not describe her murder or her return from "the other side": rather, it depicts timeless moments in which she suffered a painful isolation and separation from her people. Even though it has been many years since the Middle Passage, when captured slaves were sometimes barbarically drowned, she describes a traumatic scene of such drowning. As she says,

> They are not crouching now   we are   they are floating on the water. . . .
> I cannot find my pretty teeth   I see the dark face that is going to smile at
> me   the iron circle is around our neck . . . she goes in the water   with my
> face . . . there is no one to want me to say my name   I wait on the bridge be-
> cause she is under it[.] (212)

Like those already "floating on the water," her mother, whose "dark face that is going to smile" at her, stops crouching and showing her "pretty teeth" and "goes in the water." As a result, Beloved experiences a traumatic abandonment: "there is no one to want me to say my name." In general, unlike *Dracula* or *Wuthering Heights*, the multiple narratives of both *Absalom, Absalom!* and *Beloved* show diverse, indeterminate perspectives undermining the stories' providential import; still, the horror of *Absalom, Absalom!* stems not only from the Sutpen's single-minded pursuit of his design but also from the tragedy which, if Quentin and Shreve are right, the danger of miscegenation and the defeat of Sutpen and the South represent; more profound, the horror of *Beloved* stems from Beloved's sexual abuse or murder, her traumatizing abandonment, and slavery's forgotten brutality.

Absalom, Absalom! depicts less of a horror; in addition, in undermining gothic fiction's providential import, *Absalom, Absalom!* dismisses the South's historical progress. As Mr. Compson points out, except for General Compson's friendship, Sutpen never overcomes his

outsider status or wins the acceptance of the community, which boy-
cotts his wedding in protest. More importantly, the South's patriarchal
ideals destroy Sutpen and his family as well as plantation slavery, yet
Quentin, who struggles to find some redemptive import in Sutpen's
life, concludes only that he does not hate the South. More negatively,
Shreve, who recounts Jim Bond's idiotic yowling, warns us about
Sutpen's as well as slavery's progeny: "in time the Jim Bonds are
going to conquer the western hemisphere" (302).

Morrison's *The Bluest Eye* shares this pessimism, for the community excludes Pecola after Cholly rapes her and, despite her blue eyes,
she degenerates into insanity. By contrast, in *Sula* the indiscriminate
sexual activity of the title character changes the community for the
better; similarly, *Beloved*'s excesses force Sethe, her family, and her
community to remember their experiences and to improve themselves.
For example, after Sethe becomes so obsessed with Beloved that she
stops working or taking care of the family, Denver, who recognizes Beloved's destructiveness, leaves home to find help. The community
condemned the murder of Beloved, ostracized Sethe and her family,
resented the extravagant picnic of Baby Suggs, Denver's deceased
grandmother, but remains appreciative of her preaching. Thanks to the
community's ensuing help, Denver gets her family food, finds employment at several houses, and may even gain a male companion and an
education at Oberlin College. More importantly, Ella and other community women, who do not wish to remember that, raped by slave
masters, they too killed their unwanted babies, do not want such ghosts
to come back and haunt them. To exorcise Beloved, these community
women go to 124 to chant. Even though Denver stops Sethe from killing Bodwin, who rides up at the same time, Sethe's attack on him frees
her from Beloved, who, abandoned again, runs off in despair. Paul D
and Stamp Paid laugh at Sethe's aborted attack on Gardner, but this
time she fought the oppressor, not her offspring, and freed herself.
Ironically, once Beloved is gone, Paul D feels grateful to her because
she took him to the "ocean-deep place he once belonged to" (264).

Moreover, after Sethe retreats to her bed, Paul D comes back to reestablish their relationship and to rebuild her self-esteem: "You your best thing, Sethe. You are" (273). While Sutpen and his family succumb to the South's plantation system, whose ideals move them to destroy each other, Sethe and her family and community resist its effects and establish positive relationships.

Although *Absalom, Absalom!* and *Beloved* rework the conventions of a gothic romance, including the multiple narrators, dominating figures, tormented lovers, and troublesome ghosts, *Absalom, Absalom!* and *Beloved* present the fractured, divided perspectives making history an imaginative reinterpretation, not plain historical fact or divine providence; just the same, *Beloved* depicts a more profound horror and a more positive community—it overcomes evil and brings improvement, instead of degenerating into idiocy and justifying a modernist pessimism, as Sutpen and his family do.

Moreover, this revaluation of Faulkner's and Morrison's novels overcomes the commonly held opposition of art and politics because it rejects the autonomous or reified character of literary texts and supports the humanities' new Black, Feminist, Gay, and Cultural Studies. By contrast, the many studies comparing Faulkner and Morrison treat them as equally profound and creative geniuses who rise above their cultural contexts and grasp the common truths of our human nature or racial and sexual contexts.[3] As Weinstein says, "questions of canon evaluation" ought not "amount to nothing more than a power debate among contending subgroups' claims" (162).

Such views repudiate the intertextual generic conventions of the gothic romance and defend the autonomous or reified character of Faulkner's or Morrison's art; however, the reception of the novels reveals the cultural politics justifying the revaluation of them. For instance, in the 1930s, Faulkner's work was attacked on the grounds that it indulged sensationalist interests, neglected social justice, and fostered modernist absurdity. In the early 1940s, his major fiction was out of print, and, desperate for cash, he churned out short stories and Hollywood film scripts. The American New Critics, who established his high reputation after WWII, supported the Southern Agrarian movement and the modernist avant-garde and condemned the "progress," industry, liberalism, science, wealth, bureaucracy, and democratic equality of the Yankee North (see Jancovich 71-101). Methodologically, their influential faith in close textual analysis justified the growing specialization of literary study, which, once the model of the research university was established, divided into independent fields and opposed the classical methods of the older generalist and the public sphere and generic types of popular culture (see Graff 10-12).

A founding member of the New Critics, Cleanth Brooks, who first argued that *Absalom, Absalom!* was Faulkner's greatest work (see Parker 15), says that Sutpen is not a typical Southerner but a Yankee outsider. Ignoring the community's traditions, he pursues his private ends in the name of abstractions like his "design" but remains innocent because he never learns anything from his experiences (295-324; see also Poirier). In this way the novel does not simply depict the South alone; rather, universal in scope, the novel critiques modern rationalism, abstraction, and detachment. Moreover, Brooks claims that, far from justifying a modernist pessimism, the second generation of Henry and Judith overcomes Sutpen's failings and makes significant choices, as Catherine and Hareton do in *Wuthering Heights*. Brooks still maintains, however, that the work is not a gothic romance but a unique work whose intricate structure enhances its climatic moments.

Like Brooks, Irving Howe also defends the novel's formal autonomy, but he adopts the cultural politics of the New York intellectuals, who, to secure positions in the university, aligned themselves with the New Criticism, turning high modern art into what Lionel Trilling called "a polemical concept" (94). Repudiating their youthful Marxism, they condemned the ideological conformity and cultural decline imposed by academic disciplines, Stalinist intellectuals, popular culture, and, eventually, Black and Women's Studies (see Leitch 109-14, and Shumway 279-87).

In keeping with this cultural politics, Howe, who provided what Lawrence Schwartz terms "the sharpest definition of Faulkner's role in the 'vital center' of politics and culture" (208), grants that the novel has the conventional generic features of a gothic romance but like Brooks claims that the novel's intricate structure emphasizes its climatic moments and its moral truth. More precisely, he argues that the novel parodies the generic conventions of the gothic romance, which rather than a structuring device expressing the novel's modernist pessimism, enables Faulkner to establish his distance and to preserve his autonomy. Howe also grants that Sutpen lacks self-recognition, as Brooks says, but argues that, a tragic hero, he "strives for large ends, actively resists his fate, and fails through an inner flaw" (74-75). Moreover, his tragic failure illustrates the novel's moral truth: in Howe's terms, "[H]is failure cannot be understood without judging the moral quality of his design. Sutpen's evil and heartlessness flow from his ambition to own and dominate men" (77).

Contrary to scholars who complain that the New Criticism established a professional, textual approach destroying literature's subversive force,[4] the overlapping interpretations of Brooks and Howe suggest that at least initially the New Criticism, along with the New York intellectuals, exposed the tragic moral flaws of the enterprising bourgeois individualist. By contrast, subsequent interpretations of *Absalom, Absalom!* defend the novel's formal autonomy and/or moral truth but, except for the feminists, eschew any cultural politics.

Some of these later critics say that the novel's stylistic tensions between the "static word" and "dynamic life" explain the moral truth which Quentin and Shreve discover. In *Faulkner: Myth and Motion* (1968), Richard P. Adams claims, for example, that it "emerges from the pervasive counterpoint of static, ideal aristocracy against the concrete dynamism of rapid, chaotic, and often violent change" (213; see also Lind and Vickery). This opposition between the "pervasive counterpoint" and the "concrete dynamism" breaks down Howe's generic distinction between gothic style and moral truth. Other critics also maintain that the novel asserts a universal moral truth but, adopting a Freudian viewpoint, argue that the novel depicts the deadly familial rivalries whereby the son struggles against his father and, upon becoming a father, opposes his son in turn.[5] Still others grant that Sutpen means to make himself his own father, as the Freudians say, but in a critical feminist manner maintain that, along with Rosa's hysteria, the textual devices of the novel reveal the irrational misogyny of the patriarchal family.[6] Still other critics grant that the novel critiques Yankee rationalism, as Brooks says; depicts Sutpen as a tragic hero, as Howe says; reveals moral truth as style, as the formal critics say; and faults Sutpen's desire to make himself his own father, as the psychoanalytic and feminist critics claim; however, to defend the novel's aesthetic autonomy, these critics argue that the novel anticipates and undermines all such interpretations of Sutpen's life.[7]

Yet other critics defend the historical objectivity of Faulkner, rather than the formal autonomy of his texts. That is, they argue that what reveals the moral truth is Faulkner's critique of the South, not the familial struggles of a patriarchal society nor the stylistic devices of the autonomous text. These historical critics argue that, contrary to Adams, Sutpen does not suffer a mythic fall from an Edenic communal life when he is not allowed to enter the front door of the plantation; rather, he grasps the plantation aristocracy's "corruptions of labor" and "idleness of character" (see Railey 116 and Jehlin 60-1). Moreover, these critics claim that the novel critiques what Melvin Backman calls the "post-Civil War legend of a humane gentlemanly Southern aristocracy" and depicts the sociohistorical divisions and conflicts of the South and even the arbitrary character of racial divisions. As Kevin Railey says, "Telling a more comprehensive tale than the one each of his narrators tells," Faulkner "accurately portrays the historical Southern world and implicitly criticizes and judges this world that came to accept the Sutpens rather than the Bons."[8] Whether by critiquing Southern society, asserting a universal moral truth, or resisting interpretations of Sutpen's life, these critics show that the novel preserves its formal autonomy or historical or psychological objectivity and implicitly or explicitly resists the speculative narratives and the generic conventions of the gothic romance as well as the reader's interpretive practices.

Like Barbara Christian, who says that Morrison's work needs no validation by a "western White literary father," critics who restrict accounts of *Beloved* to African American historical or rhetorical contexts thereby establish an equally unstable opposition between the novel's formal autonomy or historical objectivity and its readers' cultural politics.[9] The difference is that in Morrison's case it is black feminism, not the New Criticism or the New York intellectuals, that established the high status of Morrison's work, which, in turn, legitimated the oppositional character of black feminism, including its revaluation of Faulkner's work.

In the 1960s and 1970s, when, thanks to the student rebellions and Civil Rights activists, Black Studies was established in major Anglo-American universities, African American literary criticism underwent what Houston Baker, echoing Thomas Kuhns, terms a "paradigm shift": the Black Power movement gave rise to a new Black Aesthetics, which dismissed the realist belief that African American literature adhered to common American ideals and which identified African American literature with peculiarly African American experience, culture, language, and history. Baker adds that this paradigm shift "made it possible for literary-critical and literary-theoretical investigators to . . . include previously 'unfamiliar' objects in an expanded (and sharply modified) American artworld."[10]

As Nancy Peterson points out, the evolution of black feminist criticism enabled Morrison's novels to receive in the 1980s the attention which they so terribly lacked in the 1970s (5). Ironically, Morrison has substantially contributed to this evolution. As an editor at the influential Random House, she published the writings of Toni Cade Bambara, Angela Davis, Gayle Jones, and others whose work contributed markedly to the black feminist discourse producing her reputation.[11] Moreover, like T. S. Eliot, whose revaluation of John Donne and the Metaphysical Poets supported his modernist poetry, she has produced *Race-ing Justice, En-gendering Power, Playing in the Dark: Whiteness and the Literary Imagination*, and other collections of nonfiction essays that foster the black feminist concerns and issues justifying her work.

Baker goes on, however, to defend the new formal or figural black critics, whom he calls "reconstructionists" because they "reconstruct" pedagogy or criticism as a matter of close textual analysis. While black feminists like Barbara Christian or Barbara Smith condemned this formal criticism because it ignored or misjudged the work of black women and sought middle-class acceptance and careerist success,[12] critics have dismissed this black cultural politics and, at least in Morrison's case, defended her work's formal autonomy or historical objectivity.

For example, many critics maintain that *Beloved* is rightly understood as a slave narrative that voices both the male and the female sexual abuse and torment repressed by traditional slave narratives.[13] As Elizabeth Fox-Genovese points out, although *Beloved* is more graphic than Harriet Jacobs's *Incidents in the Life of a Slave Girl*, both works describe women's experiences of plantation slavery: "[i]t is as if the example of abuse from which Jacobs had so carefully distanced Linda Brent [her narrator] had come to life" (106). Fox-Genovese admits that, unlike slave narratives, *Beloved* employs multiple, nonlinear narratives, but she still emphases the narrative's historical insight into plantation slavery. Such accounts forcefully articulate the harrowing African American experience of slavery, especially the female sexual experience that historians have been reluctant to discuss, but minimize the import of the novel's multiple narratives and other gothic conventions because, as Molly Travis points out, they sustain "our institutional obsession with ambiguity and undecidability" (85).

By contrast, figural literary or psychoanalytic accounts, which emphasize the disruptive effects of the multiple narratives, preserve the novel's textual autonomy but minimize the sociohistorical contexts of African American life. Catherine Kodat claims, for instance, that *Absalom, Absalom!* and *Beloved* "force us to struggle with what is most resistant to expression (the nature and purpose of Beloved herself, the ultimate ramifications of Sutpen's design) and which, in its resistance, fuels some of the novels' most breathtaking technical accomplishments" (183). She argues that these "technical accomplishments" do not preclude profound historical insight, but the history in question is mainly that of the modernist movement, whose "pure" white character *Beloved* violates (189). Similarly, Phillip Novak grants that *Absalom, Absalom!* and *Beloved* both "elucidate a central traumatic event—the killing of Sethe's 'crawling-already? baby' mirroring, in this structural sense, the killing of Charles Bon" (208). Both novels present themselves as generic and psychological types: "a ghost story, a murder mystery, and a process of psychotherapy—perhaps even of exorcism—carried out at the cultural level" (206). Novak concludes, however, that neither novel successfully reveals the meaning of the traumatic event or depicts the historical truth: "in setting itself up as the unveiling of a mystery that it nonetheless refuses to disclose, *Beloved* . . . , like *Absalom, Absalom!*, presents itself structurally as the production of an absence, as the marking of a loss" (210). Novak grants that, unlike *Absalom, Absalom!*, *Beloved* reveals the cause of this absence—the slaveowning South's drive to destroy the slave's cultural memory, but his deconstruction of the novels' techniques ultimately affirms their untranslateable autonomy, not their historical insights.

More positive figural or rhetorical accounts examine the challenging role of the reader, the historical or mythopoetic significance of mothering, or the repression of traumatic memories or of the characters' subjectivity. For example, in an essay reprinted several times, Ashraf Rushdy characterizes *Beloved* as what Henry Louis Gates calls a "speakerly text" in which "[t]he scenes of hearing the mother's tongue, understanding the mother's code, knowing the mother's history—these are themselves the very enactment of an ongoing generational oral transmission."[14] This claim forcefully articulates the novel's rhetorical practices and their oral roots but says little about the novel's gothic conventions. Moreover, like Faulkner's defenders, such accounts may go on to ignore or condemn academic or cultural institutions like Black Studies or black feminist criticism. For instance, Linda Krumholz praises the novel's fragmented plot and shifting narrative voice because it produces an engaged, "healing" notion of historical memory. At the same time, Krumholz faults academic histories because they adopt the "linguistic objectivity and scientific method" of Schoolteacher in order to mask their political motivations (85).[15] Such claims ignore the institutional divisions of literary study, which include not only traditional academic methods but also the black feminist criticism which established Morrison's reputation.

In short, most accounts of Faulkner's or Morrison's art set up a debilitating opposition between textual autonomy and historical truth, on the one hand, and the reader's generic conventions and cultural politics, on the other. Rather than allow "questions of canon evaluation" to "amount to nothing more than a power debate among contending subgroups' claims," as Weinstein says, they treat Faulkner and Morrison as equally profound and creative geniuses who rise about their cultural contexts and implicitly or explicitly repudiate established programs and studies. By contrast, I have argued that, while *Beloved* and *Absalom, Absalom!* both depict gothic romances, Faulkner's novel shares the modernist disillusionment with liberal notions of progress and freedom, whereas Morrison's novel forcefully suggests that the community can overcome these horrors and reintegrate its alienated members. Since *Beloved* proves the better romance, it justifies the black feminism supporting it even as it denies the autonomy of both African American and traditional criticism.

Courtesy of *The Faulkner Journal*, XX: 1 & 2 (Fall 2004/Spring 2005). Copyright © 2005 by the University of Central Florida. Reprinted with permission.

Notes

1. xi; Kolmerten, who is editor of *Unflinching Gaze: Morrison and Faulkner Re-Envisioned*, adds "no reader of Faulkner will ever read him in the same way after encountering the works of Morrison." See also Catherine Gunther Kodat, who claims that a large part of the new "historical" Faulkner "arises from the interaction of Faulkner's novels with works like *Beloved*" (196), and Philip Weinstein, who says that Faulkner and Morrison "are both major novelists of racial turmoil . . . each is extraordinarily invested in imagining American racial dynamics" (*What Else* xix). For an earlier discussion of Faulkner's critique of slavery, see Melvin Backman.

2. For Morrison's account of how she means to reach the "interior life" of the slaves recorded in historical records, see Plasa, 43-47; for an account of *Beloved* as both a neo-slave narrative and a gothic romance, see Bernard Bell, who calls it a "womanist neo-slave narrative" (59) and an "an extraordinarily effective Gothic blend of postmodernism and romance" (68).

3. Weinstein recognizes that "Morrison . . . refuses the plot of tragic impasse to which modernist forms tend to lead Faulkner" (178) but considers it just another sign of their different "cultural positioning." Bloom considers "the ideologies of political correctness . . . deeply embedded in *Beloved*" (Intro. 2). Other critics assume that the similar themes or subjects of Faulkner and Morrison shows their aesthetic transcendence. For example, Carolyn Denard says that Faulkner and Morrison both depict those "other" Americans, those whom Morrison calls the "discredited. . . . For Faulkner, the discredited are the defeated southern whites. . . . Morrison's discredited are American blacks, with slave and sharecropper pasts." The "great merit" of Faulkner and Morrison's work is that they imbue their subjects with a mythical "import and still . . . question, transform, and enlarge the mythical tradition to which they believe all history is connected" (21-22). John Duvall says that Faulkner and Morrison both treat outsiders; oral, blues, and folk traditions; and miscegenation, racism, or "colorism" (9-13). Catherine Gunther Kodat says that "*Absalom, Absalom!* and *Beloved* not only represent African-American history artistically: they comment upon the history of artistically representing African-Americans" (184). Michael Hogan focuses "upon Sutpen's mansion and 124 as fictional manifestations of Lincoln's American 'house'" and reads "both houses as spaces defined by individual and communal identity as well as by gender" (168).

4. Richard Ohmann argues, for example, that, to practice a genuinely radical politics, literary critics must disavow not just the New Criticism but the whole "bourgeois" institution of literary studies as well (85-88). Similarly, Paul Bové claims that, "fundamentally conservative, even reactionary," practical criticism "cannot be the ground for an oppositional intellectual practice, because it must trivialize history if it hopes to minimize the importance of change so that it can manage and perhaps even encourage the forgetting of social and gender difference" (53-55).

5. John T. Irwin claims, for example, that Quentin finds the story of Henry, Judith, and Bon so fascinating because it parallels the story of Quentin, Caddy, and Dalton Ames. Just as Quentin's desire to kill Ames and restore the Compson family honor shows an incestuous desire for Caddy, so Henry's killing Bon and preserving the

---

Absalom, Absalom! and *Beloved* as Gothic Romances

Sutpen family honor shows an incestuous desire for Judith. Quentin finds the story of Sutpen equally fascinating because Sutpen means to make himself his own father by besting the plantation owner whom he takes as a surrogate father and by besting his sons whose claims on him he denies or rejects. Similarly, Quentin means to defeat his father and remake himself by telling a better narrative than his father does (151-58; see also Bleikasten 137-40).

6. For example, Carolyn Porter says that the traumatic incident whereby Sutpen decides to become a plantation owner illustrates the ways in which patriarchy perpetuates itself not by the son's identifying with his personal father but by his preserving the father's mastery, what Lacan calls the realm of the symbolic. Indeed, Sutpen adheres to the father's law so strictly that he makes Henry kill Bon and wreck his design (194). Moreover, the outrage of Rosa, who defends the lost pleasures of virgins and the mothers with no sons, shows that patriarchy grants women only the positions of wife and mother, virgin or prostitute (193-94; see also Gwin 63-121).

7. James Guetti claims, for example, that the contrasting narratives show that Faulkner considers experience beyond human understanding (65; see also Duncan 96), while Christine de Montauzon maintains that the novel accommodates the diverse interpretive methods of diverse readers only to subvert them and reassert the openness or irreducible character that indicates Faulkner's genius (275-76).

8. Like Brooks, Railey maintains that Sutpen fails because he is "been unable to check" his "deep-seated individualism" (122), but Railey claims that the novel's sociohistorical conflict is between a Jeffersonian liberalism, whereby those individuals who, like Sutpen, possess "natural" virtues are free to rise in the social system, and a hierarchic Southern paternalism, which ruled poor whites and enslaved or freed blacks by making poor whites feel superior to enslaved blacks. Railey even takes the narrators' speculations about Bon's mixed blood to show how arbitrary Faulkner considers racial differences.

9. As Barbara Christian asks Morrison, "What is the purpose of securing a link between you and William Faulkner? . . . Is it that you . . . must have a Western white literary father?" ("Layered" 20). Morrison herself opposes Anglo-American contexts of interpretation because she fears that they produce superficial readings (see Mobley 18-19). Morrison also admits, however, that the work of Faulkner, who, along with Virginia Woolf, was the subject of her master's thesis, has influenced her (see Duvall 4-5).

10. Baker 76-77. Similarly, Barbara Herrnstein Smith says that a text may be rediscovered as an "unjustly neglected masterpiece" when "different of its properties and possible functions become foregrounded by a new set of subjects with emergent interests and purposes" (cited in Richter 1341).

11. See McKay, "Intro" 5. Richard Ohmann says that Random House publications were much more likely than other publications to be reviewed in *The New York Times Book Review* or some other prestigious review or magazine. Moreover, a novel that, thanks to Random House's extraordinary influence, has been positively reviewed is "likely to draw the attention of academic critics in more specialized academic journals . . . and by this route make its way into college curricula, where the very context—course title, academic setting, methodology—gave it de facto recognition as literature" (75). Ohmann adds that the "college classroom and the academic journal have

become in our society the final arbiters of literary merit, and even of survival. It is hard to think of a novel more than twenty-five years old . . . that still commands a large readership outside of school and college" (75).

12. See Barbara Christian, "The Race for Theory," *Cultural Critique*, 6 (1987): 51-63; Joyce A. Joyce, "The Black Canon: Reconstructing Black American Literary Criticism," *NLH*, 18 (1987): 335-44; Michele Wallace, "Negative Images: Towards a Black Feminist Cultural Criticism." *The Cultural Studies Reader*, ed. Simon During (London: Routledge, 1993): 118-31; Barbara Smith, "Toward a Black Feminist Criticism," *Feminist Literary Theory: A Reader*. 2nd ed., ed. Mary Eagleton (Oxford: Blackwells, 1996): 122-26.

13. In a frequently reprinted essay, Marilyn Mobley also considers *Beloved* a modern slave narrative which "exposes the unsaid of the narratives, the psychic subtexts" (20), but she argues that "Morrison uses the trope of memory to revise the genre of the slave narrative" (19). By means of this trope, Mobley too forcefully describes the novel's historical import, what she terms "the psychic consequences of slavery for women, who, by their very existence, were both the means and the source of production" (20); however, she goes on to equate memory and narrative. That is, memory acquires the "dialogic characteristics" which Bakhtin attributes to narrative as well as its "imaginative capacity to construct and to reconstruct the significance of the past" (20; see also Barnett 196-97, and Jill Matus 104-5).

14. (138). Similarly, Linda Krumholz argues that *Beloved* reconceptualizes the African American experience of plantation slavery as rituals promoting a "healing process for the characters, the reader, and the author" (79). The fragmented multiple narratives impel the reader to reconstruct the story and to participate in the healing, a process which, Krumholz says, "parallels Sethe's psychological recovery: repressed fragments of the (fictionalized) personal and historical past are retrieved and reconstructed" (81). See also David Lawrence, who takes the novel to recognize that the authority governing one's body is closely tied to authority over one's language and its codes; as he says, "Woven into the dense texture of the novel, . . . the interaction of language and body underlies the collective confrontation with the ghosts of memory" (46). See also Caroline Rody, who claims that "[i]n the jealous longing of the abandoned daughter, the novel figures its relationship to the unknown ancestress-muse of the African-American women's literary renaissance" (170).

15. Similarly, Rushdy considers the resurrection and articulation of the unjustly killed Beloved Morrison's "greatest achievement" because it criticizes the traditional academic history that "excluded her and her rebellious spirit" (138). Denise Heinze also claims that, because of Morrison's double consciousness, her novels subverted middle-class values and still impressed the literary establishment even though its values "perpetuate the system" (4-5). See also Sally Keenan, who says Morrison may well be a token black feminist author whom the establishment uses to show how liberal and tolerant it is (qtd. in Plasa 118-19).

Works Cited

Adams, Richard P. *Faulkner: Myth and Motion*. Princeton: Princeton UP, 1968.

Backman, Melvin. "*Absalom, Absalom!*" Goldman 59-75.

Baker, Houston A., Jr. *Blues, Ideology, and Afro-American Literature: A Vernacular Theory*. Chicago: U of Chicago P, 1984.

Barnett, Pamela E. "Figurations of Rape and the Supernatural in *Beloved*." Bloom 193-205

Bell, Bernard W. "*Beloved*: A Womanist Neo-Slave Narrative; or Multivocal Remembrances of Things Past." Bloom 57-68.

Bleikasten, André. "Fathers in Faulkner." *The Fictional Father: Lacanian Readings of the Text*. Ed. Robert Con Davis. Amherst: U of Massachusetts P, 1981. 115-46.

Bloom, Harold. Introduction. Bloom 1-3.

_____, ed. *Toni Morrison's Beloved*. New York: Chelsea House, 1999.

Bové, Paul. *In the Wake of Theory*. Hanover, N.H.: Wesleyan UP, 1992

Brooks, Cleanth. *William Faulkner: The Yoknapatawpha Country*. New Haven: Yale UP, 1963.

Christian, Barbara. "Layered Rhythms: Virginia Woolf and Toni Morrison." Peterson 19-36.

_____. "The Race for Theory," *Cultural Critique* 6 (1987): 51-64.

Denard, Carolyn. "The Convergence of Feminism and Ethnicity in the Fiction of Toni Morrison." In *Critical Essays on Toni Morrison*. Ed. Nellie Y. McKay. Boston: G. K. Hall, 1988. 171-78.

Duncan, Aswell. "The Puzzling Design of *Absalom, Absalom!*" *William Faulkner's* Absalom, Absalom!: *A Critical Casebook*. Ed. Elisabeth Muhlenfeld. New York: Garland, 1984. 93-108.

Duvall, John N. "Toni Morrison and the Anxiety of Faulknerian Influence." Kolmerten, Ross, and Wittenberg 3-16.

Faulkner, William. *Absalom, Absalom!* 1936. *The Corrected Text*. New York: Vintage International, 1990.

Fox-Genovese, Elizabeth. "Unspeakable Things Unspoken: Ghosts and Memories in the Narratives of African-American Women." Bloom 97-114.

Goldman, Arnold, ed. *Twentieth-Century Interpretations of* Absalom, Absalom! Englewood Cliffs, N.J.: Prentice-Hall, 1971.

Graff, Gerald. *Professing Literature: An Institutional History*. Chicago: U of Chicago P, 1987.

Guetti, James. "*Absalom, Absalom!* The Extended Metaphor." *William Faulkner's* Absalom, Absalom!: *A Critical Casebook*. Ed. Elisabeth Muhlenfeld. New York: Garland, 1984. 65-92.

Gwin, Minrose C. *The Feminine and Faulkner: Reading (Beyond) Sexual Difference*. Knoxville: U of Tennessee P, 1990.

Heinz, Denise. *The Dilemma of "Double-Consciousness": Toni Morrison's Novels*. Athens: U of Georgia P, 1993.

Hogan, Michael. "Built on the Ashes: The Fall of the House of Sutpen and the Rise of the House of Sethe." Kolmerten, Ross, and Wittenberg 167-81.

Howe, Irving. *William Faulkner: A Critical Study*. 2nd ed. New York: Vintage Books, 1962.

Irwin, John T. "The Dead Father in Faulkner," *The Fictional Father: Lacanian Readings of the Text*. Ed. Robert Con Davis. Amherst: U of Massachusetts P, 1981. 147-68.

Jancovich, Mark. *The Cultural Politics of the New Criticism*. Cambridge: Cambridge UP, 1993.

Jehlen, Myra. *Class and Character in Faulkner's South*. New York: Columbia UP, 1976.

Joyce, Joyce. A. "Black Woman Scholar, Critic, and Teacher: The Inextricable Relationship between Race, Sex, and Class." *NLH*, 22 (1991): 543-65.

Kodat, Catherine Gunther. "A Postmodern *Absalom, Absalom!*, a Modern *Beloved*: The Dialectic of Form." Kolmerten, Ross, and Wittenberg 181-98.

Kolmerten, Carol A., Stephen M. Ross, and Judith Bryant Wittenberg. Introduction. Kolmerten, Ross, and Wittenberg ix-xv.

_____, eds. *Unflinching Gaze: Morrison and Faulkner Re-Envisioned*. Jackson: UP of Mississippi, 1997.

Krumholz, Linda. "The Ghosts of Slavery: Historical Recovery in Toni Morrison's *Beloved*." Bloom 79-95.

Kuyk, Dirk, Jr. *Sutpen's Design: Interpreting Faulkner's* Absalom, Absalom! Charlottesville: UP of Virginia, 1990.

Langford, Gerald. *Faulkner's Revision of "Absalom, Absalom!": A Collation of the Manuscript and the Published Book*. Austin: U of Texas P, 1971.

Lawrence, David. "Fleshly Ghosts and Ghostly Flesh: The Word and the Body in *Beloved*." Bloom 45-56.

Leitch, Vincent B. *American Literary Criticism from the Thirties to the Eighties*. New York: Columbia UP, 1988.

Lind, Ilse Dusoir. "The Design and Meaning of *Absalom, Absalom!*" *William Faulkner: Three Decades of Criticism*. Ed. Frederick J. Hoffman and Olga W. Vickery. New York: Harcourt, Brace, Jovanovich, 1960, 278-304.

Matus, Jill. *Toni Morrison*. Manchester: Manchester UP, 1998.

McKay, Nellie Y. Introduction. *Toni Morrison's* Beloved: *A Casebook*. Ed. William L. Andrews and Nellie Y. McKay. New York: Oxford UP, 1999, 3-19.

Mobley, Marilyn Saunders. "A Different Remembering: Memory, History, and Meaning in Toni Morrison's *Beloved*." Bloom 189-99.

Montauzon, Christine de. *Faulkner's* Absalom, Absalom! *and Interpretability: The Inexplicable Unseen*. New York: Peter Lang, 1985.

Morrison, Toni. *Beloved*. New York: Plume, 1988.

Novak, Phillip. "Signifying Silences: Morrison's Soundings in the Faulknerian Void." Kolmerten, Ross, and Wittenberg 199-216.

Ohmann, Richard. *English in America: A Radical View of the Profession*. New York: Oxford UP, 1976.

Parker, Robert Dale. Absalom, Absalom!: *The Questioning of Fictions*. New York: Twayne, 1991.

Peterson, Nancy J. Introduction. Peterson 1-15.

_____, ed. *Toni Morrison: Critical and Theoretical Approaches*. Baltimore: Johns Hopkins UP, 1997.

Plasa, Carl. *Toni Morrison,* Beloved. New York: Columbia UP, 1998.

Poirier, Richard. "Strange Gods in Jefferson, Mississippi: Analysis of *Absalom, Absalom!*" Goldman 12-31.

Porter, Carolyn. "*Absalom, Absalom!*: (Un)Making the Father." *The Cambridge Companion to William Faulkner*. Ed. Philip M. Weinstein. New York: Cambridge UP, 1995. 168-96.

Railey, Kevin. *Natural Aristocracy: History, Ideology, and the Production of William Faulkner*. Tuscaloosa: U of Alabama P, 1999.

Richter, David, ed. *The Critical Tradition: Classic Texts and Contemporary Trends*. New York: St. Martin's Press, 1989.

Rody, Caroline. "'History,' 'Rememory,' and a 'Clamor for a Kiss.'" Bloom 155-75.

Rushdy, Ashraf H. A., "Daughters Signifyin(g) History: The Example of Toni Morrison's *Beloved*." *Toni Morrison*. Ed. Linden Peach. New York: St. Martin's Press, 1998, 140-53.

Schwartz, Lawrence H. *Creating Faulkner's Reputation: The Politics of Modern Literary Criticism*. Knoxville: U of Tennessee P, 1988.

Shumway, David. *Creating American Civilization: A Genealogy of American Literature as an Academic Discipline*. Minneapolis: U of Minnesota P, 1994.

Smith, Barbara. "Toward a Black Feminist Criticism." *Feminist Literary Theory: A Reader*. Ed. Mary Eagleton. Oxford: Blackwell, 1996, 122-26.

Trilling, Lionel. *Sincerity and Authenticity*. Cambridge, Mass.: Harvard UP, 1972.

Vickery, Olga. *The Novels of William Faulkner*. Baton Rouge: Louisiana State UP, 1959.

Wallace, Michele. "Negative Images: Towards a Black Feminist Cultural Criticism." *The Cultural Studies Reader*. Ed. Simon During. London: Routledge, 1993. 118-31.

Warren, Robert Penn. "William Faulkner." *William Faulkner: Three Decades of Criticism*. Ed. Frederick J. Hoffman and Olga W. Vickery. New York: Harcourt, 1960, 109-24.

Weinstein, Philip. *What Else But Love? The Ordeal of Race in Faulkner and Morrison*. New York: Columbia UP, 1996.

"A Shape to Fill a Lack":
Absalom, Absalom! and the Pattern of History

Deborah Wilson

In his Nobel Prize speech, William Faulkner claims that a writer (pronominally male throughout the speech) must leave "no room in his workshop for anything but the old verities and truths of the heart, the old universal truths lacking which any story is ephemeral and doomed" (*ESPL* 119). In *Absalom, Absalom!*, published fourteen years earlier, Quentin Compson's father makes a similar observation in noticing "how so often when we try to reconstruct the causes which lead up to the actions of men and women, how with a sort of astonishment we find ourselves now and then reduced to the belief, the only possible belief, that they stemmed from some of the old virtues" (96). Compson's speech occurs during his narrative of Thomas Sutpen's life, a history he tries to reconstruct as a logical series of causes and effects that he decides necessarily originates in "old virtues." The examples he uses are of a thief stealing for love rather than greed and a murderer killing out of pity rather than lust (96), but these examples appear amid his primary attempt to explain the actions of Judith Sutpen. Actually he is explaining what he sees as her inaction, for in his version of the Sutpen history, Judith waits for the struggle among her father, brother, and fiancé with "no effort to do anything else" other than wait. Thus, in spite of Compson's declared interest in the actions of men *and* women, he speaks of women as passive while the men act around them. In his version, Judith makes no investigation into the causes of the conflict among the men, nor does she engage in any "moral debate between what she wanted and what she thought was right" (96).

What appears in both these instances is the belief that action, both in fiction and in history, originates in truths and virtues *from the past* rather than from the present, a belief also apparent in Faulkner's critique of Robert Penn Warren's *All the King's Men*. In July of 1946,

---

Faulkner wrote to Lambert Davis, an editor at Harcourt, Brace, thanking him for a prepublication copy of Warren's novel and adding his appraisal of it:

> The Cass Mastern story is a beautiful and moving piece. That was his novel. The rest of it I would throw away. The Starke [sic] thing is good solid sound writing but for my money Starke and the rest of them are second rate. The others couldn't be bigger than he, the hero, and he to me is second rate. . . . He was neither big enough nor bad enough. (*SL* 239)

Faulkner then repeats his preference for the Cass Mastern section, adding his admiration for "the way Warren caught . . . the pattern of their acts," and finally claiming that "there has been little in this country since that time—1860-'70 etc. good enough to make good literature" (239).

To Faulkner, the section of Warren's novel set in the more distant past is of far greater worth than the much larger section set in his and Warren's present. In claiming that heroes since 1870 have become "second rate," not big or bad enough to "make good literature," Faulkner again expresses his preference for the past over the present as the seedbed of action. Furthermore, in referring to the "pattern" of those past heroes' actions, a pattern he claims Warren has replicated, Faulkner aligns himself with the view of history espoused by Jack Burden. Burden's task is uncovering the pattern of events and reconstructing the past in order to discover truth and understand the present, a task Faulkner sets for his own Quentin Compson in another Old South novel.

But in addition to Faulkner's belief that the heroes, truths, and virtues worth writing about are found in the past, another belief surfaces in his Nobel Prize speech and Mr. Compson's comments. Faulkner's view of history, especially in *Absalom, Absalom!*, excludes women, subordinating them to a patriarchal logic that finds only masculine patterns in both past and present (and in ways quite similar to Warren's view in *All the King's Men*). Women are outside the logic inherent in Faulkner's old, original "verities." If, as his own speech makes clear, anything outside these old truths is "ephemeral and doomed," and if women are outside (or, to use Faulkner's significantly Freudian term, "lacking"), then women are doomed to exclusion from the Faulknerian writer's workshop and the Faulknerian character's history.

In discussing his own writing process, Faulkner told an interviewer in 1956 that his stories usually begin "with a single idea or memory or mental picture," and that the actual writing that follows consists in "working up to that moment, to explain why it happened or what it caused to follow" (Cowley 133). In the midst of this causally linked series of events, he sets his characters in motion. In *As I Lay Dying*, he "subjected [the Bundrens] to the simple universal natural catastrophes which are flood and fire, with a simple natural motive to give direction to their progress" (129). This directed progress is central to his project as a writer since, in his definition, "Life is motion, and motion is concerned with what makes man move—which is ambition, power, pleasure" (138). The artist's aim, he says, is to "arrest motion, which is life" so that later when "a stranger looks at it, it moves again since it is life" (139). The only access man has to immortality is "to leave something behind him that is immortal since it will always move" (139).

The artist who creates this motion which is life has not only immortality, but Godlike power since he "can move these people around like God, not only in space but in time too" (141). And his created cosmos becomes "a kind of keystone in the universe; that, small as that keystone is, if it were ever taken away the universe itself would collapse" (141). After his last book, to be called "the Doomsday Book," he will break his pencil and have to stop (141). But what lines does that pencil draw before he breaks it? His comments indicate his interest in directed, progressive motion, as well as his admiration for writing that captures the pattern of events. He says that not only did each of his own books have "to have a design but the whole output or sum of an artist's work had to have a design" (141). Although the design of *As I Lay Dy-*

ing is apparent in its journey-plot, *The Sound and the Fury* also has a design, though one that Faulkner apparently found much more difficult. Although he claims that he knew "probably every single word right to the end" before writing the first word of *As I Lay Dying* (129), he says he wrote *The Sound and the Fury* "five separate times, trying to tell the story" (130). After having all three Compson brothers tell the story, he concludes,

> That was still not it. I tried to gather the pieces together and fill in the gaps by making myself the spokesman. It was still not complete, not until fifteen years after the book was published, when I wrote as an appendix to another book the final effort to get the story told and off my mind . . . and I never could tell it right, though I tried hard and would like to try again, though I'd probably fail again. (130-31)

The design Faulkner desires and keeps attempting to create is a peculiarly masculine narrative, similar to Warren's in *All the King's Men*, in which the pieces are gathered together into a pattern and the gaps that remain are filled in by the master narrator's (male) voice.[1] Faulkner's view of history is, like Warren's, teleological, a history in which characters move toward the inevitable doomsday book that will conclude the narrative, toward the death that will break the master narrator's phallic pencil and end the line he has drawn. But until that inevitable conclusion, the wielder of the pencil, the figure in the workshop, the prophet and the historian are inevitably masculine.[2]

The title of *Absalom, Absalom!* points toward an underlying Biblical narrative pattern that stresses patriarchal lineage, the transmission of political power from father to son, from the king to the prince intended to succeed his father. The narrative then depends upon origins, particularly upon paternity. In the Biblical story of David and his son Absalom, the son prematurely tries to take his father's place and disrupt the "logical" sequence of primogeniture (II Samuel 11-19). He murders his older brother, Amnon, who would precede him in

Critical Insights

the order of succession, and then tries to usurp his father's throne by armed revolt. As a result, he is murdered, erased from the lineage, and his position is ultimately inhabited by another of David's sons, Solomon.

David, too, is punished for failing to follow the prescribed sequence of God's plan. Because David arranged the murder of Bathsheba's husband Uriah in order to make her his wife, God promises to "raise up evil" from within David's "own house" (II Samuel 12:11), a punishment fulfilled by Absalom. Later, when David desires to build a temple, God refuses to allow it: "Thou hast shed blood abundantly, and hast made great wars: thou shalt not blind an house unto my name, because thou hast shed much blood upon the earth in my sight" (I Chron. 22:8). Instead, God promises that Solomon, a man whose very name means peaceable, will build God's house as God's son: "And he shall be my son, and I will be his father; and I will establish the throne of his kingdom over Israel for ever" (I Chron. 12:10).

Since David's design was not aligned with God's, he is displaced as his own son's father *by* God, the eternal father and the origin of all fathers. Solomon is chosen because he is an Old Testament type, or forerunner, of the Son of God, the Prince of Peace. And even though Solomon's temple is destroyed in the destruction of the Jewish state, the temple is rebuilt during the restoration of Israel recorded in Ezra, and that temple is to exist eternally in the New Jerusalem prophesied in St. John's Revelation. In the Biblical pattern, destruction of the father's house is always followed by restoration, or reconstruction of that house by the father's male descendant.[3]

The Biblical model thus establishes that, despite reversals, the patriarchy is always restored. Faulkner's title calls attention to the disparity between that model and Sutpen's attempted but unsuccessful replication of it. Sutpen's design for a father's house to be preserved by his male descendants fails in part because he proves unable to replicate the linear pattern of history so necessary to the perpetuation of patriarchal antebellum Southern culture. Like David, Sutpen is a man of war, but in Faulkner's construct, this is no cardinal sin. Instead, Sutpen's fatal flaw is his view of the past.[4] As Carl Rollyson suggests,

> Sutpen's tragedy, indeed, is his lack of historical consciousness, his inability to adjust his sense of the past to the present. . . . He could not see the past as part of the continuum of time and of his own life. (81)

In a novel preeminently about origins and paternity, Sutpen is ignorant of his origins: he does not know his age or his birthplace (*AA* 184) nor his father's origins (181). Worse yet, his progress does not follow the linear pattern of history that makes the present a product of the past and thus predetermines the future.

His family leaves their home without intention or direction, merely falling from the mountains of West Virginia into the Tidewater, sliding "like a useless collection of flotsam on a flooded river moving by some perverse automotivation such as inanimate objects sometimes show, backward against the very current of the stream" (181). Where the journey begins there are no roads, and his father makes the trip "flat on his back in the cart, oblivious among the quilts and lanterns and well buckets and bundles of clothing and children" (181), a static, passive, feminized figure aligned with children and domestic objects, and thus an unfit pattern for a father. The journey is without beginning or end, becoming a "sort of dreamy and destinationless locomotion . . . during which they did not seem to progress at all" (182). Instead, the earth seems to pass by them "as if the cart moved on a treadmill" (182) in repetitive circles without linear progression.

Not only is Sutpen's faulty historical consciousness evident in his ignorance of origins, the non-linear "destinationless locomotion" that carries him away from those origins is replicated in his version of his personal history. When Sutpen relates that history to General Compson, he tells it without regard for continuity or completeness, leaving gaps in the story, stopping abruptly and then starting again without warning or transition:

He was telling some more of it, already into what he was telling yet still without telling how he got to where he was nor even how what he was now involved in . . . came to occur . . . ; this anecdote no deliberate continuation of the other one. (198-99)

At one point Compson stops Sutpen until he starts over "with at least some regard for cause and effect even if none for logical sequence and continuity" (199). Sutpen tells a story but without "recounting" his career. Much of his story is omitted, particularly the journey to Haiti, which he forgot along with how the revolt there began (205). In fact, he apparently did not know "the steps leading up to it," a further indication of his disregard for cause and effect (203). Omitting how he subdued the revolt, recovered from his wounds and became engaged, he finally stops talking, "flat and final like that, like that was all there was, all there could be to it, all of it that made good listening from one man to another" (206). The omissions in his story and its lack of closure frustrate General Compson, whose repeated cries of "Wait wait" (199, 204) beg for the gaps to be filled. Years later those same cries are echoed by Quentin and Shreve while they try to put together a more complete history.

After leaving Virginia, Sutpen wants to "shut that door himself forever behind him on all that he had ever known, and look ahead" (210), believing the future to be more important than the past so that he can alter the pattern of events set in motion within his past. Such a view is at odds with the traditional version of the Southern historical consciousness, the obsession with the past considered a dominant Southern characteristic and certainly dominant among the other characters in this novel. During the Haitian revolt, Sutpen is nearly castrated, sustaining a scar that General Compson says "came pretty near leaving him [a] virgin for the rest of his life" (205) and thus preventing him from extending his future beyond his own lifetime through his children. That future is the focus of his design, but the narrators of the novel (including Rosa Coldfield, who has been so shaped by the patriarchy that she echoes its values) persist in linking that design to their own narrative design of linear storytelling, making of Sutpen's life a connected, causal and complete story at great odds with Sutpen's own storytelling.

When Quentin tells Shreve the story Sutpen told General Compson, Shreve refuses to accept Sutpen's abruptly halted narrative and insists that Quentin not "bother to say he stopped now; just go on. . . . Just get on with it" (208). When Quentin gets sidetracked with the story of Sutpen's financial arrangement with Mr. Coldfield, Shreve interrupts: "But Sutpen. The design. Get on, now" (209). Sutpen's design for his future thus becomes, for Shreve and Quentin as well as for the reader of Faulkner's novel, a *narrative* design in which the listeners or readers cry "wait" when there is a gap to be filled and "go on" when the story line is diverted or sidetracked. The narrative picks up speed as it progresses, and at times even the cries of "wait" do not stop or even slow the narrative flow as Quentin and Shreve switch back and forth, often resuming as if the interruption had never occurred (221) and taking the story "up in stride without comma or colon or paragraph" (225).

At one point, after Quentin has insisted on maintaining possession of the narrative ("Wait, 1 tell you! . . . I am telling" [222]), Shreve replies, "No, you wait. Let me play a while now" (224). Not only has Sutpen's story become the possession of others, an object to be fought over, it has also become a game, the game of reconstructing history. Sutpen's version is "about something a man named Thomas Sutpen had experienced, which would still have been the same story if the man had had no name at all, if it had been told about any man or no man" (199). But in the hands of the others who tell his story for him, it becomes a story that *centers* on Sutpen's name, the name of the father, and his refusal to grant that name to his eldest son.

The rules of storytelling among these other narrators—the insistence upon filling in the blanks and achieving closure—pass judgment not only upon Sutpen's narrative design but also upon the design for his life, his plan to look toward the future and forget the past. The other narrators cannot escape the past. As Quentin thinks, "I am going to have to hear it all over again I am already hearing it all over again I am listening to it all over again I shall have to never listen to anything else but this again forever" (222). Nor will the other narrators let Sutpen escape, even after his death, for they keep his ghost imprisoned within the history they keep telling and retelling.

But what motivates these narrators to take over Sutpen's story? What in his own version, his own design, is inimical to them? His resistance to linearity, his determination to look forward rather than backward and to work for a self-created future rather than one predetermined by the past contradict the logic that supports the patriarchal system in which he wishes to participate. Sutpen tells General Compson that he wants to become a wealthy planter, a planter wealthier and finer than the man whose slave had turned the boy Sutpen away from the front door. Once he had attained that position, Sutpen meant to

take that boy in . . . so that that boy, that whatever nameless stranger, could shut that door himself forever behind him on all that he had ever known, and look ahead along the still undivulged light rays in which his descendants who might not even ever hear his (the boy's) name, waited to be born without even having to know that they had once been riven forever free from brutehood just as his own (Sutpen's) children were. (210)

In *Sutpen's Design*, Dirk Kuyk, Jr., argues that Sutpen plans to become part of the plantation aristocracy and take in a nameless stranger so that he can make that stranger part of the *class* that had excluded Sutpen as a boy. Rather than replicating the scene in which he had been turned away from the plantation door, Sutpen plans to reverse the scene and act according to an opposing logic: "Sutpen intends to free the stranger's descendants from brutehood forever and, by doing so, to strike at the heart of the patriarchal structure on which not only the southern plantation but also Western culture itself had been based" (21).[5]

But Sutpen is never accepted by the plantation aristocracy and remains in the margins although he acquires all the accoutrements. They cannot accept him because he is an "underbred" man whose lower-class origins show "in all his formal contacts with people" (*AA* 34). His "trouble was innocence" (178); he does not know that his acquisitions will never include a new origin or hide his old one. On the surface, Sutpen's design should be acceptable since, as Carolyn Porter points out, it mirrors plantation society, yet the mirror of Sutpen's design is flawed by what it reflects—the "conflicts and contradictions inherent in that society" (235). In striving for his (American) dream, Sutpen is stopped dead by the contradiction at its core: the self-made man who rises from nothing still must enter a highly codified class structure obsessed with the fantasy of origins. His antagonism to the system he mimics is inherent in the system itself.

His innocence requires him to believe that "the ingredients of morality were like the ingredients of pie or cake" (*AA* 211), and he relates to General Compson the "logical steps by which he had arrived at a result absolutely and forever incredible, repeating the clear and simple synopsis of his history" (212). At this point, Sutpen is trying to explain to Compson his design, which he imagines to be logical and orderly, and is therefore unable to understand its failure. As a result, he assumes he has made a mistake, left out a step, omitted an ingredient, and that in recounting his history (something of which he earlier seemed incapable) he can find his error (215). After telling Compson his story, Sutpen rides away (ironically back to Virginia), struggling to hold on to "his code of logic and morality, his formula and recipe of fact and deduction whose balanced sum and product declined, refused to swim or even float" (221). Although he tries to ape the logic of the masculine ruling class, his logic is still associated with the feminine: his moral code is concocted as if he were baking a pie or cake.

One thing he fails to see is that his recipe lacks an ingredient he will never have—the correct origin. That lack prevents his progress and denies him active motion. The boy whose family had left Virginia like

"flotsam on a flooded river moving by some perverse automotivation . . . against the very current of the stream" (181) now appears unable to swim *or* float. Whereas his earlier journey had seemed to be locomotion without progression (182), he now seems immobile. After
the war, his acquired "shrewdness . . . broke down, it vanished into that
old impotent logic and morality which had betrayed him before," and
he "stopped dead" with the realization that he must hurry to rectify his
lack of a son (224). But his plan to have a son with Rosa fails because
he "bogged himself again in his morality which had all the parts but
which refused to run, to move" (224). His impotent, immobile (and
thus stereotypically feminized) logic does not equip him to succeed because his lack cannot be rectified by producing a son. He appears on
horseback throughout the novel, constantly riding into and out of scene
after scene, but when Wash sees him just before his death, Sutpen is an
image "galloping through avatars which marked the accumulation of
years, time, to the fine climax where it galloped without weariness or
progress" (231). His motion is without progress, and he still ends up
where he began—without prosperity or posterity, without past or future, father or son.

At this point in the narrative, the scene shifts to Quentin and
Shreve's dormitory room at Harvard, a place "dedicated to that best of
ratiocination which after all was a good deal like Sutpen's morality"
(225). Here Sutpen's logic is aligned with the logic of the Western culture that otherwise appears to exclude him. But there immediately follows a reference to Sutpen as "Quentin's Mississippi shade who in life
had acted and reacted to the minimum of logic and morality, who dying
had escaped it completely, who dead remained not only indifferent but
impervious to it" (225). This description again clarifies Sutpen's inability to acquire the logic that supports the Southern plantation aristocracy.

The men who make up that aristocracy maintain it by setting "the
order and the rule of living," and that order is based upon boundaries,
upon lines that exclude difference. The threshold that stopped Sutpen

at the door of the plantation in Virginia represents a line that separates class from class. His logic is outside a system based on difference because he *represents* difference. To include him, much less the nameless stranger he wishes to include, is to erase the order that grants the aristocracy power and privilege. Although the Biblical King David was not an aristocrat from birth, he crosses class lines with permission of the highest authority: he is chosen by God to become Israel's king.[6] Although antebellum Southerners saw themselves as a classless society since anyone at the bottom could supposedly rise to the top (one reason the poor majority fought to support the wealthy minority), there remained a desire to *believe* in aristocratic origins.[7] To take in Charles Bon as the stranger is, of course, to do away with not only the difference of class but that of race as well, and the line between the races was a much more serious division than that between classes.[8]

In the New Testament, Christ tells his followers that by taking in strangers, they are taking in Christ ("Inasmuch as ye have done it unto one of the least of these my brethren, ye have done it unto me"—Matthew 25:40), a sentiment echoed in Hebrews 13: "Be not forgetful to entertain strangers: for thereby some have entertained angels unawares" (verse 2). Furthermore, the New Testament Christ brings together the formerly divided Gentiles ("strangers from the covenants of promise") and Jews, breaking down "the middle wall of partition" that had separated them (Ephesians 2:12-14). But whereas in the New Testament, "there is neither Jew nor Greek, there is neither bond nor free, there is neither male nor female" since all are united in Christ as "Abraham's seed and heirs" (Galatians 3:28-29), the Old South in Faulkner's novel still operates under Old Testament values. The patriarchal pattern of their society depends upon divisions of class, race and gender. To erase those boundaries would be to alter the patriarchal path of history and produce an alternative future.

Absalom, Absalom! presents a history that maintains those old lines. The doorways at which both Thomas Sutpen and Charles Bon stand separate class and race, but there is another doorway, another line, other figures left standing on the outside: Judith Sutpen and Rosa Coldfield's sex leaves them outside the patriarchal house and the patriarchal narrative. In *Discourses of Desire*, Linda Kauffman comments on the "astonishing number of forbidden doors, gates, and corridors" in the novel, adding that these images "contribute to the sense of the novel as a labyrinth and to the narrative line as a thread" (252-53). Kauffman reads Rosa as Ariadne to Sutpen's Theseus but pays little attention to Rosa's role within that mythic paradigm.[9]

Faulkner's Judith Sutpen uses a weaving metaphor to describe the chaos she sees in relationships. To Judith, people are all mixed up together, attached to each other by strings, trying to achieve goals for motives they do not understand, "like five or six people all trying to make a rug on the same loom only each one wants to weave his own pattern into the rug" (101). This image embodies the recognition that there is no single pattern to be found in history, no single path that will take one out of the labyrinth that is life. But Judith's image is superseded by another, for "all of a sudden it's all over and all you have left is a block of stone with scratches on it" (101). The feminine image of the loom, of the pattern that can never become a single, discernible pattern because there are too many weavers with individual perspectives, disappears and leaves a monumental, phallic stone with a fixed, singular text inscribed upon it.

Of course, Judith adds that eventually the writing on the stone will become meaningless scratches and the name upon it forgotten. She proposes an alternative in the exchange of a letter passing from one hand or mind to another, making a mark on something living rather than dead. As Patrick McGee says of that exchange,

> In passing Bon's letter to Quentin's grandmother, Judith ties herself . . . to the descendants of the entire human community. By passing it out of her family, she passes it to the radical alterity of an indeterminate history where its trajectory and purpose cannot be governed or predicted. (50)

Because Judith privileges the letter "as *sumbolon*, a part or fragment," McGee elaborates, the letter enters into a never-completed process, "the process of symbolic exchange": "Through exchange, the letter as event (re)constitutes the human collective" (51). But such an interpretation is undercut by the fact that Judith's voice is overwhelmed by Mr. Compson's, who reminds us that the letter Judith passes on is Charles Bon's, that the text is, as always in this novel, authored by a man.[10] And in Mr. Compson's version, the letter makes its "undying mark," not on something living, but "on the blank face of the oblivion to which we are all doomed" (*AA* 102). What surfaces in his interpretation of Judith's alternative vision is the doom that awaits at the end of Faulkner's teleological historical design.

Judith's voice and vision are not the only voices supplanted in Faulkner's novel, for throughout *Absalom, Absalom!* women's voices are drowned out by male voices. Faulkner constantly reduces them from writing, speaking subjects to the blank page upon which men write. When Rosa Coldfield begins telling her story (which is actually Sutpen's), her voice "would not cease, it would just vanish" as Sutpen's ghost haunts, or inhabits her voice as if it were a house (4). His voice, unlike hers, is Godlike as he speaks Sutpen's Hundred into existence *ex nihilo*, "like the oldentime *Be Light*" (4). Yet even that diminishing of her voice is insufficient, for Quentin takes over, becoming two Quentins, both speaker and listener, with Rosa's words in parentheses.[11] Much like Sadie Burke handing over her knowledge to Jack Burden in *All the King's Men*, Rosa tells Quentin her story so that he may write it, even though a woman who could write poetry could write her own story (6). She offers the story for his profit, not hers, claiming that he may sell it to a magazine and buy domestic trinkets for his wife.[12] Faulkner, like Warren, creates an articulate female only to have her voice subsumed by the male characters around her.

But Rosa's gift is not enough for Quentin, who immediately begins rewriting her story, deciding that her stated motive is a lie, that "she wants it told" (5). In his version, the only way the story *can* be told is by a male subject who can fulfill the woman's desire to speak. Furthermore, he concludes that the purpose of the narrative is to explain "why God let us lose the War," making the story a causal history of that most masculine of historical events, war (6). He then decides that the motive behind her story is the man, Thomas Sutpen, whose ghost, "as though in inverse ratio to the vanishing voice . . . began to assume a quality almost of solidity, permanence" (8).

Rosa's narrative method disturbs Quentin, who complains that "the getting to [the reason for choosing him] . . . was taking a long time" (8), and her telling seemed "to partake of that logic- and reason-flouting quality of a dream" (15). Her narrative must be rewritten, retold through the filter of a masculine voice so that it leaves the feminine realm of the dream, in which the repressed surfaces, and returns to the masculine realm of logic and reason. Mr. Compson claims that women are "irrevocably excommunicated" from reality (156), that they draw sustenance from an unreality in which facts have no ability to hurt them, and that they can ignore "*incontrovertible evidence*" (171), all traits that disqualify them from participating in Faulkner's version of historical narrative.

Faulkner's subversion of the female narrative tacitly endorses Mr. Compson's notion that women are removed from reality. Rosa attempts an alternative, feminine version of history when she asks if "true wisdom . . . can comprehend that there is a might-have-been which is more true than truth," a might-have-been she connects with dreaming (115). She goes on to declare that "there is no such thing as memory: the brain recalls just what the muscles grope for: no more, no less: and its resultant sum is usually incorrect and false and worthy only of the name of dream" (115). Like Laurel McKelva at the end of Welty's *The Optimist's Daughter*, Rosa is aware that memory fictionalizes her historical narrative.[13] Here, as in Judith's image of the loom, Faulkner seems to offer a feminine narrative, a feminine version of history. But again, that version is subsumed by the master narrative that persists in drowning out the feminine voice, and Rosa ultimately speaks as an agent of patriarchy, supporting rather than subverting it.

Although Kauffman admits that Rosa "gets lost in translation" (267), she insists that Rosa defies the dominant logic of the phallus by positing another logic in her "true wisdom which can comprehend that there is a might-have-been which is more true than truth" (*AA* 115). After Rosa claims that "might-have-been . . . is the single rock we cling to above the maelstrom of unbearable reality," she goes on to speak of the war years when the "stable world" of peace and security, pride and hope dissolved (120). All that remained was "love and faith," but Rosa's apparent affirmation of love and faith does not actually oppose the abstracting masculine economics at work in the novel. Instead, she believes love and faith were "left with us by fathers, husbands, sweethearts, brothers" who fought the war and died "for that love and faith they left behind" (120). For Rosa, this legacy—a remnant of the dissolved, stable, masculine South before the war—is all that has been salvaged from the "old lost enchantment of the heart" (121). Here she seems to repeat the sentiment found in Faulkner's and Mr. Compson's speeches, returning us to the "old virtues," the "old verities and truths of the human heart." Faulkner makes her a mouthpiece for the masculine vision expressed in Mr. Compson's voice, and elsewhere his own, since Rosa, too, associates pride and hope and love and faith with a lost, masculine world.

In spite of Rosa's feminine narrative meandering, her vision of history and the version she tells is linear and teleological, in keeping with her Calvinist father's theology.[14] She tells Quentin at the beginning of her story that her own life "was destined," as well as the lives of her sister's "two doomed children" (12). If all their lives are moving toward some predetermined end, then she should be able to reconstruct that path those lives have followed. But, as a woman, associated by Mr. Compson with "the fluid cradle of events" (51) rather than the causal progression of events, she is still an inadequate historian.

By handing the story over to Quentin, she allows the narrative she cannot sort out, piece together and tie up ("since there is no all, no finish" [121]) to be concluded. She ultimately lets go of the threads and the loom so that the masculine pattern can be woven. Shreve claims that Rosa refused to be a ghost or let Sutpen lie in peace because she wanted closure but could not manage that closure alone:

> That even after fifty years she not only could get up and go out there to finish up what she found she hadn't quite completed, but she could find someone to go with her and bust into that locked house because instinct or something told her it was not finished yet. (290)

In spite of her masculine "instinct" that demands the story be finished, Rosa's femaleness makes her incapable of finishing the story herself. She is still on the outside of the threshold, standing outside the door of a locked house. Quentin drives her onto Sutpen's "Domain," where she is determined to discover what is hidden in the dark house of patriarchy. She seems possessed, as if "it were not she who had to go and find out but she only the helpless agent of someone or something else who must know" (292). Although she gives the directions to Quentin, as if she were in command of the events, she is in fact the agent of the patriarchal logic that will control the narrative. She cannot pass the gatepost, standing beside it whimpering until Quentin walks through it with her. Although she carries a phallic umbrella, flashlight and a hatchet, as if to compensate for her feminine lack, she still cannot walk without stumbling, finally having to grip Quentin's arm. Giving the hatchet to him, she must be guided toward the steps and "almost lifted, carried" up the steps, supported "from behind by both elbows as you lift a child" (293). Although Rosa then runs across the gallery to the door, there she is again stopped dead. When Quentin hesitates to break the door, Rosa asks him to give her back the hatchet, but the inexorable logic of Faulkner's masculine narrative cannot allow her to enter the patriarchal house unaided.[15] Instead, Quentin easily breaks through the shuttered window, the shutters proving "a flimsy and sloven barricad-

---

ing done either by an old feeble person—woman—or by a shiftless man" to Quentin's hatchet blade (294).

Once Quentin enters the house, the door can be opened for Rosa. Although Clytie is the one who actually opens the door, she does so "as if she had known all the time that this hour must come and that it could not be resisted" (295). The door must be opened once the master narrator (Clytie even calls him "young marster") is in the house so that he can discover the missing piece and finish the story. By knocking Clytie down "with a full-armed blow like a man would have" (295), Rosa is aligned with the masculine long enough to ascend the stairs. Once she comes back down, she is taken to the gate and the buggy by Jim Bond, "the scion, the heir, the apparent (though not obvious)" (296). Because she refuses Jim's arm or advice about where to walk, she stumbles and falls. After Quentin drives her back home, he has to lift her down out of the buggy, support her and lead her through the gate, up the walk and into the house (297). She moves "like a mechanical doll" into her "doll-sized" house, her "fixed" face looking like a sleep-walker's (297).

What is hidden within the Sutpen house, the secret she discovers when Quentin accompanies her, is the male heir (actually, two male heirs) to the Sutpen line. Quentin is compelled to walk up the stairway, down the hall, and, in spite of his resistance, must go through the door to find Henry Sutpen. By killing Charles Bon, Henry has redrawn the lines between the races, lines that Charles's mixed blood blurs. After the murder, Henry disappears, having "abjured his father and renounced his birthright" (62), forcing Sutpen's failed attempts to sire a new heir. Just as Henry draws a line that he forbids Charles to pass ("Dont you pass the shadow of this post, this branch" [106]), he redraws the cultural lines between race and class. And those lines result in his imprisonment within the patriarchal house, a house he cannot escape (as he cannot escape the law) without destroying both the house and himself within it. The lines that excluded women have never been threatened. When Rosa returns to the Sutpen house in an ambulance (this time without Quentin but still accompanied and driven there by men), she still cannot enter the house. The men who take her there physically restrain her from entering the now unlocked door. Although she does not die in the fire along with Henry and Clytie, she does not speak again, slipping into a coma and dying soon thereafter.

Yet the house is not destroyed by Henry, but by Clytie, a woman, and one of mixed race, a doubly marginal figure who sacrifices herself to protect the patriarchy that has kept her in the margins.[16] Like Rosa, Clytie is shut up in the father's house in spite of the keys both carry. But patriarchy has not been destroyed when Clytie sets fire to the house; Sutpen's faulty, feminized version of it has. His attempts to join, or to subvert, the patriarchy fail, but that failure is "his allotted course to its violent (Miss Coldfield at least would have said, just) end" (7). He had abrupted upon the Old South from "*out of nowhere*" (4-5) and "out of no discernible past" (7) without concern for sequence. The eldest son cannot inherit his father's kingdom because of his black blood, a taint that stems from his mother: "he had stemmed from the blood after whatever it was his mother had been or done had tainted and corrupted it" (264-65). His race excludes him from any legal lineage, nor can Sutpen acknowledge Charles Bon as his son and heir and retain his kingdom.

In one of Quentin's imagined reconstructions, Charles considers his situation a "jigsaw puzzle picture" in which the answer is "just beyond his reach, inextricable, jumbled, and unrecognizable yet on the point of falling into pattern which would reveal to him at once, like a flash of light, the meaning of his whole life, past" (250). The missing piece is the father he does not have, and he believes that the moment he sees that father "he would know; there would be that flash, that instant of indisputable recognition between them and he would know for sure and forever" (255). That these views belong to *Quentin*'s version of Charles is significant. As Quentin's voice overwhelms Rosa's (whose voice is always already overwhelmed by the patriarchal values she echoes), his Southern white male perspective swallows up the possibility of another narrative. The racially-mixed Bon, like the lower-class Sutpen, is feminized throughout the novel and, as a result, is not authorized to tell his own story. Rather than imagining other possible motivations, other narratives for these characters marginalized by race, class and gender, Faulkner makes them all become, like Shreve and Quentin, echoes of the father's voice.

In one sense, the search for the pattern of the past is the search for the father. Roland Barthes describes the "pleasure of the text" as an "Oedipal pleasure (to denude, to know, to learn the origin and the end), if it is true that every narrative (every unveiling of the truth) is a staging of the (absent, hidden, or hypostatized) father" (10). In *Absalom, Absalom!* this staging of the father is at work in Charles Bon's attempts to gain Sutpen's recognition. However, Bon's mixed race (in a white society that excludes the other race) prevents the moment of illumination and closure possible, for example, in *All the King's Men*. Instead, the ledgers are not cleared, the dark house not totally destroyed, because Jim Bond remains—uncatchable, unusable, and threatening to "conquer the Western hemisphere" (302). Once again, the imperialist father's voice takes over as Shreve assumes an equally "imperialist" motive in Jim Bond, a character not only disqualified from telling his own story by race but also denied even a comprehensible human voice. He is finally reduced to a distant, bestial howl that cannot be located (300-01).

By leaving the racially mixed heir at large, Faulkner leaves the post-Civil War South unreconstructed. That former world, that "country all divided and fixed and neat with a people living on it all divided and fixed and neat because of what color their skins happened to be and what they happened to own" (179), is irrevocably lost. Just as Charles Bon cannot be compensated for the loss of a father (since those "who could have given him a father had declined to do it, . . . revenge could not compensate him nor love assuage" [274]), there is no compensation, no pay-back or redemption for the loss of the Old South, of that "dead time" that Mr. Compson considers "simpler . . . larger, more heroic" (71). Compson considers those former heroic figures "distinct, uncomplex," unlike the fragmented people living in the present, "diffused and scattered creatures drawn blindly limb from limb from a grab bag and assembled" (71).

Much recent Faulkner criticism considers the role of loss in Faulkner's writing (Gwin, Matthews, and Mortimer). John Matthews claims that, for Faulkner, "writing itself is as much a kind of loss as it is a kind of compensation" (19). Although Matthews admits that "Faulkner's novels display a nostalgia" for the "loss of authoritative truth, the center, the signified realm, the place of origin, innocence," he also sees the apparent lack of "conclusive sense" in the novels as proof of "a spirit of lively play about the possibilities of infinite interpretation" (36). Faulkner certainly plays with the reconstructed Sutpen story in *Absalom, Absalom!*, leaving the reader with historical inventions "probably true enough" (*AA* 268) from narrators willing to accept the fictionality of truth. But the form of that historical fiction, the way in which Faulkner patterns his play, signifies more than a paradoxical, yet innocent sense of loss.

Part of what is lost in the Old South is the division between races, classes, and genders that enabled white males to maintain authority and mastery. With the blurring of those lines, the power of patriarchy is undermined and Southern white males left with a sense of powerlessness and loss that extends beyond structures of language. They have lost the ownership of the other race, part of the material base that supports their hierarchy. Heidi Hartmann defines patriarchy as "relations between men, which have a material base, and which, though hierarchical, establish or create interdependence and solidarity among men that enable them to dominate women" (14). As compensation for the losses that threaten that solidarity, Faulkner reconstructs history in forms that dominate the women within his history.

When Quentin and Shreve work to provide the closure that Rosa cannot, they engage in an all-male "marriage of speaking and hearing," creating "this shade whom they discussed (rather, existed in) and in the hearing and sifting and discarding the false and conserving what seemed true, or fit the preconceived—in order to overpass to love, where there might be paradox and inconsistency but nothing fault nor false" (253). Beginning with this passage, Matthews describes Quentin and Shreve hunting for explanations "as hunters follow tracks," on a hunt in which "the quarry seems less compelling than the excitement of the pursuit" (16). In other words, whether the shades created are true or false, whether the explanation or answer they offer is *the* answer does not matter so much as the pursuit of that answer. As Matthews says, "The trail is the destination" (16). Or, as Jack Burden claims in *All the King's Men*, "Direction is all" (384).

For both Faulkner and Warren, life is defined as motion, and the women within their narratives are outside that motion. Since the trail, the journey toward the answer at the end of narrative (which, in both Faulkner and Warren, is tied to the search for the father) is a journey through language, telling the tale gives life to the tellers. Quentin and Shreve not only tell a story, they also "exist in" the telling, in the narrative motion toward its end. As Matthews writes, "The tellers of tales seem to have no life or consciousness—no selfhood—exterior to their speech" (16), adding that for "Faulkner's characters not to speak . . . is for them not to be" (31). By denying motion and narration to his women characters, Faulkner excludes them from history and life, thus constructing a world even more patriarchal than the Old South he has lost.

However, Faulkner's created world is *not* a re-construction but a fictional realm that significantly belongs to him as its creator. He is "sole owner and proprietor" of this land and its people, more godlike in his power than the masters of the Old South ever were. He also uses his own version of Biblical history, a version that reflects his attraction to Old Testament paradigms. Faulkner placed the Old Testament first among the list of books he read as a young man and returned to repeatedly "as you do to old friends," commenting further that reading the Old Testament made him "feel good" (Cowley 129, 136). His work reflects the Puritan heritage he describes in *Absalom, Absalom!* as "a granite heritage where even the houses, let alone clothing and conduct, are built in the image of a jealous and sadistic Jehovah" (86). Although he includes the comment that people "evoke God or devil to justify them in what their glands insisted upon" (276), he also sets up the flesh ("the old mindless sentient undreaming meat") in opposition to God:

> if you dont have God and you dont need food and clothes and shelter, there isn't anything for honor and pride to climb on and hold to and flourish. And if you haven't got honor and pride, then nothing matters. (279)

Here God becomes the base upon which the old verities are founded, and he is the Old Testament God who sets history in motion at creation and predetermines the path it will follow to the apocalypse—the destruction of earth by fire and the restoration of Israel in the New Jerusalem.[17] In other words, history will return to its origin, the great Patriarch, who, with his only son, will rule his unified kingdom by his transcendent word.

Faulkner's attraction to this paradigm in writing about the history of the Old South does not include the promise of its restoration. Instead, he restores the Old South by means of narrative reconstructions that repeat the historical pattern of what has been lost. Ironically, the voice that articulates that irreparable loss and impossibility of reconstruction is the voice of a woman like Judith Sutpen or Rosa Coldfield or, in Faulkner's most extended feminine monologue, Addie Bundren in *As I Lay Dying*. The latter character embodies Faulkner's contradictory and ambivalent relation to his own view of history. Women speak the truth of history; but even as they speak, their voices are erased by the process of dying. Like Addie, Faulkner's women are neither in nor out of history.

In *The Feminine and Faulkner*, Minrose Gwin asks, "Does Faulkner want Rosa silenced, or is he writing her silence as the hysterical symptom of the Old South's narrative of mastery?" (71). Her answer depends upon reading a "bisexual artistic consciousness" within the tension between Rosa's narrative and the male voices that overwhelm it. Rosa's feminine narrative, consisting of gaps and ruptures, is powerful because it makes and unmakes Sutpen, who becomes "a castrated shadow of a man, cut off from the object of his desire—his replication in a son" (104). Responding to critics who see the father at the center of the novel, she declares *Absalom, Absalom!* "Faulkner's most sustained revocation of the Father and his mastery" (76-77) since Rosa's "mad text . . . enacts the death of the Father, the demise of Sutpen" (104). But what happens to these arguments once Sutpen's feminine subversiveness is acknowledged? What power does Rosa's narrative have if he is already "cut off" from the overwhelming patriarchal text that rewrites his story as it rewrites hers?

Even Gwin, in spite of her determination to "trust Faulkner," admits that, "as he drags us into this bog of male discourse, we must struggle to keep our heads up so that we can speak what that silence means" (105). In "Feminism and Faulkner," she admits to "second thoughts" that reveal more doubt than trust: "What he does do so well is to show the *process* of women's silencing, the appropriative gesture of white male dominance—the naturalization of systems of oppression. Ironically Faulkner does this so well because of his participation in such systems" (61). What he does not do is go beyond the gaps, the disruptions, to empower female subjects who not only unravel the patriarchal text but spin their own alternative texts. Neither Sutpen nor Faulkner finally opens the door to subversion.

When Mr. Compson declares women "irrevocably excommunicated" from reality, he adds that their funerals and graves are "of incalculable importance" (156). Women are thus connected with the grave and its dark silence in opposition to the facts and events that are to them mere "shades and shapes" (171). But the significant word in Compson's description is "excommunicated," for women are *excluded* from Faulknerian history's facts and events by *excommunication*, by being excluded from language and narration. Grandfather Compson defines language as that meagre and fragile thread . . . by which the little surface corners and edges of men's secret and solitary lives may be joined for an instant now and then before sinking back into the darkness where the spirit cried for the first time and was not heard and will cry for the last time and will not be heard then either. (202)

The grave is a place outside of language, a place from which one's voice cannot be heard, and thus a place in which women cannot find community and solidarity. By denying them the thread of language and the telling of their own stories, Faulkner, like Warren, denies women access to the loom and protects the patriarchal pattern repeatedly woven in nostalgic Southern texts. To Quentin, Rosa's summons seems "out of another world almost," her note written in a "neat faded cramped script" (5), and her voice—from that otherness of the feminine—is cramped by the male narrators' own scripts until she is mute, her story faded into oblivion. Addie Bundren proclaims her distrust of a language that has excluded her, calling words "just a shape to fill a lack" (172). For Faulkner, the shape of history in his narratives compensates for the loss of the patriarchal Old South, restoring authority to men who tell the stories over and over while the women listen silently from the grave.

Courtesy of *The Faulkner Journal*, VII: 1 & 2 (Fall 1991/Spring 1992). Copyright © 1992 by the University of Central Florida. Reprinted with permission.

Notes

1. As in Warren's novel, the narrative belongs to men. Although Faulkner claims that *The Sound and the Fury* is "a tragedy of two lost women," the story is told by the male relatives of those two women. The last section is referred to as Dilsey's, but, as Faulkner admits, he is the final spokesman.

2. In contrast to the masculine figures are Faulkner's usually enigmatic female characters, which have produced surprisingly various critical stances. Wittenberg, who concedes the prevalence of the male voice and viewpoint in Faulkner's fiction, as well as the circumscription and limited options of his fictional women (336), ulti-

mately defends him from accusations of being either pro- or anti-female. Mortimer sees Faulkner's women as representing paradoxical masculine responses to the feminine, both attraction and repulsion ("The Smooth Suave Shape of Desire" 150), and she concludes that the typical Faulkner character "experiences women in archaic ways" (159), an argument that points again to the "old verities" undergirding Faulkner's constructions of masculinity and femininity. Critics like Gwin and Donaldson argue that Faulkner's women characters subvert traditional notions of the feminine and of history; however, their interpretations valorize women's *silence* as feminine subversion. In a reversal of Gwin's claim that the feminine subverts the apparently patriarchal text, Peter Brooks argues that the primary narrative pattern is masculine: the narrative center is the history of a male character, Thomas Sutpen, and the transmission of that history is largely from father to son. As Brooks succinctly states, "Nothing can be solved or explained without getting Sutpen's story straight" (300), and the Compson lineage sets out to solve this male-centered, historical detective story. The nostalgic attempts to recover the past and to order history that in Brooks's argument merely haunt the text, are, I believe, at the center of Faulkner's project.

3. Hagopian draws other parallels between the Biblical story and Faulkner's novel but concludes that the relation between the two is "by ironic inversion" since Sutpen "neither triumphs nor survives his younger son and he does not lament his disappearance" (134).

4. Whether or not Charles Bon is of mixed race would not necessarily interfere with Sutpen's plan since Sutpen's dynasty was to be founded upon Henry rather than Bon. See Brooks (298) and Kuyk (13-14).

5. Kuyk goes on to argue that Sutpen must refuse to open his door to Charles Bon because Bon is *not* a nameless stranger but his own son (23). That Bon is of mixed race is one of five other, less important reasons Kuyk offers for Sutpen's rejection of Bon (27). Kuyk's effort to rank class difference above racial difference is unnecessary since both kinds of difference support the plantation system Sutpen tries to join.

6. While David is king, he does bring a stranger into his household, but that stranger, far from nameless, is Mephibosheth, the son of Jonathan and therefore the grandson of the former king, Saul. David not only welcomes the boy into his home but also restores to him all Saul's lands (II Samuel 9) "because of the Lord's oath that was between them, between David and Jonathan the son of Saul" (21:7). In this instance, the male heir has his property restored as a result of a homoerotic bond. Mephibosheth's lameness (a result of being dropped by his nurse; see 4:4) apparently disqualifies him for God-anointed kingship.

7. Brooks describes the "society of the lower South in the nineteenth century" as "rather fluid" with flexible class lines: "Men did rise in one generation from log cabins to great landed estates. But the past was important, blood was important, and Southern society thought of itself as traditional" (297). In *Social Relations in Our Southern States*, an 1860 defense of Southern society, Hundley describes the "Southern Gentleman" as one who "comes of a good stock . . . usually of aristocratic parentage," a man of "faultless pedigree" (27-28). For further discussion of various historians' views on the antebellum South's social structure, see Campbell.

8. In Porter's Marxist reading of the novel, Sutpen's treatment of Bon replicates

America's treatment of Native and African Americans. That Sutpen's paternal authority results in the repudiation of his son is the "logical, if self-contradictory, consequence of a paternalism generated in the interest of Capital, a paternalism which logically dictates that fathers exile and repudiate their sons" (235). The moment he comes closest to the masculine logic that excludes and evades him is the moment that irrevocably destroys his design.

9. Kauffman does note that the "male characters see female sexuality as a labyrinth" (265). But in her argument, Sutpen is the figure trying to escape, a focus which leaves the patriarchal labyrinth that entraps the women relatively unexplored.

10. Porter claims the speech is Judith's (265), but Krause argues that the "context, construction, length, style, and tone all mark it as fundamentally the (re-)invention of Compson" (231-32).

11. Weinstein argues that Rosa, unlike Mr. Compson, talks *at* Quentin rather than *to* him, and that Quentin "can only assent to" her rather than question her (91). But, in fact, Quentin not only dissents, he also rewrites her while she is still speaking.

12. Both Sadie and Rosa share the Sphinx's role in the myth of Oedipus as De Lauretis describes it: "She only served to test Oedipus and qualify him as hero. Having fulfilled her narrative function . . . , her question is now subsumed in his; her power, his; her fateful gift of knowledge, soon to be his" (112).

13. Weinstein argues that Rosa's "utterance" is "unaware of its status as a *narrative*" and that Rosa "does not ponder" or ever "say maybe" (92). Her comments on memory (quoted above) belie that argument.

14. Kauffman's claim that, "despite her imprisonment in the rigid structures of male logic and patriarchal discourse, Rosa Coldfield manages to defy those structures and to make an affirmation by embroidering her vision of what might-have-been" is seriously undercut by the footnote attached to that claim:

> I should note that even when Rosa is not being interpreted by Mr. Compson, Quentin, or Shreve, there are moments when her own voice is clearly Calvinistic. Nevertheless, those passages can be attributed to Rosa as *voice*—looking back after Sutpen injures her—rather than to Rosa as *focus*. (276)

Accepting Kauffman's odd dichotomy of voice and focus (and ignoring her focus throughout the argument on Rosa's *voice*) still does not counter the weight of Rosa's Calvinism.

15. A simpler explanation for her ineffectuality is her age. Nonetheless, that Faulkner chooses to make her a weak, doddering old lady incapable of independent prowess reinforces his pattern of portraying ineffectual women. Furthermore, Rosa is perfectly capable, once in the house, of dashing up the stairs and shoving Clytie out of her way.

16. Makowsky has drawn my attention to the possibility that Clytie, having been a black matriarch for years, may be protecting that matriarchy from Quentin, and that she may prefer destroying her world rather than having the patriarchy tie up all the loose ends and exclude truth. However, I am not convinced that Clytie's domain would qualify as a black matriarchy, in part because she is caring for the male heirs of a man

who not only fathered her but *owned* her as well. Her status, even after emancipation, does not seem authoritative. She cannot stop even the slightly-built Rosa from penetrating the recesses of her domain.

17. Bleikasten describes Joe Christmas as "much closer to the jealous Jehovah of the Old Testament than to the Man-God of the Gospels" (132), adding that "there is little Christianity in the society portrayed in *Light in August*" (135). However, he claims that the religion of Yoknapatawpha is *not* that of the Old Testament because "no covenant has sealed the mutual recognition of father and son" and Christmas's death does not discharge the debt (135). That failure to discharge the debt, the failure of the sacrifice to bring redemption, is precisely what *does* make the covenant an Old Testament one. The sacrifice of animals did not atone for sin. Only Christ's death could abolish that old code and provide redemption. In spite of Joe Christmas's name, he is no New Testament figure and therefore *cannot* discharge the debt even through a sacrificial death.

Works Cited

Barthes, Roland. *The Pleasure of the Text*. Trans. Richard Miller. New York: Hill, 1975.

Bleikasten, André. "Fathers in Faulkner." *The Fictional Father*. Ed. Robert Con Davis. Amherst: U of Massachusetts P, 1981. 115-46.

Brooks, Cleanth. *William Faulkner: Toward Yoknapatawpha and Beyond*. New Haven: Yale UT, 1978.

Brooks, Peter. *Reading for the Plot: Design and Intention in Narrative*. New York: Knopf, 1984.

Campbell, Randolph B. "Planters and Plain Folks: The Social Structure of the Antebellum South." *Interpreting Southern History*. Ed. John B. Boles and Evelyn Thomas Nolen. Baton Rouge: Louisiana State UP, 1987. 48-77.

Cowley, Malcolm, ed. *Writers at Work*. New York: Viking, 1959.

De Lauretis, Teresa. *Alice Doesn't: Feminism, Semiotics, Cinema*. Bloomington: Indiana UP, 1984.

Donaldson, Susan V. "Subverting History: Women and Narrative in *Absalom, Absalom!*" *Southern Quarterly* 4 (1988): 19-32.

Faulkner, William. *Absalom, Absalom! The Corrected Text*. New York: Vintage International, 1990.

_____. *As I Lay Dying: The Corrected Text*. New York: Vintage International, 1990.

_____. *Essays, Speeches & Public Letters by William Faulkner*. Ed. James B. Meriwether. New York: Random House, 1966.

_____. "An Introduction to *The Sound and the Fury*." *A Faulkner Miscellany*. Ed. James B. Meriwether. Jackson: UP of Mississippi, 1974.

_____. *Selected Letters of William Faulkner*. Ed. Joseph Blotner. New York: Random House, 1977.

Fowler, Doreen, and Ann J. Abadie, eds. *Faulkner and Women: Faulkner and Yoknapatawpha, 1985*. Jackson: UP of Mississippi, 1986.

Gwin, Minrose C. *The Feminine and Faulkner: Reading (Beyond) Sexual Difference*. Knoxville: U of Tennessee P, 1990.

_____. "Feminism and Faulkner: Second Thoughts or, What's a radical feminist doing with a canonical male text anyway?" *The Faulkner Journal* 4.1-2 (1988/1989): 55-65.

Hagopian, John V. "The Biblical Background of Faulkner's *Absalom, Absalom!*" *William Faulkner's* Absalom, Absalom!: *A Critical Casebook*. Ed. Elisabeth Muhlenfeld. New York: Garland, 1984. 131-34.

Hartmann, Heidi. "The Unhappy Marriage of Marxism and Feminism: Toward a More Progressive Union." *Women and Revolution: A Discussion of the Unhappy Marriage of Marxism and Feminism*. Ed. Lydia Sargent. Boston: South End, 1981. 1-41.

Hundley, D. R. *Social Relations in Our Southern States*. 1860. Baton Rouge: Louisiana State UP, 1979.

Kauffman, Linda S. *Discourses of Desire: Gender, Genre and Epistolary Fictions*. Ithaca: Cornell UP, 1986.

Krause, David. "Reading Bon's Letter and Faulkner's *Absalom, Absalom!*" *PMLA* 99 (1984): 225-41.

Kuyk, Dirk, Jr. *Sutpen's Design: Interpreting Faulkner's* Absalom, Absalom! Charlottesville: UP of Virginia, 1990.

Makowsky, Veronica. Interview. Spring 1990.

Matthews, John T. *The Play of Faulkner's Language*. Ithaca: Cornell UP, 1982.

McGee, Patrick. *Telling the Other: The Question of Value in Modern and Postcolonial Writing*. Ithaca: Cornell UP, 1992.

Mortimer, Gail L. *Faulkner's Rhetoric of Loss: A Study in Perception and Meaning*. Austin: U of Texas P, 1983.

_____. "The Smooth Suave Shape of Desire: Paradox in Faulknerian Imagery of Women." *Women's Studies* 13 (1986): 149-61.

Porter, Carolyn. *Seeing and Being: The Plight of the Participant Observer in Emerson, James, Adams, and Faulkner*. Middletown: Wesleyan UP, 1981.

Rollyson, Carl E., Jr. *Uses of the Past in the Novels of William Faulkner*. Ann Arbor: UMI Research P, 1984.

Warren, Robert Penn. *All the King's Men*. 1946. New York: Harvest-Harcourt, 1982.

Weinstein, Philip M. "Meditations on the Other: Faulkner's Rendering of Women." *Faulkner and Women: Faulkner and Yoknapatawpha, 1985*. Ed. Doreen Fowler and Ann J. Abadie. Jackson: UP of Mississippi, 1974. 81-99.

Wittenberg, Judith Bryant. "William Faulkner: A Feminist Consideration." *American Novelists Revisited: Essays in Feminist Criticism*. Ed. Fritz Fleischmann. Boston: Hall, 1982. 325-38.

Faulkner's Prose Style in *Absalom, Absalom!*_____

Robert H. Zoellner

Unsympathetic critics of Faulkner's prose style have made much of what they choose to call his lack of discipline, his verbosity, or his love of rhetoric for rhetoric's sake. There is a marked tendency in certain critical circles to label him, simply, "obscurantist." While there is a certain element of truth in such strictures, I think it can be established that there is a meaningful correlation between the dominant ideas of Faulkner's "difficult" novels and the tortured prose style he employs in expressing these ideas. A careful analysis of *Absalom, Absalom!*, for example, suggests that his obscurantism is in fact a great part of the means by which he becomes artistically intelligible. Here is a typical passage from *Absalom, Absalom!* which I propose to analyze in some detail:

1. It was a summer of wistaria. The twilight was full of it
2. and of the smell of his father's cigar as they sat on the front
3. gallery after supper until it would be time for Quentin to start,
4. while in the deep shaggy lawn below the veranda the fireflies
5. blew and drifted in soft random—the odor, the scent, which
6. five months later Mr Compson's letter would carry up from Mis-
7. sissippi and over the long iron New England snow and into Quentin's
8. sitting-room at Harvard. It was a day of listening too—the
9. listening, the hearing in 1909 mostly about that which he already
10. knew, since he had been born in and still breathed the same air
11. in which the church bells had rung on that Sunday morning in 1833
12. and, on Sundays, heard even one of the original three bells in
13. the same steeple where descendants of the same pigeons strutted
14. and crooned or wheeled in short courses resembling soft fluid
15. paint-smears on the soft summer sky. That Sunday morning in June
16. with the bells ringing peaceful and peremptory and a little
17. cacophonous—the denominations in concord though not in tune—

18. and the ladies and children, and house negroes to carry the
19. parasols and flywhisks, and even a few men (the ladies moving in
20. hoops among the miniature broadcloth of little boys and the pant-
21. alettes of little girls, in the skirts of the time when ladies did
22. not walk but floated) when the other men sitting with their feet
23. on the railing of the Holston House gallery looked up, and there
24. the stranger was.[1] (p. 31)

Putting aside for the moment the question of what total meaning Faulkner intends to convey here, let us examine the rhetorical and syntactical devices which account for the characteristically Faulknerian flavor of the passage. In line 5 the reader encounters a device which might be termed *syntactical ambiguity*. The ambiguity centers about the precise syntactical status of "the odor, the scent"; there are at least two possibilities. First, it may be the subject of a verb which will appear later (perhaps very much later) in Faulkner's often interminable sentence structure:

. . . the odor, the scent . . . [*drifted, moved, penetrated*, or some other verb].

This is the resolution which our sense of English word-order would ordinarily lead us to expect. The other possibility is that "the odor, the scent" is in apposition with a preceding element in the sentence:

. . . the *smell* of his father's cigar . . . —the odor, the scent . . .

The alert reader is thus forced to hold at least two possible readings simultaneously in his mind until the sentence is completed in line 8, when it becomes clear that Faulkner intended the second alternative.

Such syntax-traps demand an inordinate degree of attention and retention. The reader of conventional prose, accustomed to holding in the forefront of his consciousness only that relatively limited portion of the sentence which is immediately before his eyes, usually neglects the after-image; by the time he is mid-sentence the beginning has pretty well faded out. Such habits, of no great consequence in reading conventional prose, undercut the very foundations of Faulkner's aesthetic intention, which I shall try to demonstrate hinges upon a concept of life as a peculiar kind of continuum. Suffice it here to say that Faulkner demands that the reader maintain the maximum possible consciousness of the *whole* extended sentence—the sentence-continuum—from beginning to end. In this case, the syntactical ambiguity of "the odor, the scent" jars the reader out of his habitual casualness and forces him, if he hopes to maintain a sense of logical continuity, to keep the entire word-pattern in the vivid forefront of his consciousness.

A more important technique is *time-alternation*, a particularly vivid example occurring in lines 9-15. In line 9 the reader is given a specific point in time: 1909. With the introduction of the "which" clause of line 11 there is a shift to a specifically dated past: "that Sunday morning in 1833," followed by an immediate return to 1909 with "on Sundays" (line 12). The final alternation, and the most important, occurs in line 15 where "That Sunday morning" throws the reader once again into 1833. (In addition, the reader must keep in mind the "frame-time" for the entire novel, which finds Quentin Compson III at Harvard talking to Shrevlin McCannon, and viewing these antecedent points in time retrospectively.) These rapid-fire time alternations inevitably result in the atrophy of those habitual time distinctions which the reader brings to the novel; Faulkner obviously wishes different points in time to coalesce. This intention becomes clear in line 15, with "That Sunday morning in June . . . ." Since at this point Faulkner ceases to specify which time-period he means, 1909 or 1833, the average reader will very likely abandon the effort to keep the various times separate, convinced that if Faulkner will so intricately interweave his various time periods, then time distinctions must not be too important—the exact state of mind which Faulkner desires. Actually, "That Sunday morning in June" of line 15 is carefully dated by being made parallel to "that Sunday morning in 1833" of line 11, but such stylistic clues are buried too deeply to interfere with the author's calculated attack on the reader's time sense.

A third technique, *delayed modification*, springs from the fact that even for Faulkner there is generally a limit as to how involute a sentence may become. Often, what he appears to want to do is to deal not only with two (or more) time periods, but also with two or more ideas at once, to talk with two simultaneous voices. The parallel phrasing ("that Sunday morning," lines 11, 15) is a case in point. Up to line 15, despite the rapid alternations in time, Faulkner is dealing primarily with 1909, with the church bells and pigeons of 1909. Yet in the midst of this comes a reference to the earlier point in time, "that Sunday morning in 1833" (line 11), which also needs a great deal of development. To interpose a detailed explanation in the middle of line 11 would be to make the sentence impossibly complex: Faulkner, by virtue of the sequential nature of language (a limitation of his artistic medium against which he constantly struggles) must complete the description of the 1909 period, and then turn to 1833. But such sequential time distinctions are precisely those logical entities which he is attempting to suppress. He gets around the difficulty by lifting "that Sunday morning in 1833" (line 11) out of the sentence, repeating it in roughly parallel form (line 15), and then expanding and modifying it fully. It is significant that the sentence beginning in line 15 lacks an independent subject-verb pattern. Faulkner leaves it incomplete to emphasize that it is an organic part of the sentence preceding it. This delayed modification of "That Sunday morning" results in the superimposition of the 1833 period, which dominates line 15 and following, over the 1909 period handled in the preceding sentence. The Sunday mornings of 1909 coalesce inextricably with those of 1833.

A fourth stylistic technique which Faulkner utilizes repeatedly is *suspension and enclosure*. The suspension begins at the word "with" (line 16) and ends at "floated" (line 22). The basic frame-sentence, less the suspension, reads: "That Sunday morning in June . . . when the other men sitting with their feet on the railing of the Holston House gallery looked up, and there the stranger was"—this is the bare, central fact of the experience. But there is a great quantity of peripheral material, tonal shades and subtle nuances, which should be integrated with this central fact. The conventional writer would simply add this peripheral data by means of secondary sentences grouped about the primary thematic statement, but Faulkner's aesthetic will permit him no such easy solutions. He apparently feels the conventional paragraph tends to obscure the massive, monolithic quality of real experience. Faulkner will have no hierarchy of sentences or sequence of impressions; he aims at the total impression and the total sentence. To achieve this aesthetic totality, he must establish the closest possible organic relation between the central idea and the peripheral tonal material. To do this, he brings the frame-idea to an abrupt suspension at the end of the phrase "That Sunday morning in June" (line 15). This suspended phrase requires some kind of grammatical resolution, in a manner somewhat analogous to the resolution of certain musical chords. Some possible resolutions are:

(1) [That-Sunday-morning-in-June] plus a verb—functions as subject.
(2) [That-Sunday-morning-in-June] plus subject plus verb—functions as adverbial modifier.
(3) [That-Sunday-morning-in-June] modified adjectivally or adverbially. (Actually the case here, with the "when" clause of line 22.)

The point is that the reader does not immediately get any of these possible resolutions. The syntactical development is suspended while Faulkner injects the requisite peripheral detail of the bells, their sound, the floating ladies, the children, and the church-going men; only then does he allow the syntactical resolution of the "when" clause of line 22. The result is a monolithic sentence which conveys stylistically the massive quality of actual experience. The peripheral material is not relegated to a series of secondary sentences; instead, the two segments of the frame-sentence enclose this scattered detail, bringing it into an organic relationship with the narrative thread, and endowing it with dramatic power and aesthetic centrality. So effective is this fusion that terms like "central" and "peripheral" cease, in fact, to have much meaning. One other important aesthetic by-product is that the reader's habit of making a hierarchic differentiation between ideas is substantially broken down.

Finally, the "June . . . when" suspension gives a pronounced effect of *dramatic periodicity*: Faulkner builds up gradually to a final dramatic denouement for the complex tissue of impressions he has been weaving. The starkly simple resolving clause, "and there the stranger was" (lines 23-24), constitutes a massively effective entrance for Thomas Sutpen, the protagonist of *Absalom, Absalom!*

These stylistic techniques—*syntactical ambiguity, time alternation, delayed modification, suspension and enclosure*, and *dramatic periodicity*—all contribute to a specific aesthetic effect. Not only is the reader forced to hold two or more possible sense resolutions in the forefront of his consciousness as he moves along, but distinctions of time and space merge, qualitative differentiations are erased, and the neat, compartmentalized autonomy of the conventional sentence is done away with. Faulkner simply presents a mass of experience in a lump, *now*, as it enters the consciousness. Most important, the prose style of *Absalom, Absalom!* neutralizes the reader's ingrained tendency to break up experience into convenient, logically divided parcels, hierarchically arranged for painless assimilation.

But to explain the difficulty of Faulkner's prose is not to justify it. To do this, one must establish a direct connection between these formal devices and the "meaning" of the novel; the former must contribute aesthetically to the realization of the latter. While this is not the place for a detailed analysis of the "meaning" of *Absalom, Absalom!*, a few general conclusions may be offered. The action centers about Thomas Sutpen's refusal to recognize anything which is not "adjunctive to the furthering of the design," and his consequent denial of his first, part-Negro wife. This is the fountainhead of all the frustration and failure which dog

---

Sutpen's footsteps from that day forward: the whole "design" is shattered when his original sin of racial repudiation comes home to roost in the person of Charles Bon. Thus the novel deals with the pervasive and continuing consequences of moral evil, spreading like a wave in a still pool, not only through the years of Sutpen's life, but also through all the years and generations that follow, focused and ultimately distilled in the symbolic idiocy of Jim Bond. The evil is as vital in 1909 when Quentin is at Harvard as it was in 1833 when Sutpen arrived in Yoknapatawpha County with his band of wild Negroes and the frightened French architect. Sutpen's sin—his repudiation—is also the sin of the South, and thus Sutpen's story has as much impact on Quentin as it would had Sutpen been of his own blood. Quentin hates the South (despite his violent asseverations to the contrary) because Sutpen's evil is the South's evil, and Quentin is bone and gristle a Southerner.

But what I wish to examine is not so much the specific interpretation here offered as the philosophical convictions which stand behind it. First of all, *Absalom, Absalom!* is saturated by Faulkner's conception of time as a cumulative continuum—the present moment, its quality and tone, is the sum of all past moments. To relegate any event to a dead past is to miss its living, present significance. This explains Faulkner's fusion of various points in time, which might be described (rather crudely) in terms of a series of photographic transparencies, each one carrying the image of a different point in time. On one we see Sutpen arriving in Yoknapatawpha in 1833. Another shows him returning from the Civil War to a ruined plantation and a shattered "design." On a third we glimpse General Compson talking with Sutpen, learning his story. On a final transparency we find the image of Quentin III, shivering in the iron cold of an alien New England winter, living the entire saga himself, and trying futilely to explain it to Shreve, the dispassionate and isolated Canadian. The reader, however, does not view these separate images in any logical sequence: rather, they are superimposed one over the other and thus are seen all at once. Faulkner shifts so rapidly from one time to another that it soon becomes impossible to tell which image is on which transparency—logical distinctions between past time and present time cease to have any meaning.

Secondly, Faulkner suggests that moral evil is a living, inherited continuum. Evil, once generated, displays thenceforth an autonomous vitality, living independently of any single personality. The consequences of Sutpen's moral failure spread vertically to Charles Bon and Jim Bond, and horizontally through all the other inhabitants of the moral continuum, the Coldfields and the Compsons. Sutpen's repudiation of his wife and son is as vigorously alive in 1909 as in 1833.

A third concept, that tradition is a cumulative continuum, clearly underlies the passage just analyzed. Faulkner emphasizes the fact that the church bells of 1833 are the church bells of 1909, the pigeons of 1909 the descendants of those of 1833, so that the two time periods are really one, despite whatever changes in externals, in style of dress for example, may have occurred. Moreover, throughout the novel it is virtually impossible to distinguish the voices of the past from those of the present: Sutpen's comments carry the same sense of immediacy as those of Quentin or Rosa Coldfield.

A fourth aspect of Faulkner's Weltanschauung is the conviction that personality is not discrete, but part of a cumulative continuum of anterior personalities. Thus Sutpen is an essential and explanatory ingredient in the total personality of Rosa Coldfield, Jim Bond, or Quentin III. Sutpen, for good or evil, lives in the present because these people live in the present. It is this inescapable organic entanglement with a tainted past which Quentin hates, and which he denies hating.

Finally, because of the time-, moral-, historical-, and personality-continuums, spatial relationships are relatively meaningless. The events of Sutpen's early life in the West Indies, the octoroon mistress of Charles Bon in New Orleans—these spatially "distant" elements, apparently peripheral to the central narrative, have as much immediate impact and relevancy as if they were physically present in the hulking mansion at Sutpen's Hundred or Quentin's room at Harvard.

This philosophical conviction, that life is in all its aspects a massive continuum that cannot be compartmentalized without substantial loss of truth, is the ultimate foundation of the prose style of *Absalom, Absalom!* It is imperative that Faulkner break down the "logical" concepts of space, time, division, and sequence, the careful articulation of which is the purpose of most conventional prose. In this sense, one can with some justice accuse Faulkner of illogicality and obscurity, since much of his prose is not composed of sentences at all, but rather of massive doses of reality for which there is no adequate term in traditional grammar or rhetoric.[2] Syntactical ambiguity blurs the deceptively logical distinctness with which we habitually regard the written word and the reality which stands behind it. Delayed modification and suspension and enclosure both emphasize the organic, essential relevance of apparently unrelated peripheral matter, while repeated time alternations erode the reader's sequential sense of chronology—and all three assert the cumulative, living nature of the life-continuum. The result is a profound aesthetic correspondence between the "meaning" of *Absalom, Absalom!* and the tortured syntax in which it is cast.

To return to the textual analysis, here is a compressed example of alternated or superimposed time:

1. . . . and this for the same spurious delusion of reward which
2. had failed (failed? betrayed: and would this time destroy)
3. him once. . . . (p. 162)

The past-time sense of the passage is "delusion of reward which had failed him once." The present-time sense is "would this time destroy him." The precise overlap of the two time periods occurs at the word "him" (line 3), which is simultaneously the object of a past-verb, "failed" (line 2) and of a present-verb, "destroy" (line 2). The reader ignores the parenthesis marks in one case, and reads them in the other, or, to be more exact, unconsciously apprehends both readings simultaneously. The adverb "once" is also read or not read, depending upon which time period is in the focus of consciousness.

An example of both time alternation and suspension and enclosure appears in this passage:

1. He had not only public opinion but his own disinclination for the
2. big wedding to support it without incongruity or paradox. Then
3. (the tears won; Ellen and the aunt wrote out a hundred invitations
4. —Sutpen brought in one of the wild negroes who carried them from
5. door to door by hand—and even sent out a dozen more personal ones
6. for the dress rehearsal) when they reached the church for the
7. rehearsal on the night before the wedding and found the church
8. itself empty and a handful of men from the town's purlieus
9. (including two of old Ikkemotubbe's Chickasaws) standing in the
10. shadows outside the door, the tears came down again. (pp. 53-54)

The more immediate time period is the night of the dress rehearsal, beginning with "Then" (line 2). But Faulkner no sooner launches into this time period than he breaks off, institutes a suspension marked by the parenthesis of line 3, and shifts to an antecedent time dealing with the sending of wedding invitations. The frame-sentence, "Then . . . when they reached the church . . . ," set in the later time period, organically encloses the peripheral background detail. The situation of the key word "Then" (line 2) is identical with the word "him" in the passage just examined; "Then" functions in both time periods at once, the reader simultaneously reading or ignoring the parenthesis mark:

Later time: *Then* when they reached the church . . . .
Earlier time: *Then* the tears won . . . .

The reader who doubts his ability to read and not read the parenthesis of line 3 might compare Faulkner's use of it here with the conventional parenthetical element of line 9.

A vivid example of the tremendous dramatic potentialities of Faulkner's prose style is the following passage, a combination of suspension, delayed modification, and dramatic periodicity. Sutpen, upon completion of his mansion, and following a period of relative quiescence, suddenly appears in Jefferson, carrying a mysterious wicker basket. He changes clothes at the Holston House, and reappears on the hotel veranda before the waiting crowd of hostile townsfolk. At this point Faulkner remarks that "They [the townsfolk] even knew now what the basket had contained because he did not have that with him now either" (p. 46), but the reader is not yet let into the secret:

1. [Sutpen] just walked on, erect, with the new hat cocked and
2. carrying in his hand now that which must have seemed to them
3. the final gratuitous insult, with the committee riding along
4. in the street beside him and not quite parallel, and others
5. who did not happen to have horses at the moment joining in and
6. following the committee in the road, and ladies and children
7. and women slaves coming to the doors and windows of the homes
8. as they passed to watch as they went on in grim tableau, and
9. Sutpen, still without once looking back, entered Mr Coldfield's
10. gate and strode on up the brick walk to the door, carrying his
11. newspaper cornucopia of flowers. (p. 47)

Less the suspension, the two segments of the frame-sentence read: "[Sutpen] just walked on, erect, with the new hat cocked and carrying . . . his newspaper cornucopia of flowers," a sentence of admirable lucidity, but hardly calculated to convey the impression of a monolithic dramatic continuum. So Faulkner inserts a suspension, pivoted on "carrying" (line 2); the reader must hold the precise context of this word in his mind until it reappears in line 10. Meanwhile, an enormous amount of peripheral but organically essential detail is enclosed between the two segments of the frame-sentence. Early in the suspension appears the phrase "that which" (line 2); the reader is deliberately *not* told what the referent of this phrase is, only that it is the "final gratuitous insult." The final explanation is delayed until line 11 where, in a brilliant denouement, Faulkner reveals that the "that which" referred to the "newspaper cornucopia of flowers," symbolic of the fact that Sutpen has at last found the keystone, Ellen Coldfield, to cap his monomaniacal "design." The entire passage suggests how Faulkner forces the disparate elements of reality to coalesce into an indivisible whole, to fuse into one organic stream of images leading to a single climactic moment of dramatic truth. To sense the peculiar quality of his genius here, one need only imagine how this same word-pattern (it hardly does it justice to call it a sentence) would be handled by a conventional writer, how the multifarious detail would be logically parceled out among topic and subordinate sentences. The monolithic and cumulative effect of Faulkner's style here is a direct formal reflection of the continuum which is his vision of reality.

The way in which the novelist draws what would ordinarily be peripheral, tonal material into an integral relationship within the two segments of the frame-sentence is clearly illustrated in the following example. The frame-sentence reads: "So he and the twenty negroes worked together . . . in the sun and heat of summer and the mud and ice of winter, with quiet and unflagging fury."

1. So he and the twenty negroes worked together, plastered over with
2. mud against the mosquitoes *and*, as Miss Coldfield told Quentin,
3. distinguishable one from another by his beard and eyes alone
4. *and* only the architect resembling a human creature *because* of
5. the French clothes *which* he wore constantly with a sort of
6. invincible fatality *until* the day after the house was completed
7. save for the windowglass and the ironware *which* they could not
8. make by hand *and* the architect departed—working in the sun
9. and heat of summer and the mud and ice of winter, with quiet and
10. unflagging fury. (pp. 37-38)

Again, the repetition of a key word ("worked . . . working") indicates the beginning and termination of the suspension. But what I would call particular attention to is Faulkner's method of handling the contained material itself. The structure is essentially chainlike; there is no attempt to arrange the separate segments of enclosed tonal material qualitatively or quantitatively—they are indifferently linked together by conjunctive words (which I have italicized), one after another. By line 8 Faulkner has wandered so far forward in time that he is telling of the departure of the French architect, and then pulls the reader back in time to the beginning of the furious ritual of construction. This meandering linkage of apparently unrelated elements is, of course, precisely that aspect which most distinguishes the impressionistic and stream-of-consciousness techniques. Yet the prose of *Absalom, Absalom!* seldom degenerates into the undisciplined incoherency which has marred a large part of the experiments in this form; Faulkner always communicates, however turgidly. The explanation lies in the frame-sentence, which acts as a control and supporting medium for the impressionistic jumble of tonal material which it contains, and which perhaps constitutes Faulkner's most distinctive contribution to the literary articulation of the impressionistic vision. At the same time, the linked chain of tonal images is strikingly cumulative and organic, reflecting Faulkner's peculiar Weltanschauung.

This cumulative chain-effect is best illustrated by Faulkner's habit of piling "which" clauses one on the other, a technique which has been the target of much derogatory comment. Here is a description of Rosa Coldfield's musty parlor:

1. . . . a dim hot airless room with the blinds all closed and fastened for
2. forty-three summers because when she was a girl someone had believed
3. that light and moving air carried heat and that dark was always cooler,
4. and *which* (as the sun shone fuller and fuller on that side of the
5. house) became latticed with yellow slashes full of dust motes *which*
6. Quentin thought of as being flecks of the dead old dried paint itself
7. blown inward from the scaling blinds as wind might have blown them. (p. 7)

While the two linked "which" clauses here suggest the monolithic continuity of Quentin's impressions, the examination of so small a sample does not do justice to the technique. Only after wading through fifteen or twenty pages, link on endless link, can one appreciate fully how the normal insistence on compartmentalized, centralized prose structure dissolves under the impact of this kind of writing.

The following long passage typifies most fully those aspects of Faulkner's craft which have wrung pained outcries from readers and critics alike. It occurs at a moment of high emotion in the novel: Thomas Sutpen has returned to the ruins of the Hundred, where he finds nothing of his former affluence but the faded and embittered Judith. Faulkner wants to say a number of things at once, and at the same time convey the organic continuity of the experience. He resorts again to an extended tissue of linked "which" clauses:

1. As Judith and Clytie did, I stood there before the rotting portico
2. and watched him ride up on that gaunt and jaded horse on *which*
3. he did not seem to sit but rather seemed to project himself ahead
4. like a mirage, in some fierce dynamic rigidity of impatience
5. *which* the gaunt horse, the saddle, the boots, the leaf-colored
6. and threadbare coat with its tarnished and flapping braid contain-
7. ing the sentient though nerveless shell, *which* seemed to precede
8. him as he dismounted and out of *which* he said "Well, daughter"
9. and stooped and touched his beard to Judith's forehead, who had
10. not, did not, move, who stood rigid and still and immobile of
11. face, and within *which* they spoke four sentences, four sentences
12. of simple direct words behind beneath above *which* I felt that same
13. rapport of communal blood *which* I had sensed that day while Clytie
14. held me from the stairs: "Henry's not—?" "No. He's not here."
15. —"Ah. And—?" "Yes. Henry killed him." And then burst into
16. tears. (p. 159)

The first encounter with such a passage can hardly result in much more than a blurred, jumbled impression. Faulkner's "lack of discipline" is a convenient explanation, but perhaps it would be more just to say that such blurring is deliberate—moments of intense emotion do not produce precise, sharply articulated pictures. Even so, many readers would still insist that the passage leaves them dissatisfied. If pressed for an explanation, I imagine they would point to the undeniable fact that no *physical* detail or pattern of details is really developed; oddly enough, there is no impression of tactile, sensible substantiality. The "thing-ness" of our existence, the "solidity of specification" (as James calls it) by which we ordinarily measure the success or failure of fiction, are peculiarly lacking here. There is a relative absence of physical detail, and what there is runs together into an amorphous mass. The passage is, in a word, "unreal."

Such objections would be difficult to discount were it not for the fact that they fail to take into consideration the peculiar metaphysic of *Absalom, Absalom!* The critic who deprecates Faulkner's habit of reducing even the most solid objects to a ghostly, unidimensional evanescence is imposing on the novel an alien ontology. I simply mean that the elements that are "real" to Faulkner, the things that have substantial being for him, are not the physical facts, nor even in many cases whatever abstract meaning the physical facts might potentially contain. In this respect Faulkner's ontology is as extreme in one direction as Hemingway's is in the other. That is why the mansion and its rotting portico, the exhausted horse, and even the physical person of Sutpen in his tattered uniform fail to "come through," are not, one is tempted to say, really *there*. What *is* there is the abstract and dimensionless spiritual condition of the protagonist and those surrounding him. It is this aspect of the experience which is "real" for Faulkner, and it is manifestly unfair to demand another kind of reality from him, or to condemn the novel for not producing what Faulkner never intended it to produce.

To suggest the spiritual and psychological climate which the compulsive Sutpen generates, Faulkner relegates physical detail to an undifferentiated background, and fills the foreground with semi-surrealistic abstractions exceedingly difficult to visualize: the "mirage" and "fierce dynamic rigidity of impatience" (line 4), the "sentient though nerveless shell" (line 7), and the "rapport of communal blood" (line 13). These, tenuous though they may be, are the "real" elements of the experience. Even the "four sentences of simple direct words" (lines 11-12) seem to assume a dimensioned and tactile solidity as Faulkner applies no less than three prepositions to them ("behind beneath above"), at least one of which is normally reserved for the description of spatial relations between solid objects. It is this concentration on the abstract-as-most-substantial which gives his prose the peculiar unreal quality so often criticized.

I have digressed into Faulkner's metaphysic in order to call attention to the fact that the style of *Absalom, Absalom!* directly subserves the novelist's theory of what is "real" and what is not. The abstract "fierce dynamic rigidity of impatience," for example, impinges on the reader's consciousness with a sensible impact which far exceeds that of the horse, Sutpen's uniform, his physical person, or any other merely solid object. The explanation of this metaphysical sleight of hand lies, I believe, in the novelist's style, and it is perhaps here that one sees most clearly the originality of Faulkner's contribution to the development of English prose.

The key to the way in which he manages to endow abstractions with such an unwonted air of substantiality lies in his peculiar use of the "which" clause: a close examination of the passage we are discussing reveals that in this respect it is not the meandering abuse of good English that it might at first appear to be. Instead, there are two or three precisely limited control points about which all the apparently unrelated elements in the sentence pivot. The first and most important of these is the abstract "fierce dynamic rigidity of impatience" (line 4). One reading of the passage makes it possible to relate most of the apparently disparate segments of reality to this pivotal control point:

>   . . . some fierce dynamic
>
>   rigidity of impatience: *which* the gaunt horse, the saddle. . . . (line 5)
>
>   : *which* seemed to precede him. . . . (lines 7-8)
>
>   : out of *which* he said. . . . (line 8)
>
>   : and within *which* they spoke. . . . (line 11)

According to this reading, the detail of the sentence is not thrown in helter-skelter, but is all related to one point of control; the sentence is deceptively disciplined.[3] More important, because so much of the physical detail pivots about "some fierce dynamic rigidity of impatience," this abstraction is endowed with an abnormal degree of substantiality. On the other hand, since the physical detail is made subordinate both grammatically and rhetorically to this central abstraction, it is deprived of much of the sensible impact it would ordinarily have. The result is that the abstractions, the tonal qualities of the prose pattern, loom up in the foreground with a unique immediacy and relevancy, while the mere physical facts, normally so prominent, fade into the background. In this way Faulkner's prose style becomes a direct and aesthetically efficacious reflection of the ontology of *Absalom, Absalom!*

I hasten to add that I have oversimplified the analysis in order to make my point. As a matter of fact, the precise referential area of a number of the "which" clauses in the sentence is difficult, if not impossible, to determine. Three of them, the two in lines 7 and 8 and possibly the one in line 11, may refer either to "some fierce dynamic rigidity of impatience" or to "the sentient though nerveless shell" of line 7. In any case, the reader may take them one way or the other, or like many Faulknerian constructions, both ways at once, with little loss in meaning. The important point is that these linked "which" clauses are subordinated about one or another of the tonal abstractions which constitute the ontological core of the passage.

Three points remain to be made. First, the flow of the "which" clauses in this sample, and the tremendous amount of scattered detail which is brought into organic relation with the central narrative thread, constitute a direct stylistic expression of the cumulative and mono-lithic aspects of Faulkner's Weltanschauung. Second, the "behind be-neath above" of line 12 offers a peculiarly effective example of the co-alescence of spatial concepts in Faulkner's prose. This unpunctuated phrase, set in the midst of a heavily punctuated context and probably meant to be read "behindbeneathabove," expresses the utterly pervasive quality of a "rapport of communal blood" so powerful that ordinary logical distinctions sink into insignificance before it. Third, once again Faulkner masses his dramatic effects toward one climactic denoue-ment. The "And then burst into tears" of lines 15-16 represents a dra-matic resolution similar in both its psychological and stylistic aspects to the "and there the stranger was" of the first passage analyzed.

I do not suggest that any passage selected at random from *Absalom, Absalom!* will reveal such self-conscious and deliberate craftsman-ship, but the cumulative effect of the novel seems to follow the aes-thetic intention outlined here. *Absalom, Absalom!* is a history, expres-sive of Faulkner's distinctively historical sensibility. It differs from conventional history in that it is not constructed sequentially, fact by isolated fact; the reader is seldom conscious that he is being told sepa-rate facts at all. Rather, the story of Thomas Sutpen, his crime of racial repudiation and its consequences, rears up out of the living earth of Yoknapatawpha as a *fact*, abstracted from any temporal distinctions of past or present, or any qualitative distinctions of important or unimpor-tant, an organic, monolithic mass which directly reflects Faulkner's concept of life as a cumulative continuum. Finally, an analysis of the prose style of *Absalom, Absalom!* suggests that it is not the grammati-cal and rhetorical chaos it may appear to be at first glance, but rather a highly developed, extraordinarily plastic medium which the novelist uses with brilliant effect to express the labyrinthine Gothicism of his vision of life.

From *American Literature* 30.4 (January 1959): 486-502. Copyright © 1959 by Duke University Press. All rights reserved. Reprinted with permission of Duke University Press.

Notes

1. All page references in the text are to the Modern Library edition of *Absalom, Absalom!* (New York, 1951).

2. A representative example of Faulkner's more extreme attempts to make his style mirror the life-continuum appears in "The Bear," which boasts a single "sentence" 1600 words long.

3. I by no means intend to suggest that Faulkner never becomes entangled in the maze of his own syntax. The "which" clause beginning in line 5 contains an unmistakable slip, and an unfortunate one—it is not a clause at all.

Rosa Coldfield as Daughter:
Another of Faulkner's Lost Children_____

Linda Wagner-Martin

> The dungeon was Mother herself she and Father upward into weak light
> holding hands and us lost somewhere below even them without even a ray
> of light. . . .[1]

Throughout William Faulkner's fiction, the pattern of children
uncared for—ignored, isolated, used, abandoned—is relentless. Readers for more than half a century have felt inexorable pity for the Compson and Bundren children and for Joe Christmas, Gale Hightower,
Isaac McCaslin, and the countless other characters Faulkner defined as
orphaned or born late to parents who cared little about them. Similarly,
in the first chapter of *Absalom, Absalom!* Faulkner presents the character of Rosa Coldfield as a diminutive child, feet dangling from her
chair; and he reinforces the pathetic image of the Southern poetess by
using a narrative form that reflects the chronology of her life. In the
first chapter, part of her narrative occurs when she is three; part when
she is four; and another segment six years later, when she is ten. In the
fifth chapter, part of her story occurs when she is fourteen, and more
when she is nineteen. This combination of the narrative charting of her
life with the author's visualization of Rosa as childlike, or somehow
stunted, forces the reader to see that Rosa was never allowed to be a
child. Part of the looming tragedy of Faulkner's novel is that Rosa's
emotional growth was both restricted and exploited through her experiences. Faulkner gives the lengthy first and fifth chapters of *Absalom,
Absalom!* to this portrayal; these chapters are the reader's point of entry to the Sutpen story and to Rosa's own increasingly important
narrative.[2]

What such an emphasis on Rosa's childhood means for the reader is
a shift in perspective from the story of Thomas Sutpen and his surreal
creation, Sutpen's Hundred, to the more generalized tale of the South-

ern white patriarch. For Rosa's story is only partly that of Sutpen. Much of her narrative, both in Chapters 1 and 5, is that of the Coldfield family and its acquisition of place and power as well as its denouement. Even though some of her narrative deals with her role as Sutpen's beloved, more of it charts her role within the Coldfield family as youngest daughter, beholden to and thoroughly dependent on her remaining parent, her father.[3] By casting Rosa as child, by forcing the reader to see how terrorized her life was not only by Sutpen but by her father's uncaring and naive responses to both her and to life and war, Faulkner underscores the tragedy of the misuse of parental authority. *Absalom, Absalom!* becomes the story not of the quasi-heroic Sutpen, claiming accomplishment as he wrested power from poverty, but the story of various white males who destroyed families, particularly the women and children of those families, in their rapacious pursuit of what they defined as "success."

Fifty years of criticism added to the innate difficulty of Faulkner's choices in point of view. Trained to look for the Southern myth, the fall of the genteel white culture to encroaching materialism, readers sometimes overlooked the fact that Rosa's narrative provided the heart of the novel. For all Mr. Compson's, Quentin's, and Shreve's attempts to rewrite Rosa's story—to embroider, invent, and graft on new segments of her story—the force of Rosa's disinheritance should have carried through the later over-writings of her text. That it has not shows much about the kind of reception given to his fictions that attempt to move beyond codified themes.[4]

Following Faulkner's directive about Rosa's "place" in the narrative—her unquestioned role as the only living participant-narrator in the telling of the Sutpen legend—the modern reader must choose to see everything besides Rosa's narrative as further evidence of the complicit cultural support for the collusion that ensures Sutpen's "success." The way in which Mr. Compson, Quentin, and Shreve take over Rosa's story echoes the way both Sutpen and Coldfield usurped the rights that should have belonged to their wives and children, family-based rights that were instead assumed by the fathers. The way Faulkner presents this assumption in his novel is through the fathers' voices—those of Sutpen and Coldfield, as well as of Mr. Compson—as they justified their often indefensible actions. Much of that voicing is taken up with giving directives.

By following Rosa's story instead of the redactions of it, by listening and responding to the fear and pain in her primary narrative, the reader cannot fail to understand the harm done to people as Sutpen and, in his less effective way, Coldfield scramble over both traditions and human values to achieve immediate and often valueless aims. Reading *Absalom, Absalom!* as Rosa's story gives the reader a strategy to undercut the comparatively romantic appeal of the Sutpen story.[5] In the context of Southern history, Sutpen's Hundred serves no viable purpose either social or familial. Faulkner shows Thomas Sutpen to be little but animal, mating where and when he can, caring little for either his sex partners or their offspring, failing to take even perfunctory care of his family's needs. His abuse of Ellen Coldfield parallels the contempt he learned for Charles Bon's mother, for Rosa, and for Millie, whose child, if "correctly" sexed, would have earned for her at best a stable in some barn. Women having become only breeding machines, Sutpen was able to dismiss all normal human ties from his life. But first, for Sutpen to achieve his aim, he had to have as accoutrements those expected social garnishes—wife, children, social graces, religion, community.

At this point Faulkner weaves the Sutpen-Coldfield story lines together. Sutpen's most blatant affront to the community—growing out of his most audacious act—was to marry one of its upstanding, virginal women. Coldfield may have smelled financial benefit to his humble business by allowing Sutpen to court Ellen, but the fact that the eminently scrupled Methodist finds Sutpen less objectionable than does the rest of the community raises serious questions about Goodhue Coldfield's morality. Faulkner's intention as he presents the wedding scene seems to be to satirize the man's names, to paint Coldfield as thoroughly irresponsible, a characterization completed once the reader learns his reaction to the Civil War. Coldfield's mad demise suggests that he believes he can absolve himself of all responsibility for his family, his business, his community, and his region by blocking out—literally hiding from—all events of the war. Such obsessive egotism makes Coldfield much like Sutpen; they are both men who see themselves at the center of every event, who believe they can control life through sheer will. During Coldfield's last years, rather than caring for his young daughter, he treats her disdainfully, demanding sustenance and care from her. How Rosa was to secure food for him, as well as to cook and smuggle it into his nailed-shut hiding hole, was immaterial to Coldfield. For him, children were only means to ends. In this, as in all parts of *Absalom, Absalom!*, Faulkner emphasizes that Coldfield and Sutpen are both uncaring fathers. Although the ostensible plot depends on Sutpen's outrage of his role as father, Coldfield has abused the role every bit as much. Rosa's story gives the reader insight into that complicity.

Rosa's irate and sometimes hysterical lament about Sutpen's treatment of her is obviously an outcry at double injustice. In finding words for her bitterness, in belatedly choosing to tell her story, Rosa relinquishes pain and grief that has colored, and stunted, her entire life. Not only the spurned beloved, Rosa has been as well—and more consistently—the spurned daughter. Bereaved of sympathy, separated from any audience for her anguish over Ellen's madness, Rosa is driven to steal the materials to help sew Judith's trousseau. Her hatred of Coldfield is clear in that act. But so too is her great, and necessarily dependent, love for him. Her mother long dead; her sister moving further and further away from normalcy; her niece older than Rosa by four years and the product of Sutpen's tough will, a spirit very different from the Coldfield passivity; and Clytie, a strange mixture of deference and authority; Rosa had no mother, no sister, no peers. Faulkner gives the reader no evidence that Ellen ever thought about her much younger sister. So absorbed is she in maintaining her own balance, assaulted as she has been by the bestial behavior of both husband and children, Ellen gives nothing to Rosa. Faulkner's constant image of Ellen as chrysalis, of her undeveloped growth, keeps her helplessness firmly before the reader. And once she has succumbed to the horror of Henry's loss, she rouses only to ask something of Rosa. Still bereft of comfort and love, Rosa must assume the responsibility of caring for her niece Judith; that is Ellen's only legacy to her little sister.

Rosa's partially distraught monologue to Quentin Compson is both symptom and event. Her pain, so long hidden and unexpressed, breaks through the stoic shell she has assumed with some kind of primitive instinct. As her physical strength wanes, she is fired to share the one thing she has never shared, her sad emotions of loss, loss of a family who might have helped her bear what the world demanded of her, but particularly loss of the paternal love every daughter is acculturated to expect. Rosa speaks for the obverse of that Southern myth that says fathers and brothers must protect the young women of the family. In some ways, Rosa's language re-creates Caddy's less immediate, less often voiced, speech. The pain of being asked to care for everyone else, in lieu of having been cared for herself, dominates Rosa's heartbreak. (There may be an intertextual joke in Faulkner's choice of structure, as he has Quentin ask Mr. Compson why Rosa has turned to him to tell her story; in effect, Faulkner has given Quentin the little sister he sought for so earnestly in *The Sound and the Fury*. There is much he could learn from Rosa's story, if he would only listen to it rather than re-inscribing it to his own purposes.)

Faulkner's "text" of Rosa's narrative is dominated from the first by a view of her as daughter. She meets Quentin in "what Miss Coldfield still called the office because her father had called it that" (p. 7), her habits of language and behavior formed by that father-daughter relationship. The forty-three years that have passed since she assumed her black garb might mark either the death of Goodhue Coldfield in 1864 or Sutpen's insult in 1866; those years are emphasized because Faulkner's attention falls on her long-unexpressed story, her "grim haggard amazed" voice, her "impotent yet indomitable frustration" paralleling her "impotent and static rage." The "crucified child" as she is pictured—sitting in "the chair that was so tall for her that her legs hung straight and rigid as if she had iron shinbones and ankles, clear of the floor . . . like children's feet"—has remained a child because she has never expressed that static rage directed at both father and non-husband, family and world.

The language that Rosa uses reflects that rage. Rosa says "tore violently"; Quentin writes "built." Rosa says "without gentleness begot," and Quentin omits the first two words (p. 9). Though she rages within this language, she also tries to confine her image of Sutpen to "a scene peaceful and decorous as a schoolprize water color" (p. 8). Her art attempts to transform, but it fails as Quentin heightens the romantic elements of Sutpen's life. (It is Quentin's romanticism the reader responds to, not Rosa's telling, in thinking Sutpen superior in any way.) Rosa's focus is on the family of Sutpen, himself, the two children, and "the mother, the dead sister Ellen: this Niobe without tears," the mother who sacrificed everything for the children who were slain (p. 13); but Rosa insists on her own role in the configuration: "I, a child, a child, mind you" (p. 14). Keeping Quentin's attention on her role in this macabre family romance, represented by her imaginary photo of parents and children, "the conventional family group of the period" (p. 14), from which she is absent, Rosa builds her own narrative, her accumulation of bad fortune so that at twenty, "an orphan a woman and a pauper," she had to turn for existence to her only kin, the family of her sister (p. 19). The peak of Rosa's anguish occurs in the long paragraph stressing the guilt of her father's role in giving Ellen to Sutpen, in allowing that family group to exist. Her use of refrain signals her intensity: "But that it should have been our father, mine and Ellen's father of all of them that he knew. . . . That it should have been our father" (p. 20). Her jeremiad calls the reader's attention to the repetition of "our father," the prayerful term that suggests Rosa's strained apostasy, the daughter's willed deification of the father who would do no wrong but did numerous wrongs, increasing to the final one, of abandonment through voluntary separation and death.

* * *

Rosa's paragraph serves to curse the name of Goodhue Coldfield, and after it she resumes her story, with a significant change. This time when she reaches the point of Ellen's death, rather than Ellen's asking the young Rosa to look after Judith, in this version she says "protect *them*" (p. 21). Rosa's task has broadened, and into the matriarchal line come both children, Henry as well as Judith, an interruption of male power and control that unsettles Rosa. It is as if the weight of the entire South rests on her shoulders, and she cries to Quentin "even I used to wonder what our father or his father could have done before he married our mother that Ellen and I would have to expiate and neither of us alone be sufficient; what crime committed that would leave our family cursed to be instruments not only for that man's destruction, but for our own" (p. 21). Here Faulkner establishes the "plot": the house of Sutpen, aided by the minor house of Coldfield (a house Coldfield completely usurps by co-opting its attic as his hiding place, corruption weighing heavily, and inescapably, on its top story), rising or falling depending on the community reaction to its master's outrages. Yet Rosa, who is almost alone in seeing the full range of Sutpen's criminal acts, alone, childlike, and consequently powerless to prevent his success, manages to bring about the destruction of both Sutpen's house and, for practical purposes, his line.

Quentin's empathy with Rosa at this point in the narrative, before his father begins talking with him, is clear. He is able to visualize her, "to watch resolving the figure of a little girl, in the prim skirts and pantalettes, the smooth prim decorous braids, of the dead time" (p. 21). Standing by some hypothetical fence "with that air of children born too late into their parents' lives and doomed to contemplate all human behavior through the complex and needless follies of adults . . . a child who had never been young" (p. 22), Rosa begins her countdown through vivid memories that all implicate Sutpen. At three, she remembers the mad rides to church, faces like ogres leering from the carriage, although Ellen's face is "bloodless." At four, she remembers standing outside the door to the Sutpen parlor, as her father talks with Ellen about leaving Sutpen: "'Think of the children,' papa said" (p. 27). But Faulkner also gives the reader the necessary information that in this scene Goodhue Coldfield had not invited Ellen to bring the children and move back to his house, just as in the aftermath to the preceding church scene he had not responded positively when his sister had urged him to interfere for Ellen's sake. Rosa recounts hearing the pithy conversation: "'Your daughter, your own daughter' my aunt said; and papa: 'Yes. She is my daughter. When she wants me to interfere she will tell me so herself'" (p. 25). Faulkner's inclusion of this scene clearly shows Coldfield absconding from the social and familial role he should play, as he pretends that his daughter Ellen could take language, could forge a voice for herself out of the malaise of Sutpen's Hundred and its completely male power, and so thereby excuse his own inaction. Coldfield was one of Faulkner's male characters who said some of the right things but never acted, and, as Rosa could so easily see, her father was never either willing or able to change things, never able to do the protecting that should have been his responsibility. Her narrative is an account of Goodhue Coldfield's failure even more than it is a story of Sutpen's success.

Faulkner's pivotal image in Chapter 1 is that of the young Rosa, only four years old, "a child standing close beside that door because I was afraid to be there but more afraid to leave it, standing motionless beside that door as though trying to make myself blend with the dark wood and become invisible, like a chameleon" (p. 27). The child afraid to be either hovering or absent, the child wishing for invisibility, is an icon of the forgotten person. The reader is convinced of the child's near, or actual, invisibility. Faulkner's locating Rosa near the door, wishing to become part of the stability that the door represented, is an ironic echo of Sutpen's compelling "door" narrative, when he is stigmatized by being sent around to the back, by a black, and refused entrance through a front door.[6] In this scene, Rosa enters no door; she is refused any entrance. She is given the role of hiding behind the door eavesdropping while she tries to figure her fate and that of the sister she loves so much. Kept away from power, hidden behind the observable actions, Rosa learns by stealth, complicity, and fear all that she needs to know for the kind of life the Southern culture will permit her to lead. In contrast, Sutpen's tactic is to wrest power from established channels, to substitute one door for another by creating his own set of doors, front and back, and with that structure a set of rules to govern it. Rosa has no house, no door, no physical location except that of her imagination and her narrative. In this scene, Faulkner makes clear Rosa's relation to the substance of male propriety.

With emphatic concision, Faulkner's narrative jumps to Rosa at age ten, speaking matter-of-factly and without self-pity: "Our aunt was gone now and I was keeping house for papa" (p. 28). She continues, "I did not have time now to play, even if I had ever had any inclination. I had never learned how and I saw no reason to try to learn now even if I had had the time." The last "story" in this first chapter of Rosa's narrative is of Judith, Clytie, and Henry illicitly watching Sutpen fight with his blacks and Ellen's horror at the corruption of her "baby girl" (p. 30). The irony of Ellen's being so horrified, when her daughter, at fourteen, is in fact the protected and privileged (if corruptible) daughter of wealth, set beside Rosa's simultaneous acceptance of her adult role as she, at ten, cares for her father and his household, shows the utter lack of concern for Rosa as younger daughter, baby sister, child.

What Rosa becomes, if her state has allowed her any time or space to "become" a female person in this inimical Southern culture, acts as a mandala to the various narratives of *Absalom, Absalom!* Her succinct realization of the cultural patterns she has been both observing and living—what happens to women's lives in the matrix of the South—is expressed in her memory of being fourteen, written as a part of her paean to the "summer of wisteria" that begins "once there was." The pithy declaration Rosa makes has little to do with fairy tales, however, as she laments "I waited not for light but for that doom which we call female victory which is: endure and then endure, without rhyme or reason or hope of reward—and then endure" (p. 144). Faulkner's telling of *Absalom, Absalom!* extends this axiom about women characters by focusing increasingly on their lives: during and after the war, the Sutpen fortunes are controlled for the most part by Judith, Clytie, and Rosa, with Sutpen's reappearance figuring only briefly. And such focus is true of the ending of the novel, which also is the ending of both the Sutpen dynasty and Sutpen's Hundred.

Rosa speaks seldom—the narrative reinforces her sense that she has little value, little power to create voice and language, as Faulkner shows Mr. Compson and the Harvard roommates re-fashioning Rosa's passionate tale—and almost never to male characters. Even in conversation with other women characters, she is laconic, hesitant. Faulkner includes a chilling scene of Sutpen's return from war, in which Judith tells him of Charles Bon's death, finally releasing her grief into the tears she has not shed during the seven months since his murder. That image suggests the analogous outpouring of Rosa's final storying, her capture of Quentin Compson so that he will not only hear her words but help her create the last of them by accompanying her in her decisive action. Her childlike insistence on her story, on telling her story to Quentin, as well as her self-protective distance from the young man's disinterest, are integral pieces of Faulkner's characterization of how a woman would speak after forty-three years of self-imposed silence. Given what the reader comes to know about these circumstances, the mania of Rosa's story as it propels her into the later stages of her narrative is plausible.

When Faulkner allows her to resume talking, in Chapter 5, she begins with Wash Jones' calling her to Sutpen's Hundred on the occasion of Charles Bon's murder. Arriving there, now nineteen, Rosa finds that the Sutpen house has become her adversary: "Rotting portico and scaling walls, it stood, not ravaged, not invaded, marked by no bullet nor soldier's iron heel but rather as though reserved for something more: some desolation more profound than ruin" (p. 136). Coupled with the indomitable, and waiting, house, Rosa finds Clytie, also a nemesis, a "force" that was destined to keep her and all who wanted to change or subvert Sutpen's Hundred away from it. When Rosa enters the house and calls out to Judith, she reverts to being powerless and fearful: "Just as a child, before the full instant of comprehended terror, calls on the parent whom it actually knows (this before the terror destroys all judgment whatever) is not even there to hear it. I was crying not to someone, something, but (trying to cry) through something, through that force . . ." (p. 137). Rosa as abandoned, and therefore disoriented, child yet perseveres. After years of private sorrow, she has learned that her abandonment gives her a kind of power; she is immune from social conventions. In this scene with Clytie, she conquers the door that Clytie would close before her; she gains access to the upper story, even though doing so means enmity with Clytie forever. The lasting insult—Clytie's calling her "Rosa" and her calling Clytie "nigger"—reifies the conflict, makes it permanent through its inscription in language. Judith, however, does not allow Rosa through the bedroom door, so she never sees Bon, never knows that his dead body is, in fact, housed in the coffin she helps to carry. Judith closes the door to Rosa as if to comment on the power of the legitimate Sutpen heirs. The closed door trope becomes Rosa's means of expressing her isolation from the life, and power, of the Sutpen family; and in a later speculation about the sound of Henry's gunshot as he killed Bon, she uses the trope once more: "No, there had been no shot. That sound was merely the sharp and final clap-to of a door between us and all that was, all that might have been . . ." (p. 158).

With the poignancy of the doom she saw in women's lives, Rosa laments that, even though she is twenty, she is "still a child, still living in that womb-like corridor where the world came not even as living echo but as dead incomprehensible shadow" (p. 162). Her fierce desire was to know life, and for a young Southern woman, "life" translated as love and romance. But again, Faulkner's pervasive trope is of closed doors, despite Rosa's readiness to open the doors of her body in accepting Sutpen's proposal. His proposal—which ominously says nothing of "love"—is delivered as if he were speaking to a child, his hand on Rosa's head, with Judith and Clytie looking on. Fatherlike in this pose, Sutpen evokes all Rosa's feelings for her biological father as well as her fantasies about patriarchal and military power: Sutpen is an important man, a brave soldier, who somehow "deserves" her virginal love. But that obeisance is mixed with Rosa's continual despair and rage at having been abandoned by Goodhue Coldfield. She, in fact, blames Coldfield for leaving her in the circumstances that made living at Sutpen's Hundred necessary (although she has earlier denied that she needed to go there to live): "She had been right in hating her father since if he had not died in that attic she would not have had to go out there to find food and protection and shelter" (p. 169). Faulkner further plays on Rosa's confusion of Sutpen and Coldfield in a subsequent scene through the use of the indefinite pronoun *him*: "And that's what she cant forgive him for: not for the insult, not even for having jilted him: but for being dead" (p. 170).

Faulkner's plot development has allowed him to bring Rosa fully into the primary narrative, to move her out of her role as observer (and her common stance, "This is what I saw" [p. 23]). Her passion, whether vengeful or erotic or both, brings her to voice as participant, and her voice—in the passage that serves to close her inscription of the story she has lived as well as told—takes on the qualities of a fully involved woman. Her voice here can be taken for that of Judith, as Faulkner juxtaposes the scenes of the women's learning of the deaths of their lovers. Rosa's recognition of Sutpen's death, "'Dead?' I cried. 'Dead? You? You lie; you're not dead; heaven cannot, and hell dare not, have you!'" (p. 172), shows the possessiveness of the spurned woman, and her attribution of voice to him even in death suggests the heightened, raging responses she is capable of even years after her abandonment

Critical Insights

and betrayal. Faulkner opens the juxtaposed scene, in which Judith learns of Bon's death, with the image of the door, this time a door through which Henry enters Judith's room to bring her the news of Bon's murder (in contrast, Quentin cannot pass that threshold, even imaginatively):

> Now you cant marry him.
> Why cant I marry him?
> Because he's dead.
> Dead?
> Yes. I killed him. (p. 172)

The immensity of Faulkner's compassion in *Absalom, Absalom!* becomes clear through his narrative structure, as he creates loss after loss after loss, and the reader is reminded of his later praise of Hemingway's *The Old Man and the Sea*: "This time he wrote about pity: about something somewhere that made them all: the old man who had to catch the fish and then lose it, the fish that had to be caught and then lost . . . made them all and loved them all and pitied them all."[7] Faulkner's *Absalom, Absalom!* is a novel about power and loss, but it is increasingly focused on the women and children (or the women as children) of the decimated South rather than on the various father-son paradigms. Drawing near the close, Faulkner leaves the reader to experience the ashes of bitter loss in both Rosa's and Judith's speeches, their lives as Southern women doomed by the deaths of men who were their means of escaping those dusty corridors of repressed sexuality.

From this point of resonant understanding, Faulkner's narrative now embroiders the already known story. For the next four chapters, control of Rosa's story is usurped by Mr. Compson, Quentin, and Shreve (who sounds more and more like the elder Compson); and even though that usurpation is partly justified at the opening of Chapter 6, with Mr. Compson's announcement of Rosa's death, the reader remains in suspense, poised to discover the end of Rosa's story. Faulkner finally concludes the novel, and the Sutpen history, with an ending that interweaves the tropes of Rosa as voiceless child, Clytie as avenger of the Sutpen dynasty, and the house as mausoleum, complete with closed doors and an identification with human lineage. The ephemeral quality of Sutpen's Hundred—as fantastic in decline as it was in inception—dominates Faulkner's late description: the house looking as if it "were of one dimension, painted on a canvas curtain in which there was a tear . . . reek[ing] in slow and protracted violence with a smell of desolation and decay as if the wood of which it was built were flesh" (p. 366).

As Quentin drives toward Sutpen's Hundred with Rosa, she does little but "whimper." As they walk into the house, her hyperventilation continues and she trots beside him, "her hand trembling on his arm . . . not talking, not saying words, yet producing a steady whimpering, almost a moaning, sound" (p. 366). Frightened by the action she has planned and provoked, Rosa becomes once more the voiceless child she was throughout most of her life except for the years when she played the role of writer, the genteel poetess of the heroic South, living in a fantasy she found possible. Her only speech at the beginning of the journey identifies Sutpen boundaries, and her own claims to inheritance: "'Now,' she said. 'We are on the Domain. On his land, his and Ellen's and Ellen's descendants'" (p. 363). Faulkner gives Rosa such spare speech that her taut directions to Quentin, urging him to break down the front door, are particularly revealing. Convinced that the door will be nailed shut, as her father had nailed shut the attic when he abandoned her, Rosa demands revenge on both father and lover. Her act will open forever the countless doors closed against her; it will also reclaim her lost inheritances.

"Break it," she whispered. "It will be locked, nailed. You have the hatchet. Break it."

"But—" he began.

"Break it!" she hissed. "It belonged to Ellen. I am her sister, her only living heir. Break it. Hurry." (p. 367)

Three months later, Rosa returned to Sutpen's Hundred, an event that led Clytie to set the fire that destroyed the house and Henry and herself with it. Faulkner's description of Rosa as "the small furious grim implacable woman not much larger than a child," "the light thin furious creature making no sound at all now, struggling with silent and bitter fury" (p. 375), draws the reader with sympathy into the cycle of vengeance: language is sacrificed to rage, and the impassioned Rosa slips back in time, losing her human capacity to speak, to explain, to recall. Ellen Coldfield, who never learned to voice her rage, died as if turned to stone, repressing all bitter knowledge of the enormity of her life with Sutpen. Goodhue Coldfield also died without language, physically removing himself from any possibility of human community. Each adult left the child Rosa not only alone but without emotional or financial resources. And so Rosa became both the agent for vengeance and its victim.

As the Sutpen mansion burned, illustrating its "desolation more profound than ruin" (p. 136), the creation of the Sutpen legacy—with the disinherited Rosa Coldfield demanding her legacy—continued. In the immediate present of the novel, twenty-year-old Quentin, who is the same age Rosa was during the last episode she chooses to tell of her story, the episode of Sutpen's proposal and then insult, says to Shreve, "I am older at twenty than a lot of people who have died" (p. 377). The tragedy of Quentin Compson's understanding is that he sees no way to survive the pain of disinheritance; and he feels himself as abandoned by parents, community, and culture as Rosa was. As Faulkner so brilliantly charts, Rosa's aged but childlike self was the product of her abandonment by her father, her family, her lover, and her culture; yet when she finally broke through the chrysalis of self-protective fantasy, she brought down Sutpen's Hundred for all time and all memory. The concluding narrative envelope of Shreve and Quentin's dialogue, the last part of Mr. Compson's letter, and Quentin's own anguished realization subtract nothing from the poignancy and the terror of Rosa Coldfield's story. Her strangely silent discourse as the abandoned child, bereft of family and belonging, answers the elaborate rhetoric of Mr. Compson and his descendants (one linked by blood, the other by attitude) and leaves the reader wondering at the power of Rosa's largely unvoiced but ultimately assertive tale.

From *Studies in American Fiction* 19.1 (1991): 1-13. Copyright © 1991 by Northeastern University. Reprinted with permission of The Johns Hopkins University Press.

Notes

1. William Faulkner, *The Sound and the Fury* (New York: Random House, 1929), p. 215.

2. All references in the text are to William Faulkner's *Absalom, Absalom!* (New York: Random House, 1936). The quantity of criticism on this novel is staggering, but most of it does not give Rosa's story the prominence I do here. Recent criticism I have found most helpful includes John T. Matthews, *The Play of Faulkner's Language* (Ithaca: Cornell Univ. Press, 1982); Gail Mortimer, *Faulkner's Rhetoric of Loss* (Austin: Univ. of Texas Press, 1983); Elisabeth Muhlenfeld's *William Faulkner's* Absalom, Absalom!: *A Critical Casebook* (New York: Garland, 1984) and "Faulkner's Women," *MissQ*, 26 (1973), 435-40; Stephen M. Ross, "Oratory and the Dialogical in *Absalom, Absalom!*" in *Intertextuality in Faulkner*. ed. Michel Gresset and Noel Polk (Jackson: Univ. Press of Mississippi, 1985), pp. 73-86; Olga Vickery, *The Novels of William Faulkner*, 2nd ed. (Baron Rouge: Louisiana State Univ. Press, 1964); Minrose C. Gwin, *The Feminine and Faulkner, Reading (Beyond) Sexual Difference* (Knoxville: Univ. of Tennessee Press, 1990); and Wesley Morris with Barbara Alverson Morris, *Reading Faulkner* (Madison: Univ. of Wisconsin Press, 1989). My greatest agreement is with the latter two books, though the Morrises' reading does not follow the women characters so much as their critical stance would suggest and, in fact, they continuously "read" Rosa as trying to tell the Sutpen story when she is surely more interested in telling her own, and the Coldfield family, story (pp. 180-86).

3. See Lynda Boose's introduction to *Daughters and Fathers*, ed. Lynda E. Boose and Betty S. Flowers (Baltimore: Johns Hopkins Univ. Press, 1989), pp. 19-74, and André Bleikasten, "Fathers in Faulkner" in *The Fictional Father: Lacanian Readings of the Text*, ed. Robert Con Davis (Amherst: Univ. of Massachusetts Press, 1981), pp. 115-46. See also Philip M. Weinstein, "Meditations on the Other: Faulkner's Rendering of Women" and Ilse Dusoir Lind's "The Mutual Relevance of Faulkner Studies and Women's Studies: An Interdisciplinary Inquiry" in *Faulkner and Women*, ed. Doreen Fowler and Ann J. Abadie (Jackson: Univ. Press of Mississippi, 1986), pp. 81-99, 21-40, as well as Cleanth Brooks' chapter, "Faulkner's 'Motherless' Children" in his *On the Prejudices, Predilections, and Firm Beliefs of William Faulkner, Essays* (Baton Rouge: Louisiana State Univ. Press, 1987), pp. 66-79.

4. Again, there are more than a hundred readings of *Absalom, Absalom!* that might be mentioned. Among them, Michael Millgate, *The Achievement of William Faulkner* (New York: Random House, 1966); Cleanth Brooks, *William Faulkner: The Yoknapatawpha Country* (New Haven: Yale Univ. Press, 1963); Minrose C. Gwin, *Black and White Women of the Old South* (Knoxville: Univ. of Tennessee Press, 1985); Thadious M. Davis, *Faulkner's "Negro" Art and the Southern Context* (Baton Rouge: Louisiana State Univ. Press, 1983); Estella Schoenberg, *Old Tales and Talking: Quentin Compson in William Faulkner's* Absalom, Absalom! *and Related Works* (Jackson: Univ. Press of Mississippi, 1977); Joseph W. Reed, Jr., *Faulkner's Narrative* (New Haven: Yale Univ. Press, 1973); John T. Irwin, *Doubling and Incest/Repetition and Revenge: A Speculative Reading of Faulkner* (Baltimore: Johns Hopkins Univ. Press, 1975); Eric J. Sundquist, *Faulkner: The House Divided* (Baltimore: Johns Hopkins Univ. Press, 1982); Lynn Levins, *Faulkner's Heroic Design: The Yoknapatawpha Novels* (Athens: Univ. of Georgia Press, 1976); Carolyn Porter, *Seeing and Being: The Plight of the Participant-Observer in Emerson, James, Adams, and Faulkner* (Middletown: Wesleyan Univ. Press, 1981); Michael Millgate, "The 'Firmament of Man's History': Faulkner's Treatment of the Past," *MissQ*, 25 [Supplement] (1972), 25-35; John Middleton, "Shreve McCannon and Sutpen's Legacy," *SoR*, 10 (1974), 115-24.

5. Both Gwin in her 1990 study and the Morrises persistently question whether or not Faulkner knew what he was implying in Rosa's story. To adopt the dialogic stance toward Faulkner's fiction almost mandates that the critic accept that the author's intentionality was at least partly cognizant.

6. The Morrises state that "the novel's climactic moment is in Chapter 7" (p. 189), thereby locating Sutpen's door episode as the narrative center. While such configuration may be accurate, his initial door conflict is extended countless times through Rosa's text, and life, and it surely takes on different kinds of significance in these repetitions.

7. William Faulkner, "Review of *The Old Man and the Sea*," *Shenandoah*, 3 (Autumn, 1952), 55.

War and Memory:
Quentin Compson's Civil War

Lewis P. Simpson

Asked about his indebtedness to Sherwood Anderson, whom he had known personally in New Orleans in the early 1920s, William Faulkner replied, "In my opinion he's the father of my generation—Hemingway, Erskine Caldwell, Thomas Wolfe, Dos Passos." Strictly speaking, Faulkner's sense of literary genealogy may have derived more from a personal regard for Anderson than from an informed appreciation of his wider literary influence. It was Anderson who had advised the young writer from Mississippi to give up his residence in the French Quarter bohemia of New Orleans, return to his native patch of earth, and write about what life was like there. Heeding this cogent admonition had made all the difference. But neither the advice nor the stories of the well-known midwestern writer account for the compelling creative impulse that led a literary novice from Mississippi to develop into the world-famous author of the Yoknapatawpha saga. Faulkner offered a more basic, less arguable assertion about American literary genealogy, and about his own literary descent, when he rounded out his comment on the subject by declaring that the writer who may be considered Anderson's literary father, Mark Twain, "is all our grandfather."[1]

Whatever he owed to Anderson, the author of the Yoknapatawpha stories might have been more accurate in his metaphor if, ignoring generational chronology, he had described himself as also a son of Mark Twain; for Mark Twain was more than a distant forerunner of Faulkner. He created the model of the crucial role Faulkner enacted: that of the southern author as at once a participant in and ironic witness to a drama of memory and history that centered essentially in the never-ending remembrance of the great American civil conflict of 1861-1865. The obligation of the writer to serve as a witness, not to the actual historical event, but to the remembrance of it, was a force in shaping the vocation of the writer in the South from Thomas Nelson Page to Ellen Glasgow to Faulkner, Allen Tate, Katherine Anne Porter, Robert Penn Warren, and Eudora Welty; to, in fact, all of the writers associated with the flowering of southern authorship, especially novelists, in the 1920s and 1930s. The prime testimony to the shaping power of remembrance on the identity of the southern writer is offered not in the actual lives of the writers themselves but in certain implicit portrayals of the figure of the writer in their fiction, two of the notable instances being Lacy Buchan in Tate's *The Fathers* and Jack Burden in Warren's *All the King's Men*, but the supreme example being a twenty-year-old Mississippian who appears in *The Sound and the Fury* and *Absalom, Absalom!*, Quentin Compson III. On the surface these two Faulkner novels seem to bear no more than a coincidental relation to the war; but in the second of them, Faulkner's most baffling yet possibly finest single work, the portrayal of Quentin brings the drama of southern remembrance to its culminating expression.

Mark Twain's most cogent definition of the postbellum southern sensibility of memory occurs in *Life on the Mississippi*. At one point in this autobiographical work, first published in 1883, Mark Twain remarks that in the North one seldom hears the recent American civil conflict mentioned, but in the South it "is very different." Here, where "every man you meet was in the war" and "every lady you meet saw the war," it is "the great chief topic of conversation." To southerners, Mark Twain declares, the war is in fact "what A.D. is elsewhere: they date from it." Thus "all day long you hear things 'placed' as having happened since the waw; or du'in' the waw; or befo' the waw; or right aftah the waw; or 'bout two yeahs or five yeahs or ten yeahs befo' the waw or aftah the waw."[2]

Beneath the surface of the humor in *Life on the Mississippi*, the author—who had been brought up as Sam Clemens in the semifrontier Missouri extension of the southern slave society but had long since assumed the complex pseudonymous identity of "Mark Twain"—registers his realization of the profound effect of the war on his own consciousness of time and history. In his early manhood, before he became Mark Twain, Sam Clemens of Hannibal, Missouri, had permanently separated himself from the South when he withdrew from—or to speak less politely, deserted from—a ragtag volunteer company of Confederate Missourians and went adventuring on the new frontiers of Nevada and California. While in Nevada as a reporter for the Virginia City *Territorial Enterprise*, he adopted as his literary name the familiar cry of the leadsman on the Mississippi River steamboats he had piloted for three years prior to the war. It was as Mark Twain that after the war Sam Clemens went to live in the North and, later, having become a world traveler, at times in Europe. Although always haunted by a complex and troubled sense of his fundamental identity, in *Life on the Mississippi* Mark Twain writes out of a persistent, deeply empathic relationship with the South. It is in his identity as a postbellum southerner that the author speaks when he says that to grasp the significance of the war the stranger to the South must realize "how intimately every individual" southerner was involved in it. Ostensibly quoting a gentleman he had met at a New Orleans club—who, whether he was a real person or merely a convenient invention of the narrative moment, serves as an effective authorial persona—Mark Twain says that the experience of the calamity of war was so intense and encompassing in the South that each southerner, "in his own person," seems to have been intimately "visited . . . by that tremendous episode"—most notably by the "vast and comprehensive calamity" of "invasion." As a result, Mark Twain continues in the guise of the New Orleans gentleman, "each of us, in his own person, seems to have sampled all the different varieties of human experience." Inseparably connected to the war, the southern comprehension of time and history in Mark Twain's conception is such that "you can't mention an outside matter of any sort but it will certainly remind some listener of something that happened during the war—and out he comes with it." Even "the most random topic" will "load every man up with war reminiscences." As a result, "pale inconsequentialities" tend to disappear from southern conversation; "you can't talk" about business or the weather "when you've got a crimson fact or fancy in your head that you are burning to fetch out."[3]

Mark Twain's description of the effect of the Civil War on the southerner belongs to the account in the second part of *Life on the Mississippi* of his revisitation of the river in 1882. Although he had had his initial experience on the river only twenty-five years earlier, Mark Twain had returned to a world that bore only a superficial resemblance to the one he had known as a fledgling pilot, everything having been changed by the catastrophic internecine struggle that had erupted in the Republic of the United States of America in the seventh decade of its founding. Not to be generally known for a long time yet as the Civil War—often in the North still called the War of the Rebellion and in the South the War for Southern Independence—the unparalleled bloodletting that the grandchildren and great-grandchildren of the founders of the Republic were engaged in for four years had changed the meaning of time and history in the most fundamental sense. The civil slaughter and destruction had, to be sure, altered the very structure of American memory. Those Americans who had known the war intimately—and this in some way included all southerners, even those who like Mark Twain had removed themselves from the theater of war by going west—now, more self-consciously than the victors in the war, lived in two republics: the "Old Republic"—the remembered republic of the constitutional federation of self-liberated imperial colonies that had freed themselves in a war in that other time "befo' *the* waw"; and the actual republic—the integral union of states, the "Second American Republic," the "nation-state"—that had come into existence "aftah *the* waw." But for southerners, the defeated citizens of the aborted Confederate States of America, the sense of the displacement of memory was expressed in a more particular, in an essentially more intimate, historical terminology: the "Old South" and the "New South." Implying a displacement of memory different from that suggested by the terms Old Republic and New Republic, the southern effort to differentiate an Old and a New South emerged most simply and clearly, and it may be said most superficially, in the literary endeavor to create "local color" representations of the South. More deeply, the terms *Old South* and *New South* reflected the search by postbellum southern novelists for characters and situations that would transcend the regional concept of the southern literary identity. In their cultural situation, southern writers were inclined to see the life of the individual southerner as always in a dramatic tension with history; they seemed almost incapable of imagining the rejection of the historical context of the individual life. As Robert Penn Warren once said, "History is what you can't / Resign from."[4]

Yet after the War for Southern Independence had ended in the massive invasion and complete defeat of the Confederacy, southern writers—in ironic reaction to the feeling of being imprisoned in history—had commonly envisioned what amounted to a southern resignation from history. Ignoring the historical actuality of the Confederacy—a nation that in its brief existence was ever contentious and divided—writers created a rhetorical image of a unified spiritual nation. The metaphysical southern nation had, according to the rhetoric of southern nostalgia, evolved out of a stable antebellum civilization centered in the harmonious pastoral plantation and the beneficent institution of chattel slavery. Accepting such a vision of the past—out of the fear, it may be said, of the alienation of memory by history—the southerner was, as Warren observed, truly "trapped in history." The metaphysics of remembrance being equated with historical reality, one questioned the ideal image of the past at the risk of being suspected of treason.

But the literary imagination in the South did not yield altogether to delusionary remembrance. Reality at times intruded itself even into the rhetoric of an apologist like Thomas Nelson Page, creating an implied dramatic tension between memory and history. Removed sufficiently from the motive of apology, this tension promised to become highly fruitful in the case of Mark Twain's younger contemporary George Washington Cable, but faded as Cable became more and more committed to the politics of promoting equitable treatment for the freedmen.

Among the immediate postwar generation of southern writers the literary promise of the drama of memory and history reached notable fulfillment only in Mark Twain, and this in only one book, *Adventures of Huckleberry Finn*.

This was a novel Mark Twain had begun in the 1870s and put aside. When he had finished *Life on the Mississippi*, he almost immediately went back to the story of Huck and Jim and completed it in a sustained burst of energy. Obviously the experience of returning to the river and completing the book that he had begun earlier as "Old Times on the Mississippi" with an account of the river and its world fifteen years after the end of the Civil War had produced a tension lacking in the initial book about Tom Sawyer and Huck Finn. Although *The Adventures of Tom Sawyer* (1876) has its dark moments, in this book Mark Twain's recollection of life in Hannibal "befo' the waw" (in the 1840s) is informed more by nostalgia than irony. But in *Huckleberry Finn* the relationship between past and present—what was "befo' the waw" and what was "aftah the waw"—has altered. Always more significant in Mark Twain's imagination, and in the southern mind generally, than what was "du'in' the waw," what was "befo' the waw" and what was "aftah the waw" coalesce. In a novel that is basically an exploration of the southern society that fought the Civil War, Mark Twain strongly implies that history is what you can't resign from.

Or, to put it more precisely, Huck Finn implies this. Although a boy of no more than twelve or thirteen years of age, Mark Twain's persona in *Adventures of Huckleberry Finn* is not merely the narrator; writing in his own language, the vernacular of the Missouri backwoods, Huck is the highly self-conscious author, the literary artist, the authoritative maker of his own book. This is evident from the beginning, when Huck says that "you don't know about me without you have read a book . . . by Mr. Mark Twain [i.e., *The Adventures of Tom Sawyer*]," to the final moment, when he says that if he had "knowed what a trouble it was to make a book," he "wouldn't 'a' tackled it." Invested with the authority of the author—in a day when a "writer" was still an "author" and was presumed to have authority—Huck is fundamentally a reliable narrator. He tells it like it was because, in terms of Mark Twain's philosophy of history, he could not do otherwise. Much has been made of what seems to be Mark Twain's trivialization of the logical climax of *Huckleberry Finn* when, after his awesome declaration that he will defy every rule of society and society's God rather than abandon his support of a "nigger" and a slave with whom, in an act of ultimate impiety, he has entered into a bond of brotherhood, Huck becomes a tool of Tom Sawyer's devotion to the rhetoric of the romantic novelists and participates in the resolution of the story in the cruel rigmarole of the "splendid, mixed up rescue." Yet, ironically, Huck's authoritative honesty is still basically present. He has come close to experiencing the delusion of an elevation to a moral level superior to that of the society in which he lives—a society indubitably marked by its subscription not only to the God-ordained right to own human beings but, according to Huck's witness, to the right to be aggressively ignorant, like Pap Finn; to carry on murderous and meaningless feuds, like the Grangerfords and Shepherdsons; to lynch defenseless bums like Boggs; and to tar and feather con artists like the Duke and the Dauphin. In a society, in short, that wholly betrays the ideal of the rule of reason that had informed the founding of the American Republic, Huck acquiesces in the historicity of his moral condition. Indeed, almost immediately after he has spoken the "awful words" affirming his allegiance to Jim, he qualifies his declaration by saying that he will "go to work and steal Jim out of slavery again," for this is the kind of thing he ought to do, "being brung up to wickedness."

In his seemingly unsophisticated yet subtle recognition of the immanence of the conscience in society—of the historicism of his own consciousness of good and evil—Huck displays an intuitive awareness of his situation. He cannot breathe at the level of transcendent moral choice. In his way Huck is profoundly aware of the irony of living in the semifrontier microcosm of a society that had had its origin in a statement to the world proclaiming the innate sovereignty of self—and heralding a "Great Experiment" in governance that amounted to an unprecedented experiment in human nature, this to test whether human beings are endowed with a sufficient capacity for rational thought and rational behavior to govern themselves as free "selves." Yet even as it came into being, half of the nation that had invented itself on the assumption of an affirmative answer to this question was already in the process of expanding into the largest slave society in modern times. Having made a book detailing his memory of his own effort to reject this society through an aborted flight to freedom with Jim, Huck asserts that he will now exercise the prerogative of the transcendent sovereign self and "light out for the territory" to escape being "civilized." He has "been there before." But even as he announces the second flight to freedom, Huck knows the desperate futility of his gesture. He cannot escape the burden of the historical actuality of his experience with Jim by referring it to the realm of nostalgic memory.

Yet if in his effort to penetrate the inner reality of southern society Mark Twain resolved the tension between memory and history in favor of history, the influence of his exemplary effort did not appreciably undercut the subservience of the southern literary mind to the metaphysics of remembrance. This reason is no doubt to be found in the fact that Mark Twain wore the comic mask but not altogether so. The multi-volume compilation of southern literary piety called *The Library of Southern Literature* (prepared, the title page pointedly announces, under the "direct supervision of Southern men of letters") was published in the first decade of the twentieth century. While such an undertaking would not have been as feasible ten years later in the aftermath of World War I, the drama of the tension between memory and history created in the southern literary imagination by a war that had ended over fifty years earlier not only was still present but—in spite of the preoccupation with the before and after of the "Great War"—found its fulfillment as the definitive force in the writers of the Southern Renascence: in (to speak only of a few novelists) Allen Tate, Caroline Gordon, Andrew Lytle, Robert Penn Warren, and, most profoundly,

Faulkner.

The question of how the memory of World War I enhanced the memory of the Civil War in the twentieth-century southern literary imagination is illuminated by a comparison of the difference between the attitude toward the memory of war assumed on the one hand by Faulkner and on the other by his precise contemporary Ernest Hemingway. Like Faulkner, Hemingway acknowledged the primary significance of Mark Twain, even to the point of saying in *The Green Hills of Africa* that "all modern American literature comes from one book . . . *Huckleberry Finn*. . . . There was nothing before. There has been nothing since."[5] But in this hyperbolic theory of American writing, the midwesterner Hemingway ignored entirely the question of Huck's historical context and made him into a "Hemingway hero," who, however incongruously, may be compared to Jake Barnes in *The Sun Also Rises*. A figure of the writer (or the "author") and the chief actor in his own story, Jake, like all Hemingway heroes, finds the major motive of his life in the self-creation of a strangely stripped-down image of a world that, in contrast to the memory-obsessed world of Quentin Compson (in which "the past is not even past"), is preoccupied with the presentness of the present, even to the point of rejecting all traditional associations, including that of the family.

To speak of the role of Quentin in *Absalom, Absalom!* is to raise a much discussed problem. As we read the story of the Sutpens in its various reconstructions by the several narrators, do we discover any single character who serves as a focus of the authorial consciousness? On the face of it, is Quentin not simply one among the several characters in the novel, each obsessed by memory, each—including the third-person narrator—a self-conscious narrator (and actor), each the contributor of a highly subjective interpretative version of the fall of the House of Sutpen? The voluminous library of Faulkner criticism offers such different, and at times contradictory, responses to the narrators' interpretations of the story of the Sutpens that we may well reach the conclusion that the underlying motive of *Absalom, Absalom!* is contradictory: a strenuous effort to recover the past, the novel is yet a demonstration of the ambivalence of the effort. Yet in spite of the narrative maze we encounter in *Absalom, Absalom!*—which is further complicated, it should be added, by the presence of the unidentified third-person voice amid the identifiable voices—there is reason to interpret it as finding its ultimate focus in Quentin. "Ishmael is the witness in *Moby-Dick*," Faulkner once commented, "as I am Quentin in *The Sound and the Fury*."[6] It may be argued with some plausibility that Quentin not only is the chief participant-witness in *Absalom, Absalom!* but in his imaginative struggle to grasp the meaning of the lives of Henry Sutpen and his family, white and black, is—as a persona of Faulkner, the author, the maker, the ordering artist—the same enclosing presence in the story of the Sutpens that Faulkner had conceived him to be in his earlier story about the Compsons.

Powerfully established at the beginning of the novel, when Quentin sits with Miss Rosa in the September heat of the "dim airless room" of Sutpen's mansion—and powerfully reasserted at its end, when Quentin lies in bed talking with Shreve in the "iron" winter dark of a Harvard dormitory room—the presence of the twenty-year-old Mississippian in *Absalom, Absalom!* is more compelling than that of any other character. Hearing Miss Rosa's version of the story about the "demon" Sutpen in the initial scene of *Absalom, Absalom!*—listening to her speak "in that grim haggard amazed voice"—Quentin, a grandchild of the generation of Mississippi warriors who had fought in the Civil War, discovers after a time that he is no longer listening to the voice of Miss Rosa but is hearing "two separate" voices in himself: one voice is that of the "Quentin Compson preparing for Harvard in the South, the deep South dead since 1865 and peopled with garrulous outraged baffled ghosts"; the other voice in this inward dialogue is that of the Quentin "who was still too young to deserve yet to be a ghost, but nevertheless having to be one for all that, since he was born and bred in the deep South the same as she [Miss Rosa] was." The two Quentins talk "to one another in the long silence of notpeople, in notlanguage, like this: *It seems that this demon—his name was Sutpen—(Colonel Sutpen)—Colonel Sutpen. Who came out of nowhere and without warning upon the land with a band of strange niggers and built a plantation.*"[7]

At this point his dialogic interiorizing of the Sutpen story is interrupted when Quentin becomes aware that Miss Rosa is directly addressing him:

> Because you are going away to attend the college at Harvard they tell me. . . . So I dont imagine you will ever come back here and settle down as a country lawyer in a little town like Jefferson, since Northern people have already seen to it that there is little left in the South for a young man. So maybe you will enter the literary profession as so many Southern gentlemen and gentlewomen too are doing now and maybe some day you will remember this and write about it. You will be married then I expect and perhaps your wife will want a new gown or a new chair for the house and you can write this and submit it to the magazines. (5)

Why, Quentin wonders, does Miss Rosa need to suggest that he become a writer so that he can be the teller of her tale? If her need to tell the story of her relationship with Sutpen is so coercive, why does not she herself tell it? She is a writer, well-known as Yoknapatawpha County's "poetess laureate," who "out of some bitter and implacable reserve of undefeat" has frequently celebrated the heroes of the Lost Cause in odes, eulogies, and epitaphs published in the county newspaper. Quentin's question remains unanswered, at least explicitly. The implicit answer lies in Miss Rosa's recognition of Quentin as a potential literary witness in the first scene of *Absalom, Absalom!* Here Faulkner indicates his intention to repeat, in a more complex way, what he had done in *The Sound and the Fury* six years earlier, namely, to project Quentin as an incarnation of the fundamental, and inescapable, motive of the postbellum southern writer's imagination: the importunate sense, stemming from a compulsive memory of the Civil War, not simply of a personal intimacy with history but, as in the case of Huck Finn, of a connection with history so absolute that it is the very source of his being. When his father tells Quentin that Miss Rosa has a vengeful motive in her idea of involving him in the story of her dastardly treatment by the "demon"—this because she believes, or wants to believe, that her fateful association with Sutpen would never have occurred if the "demon" had not come to Mississippi as the consequence of a friendship with Quentin's grandfather—Quentin counters with an explanation of epic grandeur: "*She wants it told . . . so that people whom she will never see and whose names she will never hear and who have never heard her name nor seen her face will read it and know at last why God let us lose the War: that only through the blood of our men and the tears of our women could He stay this demon and efface his name and lineage from the earth*" (6).

Although Quentin himself immediately rejects his bardic explanation of Miss Rosa's solicitation of his pen, he is, as the third-person narrator indicates, not merely playing a game with his father. His conception of Miss Rosa's appeal to the "God who let us lose the War" indirectly reflects the fact that Quentin knows that he and Miss Rosa (and for that matter his father) are as profoundly entangled in the history of Sutpen's struggle to found the House of Sutpen as is Miss Rosa's older sister, Ellen Coldfield, the wife Sutpen takes from a prominent Yoknapatawpha family to be the bearer of his heirs; or Henry and Judith Sutpen, the children Ellen bears; or Charles Bon, the son and heir Sutpen has earlier fathered in Haiti, only to reject him upon discovering that his mother is partly Negro; or Clytie, Sutpen's daughter by one of the "wild" slaves he brings to Yoknapatawpha. And Quentin knows that, in a larger sense, he and Miss Rosa and Mr. Compson are also implicated in the anomalies and ironies of a shaping cultural ethos that paradoxically at once commemorates and celebrates the world-historical self-defeat of a house that was not only a part of that larger house Lincoln said could not stand divided against itself but was significantly in itself a divided house.

Without insisting at all on a literal correspondence between the House of Sutpen and the House of the South, one can hardly fail to discern implicit symbols of the southern divisiveness in Quentin's knowledge of the Sutpens. He knows, for one thing, that Miss Rosa had a father "who as a conscientious objector on religious grounds, had starved to death in the attic of his own house, hidden (some said, walled up) there from Confederate provost marshals' men and fed secretly at night by the same daughter [Miss Rosa] who at the very time was accumulating her first folio in which the lost cause's unregenerate vanquished were name by name embalmed." Quentin also knows the more fateful fact that Miss Rosa had a "nephew [Henry Sutpen] who served for four years in the same company with his sister's fiance [Charles Bon] and then shot the fiance to death before the gates to the house where the sister waited in her wedding gown on the eve of the wedding and then fled, vanished, none knew where" (6). And Quentin knows much more, too much for any peace of mind. Having "grown up" with all the names associated with the story of Sutpen, Quentin, the third-person narrator tells us, has become a symbolic repository of the memory of the destroyed House of Sutpen and the remembrance of the southern defeat. "He was a barracks filled with stubborn back-looking ghosts still recovering, even forty-three years afterward, from the fever which had cured the disease, waking from the fever without even knowing that it had been the fever itself which they had fought against and not the sickness, looking with stubborn recalcitrance backward beyond the fever and into the disease with actual regret, weak from the fever yet free of the disease and not even aware that the freedom vas that of impotence" (7).

Described by the third-person narrator as "not a being, an entity," but, in metaphors of Shakespearean intensity, as a "barracks" filled with ghosts, or more expansively, a ghostly "commonwealth," Quentin emerges more clearly in *Absalom, Absalom!* than in *The Sound and the Fury* as a highly self-conscious, romantic, doomed embodiment of the lost Confederacy. Out of the deepest levels of his imagination of memory and history, he subtly transforms the story of the House of Sutpen into a deeply introverted, and deeply ironic, vision of the drama of the inner history of the War for Southern Independence. Even as southern society was engaged in a massive struggle to preserve itself as a slave society, the third-person narrator intimates in his description of Quentin, it had a secret motive, inarticulate, hidden even from itself: a desire to free itself from its enslavement to the "disease" of slavery. Yet, having been forced by military catastrophe to accept the fulfillment of its hidden desire, this society looks back with regret at having been freed by the "fever" of war from the "disease" of slavery. Until the South can openly accept the historical implications of its desire to be free from the social and economic institution of chattel slavery—which, although *Absalom, Absalom!* does not quite make this explicit, had been rationalized by antebellum southerners as their necessary source of freedom—the revolutionary shift from a slave society to a free society is historically "impotent." As the drama of the House of Sutpen unfolds through the witness of Miss Rosa and Mr. Compson, Quentin's struggle to interpret it almost half a century after the end of the War for Southern Independence becomes the focal revelation of this powerful irony. In an earlier age, Quentin would have been a bardic voice speaking of the glory of "olden times." But in the first decade of the twentieth century—not so much a grandchild as a ghost of the generation of the 1860s—a poet of the American South assumes not only the role of a witness to the unending drama of his own personal struggle to interpret the meaning of the vexed and tortuous history of the South but, like Faulkner, the self-conscious role of an actor in a drama he is both composing and enacting in his own consciousness.

The problem of interpretation that preoccupies Quentin in this drama is the central problem in *Absalom, Absalom!*: Why does Henry kill Charles Bon? Three poignant scenes are particularly illuminating. One occurs toward the end of the fifth chapter, when the third-person narrator interrupts Miss Rosa's narrative to present what he imagines to be Quentin's creation for himself of a part of the story of Sutpen's children, this being the moment when Henry, having just shot Charles Bon as the two soldiers arrive back at Sutpen's place after Appomattox, runs up the stairs and bursts into his sister's bedroom. Here he sees Clytie and Ellen, "the white girl in her underthings (made of flour sacking when there had been flour, of window curtains when not)." He sees too Judith's wedding dress,

> the yellowed creamy mass of old intricate satin and lace spread carefully on the bed and then caught swiftly up by the white girl and held before her as the door crashed in and the brother stood there, hatless, with his shaggy bayonet-trimmed hair, his gaunt worn unshaven face, his patched and faded gray tunic, the pistol still hanging against his flank: the two of them, brother and sister, curiously alike as if the difference in sex had merely sharpened the common blood to a terrific, an almost unbearable, similarity, speaking to one another in short brief staccato sentences like slaps, as if they stood breast to breast striking one another in turn neither making any attempt to guard against the blows.
> *Now you cant marry him.*
> *Why cant I marry him?*
> *Because he's dead.*
> *Dead?*
> *Yes. I killed him.* (139)

Another illuminating scene in *Absalom, Absalom!* occurs when Quentin, listening to his father's account of the relationship between Bon and Judith, sees the one letter Bon—at Henry's urging—wrote to Judith during his entire four years in the Confederate army. Taking the letter in hand, Quentin imagines as he reads "the faint spidery script"— written nearly fifty years before on elegant French notepaper from a gutted southern mansion with a pen dipped in stove polish captured from the Yankees—that he is listening to Bon's "gentle sardonic whimsical and incurably pessimistic" voice telling Judith in the final days of the Confederacy that he has come to believe they are, *"strangely enough, included among those who are doomed to live"* (105). Although Bon's message is enigmatic, Judith takes it to be a proposal of marriage.

While Mr. Compson talks on about Henry and Bon—wondering whether Henry had warned Bon not to come back to Judith and describing the scene of their encounter outside the gate of the Sutpen place as they arrive back from the war ("the two of them must have ridden side by side almost")—Quentin, once again "hearing without having to listen," according to the intervening imagination of the narrator, is depicted as silently imagining the scene for himself.

(It seemed to Quentin that he could actually see them, facing one another at the gate. Inside the gate what was once a park now spread, unkempt, in shaggy desolation, with an air dreamy remote and aghast like the unshaven face of a man just waking from ether, up to a huge house where a young girl waited in a wedding dress made from stolen scraps, the house partaking too of that air of scaling desolation, not having suffered from invasion but a shell marooned and forgotten in a backwater of catastrophe—a skeleton giving of itself in slow driblets of furniture and carpet, linen and silver, to help to die torn and anguished men who knew, even while dying, that for months now the sacrifice and the anguish were in vain. They faced one another on the two gaunt horses, two men, young, not yet in the world, not yet breathed over long enough, to be old but with old eyes, with unkempt hair and faces gaunt and weathered as if cast by some spartan and even niggard hand from bronze, in worn and patched gray weathered now to the color of dead leaves, the one with the tarnished braid of an officer, the other plain of cuff, the pistol lying yet across the saddle bow unaimed, the two faces calm, the voices not even raised: *Dont you pass the shadow of this post, this branch, Charles*; and *I am going to pass it, Henry*). (105-106)

The conclusion of the scene is in Mr. Compson's voice: "and then Wash Jones sitting that saddleless mule before Miss Rosa's gate, shouting her name into the sunny and peaceful quiet of the street, saying, 'Air you Rosie Coldfield? Then you better come on out yon. Henry has done shot that durn French feller. Kilt him dead as a beef'" (106).

Why does Bon want to marry his sister? Is he in love with her? If so, his love is clearly subordinated to his passion for revenge on a father who refuses to acknowledge him. Sutpen had a vivid chance to accept Bon as his son when the elegant and handsome New Orleanian came to visit Sutpen's Hundred as Henry's fellow student and friend at the University of Mississippi. He had a still more vivid chance to accept Bon as his son toward the end of the war when the unit Bon and Henry were in became attached to a regimental unit commanded by their father. If Sutpen had recognized Bon at either time, presumably things would have been different. But he cannot acknowledge an heir who has a tincture of black blood. Bon—with no trace of the negroid in his appearance, handsome, urbane, ten years older than Henry—becomes Henry's idol, and no less a fatal attraction for Judith. Undergoing the experience of war with Bon, Henry, who has known since 1861 that he and Judith are half brother and half sister to Bon (and has known as well, though this knowledge is of lesser import, that Bon is the father of a boy by a New Orleans octoroon), has, it would seem, overcome his revulsion against its incestuous nature and reconciled himself to a union between Bon and Judith. How has this incredible adjustment taken place? Has the war experience rendered Henry's feeling toward Bon an emotion transcendent over any other emotion? Or does Henry, unconsciously harboring incestuous feelings both for his brother and for his sister, somehow imagine their marriage as a consummation of his desire? Does Bon desire the marriage only for revenge on Sutpen? Or is he in love with Judith? For that matter, is Judith in love with Bon?

In any event it is not until the very end of the war that Henry learns of an impediment to the marriage of Bon and Judith that love, normal or abnormal, can in no wise blink. When he responds to a command to come to Colonel Sutpen's tent (Sutpen has organized a command and gone to the war not long after Henry and Bon), he is told by Sutpen that after Bon's birth he had discovered that Bon's mother, a planter's daughter he had taken as his wife while he was an overseer on a Haitian plantation, had Negro blood. Henry is given an injunction by his father that, issuing from the lips of his commanding officer, has something of the force of a military order: "*He must not marry her, Henry*" (283).

We do not know about the meeting of Henry and his father until the culminating, and concluding, scene in *Absalom, Absalom!* In their chilly Harvard dormitory room on a snowy night in January, 1910, Quentin and his roommate, the Canadian Shreve McCannon, discuss at great length the question of why Henry killed Bon. As they talk they engage in a speculative reconstruction of what led to this event. But significantly we learn about Sutpen's injunction to Henry not through Shreve's and Henry's speculative reconstruction of the meeting in Sutpen's tent. What happened there comes to us only in Quentin's un-spoken re-creation. At first, Quentin imagines, Henry refused the order.

> —*You are going to let him marry Judith, Henry.*
>
> *Still Henry does not answer. It has all been said before, and now he has had four years of bitter struggle following which, whether it be victory or defeat which he has gained, at least he has gained it and has peace now, even if the peace be mostly despair.*
>
> —*He cannot marry her, Henry.*
>
> *Now Henry speaks.*
>
> —*You said that before. I told you then. And now, and now it wont be much longer now and then we wont have anything left: honor nor pride nor God since God quit us four years ago only He never thought it necessary to tell us; no shoes nor clothes and no need for them; not only no land to make food out of but no need for the food and when you dont have God and honor and pride, nothing matters except that there is the old mindless meat that dont even care if it was defeat or victory, that wont even die, that will be out in the woods and fields, grubbing up roots and weeds.—Yes. I have decided, Brother or not, I have decided. I will. I will. . . .*

—He must not marry her, Henry. His mother's father told me that her mother had been a Spanish woman. I believed him; it was not until after he was born that I found out that his mother was part negro. (283)

Quentin's imagination of it is also the only source of the moment that follows immediately after the scene in Colonel Sutpen's tent, the encounter between Bon and Henry at the campfire.

—So it's the miscegenation, not the incest, which you cant bear.
Henry doesn't answer.
—And he sent me no word? He did not ask you to send me to him? No word to me, no word at all? That was all he had to do, now, today; four years ago or at any time during the four years. That was all. He would not have needed to ask it, require it, of me. I would have offered it. I would have said, I will never see her again before he could have asked it of me. He did not have to do this, Henry. He didn't need to tell you I am a nigger to stop me. He could have stopped me without that, Henry. (285)

In Quentin's private re-creation of what happened next, Bon extends a pistol and commands Henry to shoot him (Bon is also Henry's superior officer), but Henry refuses, saying, "*You are my brother.*" He continues to refuse even though Bon says, "*No I'm not. I'm the nigger that's going to sleep with your sister. Unless you stop me, Henry*" (286). Henry does not stop Bon until the two arrive at the very gate to Sutpen's Hundred.

By this juncture in the novel Quentin's telling Shreve about his going out to Sutpen's Hundred with Miss Rosa, discovering the dying Henry there, and then witnessing the burning of Sutpen's mansion can only come as an anticlimax. It is instructive to learn that in the short story out of which Faulkner's novel grew, this is not the case. Unpublished until Joseph Blotner's edition of *The Uncollected Stories of William Faulkner* came out in 1979, this story, entitled "Evangeline," like another Faulkner short story called "Mistral," is developed through the use of an "I" narrator and the narrator's friend Don Giovanni. Don has put the narrator onto a "ghost story" about the mystery surrounding a decaying Mississippi plantation house belonging to a family named Sutpen. Although the details of the plot are somewhat different and not nearly so elaborate, "Evangeline" centers on the narrator's investigation of the story of Judith, Bon, and Henry, and his discovery of Henry's presence in the Sutpen house, where throughout the forty years since his fratricidal act he has lived secretly under the protection of a black woman named Raby. Raby, it turns out, is Sutpen's child by one of his slaves and the sister of Judith, Bon, and Henry (she becomes Clytie in *Absalom, Absalom!*). As though he was unable to assimilate the experience of verifying the secret presence of Henry Sutpen in the Sutpen mansion, the narrator's account of the event is fragmentary and impressionistic. Yet it is strangely emphatic; the narrator feels a certain identity with Henry:

> It was quite still. There was a faint constant sighing high in the cedars, and I could hear the insects and the mockingbird. Soon there were two of them, answering one another, brief, quiring, risinginflectioned [*sic*]. Soon the sighing cedars, the insects and the birds became one peaceful sound bowled inside the skull in monotonous miniature, as if all the earth were contracted and reduced to the dimensions of a baseball, into and out of which shapes, fading, emerged fading and faded emerging:
> "And you were killed by the last shot fired in the war?"
> "I was so killed. Yes."
> "Who fired the last shot fired in the war?"
> "Was it the last shot you fired in the war, Henry?"
> "I fired a last shot in the war; yes."
> "You depended on the war, and the war betrayed you too; was that it?"
> "Was that it, Henry?"[8]

In *Absalom, Absalom!* Quentin's visit to the dark room of the Sutpen mansion where Henry lies dying is more ambiguous in its presentation. In the novel, in contrast to "Evangeline," Henry flees after he kills Bon and returns four years before Miss Rosa and Quentin find him there under the zealous protection of a "tiny gnomelike creature in headrag and voluminous skirts" with "a worn coffee-colored face," his sister Clytie. In the discovery scene in *Absalom, Absalom!* no reference is made to a last shot in the war; Quentin's interrogation of Henry is elliptical. But the scene brings to a subtle climax the increasingly close relationship the doomed Quentin feels with Sutpen's tragic children. The sealing of this relationship is indicated by so small a sign as the colon that marks the transition from the narrator's objective description of how Quentin enters the shuttered "bare stale room" where Henry lies dying to the portrayal of the interior scene in which the identity of Henry is established.

> The bed, the yellow sheets and pillow, the wasted yellow face with closed, almost transparent eyelids on the pillow, the wasted hands crossed on the breast as if he were already a corpse; waking or sleeping it was the same and would be the same forever as long as he lived:
> *And you are——?*
> *Henry Sutpen.*
> *And you have been here——?*
> *Four years.*
> *And you came home——?*
> *To die. Yes.*
> *Yes. To die.*
> *And you have been here——?*
> *Four years.*
> *And you are——?* (298)

In the exact use of a colon instead of a parenthesis ["(*—the winter of '64 now, the army retreated*," etc.] to denote the shift from the objective to the subjective mode (*i.e.*, the entry into Quentin's consciousness), the subtle authority of the third-person narrator becomes explicit. His consciousness has become identical with Quentin's. For those who know "Evangeline" an anticipation of this moment may be seen in the "I" narrator's strange rapport with Bon, Henry, and Raby [Clytie] in that story. When both the *Saturday Evening Post* and the *Woman's Home Companion* rejected "Evangeline," Faulkner put the story aside, but finding that it would not let him alone, he came back to it after a couple of years and sought to make it work better by replacing the "I" narrator and Don with two characters he called Chisholm and Burke. Eventually, the grip of the story on him becoming stronger, he thought of transforming Chisholm and Burke into Quentin and Shreve and making them interpreter-participants in a story that, greatly expanded and far more sophisticated in technique, would have a suggestive frame of reference in the Old Testament epic of David and his sons and be a major part of his symbol of the history of the South, the fictional history of Yoknapatawpha County, Mississippi. The expanded story, in other words, would have its center not in the account of Sutpen and the exploitative invasion of the wilderness that in not much more than two short generations produced the rise and fall of the Cotton Kingdom but in a story allusive of the biblical story of King David and his sons. In this story the murder of Amnon by Absalom occurs just after the two brothers have concluded four long years of fighting against great odds for a common cause. Ironically, in a civil conflict that has often been called "the brothers' war"—and in which brothers, not only in a figurative but in some cases in a literal sense, were engaged on opposing sides—the sons of Sutpen were on the same side. Like most southerners, slaveholders and nonslaveholders, they fought to uphold the more or less official doctrine that the preservation of slavery was necessary for the preservation of a sacred guarantee of constitutional freedom that included their right to own slaves. Forcibly dispossessed of this right, they believed, they would become slaves themselves. The murdered brother and the murdering brother had no quarrel in this respect.

But the narrator in "Evangeline," asking Bon if he had been killed by the last shot fired in the war and Henry if he had pulled the trigger, was moved by the knowledge that Bon had died not in the war between the North and the South but in a struggle within a society that, even as it fought against the brothers with whom, only three generations earlier, it had made common cause in the American Revolution, was rent by its need for a more coherent, convincing definition of its historical character than the Revolution had provided. The southern struggle for historical self-representation was rendered all the more intense because of the fact that even as the South sought to express its destiny, the effort was repressed by the need to present the image of a society united in support of slavery. In its uncertainty about itself the southern slave society placed an extreme premium on an ideal of order that held above all, as Faulkner said in speaking of Andrew Jackson, that "the principle that honor must be defended whether it was or not because defended it was whether or not."[9] Equating the principle of family honor with the ideal of feminine chastity and the protection of the purity of the bloodline, Henry had finally to slay Bon, even though Mr. Compson says Henry loved Bon, and in "Evangeline" Don says the two were "close as a married couple almost."[10]

In their conversation in the cold dark after they finally go to bed, Shreve keeps on baiting Quentin about the South. Referring to the Canadians, he says, "We dont live among defeated grandfathers and freed slaves (or have I got it backward and was it your folks that are free and the niggers that lost?) and bullets in the dining room table and such, to be always reminding us to never forget." When Shreve, warming to his subject, observes that the southern memory of General Sherman is perpetual, so that "forevermore as long as your children's children produce children you wont be anything but a descendant of a long line of colonels killed in Pickett's charge at Manassas," Quentin at once corrects Shreve's factual error about the battle in which Pickett's charge occurred, adding, in the second most famous statement in the novel, "You cant understand it. You would have to be born there." But when Shreve—in a passage not often noticed in the voluminous critical interpretation of *Absalom, Absalom!*—continues to challenge Quentin about the southern culture of memory, "Would I then? [*i.e.*, have to be born there]. . . . Do you understand it?" Quentin equivocates: "'I dont know. . . . Yes, of course I understand.' They breathed in the darkness. After a moment Quentin said: 'I dont know'" (289).

When Shreve presents his most dramatic challenge to Quentin: "Now I want you to tell me just one thing more. Why do you hate the South?," the heir of the Compsons replies "quickly, at once, immediately," in the best-known words of the novel. "'I dont hate it,' he said. *I dont hate it* he thought, panting in the cold air, the iron New England dark; *I dont. I dont! I dont hate it! I dont hate it!*" (303). If, as has been said, Quentin protests Shreve's challenge too much, he has reason to. His very identity, in a way his very existence, is suddenly and irrevocably at stake.

"Ishmael is the witness in *Moby-Dick* as I am Quentin in *The Sound and the Fury*": If in his imagination of his authorial role, Faulkner identifies with Quentin in the comparatively simple structure of the story of the doomed Compsons, he does so even more surely, if more subtly, in the intricately structured story involving the relationship between the memorial reconstruction of the doom of the House of Sutpen on the one hand and the doom of the House of Compson on the other. Thought of by Faulkner as a symbol of the second—or, it may be said, the first full—literary generation of the postbellum South, Quentin (born 1890) could scarcely have been conceived by a writer of his own generation. A symbolic embodiment of the culmination of the drama of memory and history in Faulkner's generation (Faulkner was born in 1897)—the generation that became the post-World War I generation— Quentin incarnates more powerfully than any other character in southern fiction the drama of the ironic equivocation of the southern literary mind in its quest to discover in the southern memory a postbellum southern identity. The revelation of the inner civil war in the South in the story of Henry, Bon, and Judith reveals how, in his effort to come to terms with the South, Quentin, a romantic southern Puritan, is the doomed reincarnation of an earlier young southern Puritan, Henry Sutpen. In the last moment of a difficult journey back from the war, obeying the southern mode of the murderous defense of family honor—defending an abstract principle that had to be defended lest the order of the world be lost—Henry had not only killed his brother and made himself into a ghost, he had made Quentin, who would not be born for another fifteen years, into a ghost. "'I am older at twenty than a lot of people who have died,' Quentin said" (301).

Before he called on Quentin Compson to be a witness to, and an actor in, the drama of Henry Sutpen's desperate and despairing defense of the principle of honor in *Absalom, Absalom!*, Faulkner had of course in *The Sound and the Fury* already depicted the ultimate fate of his surrogate. Drowning himself in the Charles River in Cambridge, Massachusetts, on June 2, 1910, Quentin had signaled the despair of those bound by the poetry of memory to a world no longer believed in. In this case it was the world the slaveholders—and, however unwillingly, the enslaved themselves—had made in the American South. Equating freedom with the defense of an illusory principle that they nonetheless conceived to be the vital basis of order, the slave masters had littered battlefield after battlefield with the sacrificial victims of a War for Southern Independence. Like the subtly ironic pathos of Mark Twain's representation of Huckleberry Finn's memory of the antebellum South, the still more refined distillation of pathos in Faulkner's representation of Quentin's memory of the Confederacy, and of the postbellum South, does not simply reflect the drama of the literary representation of the inner history of the Civil War, it is part and parcel of this history. If, moreover—and we must admit the possibility—either Mark Twain's or Faulkner's representation of the war be deemed at times to be misrepresentation, it is not less integral to the war's inner history.

From *The Fable of the Southern Writer* (1997) by Louis P. Simpson. Copyright © 1997 by Louisiana State University Press. Reprinted with permission of Louisiana State University Press.

Notes

1. Frederick L. Gwynn and Joseph L. Blotner, eds., *Faulkner in the University: Class Conferences at the University of Virginia, 1957-1958* (New York, 1965), 281.

2. Mark Twain, *Life on the Mississippi*, in *Mississippi Writings*, ed. Guy Cardwell (New York, 1982), 491-92.

3. *Ibid.*

4. Robert Penn Warren, *Selected Poems, 1923-1975* (New York, 1972), 159.

5. Ernest Hemingway, *The Green Hills of Africa* (New York, 1954), 19.

6. Joseph Blotner, *Faulkner: A Biography* (2 vols; New York, 1974), II, 1522.

7. William Faulkner, *Absalom, Absalom! The Corrected Text* (New York, 1986), 4-5. Hereafter references to this work will be made parenthetically in the text.

8. William Faulkner, "Evangeline," in *The Uncollected Stories of William Faulkner*, ed. Joseph Blotner (New York, 1979), 685-86. *Cf.* below, 176-81.

9. Appendix to *The Portable Faulkner*, ed. Malcolm Cowley (New York, 1964), 738.

10. Faulkner, "Evangeline," in *Uncollected Stories*, ed. Blotner, 587.

The Dead Father in Faulkner_____

John T. Irwin

Father Time is an ancient conflation, based in part on a similarity of names, of two figures—Kronos, Zeus' father, and Chronos, the personification of time. As we know, that conflation ultimately led to the attachment of at least two of the major legends of Kronos to Father Time—first, that Kronos is a son who castrated his father, Ouranos, and was in turn castrated by his own son Zeus, and second, that Kronos is a father who devours his children. Discussing the evolution of the iconography of Father Time, the art historian Erwin Panofsky notes that the learned writers of the fourth and fifth centuries A.D. began to provide the old figure of Kronos/Saturn with new attributes and "reinterpreted the original features of his image as symbols of time. His sickle, traditionally explained either as an agricultural symbol or as the instrument of castration, came to be interpreted as a symbol of *tempora quae sicut falx in se recurrent*; and the mythical tale that he had devoured his children was said to signify that Time, who had already been termed 'sharp-toothed' by Simonides and *edax rerum* by Ovid, devours whatever he has created."[1]

In discussing the nature of time, Nietzsche alludes to both the legends of Kronos that became associated with Father Time. In the passage from *Zarathustra* in which he talks about the revenge against time, he mentions "this law of time that it must devour its children" (252), and in *Philosophy in the Tragic Age of the Greeks* he says, "As Heraclitus sees time, so does Schopenhauer. He repeatedly said of it that every moment in it exists only insofar as it has just consumed the preceding one, its father, and then is immediately consumed likewise."[2] One might say that the struggle between the father and the son inevitably turns into a dispute about the nature of time, not just because the authority of the father is based on priority in time, but because the essence of time is that in the discontinuous, passing moment it is experienced as a problem of the endless displacement of the generator by

330

Critical Insights

the generated, while in the continuity of the memory trace it is experienced as a problem of the endless destruction of the generated by the generator. In this last sense, we refer not just to the experience that what is generated in and by time is as well consumed in and by time, but also to the experience that the price which the generative moment exacts for its displacement into the past is a castration of the present through memory. In tropes such as "the golden age," "the lost world," "the good old days," the past convicts the present of inadequacy through lack of priority, lack of originality, since to be a copy is to be a diminution, because the running on of time is a running down, because to come after is to be fated to repeat the life of another rather than to live one's own.

In *The Sound and the Fury*, the struggle between Quentin and his father that runs through the stream-of-consciousness narrative of Quentin's last day is primarily a dispute about time. The narrative begins with Quentin's waking in the morning ("I was in time again")[3] to the ticking of his grandfather's watch, the watch that his father had presented to him, saying, "I give it to you not that you may remember time, but that you may forget it now and then for a moment and not spend all your breath trying to conquer it" (95). Quentin twists the hands off his grandfather's watch on the morning of the day when he forever frees himself and his posterity from the cycles of time and generation. When Quentin is out walking that morning, he passes the shopwindow of a watch store and turns away so as not to see what time it is, but there is a clock on a building and Quentin sees the time in spite of himself: he says, "I thought about how, when you dont want to do a thing, your body will try to trick you into doing it, sort of unawares" (102). And that, of course, is precisely Quentin's sense of time—that it is a compulsion, a fate. For his father has told him that a man is the sum of his misfortunes and that time is his misfortune like "a gull on an invisible wire attached through space dragged" (123). In his struggle against his father and thus against time, Quentin must confront the same problem that he faces in the story of Sutpen and his sons—

whether a man's father is his fate. In *Absalom, Absalom!* when Shreve begins to sound like Quentin's father, Quentin thinks, "*Am I going to have to have to hear it all again. . . . I am going to have to hear it all over again I am already hearing it all over again I am listening to it all over again I shall have to never listen to anything else but this again forever so apparently not only a man never outlives his father but not even his friends and acquaintances do.*"[4]

When Quentin demands that his father act against the seducer Dalton Ames, Quentin, by taking this initiative, is in effect trying to supplant his father, to seize his authority. But Quentin's father refuses to act, and the sense of Mr. Compson's refusal is that Quentin cannot seize his father's authority because there is no authority to seize. Quentin's alcoholic, nihilistic father presents himself as an emasculated son, ruined by General Compson's failure. Mr. Compson psychologically castrates Quentin by confronting him with a father figure, a model for manhood, who is himself a castrated son. Mr. Compson possesses no authority that Quentin could seize because what Mr. Compson inherited from the General was not power but impotence. If Quentin is a son struggling in the grip of Father Time, so is his father. And it is exactly that argument that Mr. Compson uses against Quentin. When Quentin demands that they act against the seducer, Mr. Compson answers in essence, "Do you realize how many times this has happened before and how many times it will happen again? You are seeking a once-and-for-all solution to this problem, but there are no once-and-for-all solutions. One has no force, no authority to act in this matter because one has no originality. The very repetitive nature of time precludes the existence of originality within its cycles. You cannot be the father because I am not the father—only Time is the father." When Quentin demands that they avenge Candace's virginity, his father replies, "Women are never virgins. Purity is a negative state and therefore contrary to nature. Its nature is hurting you not Caddy and I said That's just words and he said So is virginity and I said you dont know. You cant know and he said Yes. On the instant when we come to realise that tragedy is second-hand" (135). In essence Quentin's father says, "We cannot act because there exists no virginity to avenge and because there exists no authority by which we could avenge since we have no originality. We are second-hand. You are a copy of a copy. To you, a son who has only been a son, it might seem that a father has authority because he comes first, but to one who has been both a father and a son, it is clear that to come before is not necessarily to come first, that priority is not necessarily originality. My fate was determined by my father as your fate is determined by yours." Quentin's attempt to avenge his sister's lost virginity (proving thereby that it had once existed) and maintain the family honor is an attempt to maintain the possibility of "virginity" in a larger sense, the possibility of the existence of a virgin space within which one can still be first, within which one can have authority through originality, a virgin space like that Mississippi wilderness into which the first Compson (Jason Lycurgus I) rode in 1811 to seize the land later known as the Compson Domain, the land "fit to breed princes, statesmen and generals and bishops, to avenge the dispossessed Compsons from Culloden and Carolina and Kentucky" (7), just as Sutpen came to Mississippi to get land and found a dynasty that would avenge the dispossessed Sutpens of West Virginia. In a letter to Malcolm Cowley, Faulkner said that Quentin regarded Sutpen as "originless."[5] Which is to say that, being without origin, Sutpen tries to become his own origin, his own father, an attempt implicit in the very act of choosing a father figure to replace his real father. When Quentin tells the story of the Sutpens in *Absalom, Absalom!*, he is not just telling his own personal story, he is telling the story of the Compson family as well.

The event that destroyed Sutpen's attempt to found a dynasty is the same event that began the decline of the Compson family—the Civil War closed off the virgin space and the time of origins, so that the antebellum South became in the minds of postwar Southerners that debilitating "golden age and lost world" in comparison with which the present is inadequate. The decline of the Compsons began with General

Compson "who failed at Shiloh in '62 and failed again though not so badly at Resaca in '64, who put the first mortgage on the still intact square mile to a New England carpetbagger in '66, after the old town had been burned by the Federal General Smith and the new little town, in time to be populated mainly by the descendants not of Compsons but of Snopeses, had begun to encroach and then nibble at and into it as the failed brigadier spent the next forty years selling fragments of it off to keep up the mortgage on the remainder" (7). The last of the Compson Domain is sold by Quentin's father to send Quentin to Harvard.

Mr. Compson's denial of the existence of an authority by which he could act necessarily entails his denial of virginity, for there is no possibility of that originality from which authority springs if there is no virgin space within which one can be first. And for the same reason Quentin's obsession with Candace's loss of virginity is necessarily an obsession with his own impotence, since the absence of the virgin space renders him powerless. When Mr. Compson refuses to act against Dalton Ames, Quentin tries to force him to take some action by claiming that he and Candace have committed incest—that primal affront to the authority of the father. But where there is no authority there can be no affront, and where the father feels his own inherited impotence, he cannot believe that his son has power. Mr. Compson tells Quentin that he doesn't believe that he and Candace committed incest, and Quentin says, "If we could have just done something so dreadful and Father said That's sad too, people cannot do anything that dreadful they cannot do anything very dreadful at all they cannot even remember tomorrow what seemed dreadful today and I said, You can shirk all things and he said, Ah can you" (99). Since Mr. Compson believes that man is helpless in the grip of time, that everything is fated, there is no question of shirking or not shirking, for there is no question of willing. In discussing the revenge against time, Nietzsche speaks of those preachers of despair who say, "Alas, the stone *It was* cannot be moved" (252), and Mr. Compson's last words in Quentin's narrative are "was the saddest word of all there is nothing else in the world its not despair until time its not even time until it was" (197).

Is there no virgin space in which one can be first, in which one can have authority through originality? This is the question that Quentin must face in trying to decide whether his father is right, whether he is doomed to be an impotent failure like his father and grandfather. And it is in light of this question that we can gain an insight into Quentin's act of narration in *Absalom, Absalom!*, for what is at work in Quentin's struggle to bring the story of the Sutpens under control is the question of whether narration itself constitutes a space in which one can be original, whether an "author" possesses "authority," whether that repetition which in life Quentin has experienced as a compulsive fate can be transformed in narration, through an act of the will, into a power, a mastery of time. Indeed, Rosa Coldfield suggests to Quentin when she first involves him in the story of the Sutpens that becoming an author represents an alternative to repeating his father's life in the decayed world of the postwar South: "'Because you are going away to attend the college at Harvard they tell me,' Miss Coldfield said. 'So I dont imagine you will ever come back here and settle down as a country lawyer in a little town like Jefferson, since Northern people have already seen to it that there is little left in the South for a young man. So maybe you will enter the literary profession as so many Southern gentlemen and gentlewomen too are doing now and maybe some day you will remember this and write about it'" (9-10). We noted earlier that the dialogue between Quentin and his father about virginity that runs through the first part of *Absalom, Absalom!* appears to be a continuation of their discussions of Candace's loss of virginity and Quentin's inability to lose his virginity contained in Quentin's section of *The Sound and the Fury*. Thus, the struggle between father and son that marked their dialogue in *The Sound and the Fury* is continued in their narration of *Absalom, Absalom!* For Quentin, the act of narrating Sutpen's story, of bringing that story under authorial control, becomes a struggle in which he tries to best his father, a struggle to seize "authority" by achieving temporal priority to his father in the narrative act. At the beginning of the novel, Quentin is a passive narrator. The story seems to choose him. Rosa involves him in the narrative against his will, and he spends the first half of the book listening to Rosa and his father tell what they know or surmise. But in the second half, when he and Shreve begin their imaginative reconstruction of the story, Quentin seems to move from a passive role to an active role in the narrative repetition of the past.

So far I have mainly discussed the experience of repetition as a compulsion, as a fate, using Freud's analysis of the mechanism of the repetition compulsion in *Beyond the Pleasure Principle* as the basis for my remarks. But in that same text, Freud also examines the experience of repetition as a power—repetition as a means of achieving mastery. He points out that in children's play an event that the child originally experienced as something unpleasant will be repeated and now experienced as a source of pleasure, as a game. He describes the game of *fort/da* that he had observed being played by a little boy of one and a half. The infant would throw away a toy and as he did, utter a sound that Freud took to be the German word *fort*—"gone." The child would then recover the toy and say the word *da*—"there." Freud surmised that the child had created a game by which he had mastered the traumatic event of seeing his mother leave him and into which he had incorporated the joyful event of her return. Freud points out that the mechanism of this game in which one actively repeats an unpleasant occurrence as a source of pleasure can be interpreted in various ways. First of all, he remarks that at the outset the child "was in a *passive* situation—he was overpowered by the experience; but, by repeating it, unpleasurable though it was, as a game, he took on an *active* part. These efforts might be put down to an instinct for mastery that was acting independently of whether the memory was in itself pleasurable or not. But still another interpretation may be attempted. Throwing away the object so that it was 'gone' might satisfy an impulse of the child's, which was suppressed in his actual life, to revenge himself on his mother for going away from him. In that case it would have a defiant meaning: 'All right, then, go away! I don't need you. I'm sending you away myself'" (*SE*, 18:16).

Freud makes a further point about the nature of children's games that has a direct bearing on our interest in the son's effort to become his father: ". . . it is obvious that all their play is influenced by a wish that dominates them the whole time—the wish to be grown-up and to be able to do what grown-up people do. It can also be observed that the unpleasurable nature of an experience does not always unsuit it for play. If the doctor looks down a child's throat or carries out some small operation on him, we may be quite sure that these frightening experiences will be the subject of the next game; but we must not in that connection overlook the fact that there is a yield of pleasure from another source. As the child passes over from the passivity of the experience to the activity of the game, he hands on the disagreeable experience to one of his playmates and in this way revenges himself on a substitute" (*SE*, 18:17). Significantly, Freud refers to this mastery through repetition as "revenge," and his remarks suggest that this revenge has two major elements–*repetition* and *reversal*. In the game of *fort/da* the child repeats the traumatic situation but reverses the roles. Instead of passively suffering rejection when his mother leaves, he actively rejects her by symbolically sending her away. And in the other case, the child repeats the unpleasant incident that he experienced but now inflicts on a playmate, on a substitute, what was formerly inflicted on him.

In this mechanism of a repetition in which the active and passive roles are reversed, we have the very essence of revenge. But we must distinguish between two different situations: in the ideal situation, the revenge is inflicted on the same person who originally delivered the affront—the person who was originally active is now forced to assume the passive role in the same scenario; in the other situation, the revenge is inflicted on a substitute. This second situation sheds light on Sutpen's attempt to master the traumatic affront that he suffered as a boy from the man who became his surrogate father, to master it by repeating that affront in reverse, inflicting it on his own son Charles Bon. This scenario of revenge on a substitute sheds light as well on the connection between repetition and the fantasy of the reversal of generations and on the psychological mechanism of generation itself. The primal affront that the son suffers at the hands of the father and for which the son seeks revenge throughout his life is the very fact of being a son—of being the generated in relation to the generator, the passive in relation to the active, the effect in relation to the cause. He seeks revenge on his father for the generation of an existence which the son, in relation to the father, must always experience as a dependency. But if revenge involves a repetition in which the active and passive roles are reversed, then the very nature of time precludes the son's taking revenge on his father, for since time is irreversible, the son can never really effect that reversal by which he would become his father's father. The son's only alternative is to take revenge on a substitute—that is, to become a father himself and thus repeat the generative situation as a reversal in which he now inflicts on his own son, who is a substitute for the grandfather, the affront of being a son, that affront that the father had previously suffered from his own father. We can see now why Nietzsche, in connecting the revenge against time with the "envy of your fathers" (that envy which the son feels for his father and which the son has inherited from his father, who was himself a son), says, "What was silent in the father speaks in the son; and often I found the son the unveiled secret of the father."

When Sutpen takes revenge on a substitute for the affront that he received as a boy, he takes revenge not just on Charles Bon but on Henry as well. For if the primal affront is the very fact of being a son, then acknowledgment and rejection, inheritance and disinheritance are simply the positive and negative modes of delivering the affront of the son's dependency on the father. Further, we can see the centrality of the notion of revenge on a substitute to the figure of the double. The brother avenger and the brother seducer are, as I have pointed out, substitutes for the father and the son in the Oedipal triangle, but if the revenge which the father inflicts on the son is a substitute for the revenge that the father wishes to inflict on his own father, then the brother avenger's killing of the brother seducer becomes a double action: the avenger's murder of the seducer (son) is a symbolic substitute for the seducer's murder of the avenger (father). This adds another dimension to Henry's murder of Bon: Henry is the younger brother and Bon the older, and the killing of the older brother by the younger is a common substitute for the murder of the father by the son. Thus, when Henry kills Bon, he is the father-surrogate killing the son, but since Henry, like Bon, is also in love with their sister Judith, he is as well the younger brother (son) killing the older brother who symbolizes the father, the father who is the rival for the mother and who punishes the incest between brother and sister, son and mother. The multiple, reversible character of these relationships is only what we would expect in a closed system like the Oedipal triangle, and it is precisely this multiple, reversible character that gives the Oedipal triangle a charge of emotional energy that becomes overpowering as it cycles and builds. The very mechanism of doubling is an embodiment of that revenge on a substitute which we find in generation, for it is the threat from the father in the castration fear that fixes the son in that secondary narcissism from which the figure of the double as ambivalent Other springs. When the bright self (the ego influenced by the superego) kills the dark self (the ego influenced by the unconscious), we have in this murder of the son as related to his mother by the son as related to his father the reversed repetition of that repressed desire which the son felt when he first desired his mother and was faced with the threat of castration— the desire of the son to murder his father. For the psychologically impotent son who cannot have a child, the act of generating a double is his equivalent of that revenge on the father through a substitute which the potent son seeks by the act of generating a son.

Keeping in mind this notion of revenge on a substitute, we can now understand how Quentin's act of narration in *Absalom, Absalom!* is an attempt to seize his father's authority by gaining temporal priority. In the struggle with his father, Quentin will prove that he is a better man by being a better narrator—he will assume the authority of an author because his father does not know the whole story, does not know the true reason for Bon's murder, while Quentin does. Instead of listening passively while his father talks, Quentin will assume the active role, and his father will listen while Quentin talks. And the basis of Quentin's authority to tell the story to his father is that Quentin, by a journey into the dark, womblike Sutpen mansion, a journey back into the past, has learned more about events that occurred before he was born than either his father or grandfather knew:

> "Your father," Shreve said. "He seems to have got an awful lot of de-
> layed information awful quick, after having waited forty-five years. If he
> knew all this, what was his reason for telling you that the trouble between
> Henry and Bon was the octoroon woman?"
> "He didn't know it then. Grandfather didn't tell him all of it either, like
> Sutpen never told Grandfather quite all of it."
> "Then who did tell him?"
> "I did." Quentin did not move, did not look up while Shreve watched
> him. "The day after we—after that night when we—"
> "Oh," Shreve said. "After you and the old aunt. I see. Go on. . . ." (266)

In terms of the narrative act, Quentin achieves temporal priority over his father, and within the narrative Quentin takes revenge against his father, against time, through a substitute—his roommate Shreve. As Quentin had to listen to his father tell the story in the first half of the novel, so in the second half Shreve must listen while Quentin tells the story. But what begins as Shreve listening to Quentin talk soon turns into a struggle between them for control of the narration with Shreve frequently interrupting Quentin to say, "Let me tell it now." That struggle, which is a repetition in reverse of the struggle between Mr. Compson and Quentin, makes Quentin realize the truth of his father's argument in *The Sound and the Fury*—that priority is not necessarily originality, that to come before is not necessarily to come first. For Quentin realizes that by taking revenge against his father through a substitute, by assuming the role of active teller (father) and making Shreve be the passive listener (son), he thereby passes on to Shreve the affront of sonship, the affront of dependency, and thus ensures that Shreve will try to take revenge on him by seizing "authority," by taking control of the narrative. What Quentin realizes is that generation as revenge on a substitute is an endless cycle of reversibility in which revenge only means passing on the affront to another who, seeking revenge in turn, passes on the affront, so that the affront and the revenge are self-perpetuating. Indeed, the word "revenge," as opposed to the word "vengeance," suggests this self-perpetuating quality—*re*-, again + *venger*, to take vengeance—to take vengeance again and again and again, because the very taking of revenge is the passing on of an affront that must be revenged. We might note in this regard that the repetition compulsion is itself a form of revenge through a substitute. If, as Freud says, the act of repression always results in the return of the repressed, that is, if repression endows the repressed material with the repetition compulsion, and if the repressed can return only by a displacement, can slip through the ego's defenses only by a substitution in which the same is reconstituted as different, then the repetition compulsion is a revenge through substitution, wherein the repressed takes revenge on the ego for that act of will by which the repressed material was rejected, takes revenge by a repetition in reverse, by a return of the repressed that is experienced as a compulsive overruling of the will, a rendering passive of the will by the unwilled return of that very material which the will had previously tried to render passive by repressing it. As revenge on a substitute is a self-perpetuating cycle of affront and revenge, so too repression, return of the repressed, re-repression, and re-return are self-perpetuating. In his work on compulsion neurosis, the psychoanalyst Wilhelm Stekel discusses the case of a patient who reenacted the Oedipal struggle with his father through the scenario of an incestuous attachment to his sister and a struggle with his brother. Stekel notes that the patient's compulsive-repetitive acts were a "correction of the past," and he links this impulse to correct the past to that "unquenchable thirst for revenge so characteristic of compulsion neurotics."[6] At one point in the analysis, the patient describes his illness as an "originality neurosis" (449).

In his narrative struggle with Shreve, Quentin directly experiences the cyclic reversibility involved in revenge on a substitute—he experiences the maddening paradox of generation in time. At the beginning of their narrative, Quentin talks and Shreve listens, and in their imaginative reenactment of the story of the Sutpens, Quentin identifies with Henry, the father-surrogate, and Shreve identifies with Charles Bon, the son, the outsider. But as the roles of brother avenger and brother seducer are reversible (precisely because the roles for which they are substitutes—father and son—are reversible through substitution), so Quentin and Shreve begin to alternate in their identifications with Henry and Bon, and Quentin finds that Shreve is narrating and that he (Quentin) is listening and that Shreve sounds like Quentin's father. Quentin not only learns that "*a man never outlives his father*" and that he is going to have to listen to this same story over and over again for the rest of his life, but he realizes as well that in their narration he and Shreve "*are both Father*"—"*Maybe nothing ever happens once and is finished. . . . Yes, we are both Father. Or maybe Father and I are both Shreve, maybe it took Father and me both to make Shreve or Shreve and me both to make Father or maybe Thomas Sutpen to make all of us.*" In terms of a generative sequence of narrators, Mr. Compson, Quentin, and Shreve are father, son, and grandson (reincarnation of the father). Confronting that cyclic reversibility, Quentin realizes that if sons seek revenge on their fathers for the affront of sonship by a repetition in reverse, if they seek to supplant their fathers, then the very fathers whom the sons wish to become are themselves nothing but sons who had sons in order to take that same revenge on their own fathers. Generation as revenge against the father, as revenge against time, is a circular labyrinth; it only establishes time's mastery all the more, for generation establishes the rule that a man never outlives his father, simply because a man's son will be the reincarnation of that father. And if for Quentin the act of narration is an analogue of this revenge on a substitute, then narration does not achieve mastery over time; rather, it traps the narrator more surely within the coils of time. What Quentin realizes is that the solution he seeks must be one that frees him alike from time and generation, from fate and revenge: he must die childless, he must free himself from time without having passed on the self-perpetuating affront of sonship. What Quentin seeks is a once-and-for-all solution, a non-temporal, an eternal solution. When Mr. Compson refuses to believe that Quentin and Candace have committed incest and simply says, "we must just stay awake and see evil done for a little while its not always," Quentin replies, "it doesnt have to be even that long for a man of courage":

and he do you consider that courage and i yes sir dont you and he every man is the arbiter of his own virtues whether or not you consider it coura- geous is of more importance than the act itself than any act otherwise you could not be in earnest . . . but you are still blind to what is in yourself to that part of general truth the sequence of natural events and their causes which shadows every mans brow even benjys you are not thinking of fini- tude you are contemplating an apotheosis in which a temporary state of mind will become symmetrical above the flesh and aware both of itself and of the flesh it will not quite discard you will not even be dead and i temporary. . . . (196)

Of Quentin's search for an eternal solution Faulkner says, in the appen- dix to *The Sound and the Fury*, that as Quentin "loved not his sister's body but some concept of Compson honor precariously and (he knew well) only temporarily supported by the minute fragile membrane of her maidenhead," so he "loved not the idea of incest which he would not commit, but some presbyterian concept of its eternal punishment:

---

he, not God, could by that means cast himself and his sister both into hell, where he could guard her forever and keep her forevermore intact amid the eternal fires" (9).

From Mr. Compson's statement and from Faulkner's, we can abstract the elements of the solution that Quentin seeks. First, it will be an action that transforms the temporal into the eternal: "a temporary state of mind will become symmetrical above the flesh"; a temporary virginity will, by an eternal punishment, be rendered "forevermore intact." Second, the action, a death, will be a punishment in which the one who punishes and the one punished will be the same, it will be self-inflicted—a suicide. Quentin, not God, will cast himself and his sister into the eternal fires, cast not just himself but Candace as well, so that Quentin's suicide will also be a symbolic incest (a return to the waters of birth, to the womb) that maintains not just Candace's virginity but Quentin's too. Third, this action, this death, will be an "apotheosis," a deification. And finally, in this death whereby "a temporary state of mind will become symmetrical above the flesh and aware both of itself and of the flesh it will not quite discard," Quentin "will not even be dead." Considering these elements, we can see who the model is for Quentin's solution and why Faulkner places Quentin's suicide in the context of Christ's passion—that self-sacrifice of the son to satisfy the justice of the father, that active willing of passivity as a self-inflicted revenge. When Quentin tries to clean the blood off his clothes from the fight with Gerald Bland, he thinks, "Maybe a pattern of blood he could call that the one Christ was wearing" (190).

As the central enigmatic event in *Absalom, Absalom!* is Henry's murder of Bon, so its equivalent in *The Sound and the Fury* is Quentin's suicide, and the structures of both books, with their multiple perspectives in narration, point up the fact that the significance of these events is irreducibly ambiguous. Thus, Henry's murder of Bon can be seen as the killing of the son by the father, but it can also be seen as the killing of the father by the son. And what of Quentin's suicide—is it finally an act of nihilistic despair, or a last desperate effort of the will to assert its mastery over time, or is it an active willing of passivity that, as a distorted image of Christ's death, is meant to be "redemptive" of Quentin's unborn, and now never to be born, progeny, who have been freed once and for all from mortality and from the spirit of revenge that is generation? Certainly, by putting Quentin's suicide in the context of Christ's death, Faulkner makes the significance of Quentin's act more ambiguous, but this strategy works in two directions, for it also points up the irreducible ambiguities in the significance of Christ's death itself. With characters like Quentin and Joe Christmas, Faulkner uses the context of Christ's death to raise questions about the actions of these characters, and he uses their actions to question the meaning of the Christ role. His most explicit questioning of the ambiguous significance of Christ's redemptive act occurs in *A Fable* (1954), where Christ's Passion and death are reenacted during World War I in that struggle between the old general and the corporal, between the father who has supreme authority and the illegitimate son who is under a sentence of death.

Viewing Quentin's suicide in the context of Christ's willing sacrifice of his own life, we find in the very concept of sacrifice a link that joins those two triadic structures whose interplay shapes *The Sound and the Fury* and *Absalom, Absalom!*—the Oedipal triangle (father, mother, son) and the three generations of patrilinearity (grandfather, father, son, or father, son, grandson). The psychoanalyst Guy Rosolato has discussed the way in which the fantasy of the murder of the father sustains the movement from the closed Oedipal triangle to the indefinite linearity of generation (three generations of men) within the religious structure of sacrifice. Rosolato argues that all sacrifice is a putting to death of the father through the victim, and he discusses the sacrifices of Isaac and Jesus as structures in which the lethal confrontation between the father and the son in the Oedipal triangle is transformed into an alliance between the father and the son by the substitution of another male figure for the female figure in the triad. This transformation involves a mutation in the image of the father. What

Rosolato calls the "idealized father" (the father of prehistoric times, "ferocious, jealous, all-powerful, whose control over others and over his sons is unlimited, a protector in exchange for total submission, and absolute master of the laws of which he is the sole origin")[7] is a figure whose relationship with the son follows the rule of two, that is, there exist only two alternatives in the son's relationship with his father—all or nothing, victory or defeat. The relationship of the son to the idealized father is a fight to the death in which, from the son's point of view, the idealized father must become the "murdered father." Sacrifice transforms this situation by means of the rule of three, the rule of mediation. Through the use of a substitute, the murder of the father can be accomplished in an indirect, in a symbolic manner, so that the figure of the "dead father" takes the place of the figure of the murdered father. Through the symbolic substitution inherent in the mediating sacrifice, the Oedipal situation is surmounted, and one passes into the patrilineal situation.

Discussing the sacrifice of Isaac, Rosolato points out that in that covenant between God and Abraham which is to become the covenant between the father and the son, there exist two different times. First, a time of preparation (Gen. 17), in which the marks of that covenant are established, so that it is as if the law were imposed in anteriority without the knowledge of either Abraham or Isaac. Thus, the father, Abraham, is not the origin of the law but must submit to it just like his son Isaac. There are three marks of the covenant between God and Abraham: in the name, in the flesh, and in the future promise. First, God changes Abram's name to Abraham as a sign of his nomination; second, God establishes circumcision as a visible sign of the agreement between God, Abraham, and his posterity; and finally, God promises Abraham and Sara a son in their old age. With the birth of Isaac, who bears the name designated by God and who is circumcised eight days after his birth according to God's command, the third masculine person is now present and the alliance between the father and the son can now supplant their conflict in the Oedipal triangle, an alliance between God and Abraham that the sacrifice of Isaac will "definitively confirm" (65). In that sacrifice, God, Abraham, and Isaac are related as grandfather, father, and son, so that when Abraham raises the knife over Isaac it is the father threatening the son, but since the son is the reincorporation of the grandfather, it is also the son threatening the father, and at that moment Abraham realizes the principle on which the alliance is based—that the death wish against one's father means the death of one's son. When God suspends the sacrifice of Isaac, God, the idealized father, is transformed into the dead father, for God takes upon himself the death that would have been meted out to the son. The angel that stops Abraham from killing Isaac shows him the ram that will take the place of the son in the sacrifice—a substitution indicative of the fact that Isaac is himself a substitute. The ram will now take the place of God in the sacrifice, and by accepting this death, God, the idealized father (the sole origin of the law, the one to whom the law is responsible and who can abrogate it at will), is transformed into the dead father (one who is responsible *to* the law, one who is bound by a covenant).

When Abraham suspends the threat against his son, "he opts for a law: precisely that of an order, of a succession of generations in death" (68). The law that Abraham accepts is that in time fathers die before their sons—as opposed to the law of the idealized father in the Oedipal triangle whereby sons die before their fathers. Abraham "accepts this succession, and refuses, what was possible for him, to destroy Isaac; he admits this new generation which he could have destroyed, repulsed or denied. He recognizes Isaac" (68). And the mark of that recognition is circumcision, the mark that the father has accepted his own death, has accepted his displacement, his succession by his son—the mark on the son's phallus that is a sign of the surmounting of the Oedipal castration threat. Isaac carries this mark of recognition as an "assurance that he (Isaac) will have in turn to experience a similar mutation and recognition" (68). Abraham "accepts the fact that Isaac could harbor toward him the same death wish; he assumes that danger: circumcision is still there to testify to the surmounting; it is an assurance of his confidence in the identical progression by Isaac" (68). Rosolato points out that the ram, Isaac's substitute in the sacrifice, is an animal with seminal connotations, and that in the sacrifice the ram represents a "partial object"—the penis. The destruction of the ram represents the father's renunciation of the phallic power in favor of his successor, his son, renunciation that has its reward in the son's progeny. Thus, when Abraham returns from the sacrifice, he learns that children have been born in his absence, one of whom, Rebecca, will be Isaac's future wife.

Circumcision as a mark of recognition that the father confers on the son points up the fact that, in the alliance, paternity involves two acts: generation and acknowledgment. The very nature of birth makes it clear who the son's mother is, but the establishment of who the son's father is requires an act of acknowledgment—the father must "recognize" the child as his son. The substitutive, sacrificial ram considered as a partial object, as the penis, emphasizes the fact that the whole basis of the sacrificial structure is the intermediary third term, the substitute, the link. Like God's recognition of Abraham, Abraham's recognition of Isaac involves three marks of identification: circumcision (the visible marking of the penis), the conferring of a name, and the promise that Isaac will now have sons in turn. Thus there is an equivalence established between the grandson, the penis, and the name as intermediary third terms linking the grandfather and the father (i.e., the father and the son), for the law of succession that Abraham accepts is also a law of transmission. The father's acceptance of his own death, of his succession by his son, his renunciation of the phallic power, is a transmission of that phallic power to his son, a transmission that requires identifying marks precisely because what is transmitted is not just the power to generate, but the power to generate *in a line descending from the father*. And that is why the religion that is established by God's covenant with Abraham (a covenant confirmed by Isaac's sacrifice) is a religion of patriarchs, a religion of genealogy. Rosolato points out that in the one, two, three order of succession of grandfather, father, son, the zero point is the death of the father, and he notes that the succession, the transmission in which the father dies while the name identified with the generative power is passed on and the phallic, linking power is reborn "corresponds to the act of symbolization where the thing 'dies' in order to be reborn with renewed vigor in the network of the laws of language" (70).

Comparing the sacrifice of Isaac with that of Jesus, Rosolato notes that in the latter case the two triadic structures linked by the death of the father are apparent: the Oedipal triangle (the Holy Family) and the three masculine persons (the Trinity). Rosolato contends that though the elements of the Oedipal triangle are present in the Holy Family, the corresponding desires do not appear. Yet one must point out that the fecundation of Mary by God is a supplanting of Joseph in that triangle, and since Jesus, the son, is himself that God, then it is, in a sense, the son who has impregnated his own mother, and Jesus' birth, as befits the birth of a god, is incestuous. By an incestuous birth that somehow preserves the virginity of his mother, Jesus is born in order to sacrifice himself, thereby redeeming man from time and mortality by giving him eternal life. One thinks of Quentin's distorted solution in which a suicide, a putting to death of oneself, as a symbolic incest (the return to the womb) is meant to preserve eternally intact the temporary virginity of his sister and himself as well as free his descendants from time and death by freeing them from generation.

The numerous differences that exist between the sacrifices of Isaac and Jesus pertain to a shift in the concept of genealogy. The first and most notable difference is that in the sacrifice of Isaac the son is spared, while in the sacrifice of Jesus the son dies. With Isaac, the ram is substituted for the son, but with Jesus, the son is substituted for the paschal lamb (the male lamb that was killed so that the firstborn would be spared). In the sacrifice of Jesus, the son offers himself up (Jesus is both the priest and the victim) as an atonement for man's offense against God. Thus, the son is put to death to satisfy the guilt that man feels for the Oedipal death wish against the father, but since the son is the father ("I and the Father are one," John 10:30), then "this sacrifice allows beneath the cover of the Son the representation of the Oedipal wishes (the death of the Father, or of God)" (78). In the sacrifice of Jesus, the sovereignty of a single God is put to death: the death of the supreme authority of the idealized father. As in the sacrifice of Isaac where the idealized father, who is the origin of the law and who can abrogate the law at will, is transformed, by God's taking death upon himself, into the dead father, who is responsible to the law (the covenant between God and Abraham—the old law), so in the sacrifice of Jesus, the unlimited authority of the idealized father is slain by God's taking death upon himself, and the dead father is now responsible to the new law. The old law is a law of genealogical succession and transmission: the father accepts the law that fathers die before their sons. Thus, Isaac is spared, and the covenant is transmitted to and by his progeny. But in the sacrifice of Jesus, the only son dies, and here we find that shift in the concept of genealogy that is the principal difference between the sacrifices of Isaac and Jesus, for the sacrifice of the childless only son marks an "interruption of genealogy" (82). Judaism is a religion of progeniture, a religion of continuity according to the blood, of physical descent from the fathers. Christianity, on the other hand, is a religion not of physical genealogy but of conversion. That interruption of genealogy represented by the sacrifice of Jesus is, in fact, a substitution of a spiritual genealogy for a physical genealogy. In the sacrifice of Isaac, the promise of the phallic power to generate new physical life in the face of death is transmitted by a line of physical descent from father to son, but with the sacrifice of Jesus, the promise is no longer one of a new physical life but of a new spiritual life. No longer is it a question of that physical immortality which one achieves through one's children; it is, rather, a question of personal immortality in an afterlife. And that future promise is transmitted not according to a physical genealogy but according to a spiritual one, and thus it is open through conversion to any man who accepts the sacrifice of Jesus. The priests who renew that sacrifice in the Mass are, like Jesus, celibate, partly as a sign that they have to do not with the generation of new physical life, a physical life that must always be in bondage to death, but with the generation of a new spiritual life—they are ghostly fathers.

This shift in the concept of genealogy between the sacrifices of Isaac and Jesus takes the form of a shift within the triadic structures pertaining to each sacrifice. In the triad of God, Abraham, and Isaac, the person who is to be sacrificed is the third member, Isaac, while in the triad of the Father, the Son, and the Holy Spirit it is the second member, Jesus, who is sacrificed. By the substitution of the sacrificial ram for Isaac, the father can renounce the phallic power by the *physical* destruction of the ram and then have that power restored to *physical* life in Isaac and his progeny. But with the sacrifice of Jesus, we have the destruction of *physical* life in the Crucifixion and the restoration of *spiritual* life in the Resurrection. When Jesus, the second member of the triad, offers himself up, it is as if, in the earlier triad, Abraham had turned the sacrificial knife on himself, as if Abraham had become the sacrificial ram. And indeed, one of the titles of Jesus is the "lamb of god." In the Christian triad, that phallic, intermediary term whereby the power to generate spiritual life is transmitted is not the Son, who after his sacrifice returns to the Father, but the Holy Spirit, whom the Son asks the Father to send into the world: "And I will ask the Father, and he shall give you another Paraclete, that he may abide with you forever" (John 14:16). The very name "Paraclete"—advocate, pleader, intercessor, comforter—indicates the mediatory role of the third person, and his phallic power is shown in the spiritual fecundation that takes place at Pentecost, and in the phallic representation of the third person as a dove (Rosolato, 79-80).

The procession of the persons within the Trinity sheds further light on the shift that takes place between the sacrifices of Isaac and Jesus. In terms of Christian dogma, the relationship between the Father and the Son is called *generation*: active on the part of the Father as *paternity*; passive on the part of the Son as *filiation*. The Father is without antecedents; he is his own origin. The procession of the Son is a procession of knowledge. The Father comprehends himself, that is, he knows himself insofar as he is knowable; he puts himself so wholly into that idea of himself that that idea constitutes a separate person—the Son. We noted earlier that fatherhood involved not just generation but acknowledgment as well—the father's recognition of himself in the son. In the Trinity, the Father's act of self-knowledge, of self-recognition, is the generation of the Son—the Logos, the knowledge of the Father. The procession of the Holy Spirit differs from that of the Son, for the Holy Spirit proceeds from both the Father *and* the Son by an act known as *spiration*: "active on the part of the Father and the Son, and passive on the part of the Holy Spirit" (79). As the procession of the second person was an act of knowledge, so that of the third person is an act of will, an act of love between the Father and the Son. The Father and the Son look at each other and seeing that each is perfect, they love each other completely, putting themselves so wholly into that love that that love constitutes a separate person—the Holy Spirit. We should note that the processions of the Son and the Holy Spirit represent a kind of narcissistic doubling in which God makes himself, first, the sole object of his own knowledge, and then the sole object of his own love. Further, the generative relationship of the Son to the Father—filiation—is a passive relationship, and the climax of that sacrifice, whose denouement is the Crucifixion, is Jesus' active willing of his own passivity in the hands of the Father: "My Father, if it be possible, let this chalice pass from me. Nevertheless, not as I will, but as thou wilt" (Matt. 26:39). The climax of the sacrifice is the total submission of the Son's will to the Father's will, so that the Son's will becomes one with, is wed to, that of the Father. In this connection, we should also note that in some heterodox Christian traditions a feminine element is reintroduced into the masculine triad, thus reproducing the Oedipal triangle. Sometimes it is the Son who is feminized, as with the medieval mystic Julian of Norwich, who, discussing the "motherhood of God" in *The Revelations of Divine Love*, speaks of "Mother Jesus."[8] Sometimes it is the Holy Spirit, as with certain early Christian sects for whom the Paraclete was a feminine principle (Rosolato, 87). Yeats refers to these traditions of a feminine element in the Trinity in his series of poems called "Supernatural Songs." One need only add that there is an obvious movement from the Son's passivity in relation to the Father and their generation of a third person between them to a concept of the second person as feminine. Indeed, the imagery of the climactic moment when Jesus accepts his Father's will suggests the feminization of the Son. Referring to his approaching death, Jesus does not say, "Let this sword pass from me," but, "Let this chalice pass from me." The image of the cup, with its feminine connotations, accords with that death in which, by an active willing of his own passivity, Jesus will have his hands and feet pierced by nails and his side pierced by a lance. Indeed, one could view that death as a *liebestod*, a sexual act that, because Jesus is both the priest and the victim, is incestuous.

Rosolato points out that there exists, on the margins of Christianity, the aim of "a sort of revenge against God" by means of the sacrifice itself (82). Since Jesus' sacrifice is an atonement for an offense of man against God, justice requires that the sacrificial victim be both man and God. In that sacrifice, man puts God to death in an action symbolic of man's attempt to supplant God (the son to supplant the father, i.e., the doctrine of equality) within the context of religion as evolving humanism. In Christianity, not only does God become man, and man put God to death, but as a result of that death, man now enjoys a privilege that formerly belonged only to the gods—immortality. The structure of atonement by means of a sacrificial victim is, of course, that of revenge on a substitute. The collective guilt that the sons feel for the death wish against the father is discharged by putting that guilt on a scapegoat who will represent the son in relation to the communal priest (the father), but that sacrifice of a substitute allows a further unconscious substitution in which the victim represents the father, and the community (the band of brothers) is able to act out the death wish against him.

From *Doubling and Incest/Repetition and Revenge: A Speculative Reading of Faulkner* (1996), pp. 124-135. Copyright © 1996 by The Johns Hopkins University Press. Reprinted with permission of The Johns Hopkins University Press.

Notes

1. Erwin Panofsky, *Studies in Iconology* (New York: Harper and Row, 1962), p. 74.

2. Friedrich Wilhelm Nietzsche, *Philosophy in the Tragic Age of the Greeks*, trans. Marianne Cowan (Chicago: Henry Regnery, 1962), pp. 52-53.

3. *The Sound and the Fury* (New York: Random House, 1946), p. 95. All subsequent quotations from this novel will be shown in the text.

4. *Absalom, Absalom!* (New York: Random House, 1964), Modern Library College Edition, p. 277. All subsequent references to this novel will be shown in the text.

5. Malcolm Cowley, *A Second Flowering* (New York: Viking Press, 1974), p. 143.

6. Wilhelm Stekel, *Compulsion and Doubt*, trans. Emil A. Gutheil (New York: Washington Square Press, 1967), p. 474. Subsequent references to this book will be shown in the text.

7. Guy Rosolato, *Essai sur le symbolique* (Paris: Gallimard, 1969), p. 63. All subsequent quotations from Rosolato are taken from this edition.

8. Julian of Norwich, *The Revelations of Divine Love*, trans. Clifton Wolters (Harmondsworth, Middlesex, England: Penguin Books, 1966), pp. 164-70.

RESOURCES

Chronology of William Faulkner's Life _____

1897	William Cuthbert Falkner (later Faulkner) is born on September 25 to Maud Butler Falkner and Murray Charles Falkner in New Albany, Mississippi.
1902	Faulkner's family moves to Oxford, Mississippi.
1905	Faulkner enters Oxford Grade School.
1906	Faulkner skips to the third grade in school. His paternal grandmother, Sallie Murray Falkner, dies.
1907	Faulkner's maternal grandmother, Lelia Dean Swift Butler, dies.
1908	Faulkner likely witnesses the lynching of a black man, Nelse Patton.
1909	Faulkner works in his father's livery stable.
1911	Faulkner, in the eighth grade, skips school regularly.
1914	Faulkner reads the works of Ezra Pound, William Butler Yeats, T. S. Eliot, and other modern poets. He begins a longtime friendship with Phil Stone, who reads Faulkner's poetry.
1915	Faulkner returns to school to play football but quits again after he breaks his nose.
1916	Faulkner works as a clerk in his grandfather's bank. He visits the University of Mississippi campus frequently and writes poetry.
1917	Faulkner's drawings appear in the University of Mississippi yearbook.
1918	Estelle Oldham, Faulkner's boyhood girlfriend, marries Cornell Franklin. Faulkner follows Stone to New Haven, Connecticut. Turned down by the U.S. Army because he does not meet of its height requirement, Faulkner is accepted by the Canadian Royal Air Force as a cadet. Temporarily discharged from the Royal Air Force, he returns to Oxford, Mississippi.

1919	Faulkner's poem "L'Après-Midi d'un Faune" is published in *The New Republic*. He attends the University of Mississippi as a special student. He publishes poems in the Oxford *Eagle* and *The Mississippian*.
1920	Faulkner joins the university drama club. He hand-letters six copies of the verse play *The Marionettes*.
1921	Faulkner gives *Vision in Spring*, a volume of poems, to Estelle. On Stark Young's invitation, he visits New York City, where he works in a bookstore. He becomes postmaster at the University of Mississippi.
1922	Faulkner's paternal grandfather, J. W. T. Falkner, Jr., dies. Faulkner becomes a Boy Scout scoutmaster in Oxford. His poem "Portrait" is published in *The Double-Dealer* in New Orleans.
1924	*The Marble Faun*, Faulkner's first volume of poetry, is published upon the recommendation of Phil Stone. Faulkner is fired by the Oxford Boy Scouts for excessive alcohol use and loses his postmaster job for misconduct.
1925	Faulkner plans to sail to Europe but stays a while in New Orleans, writing a novel. He contributes to the local newspaper, the *Times-Picayune*, before sailing to Europe with William Spratling on a tramp steamer. He travels in Italy and stays a while in Paris.
1926	*Soldiers' Pay*, Faulkner's first novel, is published. Faulkner moves in with Spratling in New Orleans. He meets Sherwood Anderson and writes *Mayday* for Helen Baird.
1927	*Mosquitoes* is published.
1929	*Sartoris*, Faulkner's first novel set in Yoknapatawpha County, is published. *The Sound and the Fury* is published. Faulkner marries Estelle Oldham (who earlier divorced Cornell Franklin) in College Hill, Mississippi. Estelle attempts suicide. Faulkner works at the university power plant.

1930	*As I Lay Dying* is published. Faulkner also publishes short stories in national magazines. He buys a house that he later names Rowan Oak.
1931	Faulkner's daughter Alabama is born and dies nine days later. *Sanctuary* is published and becomes a best seller (it is later adapted into the movie *The Story of Temple Drake*, released in 1933)." The short-story collection *These Thirteen* is published.
1932	Faulkner's father dies. *Light in August* is published. Faulkner begins working as a contract writer for Metro-Goldwyn-Mayer.
1933	Faulkner begins taking flying lessons. *A Green Bough*, a collection of poetry, is published. Faulkner's daughter Jill is born.
1934	*Doctor Martino, and Other Stories* is published. Faulkner works on assignment to Universal Studios for three weeks.
1935	*Pylon* is published. Faulkner's youngest brother, Dean, crashes the airplane Faulkner bought for him. Faulkner works on assignment for five weeks at Twentieth Century-Fox. He begins a fifteen-year love affair with Meta Dougherty Carpenter.
1936	*Absalom, Absalom!* is published.
1937	Faulkner goes on a three-week drinking binge in New York that results in serious injury.
1938	*The Unvanquished* is published, and Faulkner sells the movie rights to the novel.
1939	*The Wild Palms* is published. Faulkner is elected to the National Institute of Arts and Letters.
1940	*The Hamlet* is published.
1942	*Go Down, Moses* and *Three Famous Short Novels* are published. Faulkner works for five months writing scripts at Warner Bros.
1946	*The Portable Faulkner*, edited by Malcolm Cowley, is published, stimulating sales of Faulkner's novels.

1948	*Intruder in the Dust* is published, and MGM buys the movie rights to the novel; the film adaptation, released in 1949, is filmed in Oxford, Mississippi. Faulkner is elected to the American Academy of Arts and Letters.
1949	The short-story collection *Knight's Gambit* is published. Faulkner meets Joan Williams.
1950	*Collected Stories* is published. Faulkner is awarded the Nobel Prize in Literature.
1951	*Requiem for a Nun* is published, and Faulkner spends time in New York working on a stage version of the novel. He receives the National Book Award for *Collected Stories* and is made an officer of the French Legion of Honor in New Orleans.
1954	*A Fable* is published. Faulkner visits England, France, Switzerland, and Brazil, where he attends the International Writers Conference as U.S. delegate. His daughter Jill marries Paul D. Summers, Jr.
1955	The short-story collection *Big Woods* is published. Faulkner receives the Pulitzer Prize and the National Book Award for *A Fable*. He visits Japan for the U.S. State Department.
1956	Faulkner's grandson Paul D. Summers III is born. Faulkner goes to Washington, D.C., as chairman of the writers' group of the People-to-People program.
1957	*The Town* is published. Faulkner becomes University of Virginia writer-in-residence in Charlottesville. He visits Athens, Greece.
1958	Faulkner's grandson William Cuthbert Falkner Summers is born. Faulkner returns to the University of Virginia as writer-in-residence.
1959	*The Mansion* is published. The stage version of *Requiem for a Nun* opens on Broadway. Faulkner buys a home in Charlottesville. He fractures his collarbone in a fall from a horse.
1960	Faulkner's mother, Maud Butler Falkner, dies at the age of eighty-eight.

| 1961 | Faulkner's grandson A. Burks Summers is born. Faulkner visits Venezuela for the U.S. State Department. He receives the Gold Medal for Fiction from the National Institute of Arts and Letters. |
| 1962 | Faulkner is injured in a fall from a horse in Charlottesville. *The Reivers* is published. After another fall from a horse, in Oxford, Faulkner enters Wright's Sanatorium in Byhalia, Mississippi. He dies of a heart attack on July 6 and is buried in St. Peter's Cemetery in Oxford. |

Works by William Faulkner

Long Fiction
Soldiers' Pay, 1926
Mosquitoes, 1927
Sartoris, 1929
The Sound and the Fury, 1929
As I Lay Dying, 1930
Sanctuary, 1931
Light in August, 1932
Pylon, 1935
Absalom, Absalom!, 1936
The Unvanquished, 1938
The Wild Palms, 1939 (also published as *If I Forget Thee, Jerusalem*, 1990)
The Hamlet, 1940
Go Down, Moses, 1942
Intruder in the Dust, 1948
Requiem for a Nun, 1951
A Fable, 1954
The Town, 1957
The Mansion, 1959
The Reivers: A Reminiscence, 1962
The Wishing Tree, 1964 (fairy tale)
Flags in the Dust, 1973 (original unabridged version of *Sartoris*)
Mayday, 1976 (fable)
Novels, 1926-1929, 2006

Short Fiction
These Thirteen, 1931
Doctor Martino, and Other Stories, 1934
The Bear, 1942 (novella)
Three Famous Short Novels, 1942
The Portable Faulkner, 1946, 1967
Knight's Gambit, 1949
Collected Stories, 1950
Big Woods, 1955
Faulkner's County: Tales of Yoknapatawpha County, 1955
Uncollected Stories of William Faulkner, 1979

Poetry

The Marble Faun, 1924
A Green Bough, 1933

Nonfiction

New Orleans Sketches, 1958
Faulkner in the University, 1959
Faulkner at West Point, 1964
Essays, Speeches, and Public Letters, 1965
The Faulkner-Cowley File: Letters and Memories, 1944-1962, 1966 (Malcolm Cowley, editor)
Lion in the Garden, 1968
Selected Letters, 1977

Screenplays

Today We Live, 1933
To Have and Have Not, 1945
The Big Sleep, 1946
Faulkner's MGM Screenplays, 1982

Miscellaneous

The Faulkner Reader: Selections from the Works of William Faulkner, 1954
William Faulkner: Early Prose and Poetry, 1962

Bibliography

Adamowski, T. H. "Children of the Idea: Heroes and Family Romances in *Absalom, Absalom!*" *Mosaic* 10 (Fall 1976): 115-31.

Adams, Richard P. "Work." *Faulkner: Myth and Motion*. Princeton, NJ: Princeton University Press, 1968.

Backman, Melvin. *Faulkner, the Major Years: A Critical Study*. Bloomington: Indiana University Press, 1966.

Bleikasten, André. "Fathers in Faulkner." *The Fictional Father: Lacanian Readings of the Text*. Ed. Robert Con Davis. Amherst: University of Massachusetts Press, 1981. 115-46.

Bloom, Harold, ed. *William Faulkner's "Absalom, Absalom!"* New York: Chelsea House, 1987.

Blotner, Joseph. *Faulkner: A Biography*. New York: Random House, 1974.

Brooks, Cleanth. "The Narrative Structure of *Absalom, Absalom!*" *William Faulkner: Toward Yoknapatawpha and Beyond*. New Haven, CT: Yale University Press, 1978. 301-28.

_____. "Notes to *Absalom, Absalom!*" *William Faulkner: The Yoknapatawpha Country*. New Haven, CT: Yale University Press, 1963. 429-36.

Brown, Joseph. "To Cheer the Weary Traveler: Toni Morrison, William Faulkner, and History." *Mississippi Quarterly* 49 (Fall 1996): 709-26.

Coindreau, Maurice Edgar. *The Time of William Faulkner: A French View of Modern American Fiction*. Columbia: University of South Carolina Press, 1971.

Cowley, Malcolm, ed. *The Portable Faulkner*. New York: Viking Press, 1946.

Davis, Thadious M. *"Absalom, Absalom!" Faulkner's "Negro": Art and the Southern Context*. Baton Rouge: Louisiana State University Press, 1983.

Egan, Philip J. "Embedded Story Structures in *Absalom, Absalom!*" *American Literature* 55 (May 1983): 199-214.

Faulkner, William. "The Art of Fiction No. 12." Interview with Jean Stein vanden Heuvel. *The Paris Review* 12 (Spring 1956).

_____. "Remarks on *Absalom, Absalom!*" *William Faulkner's "Absalom, Absalom!"* Ed. Fred Hobson. New York: Oxford University Press, 2003.

Fowler, Doreen. "Reading for the Repressed: *Absalom, Absalom!*" *Faulkner: The Return of the Repressed*. Charlottesville: University Press of Virginia, 1997. 95-127.

Godden, Richard. *"Absalom, Absalom!*, Haiti, and Labor History: Reading Unreadable Revolutions." *EHL* 61.3 (1994): 685-720.

Goldman, Arnold, ed. *Twentieth Century Interpretations of "Absalom, Absalom!"* Englewood Cliffs, NJ: Prentice Hall, 1971.

Gray, Richard. "History Is What Hurts: *Absalom, Absalom!*" *The Life of William Faulkner: A Critical Biography*. Malden, MA: Blackwell, 1994. 203-25.

Guerard, Albert J. "*Absalom, Absalom!*: The Novel as Impressionist Art." *The Triumph of the Novel: Dickens, Dostoevsky, Faulkner*. New York: Oxford University Press, 1976. 302-39.

Guetti, James. "*Absalom, Absalom!*: The Extended Simile." *The Limits of Metaphor: A Study of Melville, Conrad, and Faulkner*. Ithaca, NY: Cornell University Press, 1967.

Gwin, Minrose C. "Feminism and Faulkner: Second Thoughts; or, What's a Radical Feminist Doing with a Canonical Male Text Anyway?" *The Faulkner Journal* 4 (1988-89): 55-65.

_____. "The Silencing of Rosa Coldfield." *The Feminine and Faulkner: Reading (Beyond) Sexual Difference*. Knoxville: University of Tennessee Press, 1990.

Hamblin, Robert W. "'Longer than Anything': Faulkner's 'Grand Design' in *Absalom, Absalom!*" *Faulkner and the Artist*. Ed. Donald M. Kartiganer and Ann J. Abadie. Jackson: University Press of Mississippi, 1996. 269-93.

Handley, George B. "Oedipal and Prodigal Returns in Alejo Carpentier and William Faulkner." *Mississippi Quarterly* 52 (Summer 199): 421-58.

Hobson, Fred, ed. *William Faulkner's "Absalom, Absalom!"* New York: Oxford University Press, 2003.

Hoffman, Frederick J., and Olga W. Vickery, eds. *William Faulkner: Three Decades of Criticism*. East Lansing: Michigan State University Press, 1960.

Holman, Hugh C. "*Absalom, Absalom!*: The Historian as Detective." *The Roots of Southern Writing: Essays on the Literature of the American South*. Athens: University of Georgia Press, 1972. 168-76.

Honnighausen, Lothar. "Metaphor and Narrative in *Absalom, Absalom!*" *Faulkner: Masks and Metaphors*. Jackson: University Press of Mississippi, 1997. 157-81.

Howe, Irving. *William Faulkner: A Critical Study*. 4th ed. Chicago: Ivan R. Dee, 1991.

Hunt, John W. *William Faulkner: Art in Theological Tension*. Syracuse, NY: Syracuse University Press, 1965.

Irwin, John T. *Doubling and Incest/Repetition and Revenge: A Speculative Reading of Faulkner*. Expanded ed. Baltimore: Johns Hopkins University Press, 1996.

Jones, Norman W. "Coming Out Through History's Hidden Love Letters in *Absalom, Absalom!*" *American Literature* 76.2 (June 2004): 1-28.

Justice, James H. "The Epic Design of *Absalom, Absalom!*" *Texas Studies in Literature and Language* 4 (Summer 1962): 157-76.

Karl, Frederick. "Race, History, and Technique in *Absalom, Absalom!*" *Faulkner and Race*. Ed. Doreen Fowler and Ann J. Abadie. Jackson: University Press of Mississippi, 1987. 209-21.

Kartiganer, Donald M. "Toward a Supreme Fiction: *Absalom, Absalom!*" *The Fragile Thread: The Meaning of Form in Faulkner's Novels*. Amherst: University of Massachusetts Press, 1979. 69-106.

Kauffman, Linda. "Devious Channels of Decorous Ordering: A Lover's Discourse in *Absalom, Absalom!*" *Modern Fiction Studies* 290 (Summer 1983): 183-200.

King, Richard. "From Time and History: The Lacerated Consciousness of Quentin Compson." *A Southern Renaissance: The Cultural Awakening of the American South, 1930-1955*. New York: Oxford University Press, 1980. 111-29.

Kinney, Arthur F., ed. *Critical Essays on William Faulkner: The Sutpen Family*. New York: G. K. Hall, 1996.

Krause, David. "Reading Bon's Letter and Faulkner's *Absalom, Absalom!*" *PMLA* 99 (March 1984): 225-41.

Kuyk, Dirk, Jr. *Sutpen's Design: Interpreting Faulkner's "Absalom, Absalom!"* Charlottesville: University Press of Virginia, 1990.

Ladd, Barbara. "'The Direction of the Howling': Nationalism and the Color Line in *Absalom, Absalom!*" *American Literature* 66.3 (1994): 525-51.

Langford, Gerald. *Faulkner's Revision of "Absalom, Absalom!": A Collation of the Manuscript and the Published Book*. Austin: University of Texas Press, 1971.

Lensing, George S. "The Metaphor of Family in *Absalom, Absalom!*" *Southern Review* 11 (Winter 1975): 99-117.

Levins, Lynn G. "The Four Narratives: Perspectives in *Absalom, Absalom!*" *PMLA* 85 (1970): 35-47.

Liles, Don Merrick. "William Faulkner's *Absalom, Absalom!* An Exegesis of the Homoerotic Configurations in the Novel." *Literary Visions of Homosexuality*. Ed. Stuart Kellogg. New York: Haworth, 1983. 99-111.

Lind, Ilse Dusoir. "The Design and Meaning of *Absalom, Absalom!*" *William Faulkner: Three Decades of Criticism*. Ed. Frederick J. Hoffman and Olga W. Vickery. East Lansing: Michigan State University Press, 1960.

Longley, John Lewis, Jr. "Thomas Sutpen: The Tragedy of Aspiration." *The Tragic Mask: A Study of Faulkner's Heroes*. Chapel Hill: University of North Carolina Press, 1963.

Lurie, Peter. "'Some Trashy Myth of Reality's Escape': Romance, History and Film Viewing in *Absalom, Absalom!*" *American Literature* 73 (September 2001): 563-97.

MacKethan, Lucinda Hardwick. "Faulkner's Sins of the Fathers: How to Inherit the Past." *The Dream of Arcady: Place and Time in Southern Literature*. Baton Rouge: Louisana State University Press, 1980. 153-80.

Matthews, John T. "Marriages of Speaking and Hearing in *Absalom, Absalom!*" *The Play of Faulkner's Language*. Ithaca, NY: Cornell University Press, 1982. 115-61.

Millgate, Michael. "*Absalom, Absalom!*" *The Achievement of William Faulkner*. New York: Random House, 1966.

Minter, David. "Apotheosis of the Form: Faulkner's *Absalom, Absalom!*" *The Interpreted Design as a Structural Principle in American Prose*. New Haven, CT: Yale University Press, 1969. 191-219.

Moreland, Richard C. "Nausea and Irony's Failing Distances in *Absalom, Absalom!*" *Faulkner and Modernism: Rereading and Rewriting*. Madison: University of Wisconsin Press, 1990. 79-121.

Mortimer, Gail L. "Significant Absences." *Faulkner's Rhetoric of Loss: A Study in Perception and Meaning*. Austin: University of Texas Press, 1983. 72-96.

Muhlenfeld, Elisabeth. "'We Have Waited Long Enough': Judith Sutpen and Charles Bon." *Southern Review* 14 (Winter 1978): 66-80.

_____, ed. *William Faulkner's "Absalom, Absalom!": A Critical Casebook*. New York: Garland, 1984.

Oates, Stephen B. *William Faulkner: The Man and the Artist*. New York: Harper & Row, 1987.

O'Connor, William Van. "Rhetoric in Southern Writing: Faulkner." *The Georgia Review* 112 (Spring 1958): 83-86.

Parker, Robert Dale. *"Absalom, Absalom!": The Questioning of Fictions*. New York: Twayne, 1991.

_____. "The Chronology and Genealogy of *Absalom, Absalom!*: The Authority of Fiction and the Fiction of Authority." *Studies in American Fiction* 14 (1986): 191-98.

Patterson, John. "Hardy, Faulkner, and the Prosaics of Tragedy." *Centennial Review* 5 (1961): 160-75.

Poirier, William R. "'Strange Gods' in Jefferson, Mississippi: Analysis of *Absalom, Absalom!*" *William Faulkner: Two Decades of Criticism*. Ed. Frederick J. Hoffman and Olga Vickery. East Lansing: Michigan State University Press, 1951. 217-43.

Polk, Noel. "The Manuscript of *Absalom, Absalom!*" *Mississippi Quarterly* 25 (Summer 1972): 359-67.

Polk, Noel, and John D. Hart, eds. *"Absalom, Absalom!": A Concordance to the Novel*. West Point, NY: Faulkner Concordance Advisory Board, 1989.

Railey, Kevin. "*Absalom, Absalom!* and the Southern Ideology of Race." *The Faulkner Journal* 14.2 (Spring 1999): 41-55.

Roberts, Diane. "'But Let Flesh Touch with Flesh': The Terror of the Self-Same in *Absalom, Absalom!*" *Faulkner and Southern Womanhood*. Athens: University of Georgia Press, 1994. 89-101.

_____. "The Ghostly Body in *Absalom, Absalom!*" *Faulkner and Southern Womanhood*. Athens: University of Georgia Press, 1994. 25-40.

Ross, Stephen M. "Oratorical Voice: *Absalom, Absalom!*" *Fiction's Inexhaustible Voice: Speech and Writing in Faulkner*. Athens: University of Georgia Press, 1989. 212-33.

Rubin, Louis D., Jr. "Scarlett O'Hara and the Two Quentin Compsons." *A Gallery of Southerners*. Baton Rouge: Louisiana State University Press, 1982. 2-48.

Schmitter, Dean Morgan, ed. *William Faulkner: A Collection of Criticism*. New York: McGraw-Hill, 1973.

Sewall, Richard B. *The Vision of Tragedy*. New Haven, CT: Yale University Press, 1959. 133-47.

Snead, James. "The Joint of Racism: Withholding the Black in *Absalom, Absalom!*" *William Faulkner's "Absalom, Absalom!"* Ed. Harold Bloom. New York: Chelsea House, 1987. 129-41.

Spiller, Hortense. "Faulkner Adds Up: Reading *Absalom, Absalom!* and *The Sound and the Fury*." *Faulkner in America*. Ed. Joseph R. Urgo and Ann J. Abadie. Jackson: University Press of Mississippi, 2001. 24-44.

Stanchich, Maritza. "The Hidden Caribbean 'Other' in William Faulkner's *Absalom, Absalom!*: An Ideological Ancestry of U.S. Imperialism." *Mississippi Quarterly* 49 (Summer 1996): 603-17.

Sugimori, Masami. "Racial Mixture, Racial Passing, and White Subjectivity in *Absalom, Absalom!*" *The Faulkner Journal* (Spring 2008): 1-18.

Sundquist, Eric. "*Absalom, Absalom!* and the House Divided." *Faulkner: The House Divided*. Baltimore: Johns Hopkins University Press, 1983.

Swiggart, Peter. *The Art of Faulkner's Novels*. Austin: University of Texas Press, 1962. 149-70.

Thompson, Lawrence. *William Faulkner: An Introduction and Interpretation*. 2d ed. New York: Holt, Rinehart, 1967.

Urgo, Joseph R. "*Absalom, Absalom!*: The Movie." *American Literature* 62 (March 1990): 56-73.

Vickery, Olga. "The Idols of the South: *Absalom, Absalom!*" *The Novels of William Faulkner: A Critical Interpretation*. Rev. ed. Baton Rouge: Louisiana State University Press, 1964. 84-102.

Volpe, Edmond L. "*Absalom, Absalom!*" *A Reader's Guide to William Faulkner: The Novels*. 1964. Syracuse, NY: Syracuse University Press, 2003. 184-211.

Wadlington, Warwick. "The House of *Absalom, Absalom!* Voices, Daughter, and the Question of Catharsis." *Reading Faulknerian Tragedy*. Ithaca, NY: Cornell University Press, 1987.

Wagner-Martin, Linda, ed. *William Faulkner: Six Decades of Criticism*. East Lansing: Michigan State University Press, 2002.

Warren, Robert Penn. "Faulkner: Past and Present." *Faulkner: A Collection of Critical Essays*. Ed. Robert Penn Warren. Englewood Cliffs, NJ: Prentice Hall, 1966.

Watson, Jay. "And Now What's to Do: Faulkner, Reading, Praxis." *The Faulkner Journal* 14 (Fall 1998): 67-74.

Westling, Louise. "Thomas Sutpen's Marriage to the Dark Body of the Land." *Faulkner and the Natural World*. Ed. Donald M Kartiganer and Ann J. Adabie. Jackson: University Press of Mississippi, 1999. 126-42.

CRITICAL
INSIGHTS

About the Editor

David Madden is Robert Penn Warren Professor Emeritus at Louisiana State University. He is the author and editor of some fifty books, including studies of Wright Morris, James M. Cain, Nathanael West, James Agee, and Robert Penn Warren. Among the many other writers about whom he has written essays are Albert Camus, James Joyce, Katherine Anne Porter, Katherine Mansfield, Michel Tournier, William Gaddis, Jules Romains, Emily Brontë, Edward Albee, Graham Greene, Richard Wilbur, Tennessee Williams, Carson McCullers, Joseph Conrad, Eugene O'Neill, Ross Macdonald, Flannery O'Connor, Thomas Wolfe, James Dickey, Ingmar Bergman, and William Faulkner, including pieces on *The Sound and the Fury* and "A Rose for Emily." His other publications include two collections of his literary essays, *The Poetic Image in Six Genres* and *Touching the Web of Southern Novelists*. Among his edited books are *A Primer of the Novel*, *Harlequin's Stick*, *Charlie's Cane*, *Revising Fiction*, *Rediscoveries* (*I* and *II*), *Classics of Civil War Fiction*, *Thomas Wolfe's Civil War*, and *Loss of the Sultana and Reminiscences of the Survivors*. He has written ten novels, including *The Suicide's Wife*, made into a movie, and *Sharpshooter: A Novel of the Civil War*, both of which were nominated for the Pulitzer Prize, and two collections of stories. His first novel appeared in 1961; *Abducted by Circumstance* appeared in 2010. Soon to be published is his tenth novel, *London Bridge Is Falling Down*. His fiction has won a Rockefeller Grant and several grants and awards. *David Madden: A Writer for All Genres* is collection of essays by critics and creative writers about his works. He is founding director of the United States Civil War Center.

About *The Paris Review*

The Paris Review is America's preeminent literary quarterly, dedicated to discovering and publishing the best new voices in fiction, nonfiction, and poetry. The magazine was founded in Paris in 1953 by the young American writers Peter Matthiessen and Doc Humes, and edited there and in New York for its first fifty years by George Plimpton. Over the decades, the *Review* has introduced readers to the earliest writings of Jack Kerouac, Philip Roth, T. C. Boyle, V. S. Naipaul, Ha Jin, Ann Patchett, Jay McInerney, Mona Simpson, and Edward P. Jones, and published numerous now-classic works, including Roth's *Goodbye, Columbus*, Donald Barthelme's *Alice*, Jim Carroll's *Basketball Diaries*, and selections from Samuel Beckett's *Molloy* (his first publication in English). The first chapter of Jeffrey Eugenides's *The Virgin Suicides* appeared in the *Review*'s pages, as have stories by Rick Moody, David Foster Wallace, Denis Johnson, Jim Crace, Lorrie Moore, and Jeanette Winterson.

The Paris Review's renowned Writers at Work series of interviews, whose early installments include legendary conversations with E. M. Forster, William Faulkner, and

Ernest Hemingway, is one of the landmarks of world literature. The interviews received a George Polk Award and were nominated for a Pulitzer Prize. Among the more than three hundred interviewees are Robert Frost, Marianne Moore, W. H. Auden, Elizabeth Bishop, Susan Sontag, and Toni Morrison. Recent issues feature conversations with Jonathan Franzen, Norman Rush, Louise Erdrich, Joan Didion, Norman Mailer, R. Crumb, Michel Houellebecq, Marilynne Robinson, David Mitchell, Annie Proulx, and Gay Talese. In November 2009, Picador published the final volume of a four-volume series of anthologies of *Paris Review* interviews. The *New York Times* called the Writers at Work series "the most remarkable and extensive interviewing project we possess."

The *Paris Review* is edited by Lorin Stein, who was named to the post in 2010. The editorial team has published fiction by Lydia Davis, André Aciman, Sam Lipsyte, Damon Galgut, Mohsin Hamid, Uzodinma Iweala, James Lasdun, Padgett Powell, Richard Price, and Sam Shepard. Recent poetry selections include work by Frederick Seidel, Carol Muske-Dukes, John Ashbery, Kay Ryan, Mary Jo Bang, Sharon Olds, Charles Wright, and Mary Karr. Writing published in the magazine has been anthologized in *Best American Short Stories* (2006, 2007, and 2008), *Best American Poetry*, *Best Creative Non-Fiction*, the Pushcart Prize anthology, and *O. Henry Prize Stories*.

The magazine presents three annual awards. The Hadada Award for lifelong contribution to literature has recently been given to Joan Didion, Norman Mailer, Peter Matthiessen, John Ashbery, and, in 2010, Philip Roth. The Plimpton Prize for Fiction, awarded to a debut or emerging writer brought to national attention in the pages of *The Paris Review*, was presented in 2007 to Benjamin Percy, to Jesse Ball in 2008, and to Alistair Morgan in 2009. In 2011, the magazine inaugurated the Terry Southern Prize for Humor.

The *Paris Review* was a finalist for the 2008 and 2009 National Magazine Awards in fiction and won the 2007 National Magazine Award in photojournalism. The *Los Angeles Times* recently called *The Paris Review* "an American treasure with true international reach," and the *New York Times* designated it "a thing of sober beauty."

Since 1999 *The Paris Review* has been published by The Paris Review Foundation, Inc., a not-for-profit 501(c)(3) organization.

The Paris Review is available in digital form to libraries worldwide in selected academic databases exclusively from EBSCO Publishing. Libraries can contact EBSCO at 1-800-653-2726 for details. For more information on *The Paris Review* or to subscribe, please visit: www.theparisreview.org.

Contributors

David Madden is Robert Penn Warren Professor Emeritus at Louisiana State University. He is the author and editor of some fifty books, including studies of Wright Morris, James M. Cain, Nathanael West, Robert Penn Warren, Thomas Wolfe, and books on the Civil War. He has written ten novels, including *The Suicide's Wife*, made into a movie, and *Sharpshooter: A Novel of the Civil War* (both nominated for the Pulitzer Prize), and two collections of stories. *Abducted by Circumstance* appeared in 2010, and *London Bridge Is Falling Down* is forthcoming. *David Madden: A Writer for All Genres* is a collection of essays by critics and creative writers about his works. He is founding director of the United States Civil War Center.

Lorie Watkins Fulton is Assistant Professor of English at William Carey University. She is the author of *William Faulkner, Gavin Stevens, and the Cavalier Myth* and has published essays in such journals as *The Faulkner Journal, The Hemingway Review, African American Review, The Mississippi Quarterly, The Southern Literary Journal*, and *Modern Philology*.

Nathaniel Rich, a former fiction editor of *The Paris Review*, is the author of *The Mayor's Tongue*, a novel. He lives in New Orleans.

Nicole Moulinoux is Professor of American Literature at Rennes 2 University (France). She has collaborated in the William Faulkner Pléiade Edition and is also a specialist on contemporary American southern literature. She is Founder and President of the William Faulkner Foundation (Europe) and Editor of the Collection Etudes Faulknériennes. In a forthcoming book, she will examine and evaluate the French face of Faulkner.

Ted Atkinson is Assistant Professor of English at Mississippi State University. He is the author of *Faulkner and the Great Depression: Aesthetics, Ideology, and Cultural Politics* and essays on Faulkner, Erskine Caldwell, Larry Brown, and Lewis Nordan. He is currently working on a book about representations of Mississippi in dominant national narratives about civil rights history, racial identity and race relations, debilitating social ills, the ideological divide in U.S. politics, and natural and human-made disasters.

Randy Hendricks is Professor of English and Chair of the Department of English and Philosophy at the University of West Georgia, where he teaches courses on William Faulkner, Robert Penn Warren, and Herman Melville, as well as courses in creative writing. He is the author of *Lonelier Than God: Robert Penn Warren and the Southern Exile* and the short-story collection *The Twelfth Year, and Other Times*. With William Bedford Clark and James A. Perkins, he is coeditor of the six-volume *Selected Letters of Robert Penn Warren*. He also coedited, with James A. Perkins, *For the Record: A Robert Drake Reader* and *David Madden: A Writer for All Genres*.

Kevin Eyster is Professor of English in the Department of Language and Literature at Madonna University in Livonia, Michigan. He has published essays on a number of American writers, including William Faulkner, Eudora Welty, Nella Larsen, August Wilson, Gurney Norman, and Colson Whitehead. He teaches a seminar on William Faulkner and Toni Morrison.

Aimee E. Berger holds an MFA in creative writing and a graduate certificate in women's studies from the University of South Carolina and a doctorate in English from the University of North Texas. She has published scholarly and literary essays on a variety of subjects, including the works of Robert Penn Warren, David Madden, Dorothy Allison, Margaret Mitchell, and Louise Erdrich, as well as on Hurricane Katrina. She currently works in publishing and teaches literature at the University of Texas at Arlington.

Hyatt H. Waggoner, a specialist on the works of Nathaniel Hawthorne, was the author of several books, including *Hawthorne: A Critical Study*, *William Faulkner: From Jefferson to the World*, and *American Poetry: From the Puritans to the Present*. He was a professor at Brown University from 1956 to 1979. He died of emphysema at Hanover Terrace Health Care in New Hampshire at the age of seventy-four.

Susan V. Donaldson, National Endowment for the Humanities Professor of English, teaches in the English and American Studies departments at William and Mary. A leading scholar on the literature of the American South, and a highly accomplished writer and editor, she is the author of *Competing Voices: The American Novel, 1865-1914* (1998), which was named an Outstanding Academic Book by *Choice* magazine. She has also authored more than forty essays or book chapters and given more than one hundred lectures and conference papers, including many she delivered on American literature to universities in Central and Eastern Europe when she held a Senior Fulbright Lectureship at the University of Bonn in Germany. She has served as an associate editor and advisory board member for *The Faulkner Journal*, as an advisory board member of *The Eudora Welty Review*, and for two years as president of the Eudora Welty Society.

Richard Forrer is Assistant Professor of Religion at Texas Christian University. He has published essays on the interrelationships between religion and literature, including "*Oedipus at Colonus*: A Crisis in the Greek Notion of Deity" (*Comparative Drama*, Winter 1974-75).

Philip Goldstein earned a Ph.D. in English from Temple University in 1984. Since 1977 he has taught English and philosophy at the University of Delaware, since 2001 as full professor. His recent books include *Post-Marxist Theory: An Introduction* (2005) and *Modern American Reading Practices: Between Aesthetics and History* (2009). With James Machor, he has edited *Reception Study: Theory, Practice, History* (2000) and *New Directions in Reception Study* (2008).

Deborah Wilson is Professor of English and Director of the Masters in Liberal Arts Program at Arkansas Tech University, where she teaches American and southern literature, film, and theory. She has published onVirginia Woolf, Ellen Douglas, Faulkner, Robert Penn Warren, and Eudora Welty.

Robert H. Zoellner is the author of *The Salt-Sea Mastadon: A Reading of Moby-Dick* (1973) and coauthor of *Strategies of Composition* (1968). Interested in James Fenimore Cooper, Herman Melville, and William Faulkner, he has published articles in *American Literature, American Quarterly*, and *College English*. He formerly taught English at Colorado State University.

Linda Wagner-Martin is Frank Borden Hanes Professor of English at the University of North Carolina at Chapel Hill. She has edited and written fifty books, among which are biographies of Sylvia Plath, Gertrude Stein, Ellen Glasgow, Barbara Kingsolver, and Zelda Sayre Fitzgerald; *The Oxford Companion to Women's Writing in the United States* and its accompanying anthology (with Cathy N. Davidson); *Telling Women's Lives: The New Biography*; and *The Modern American Novel, 1914-1945*, followed by *The Mid-Century American Novel, 1935-65*. Among her recent books are *The Portable Edith Wharton* and *William Faulkner: Six Decades of Criticism*. She is currently completing a study of the 1930s in American literature. She has won teaching awards at both Michigan State University and UNC, and has been a sponsor of many women's groups on both campuses. She has been a Guggenheim fellow, a Bunting Institute fellow, a senior National Endowment for the Humanities fellow, and (twice) a resident at the Rockefeller Foundation Study Center in Bellagio, Italy. She has been president of a number of professional groups, including the American literature division of the Modern Language Association and, currently, the Ernest Hemingway Foundation.

Lewis P. Simpson was Boyd Professor Emeritus of English at Louisiana State University, where he taught for forty years. Among his many articles and books are *Mind and the American Civil War: A Meditation on Lost Causes, The Brazen Face of History: Studies in the Literary Consciousness in America*, and *The Dispossessed Garden: Pastoral and History in Southern Literature*. He was the recipient of numerous awards, including the 1990 Avery O. Craven Award of the Organization of American Historians and the 1987 Humanist of the Year Award from the Louisiana Endowment for the Humanities. He also received the 1991 Hubbell Medal for distinguished contribution to the study of American letters from the American Literature Section of the Modern Language Association. In 1996, he received the inaugural Robert Penn Warren-Cleanth Brooks Award from the Center for Robert Penn Warren Studies at Western Kentucky University. From the early 1960s until 1987, he was coeditor of *The Southern Review*.

John T. Irwin is Decker Professor in the Humanities and Professor in the Writing Seminars and the English Department at the Johns Hopkins University. He served as editor of *The Georgia Review* at the University of Georgia. His first book of literary criticism, *Doubling and Incest/Repetition and Revenge: A Speculative Reading of Faulkner*, was published in 1975, soon followed by his first book of poems, *The Heisenberg Variations*, under his pen name John Bricuth. He returned to Johns Hopkins University as Professor and Chairman of the Writing Seminars. In 1980 he published his second book of literary criticism and scholarship, *American Hieroglyphics: The Symbol of the Egyptian Hieroglyphics in the American Renaissance*, and in 1994 he published his third book of criticism, *Mystery to a Solution: Poe, Borges, and the Analytical Detective Story*, which won the Christian Gauss Prize from Phi Beta Kappa for the best scholarly book in the humanities published in 1994 and also won the Aldo Scaglione Prize in comparative literature from the Modern Language Association for the best scholarly book published in the field of comparative literature that year. In 1996, he stepped down as Chairman of the Writing Seminars after nineteen years but still continues as a Professor in the Writing Seminars and in English, teaching full-time and writing. In 1998 he published his long narrative poem *Just Let Me Say This About That*, under his pen name John Bricuth, with the Overlook Press as the first volume in the Sewanee Writers' series. Currently, he is at work on another long narrative poem about marriage called *As Long As It's Big* and on a book of literary criticism on the American poet Hart Crane and another book on hard-boiled detective fiction and film noir.

Acknowledgments_____

"The *Paris Review* Perspective" by Nathaniel Rich. Copyright © 2012 by Nathaniel Rich. Special appreciation goes to Christopher Cox, Nathaniel Rich, and David Wallace-Wells, editors at *The Paris Review*.

Maps included in "From Mapmaker to Geographer: Faulkner's Sense of Space in *Absalom, Absalom!*" by Nicole Moulinoux. Copyright © the Literary Estate of William Faulkner. Reprinted by permission.

"Past as Present: *Absalom, Absalom!*" by Hyatt H. Waggoner. From *William Faulkner: From Jefferson to the World* (1959), pp. 149-169. Copyright © 1959 by The University Press of Kentucky. Reprinted with permission of The University Press of Kentucky.

"Quentin! Listen!" by David Madden. From *Faulkner and War* (2004) edited by Noel Polk and Ann J. Abadie. Copyright © 2004 by David Madden. Reprinted with permission of David Madden.

"Subverting History: Women, Narrative, and Patriarchy in *Absalom, Absalom!*" by Susan V. Donaldson. From *Southern Quarterly* 26 (Summer 1988): 19-32. Copyright © 1988 by University of Southern Mississippi. Reprinted with permission of University of Southern Mississippi.

"*Absalom, Absalom!*: Story-Telling as a Mode of Transcendence" by Richard Forrer. From *The Southern Literary Journal*, Volume 9, no. 1. Copyright © 1976 by the Department of English and Comparative Literature of the University of North Carolina at Chapel Hill. Published by the University of North Carolina Press. Used by permission of the publisher. www.uncpress.unc.edu

"Black Feminism and the Canon: Faulkner's *Absalom, Absalom!* and Morrison's *Beloved* as Gothic Romances" by Philip Goldstein. From *The Faulkner Journal*, XX: 1 & 2 (Fall 2004/Spring 2005). Copyright © 2005 by the University of Central Florida. Reprinted with permission.

"'A Shape to Fill a Lack': *Absalom, Absalom!* and the Pattern of History" by Deborah Wilson. From *The Faulkner Journal*, VII: 1 & 2 (Fall 1991/Spring 1992). Copyright © 1992 by the University of Central Florida. Reprinted with permission.

"Faulkner's Prose Style in *Absalom, Absalom!*" by Robert H. Zoellner. From *American Literature* 30.4 (January 1959): 486-502. Copyright © 1959 by Duke University Press. All rights reserved. Reprinted with permission of Duke University Press.

"Rosa Coldfield as Daughter: Another of Faulkner's Lost Children" by Linda Wagner-Martin. From *Studies in American Fiction* 19.1 (1991): 1-13. Copyright © 1991 by Northeastern University. Reprinted with permission of The Johns Hopkins University Press.

"War and Memory: Quentin Compson's Civil War" by Lewis P. Simpson. From *The Fable of the Southern Writer* (1997) by Louis P. Simpson. Copyright © 1997 by

Louisiana State University Press. Reprinted with permission of Louisiana State University Press.

"The Dead Father in Faulkner" by John T. Irwin. From *Doubling and Incest/Repetition and Revenge: A Speculative Reading of Faulkner* (1996), pp. 124-135. Copyright © 1996 by The Johns Hopkins University Press. Reprinted with permission of The Johns Hopkins University Press.

Index

Vaughn, Matthew R., 109
Vengeance. *See* Revenge
Vicarious experience, 18, 168-169
Vickery, Olga, 96

Waggoner, Hyatt H., 374
Wagner-Martin, Linda, 375
Weaving metaphor, 89, 251
Weinstein, Philip M., 118, 218, 225, 232, 265
Wild Palms, The (Faulkner), 29

Wilson, Deborah, 374
Wittenberg, Judith Bryant, 108, 263
Women. *See* Female characters
Woodward, C. Vann, 66
Wuthering Heights (Brontë), 218

Yoknapatawpha County, 27, 325; maps, 39-41, 46, 48

Zoellner, Robert H., 375

DATE DUE

BRODART, CO.   Cat. No. 23-221